THE CATALOGUE OF IVORIES FROM HASANLU, IRAN

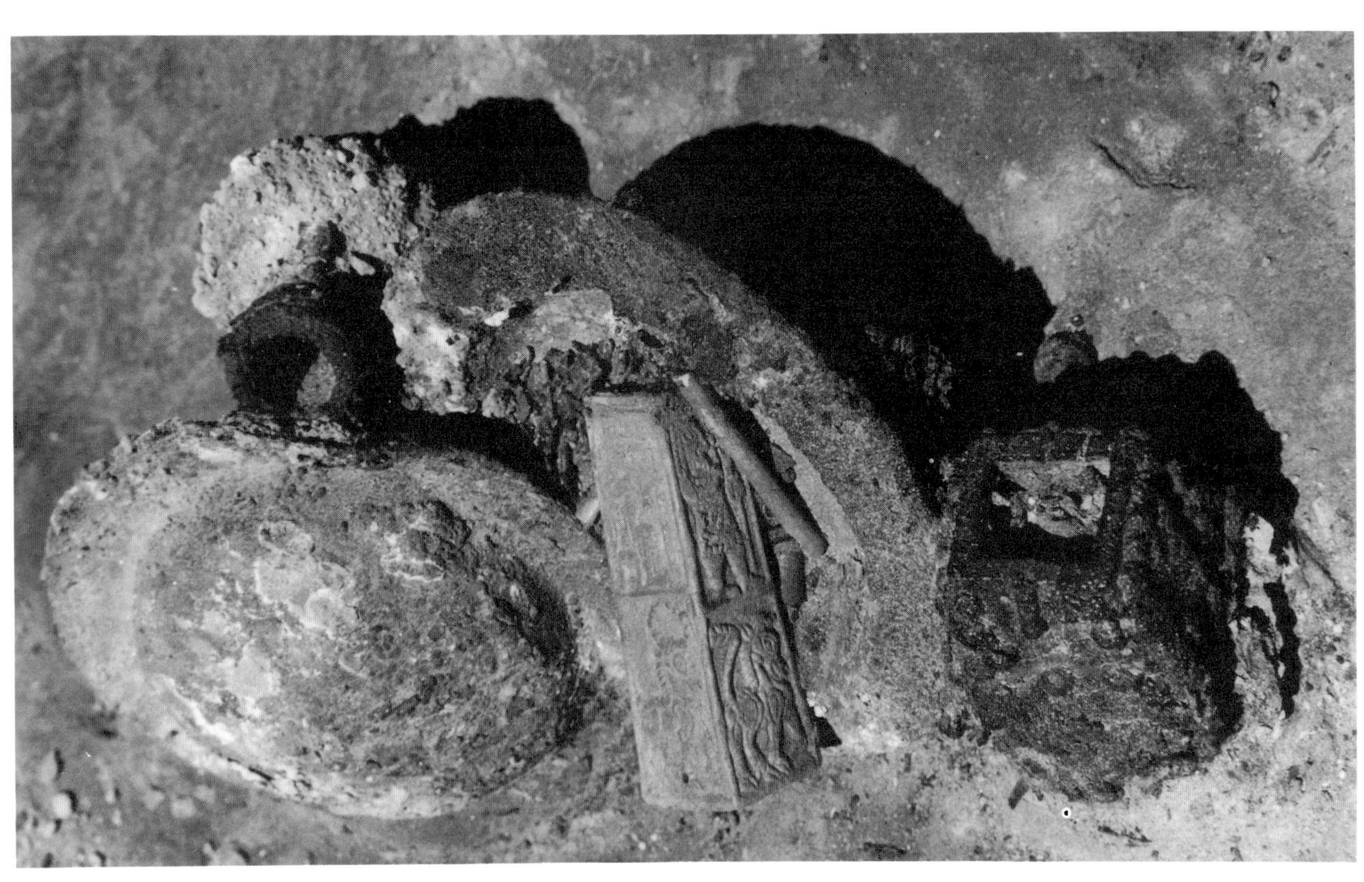

Cosmetic container, number 73, in the cluster of bronze, wood, and bone objects excavated in the great hall of Burned Building II in 1962

UNIVERSITY MUSEUM MONOGRAPH 40

HASANLU SPECIAL STUDIES
Robert H. Dyson, Jr., General Editor
VOLUME II

THE CATALOGUE OF IVORIES FROM HASANLU, IRAN

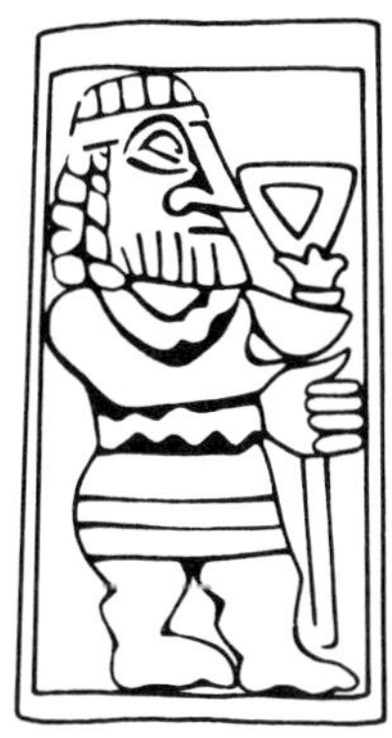

Oscar White Muscarella

Published by
THE UNIVERSITY MUSEUM
University of Pennsylvania
Philadelphia
1980

Photographs
Hasanlu Project, The University Museum
The Iran Bastan Museum, Teheran
The Metropolitan Museum of Art, New York

Drawings and plans
Hasanlu Project
Elizabeth Simpson (book colophon and no. 187)

Design, editing, production
Publication Services Division, The University Museum

Typesetting
Deputy Crown Inc., Camden, N.J.

Printing
Lithographic Publications Incorporated, Philadelphia

Library of Congress Cataloging in Publication Data

Muscarella, Oscar White.
The catalogue of ivories from Hasanlu, Iran.

(Hasanlu special studies ; v. 2) (University Museum monograph ; 40)
Bibliography: p.
1. Hasanlu site, Iran. 2. Ivories—Iran—Hasanlu site—Catalogs. I. Title. II. Series.
III. Series: Pennsylvania. University. University Museum. University Museum monograph ; 40.
DS262.H37M87 935 80-16774
ISBN 0-934718-33-4

THE UNIVERSITY MUSEUM
University of Pennsylvania
Philadelphia

Printed in the United States of America

FOR MY WIFE

GRACE FREED MUSCARELLA

PUBLICATION FUNDING

Generous grants from the Kevorkian Fund and the Schimmel Foundation of New York have made the publication of this volume possible, with additional funding provided by The University Museum, University of Pennsylvania.

UNIVERSITY MUSEUM MONOGRAPHS

A list of the Monographs published by The University Museum over the last thirty years appears at the back of this volume, followed by some of the Monographs, Special Papers, and Catalogues now in preparation.

Prices may be obtained by request and publications ordered from the Publication Services Division, The University Museum, University of Pennsylvania, 33rd and Spruce Streets, Philadelphia, PA 19104, U.S.A.

CONTENTS

CATALOGUE

COMMENTARY

FOREWORD

The Catalogue of Ivories is the second Special Study of materials from the excavations carried out at Hasanlu, Iran, between 1957 and 1974. Each of these volumes is devoted to a special object or category of objects deserving of special attention. This volume presents a small but unique corpus of ivory fragments found in the burned buildings of period IV at the site. Dated prior to 800 B.C., therefore, they provide a body of comparative material for the little-known early first millennium in northwest Iran. By virtue of their controlled stratigraphic context they assume special importance in relation to the ivories said to have come from nearby Ziwiye. They are equally important for the study of the large collection excavated by the late Sir Max Mallowan at the Assyrian capital of Nimrud. In many respects the miniature scenes of warfare and processions on the Hasanlu fragments seem to take their inspiration from the ninth century palace reliefs of Assyria, although the details of style appear quite different. The collection thus focuses our attention on the fascinating question of how concepts are transferred from cultural area to cultural area, from large to small scale, and from artistic medium to artistic medium.

The organization adopted for this volume, to be used for the others that will follow, places the catalogue of objects first, followed by an extended commentary by the author on the wider significance and context of the material.

The presentation of the ivories in this volume has been made particularly difficult by the degree of damage they suffered in the sacking of the site around 800 B.C. and by subsequent deterioration while still buried in the mound. The Hasanlu Project is indebted to all those who excavated and recorded the pieces over the years, and especially to Oscar White Muscarella for undertaking the catalogue. We are also indebted to Maude de Schauensee, who assisted in the preparation of the material for study and publication.

The ivories from Hasanlu are largely in the collection of the Iran Bastan Museum in Teheran except for selected pieces presented by the Iranian government, in accordance with the law regulating the disposition of antiquities, to The Metropolitan Museum of Art in New York and to The University Museum, University of Pennsylvania, in Philadelphia.

ROBERT H. DYSON, JR.
Director, Hasanlu Project

PREFACE

The aims of this monograph are to publish the ivories and the related decorated wood and bone objects excavated at Hasanlu over several seasons: to illustrate them, describe them and, where possible, relate them both to their immediate environment, to their find spots and to the other works of art recovered at Hasanlu, and to Near Eastern art in general. I have attempted to discuss the Hasanlu ivories with respect to other ivory groups excavated at various Near Eastern sites and to discuss the importance of the former as establishing a cultural and chronological background against which the others might be evaluated. While I discuss the ivory groups in relevant contexts, I have made no attempt to write a history of ancient ivories; my primary aim is to make the Hasanlu ivories available to scholars and interested students as soon as possible.

No book is ever written without the cooperation and work of many people. My bibliography lists the books and articles used by me, works that have enabled me to go beyond a mere description of the ivories. A few scholars listed there should be singled out for special mention because their work has proved invaluable not only to me but to anyone who has studied ancient ivories. First of all, of course, is R. D. Barnett, whose indispensable book on the Nimrud and other ancient Near Eastern ivories is mentioned numerous times in the following pages. Then I should like to acknowledge Helene Kantor, Max Mallowan, Georgina Herrmann and Brigitte Freyer–Schauenburg, whose publications of ancient ivories have helped me enormously, and whose works must be studied by any student of these extraordinary objects.

Others have been of help to me by giving me encouragement and their ideas and thoughts freely and generously: Robert H. Dyson, Jr., Günter Kopcke and Irene Winter. After completing the present study I read Dr. Winter's Ph.D. dissertation [see addendum to References] on North Syrian art, which includes a discussion of the ivories. In several areas of thought our ideas coincide and overlap; in other areas she goes beyond my discussions [I have cited some of her comments within brackets]. Robert H. Dyson, Jr. and Maude de Schauensee cooperated most generously by making available to me the ivories in the University Museum of the University of Pennsylvania, and by supplying me with many photographs and drawings. Dyson also answered numerous questions asked by me over the years. He and Irene Winter read the manuscript of the present work and both gave me valuable criticisms and suggestions. I should also wish to express my thanks to Dr. Firouz Bagherzadeh and his assistant Mlle. Anne Saurat of the Muzeh-e Iran-e Bastan in Teheran, who supplied me with photographs of the ivories housed in their museum.

OSCAR WHITE MUSCARELLA

New York
May 1977

INTRODUCTION

The quantity of ivories and other objects recovered at Hasanlu have been preserved to us because the fire that destroyed the citadel apparently spread fast and caused the buildings to collapse before much, if any, looting could have occurred. The violence of the destruction and collapse caused most of the ivories to break into small fragments, a situation in contrast with ivories preserved at other sites. The rapid collapse also caused the death of many of the site's inhabitants, scores of whose crushed skeletons were found *in situ* where they fell. That the enemy actually penetrated into the citadel shortly before the collapse is all too clear from the unfortunate evidence of mutilated skeletons, some of whom have arms or legs hacked off or other visible body wounds. The enemy apparently got very little loot from their efforts but they left a destroyed city, which served as a burial mound for many of the inhabitants and their precious possessions. Hasanlu thus has the dubious reputation of yielding archaeological information that grimly illustrates the events occurring when an ancient city was attacked, events so often discussed in detail in Assyrian texts.

That the citadel was burned to the ground a few years before 800 B.C. and that the destroyers may have been Urartians is generally accepted and has been discussed often (Dyson 1965b, 202; Muscarella 1971b, 48; 1974c, 82; cf. Calmeyer 1969, 63, N. 218). But while we may feel fairly secure that we know who destroyed Hasanlu and when, what still remains unknown to us is the ethnic and linguistic background of the people who lived there, and the ancient name of the city. Thus the ivories can at present only be called "the Hasanlu ivories," using the modern name of the site, rather than be assigned a much desired ancient attribution.

From their stratigraphic position in the fill within the burned buildings it is clear that all the ivories, as well as the majority of the other objects recovered, were originally placed in the second storey. The ivories were scattered in different directions when the buildings collapsed as a result of the fire that destroyed the citadel. Therefore, both their contexts within their original areas of use and the nature of the original units that must have held the various panels and sculpture in place have been lost to us. Nevertheless, we know which ivories came from which buildings and this information is not without value (see Concordance). It is also significant that at least with respect to other collections of ivories from the first millennium B.C. those from Hasanlu are the only examples that without doubt were in actual use and in their original positions up to the very moment of destruction.

Four distinct groups of ivories have been excavated at Hasanlu: a local style, an apparent Iranian style of unknown provenience, North Syrian style, and Assyrian style. These groups are discussed separately in the text but the first group, the ivories in the local style, warrant special mention here. I have elsewhere stated that "many of the ivories appear to be products of local craftsmen, since stylistic details are seen to be similar to those of other objects considered to be locally made, and because no immediate parallels are forthcoming from foreign centers" (1966, 127). The ivories that I consider to have been locally carved have representations that share characteristics in the manner of depicting physiognomy, and in details, proportions and forms (see *infra* and Conclusion). Collectively these specifics, or characteristics, form a recognizable group that allows them to be readily distinguishable from the style of both ivories and art objects known from other regions and sites. In addition, objects of other materials with representations that share the same features and style of the ivories have been excavated at Hasanlu. This style is at present known only at Hasanlu; the variety of locally excavated material that bears it, which indicates that different craftsmen followed basic, commonly understood artistic views and experiences, surely suggests that we are correct in recognizing a local style at Hasanlu. Of some interest with regard to distribution is the fact that the local-style ivories were recovered from only two buildings, BB I West and II. The three ivories from BB IV East are Assyrian and apparently all the ivories recovered from BB V are North Syrian.

All the ivories derive from a single chronological context, from the debris of the major destruction level, period IVB. A few ivories were first found in 1958 in BB I West (nos. 62, 63, 159, 201, 202); others, in small quantity, were excavated in 1960 and 1962 in BB II, while the great majority were recovered from BB II in 1964. When excavations commenced again in 1970, 1972 and 1974, ivories were excavated in BB IV East (nos. 281, 282, 283) and BB V (nos. 137, 223, 224, 225, 228, 237, 238, 241, 245, 250, 252, 256, 259, 261, 271, 278). See plans I and II, which show BB I, II, IV and V. The majority of the ivories recovered are from BB II, the largest of the great columned halls at Hasanlu (plan II); a few are from BB I West and BB IV East; the rest, the second largest group, are from BB V, adjacent and directly to the northeast of BB II (plan I). No ivories were found in BB III to the north of the main cluster of buildings.

Some of the ivories recovered in 1964 were catalogued only as BB II without any reference to a specific room location, and some of these ivories lack a field number and measurements. This situation exists because so many fragments were found up to the final day of excavation that there was time only to list them before they were shipped to Teheran. From the field notes and personal observation, however, it can be unequivocally stated that these ivories derive from the same proveniences as the other ivories from BB II, the southern and eastern areas. Note that no ivories were recovered from the western and northern areas or rooms of BB II, and that all the ivories from BB V were from the fill of the rooms 3 and 8 in the southeastern area of the building.

Each ivory fragment is published in the Catalogue section with its grid provenience first, and its find spot within a particular building, that is, its room or area provenience: CC31 [2] (7), for example, means area 2 of grid CC31, which is Room 7 of BB II. Room designation (5,E) or (5,N) or (5,C) means the eastern or northern or central area of Room 5, the great hall, of BB II. Unless otherwise stated, all the ivories marked simply with a grid and area designation are from BB II; ivories from BB I West, IV East and V are specifically labeled: BB V 8 means Room 8 of BB V. The provenience is followed by the Hasanlu field catalogue number, the first two figures being the year of the find; in the permanent records this number has the prefix HAS, omitted here. Next are letters giving the present location of the piece (T is the Musée Iran Bastan in Teheran; UM is the University Museum of the University of Pennsylvania; MMA is the Metropolitan Museum of Art) and its accession number. The measurements are given in centimeters. They are followed by a bibliographical reference if the ivory has been published elsewhere. About twenty carvings in bone, wood, or shell are included, and the material noted; all others are ivory. Each piece is described briefly, leaving general discussion for the Commentary. Throughout, *right* or *left* refers to the direction a figure is facing or moving, from the reader's viewpoint.

The Commentary follows the same sequence as the Catalogue. Presented first are the local-style ivories distinguished by motif and execution, relief or sculpture in the round, followed by chapters concerned with those ivories that are considered to have been imported into Hasanlu, rather than locally made. For convenience there is occasionally an overlapping of one category with another. Thus, nos. 92, 93 and 175 are catalogued with the reliefs although they are also obviously sculpture in the round. Finally, there are chapters concerned with problems related to a general discussion of ivory workshops, suggested uses of the ivories, foreign trade relations, and chronology.

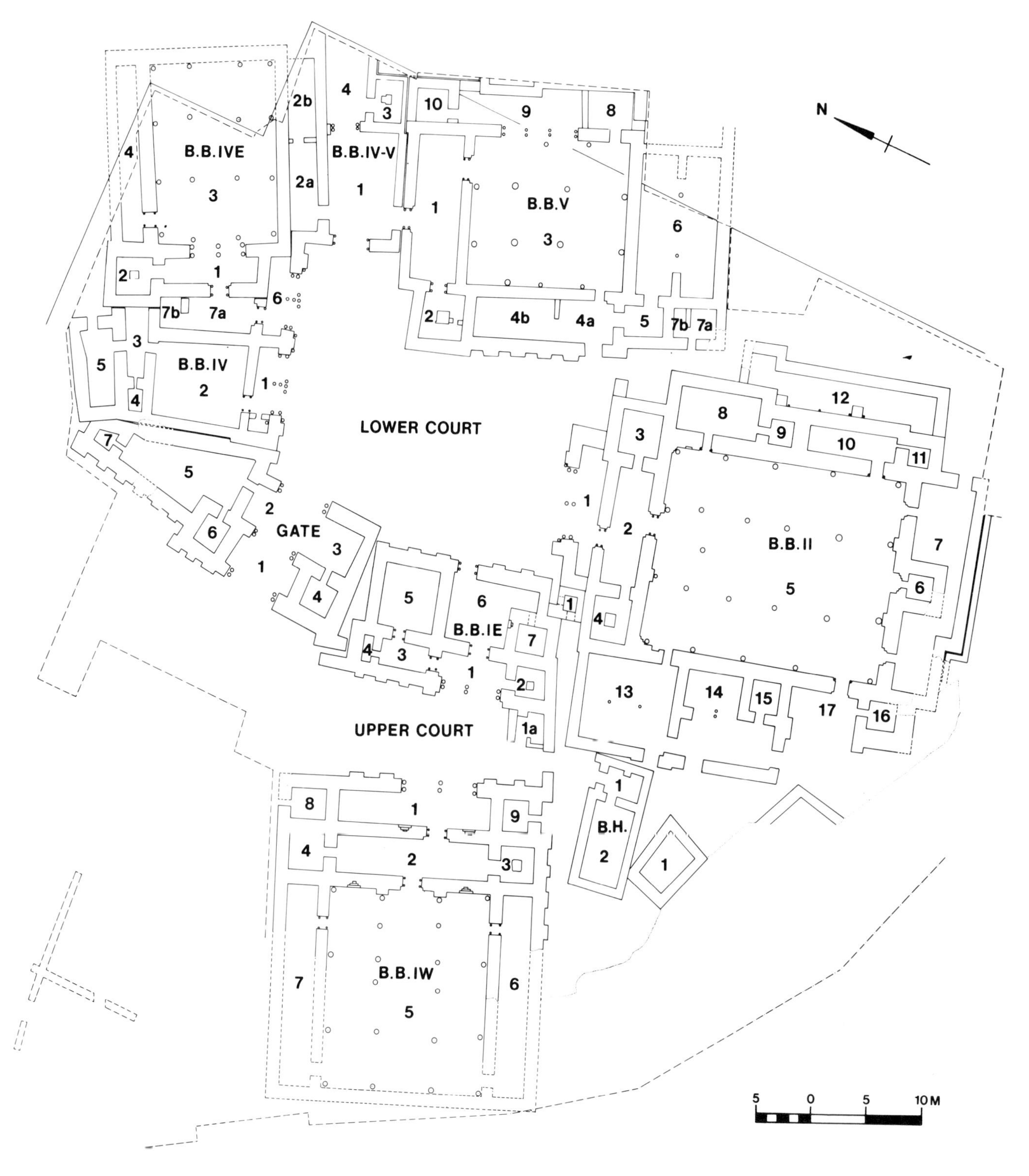

Plan I. The citadel of Hasanlu at the time of its destruction (period IVB)

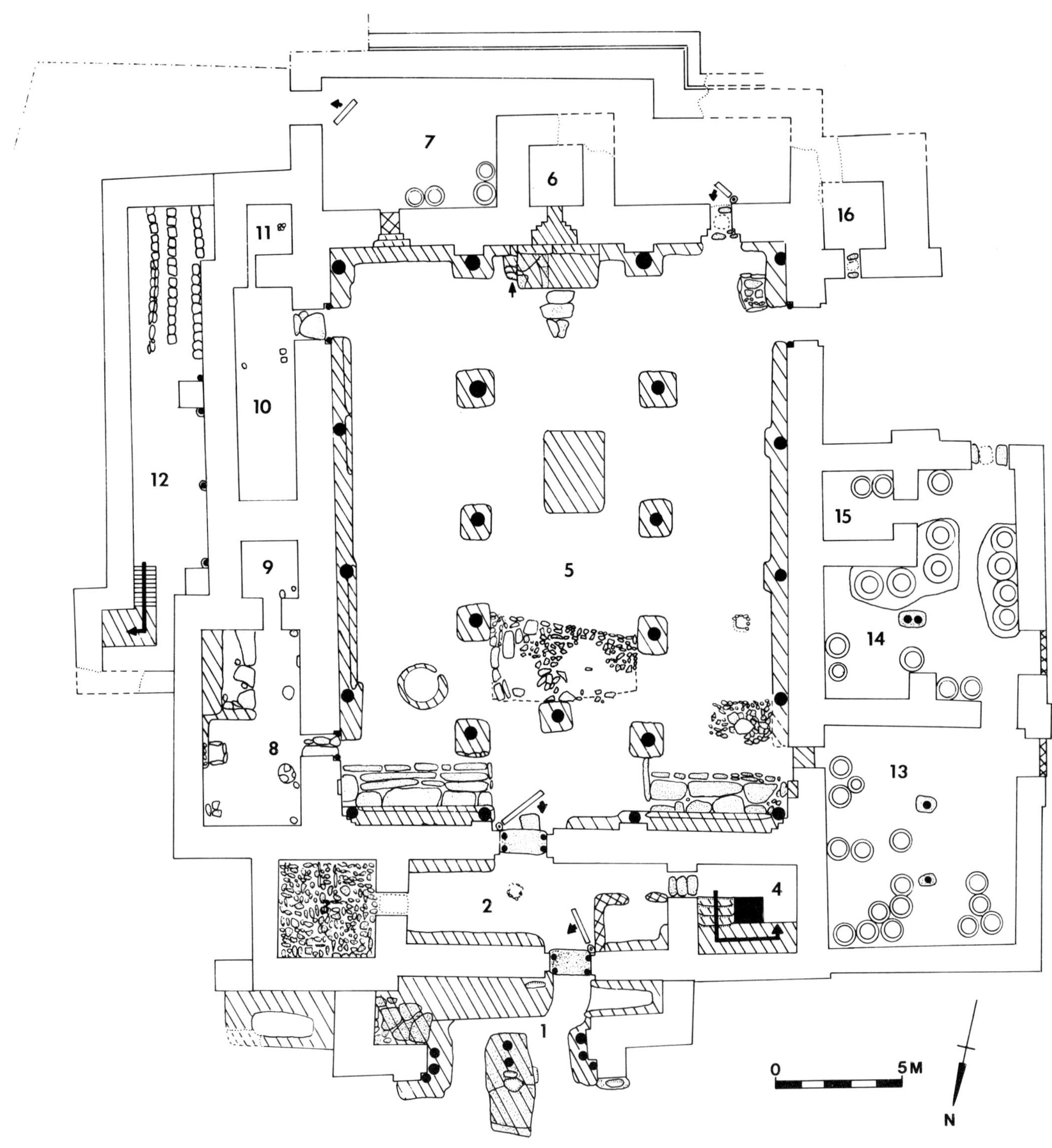

Plan II. Burned Building II (BB II) at the time of its destruction (period IVB)

CONCORDANCE

BUILDING AND ROOM PROVENIENCE OF THE IVORIES

BB 1 WEST

62, 63, 159, 201, 202

BB II

Room 6

6, 7, 39, 42, 43, 44, 50, 72, 75, 113, 119, 127, 130, 143, 144, 150, 156, 163, 164, 165, 166, 167, 182, 183, 189, 194, 195, 196, 230 N, 255 N, 273 N

Room 7

2, 5, 10, 13, 17, 24, 45, 48, 53, 59, 61, 64, 65, 80, 92, 95, 97, 105, 123, 125, 136, 138, 145, 146, 147, 148, 152, 154, 155, 160, 161, 170, 175, 177, 187, 188, 191, 221 bis I, 226 N, 227 N, 229 N, 231 N, 232 N, 234 N, 235 N, 236 N, 242 N, 243 N, 244 N, 249 N, 253 N, 257 N, 262 N, 264 N, 265 N, 266 N, 270 N, 272 N

Area East of Room 7

21, 22, 58, 93, 141, 178, 213, 233 N, 263 N

Room 8

1, 3, 4, 8, 9, 11, 12, 14, 15, 18, 19, 20, 23, 25, 26, 27, 28, 29, 30, 31, 32, 33, 35, 40, 46, 47, 49, 51, 52, 54, 55, 56, 57, 60, 66, 67, 68, 69, 71, 74, 76, 77, 78, 79, 81, 82, 83, 84, 85, 86, 87, 88, 89, 90, 91, 94, 99, 100, 101, 102, 103, 104, 107, 108, 109, 110, 111, 112, 114, 115, 116, 117, 118, 120, 121, 122, 124, 126, 128, 132, 142, 149, 151, 153, 157, 158, 162, 168, 171*, 172, 173, 174, 176, 180, 181, 184, 185, 186, 193, 198, 199, 203, 206, 207, 208, 209, 210 a, 211, 218 I, 219 I, 246 N, 251 N, 254 N, 260 N, 267 N, 274 N, 285 A, 286 A, 290 A, 292 A

Room 10

214 I, 215 I, 216 I, 217 I, 220 I, 221 I, 280 A, 284 A, 293 A

Room 5 Great Hall

34, 36, 38, 41, 70, 73, 96, 98, 131, 133, 169, 204, 205, 210 b, 275 N, 276 N, 277 N, 279 N, 287 A, 288 A, 289 A

General

16, 37, 106, 129, 134, 135, 139, 140, 179, 190, 192, 197, 200, 212, 213 bis, 222 N, 239 N, 240 N, 247 N, 248 N, 258 N, 269 N

BB IV EAST

Room 3

281 A, 282 A, 283 A

BB V

Room 3

137, 223 N, 237 N, 241 N, 250 N, 252 N**, 259 N, 271 N**, 278 N

Room 8

224 N, 225 N, 228 N, 238 N, 245 N, 252 N**, 256 N, 261 N, 271 N**

Purchased

268 N

TOWER 5

291 A

I, Iranian ivory
N, North Syrian ivory
A, Assyrian ivory.

*Actually found in corridor to the east of Room 8
**Found in adjacent parts of Rooms 3 and 8

ABBREVIATIONS

AJA:	*American Journal of Archaeology*
AfO:	*Archiv für Orientforschung*
Anat. Stud.:	*Anatolian Studies*
ANEP:	*Ancient Near East in Pitcures*, edited by James B. Pritchard (Princeton, 1954)
Bagd. Mitt:	*Baghdader Mitteilungen*
BASOR:	*Bulletin of the American Schools of Oriental Research*
BCH:	*Bulletin de Correspondance Hellénique*
BJV:	*Berliner Jahrbuch für Ver- und Frühgeschichte*
ILN:	*Illustrated London News*
JANES:	*Journal of the Ancient Near Eastern Society of Columbia University*
JAOS:	*Journal of the American Oriental Society*
JdI:	*Jahrbuch des k. deutschen archäologischen Instituts*
JESHO:	*Journal of the Economic and Social History of the Orient*
JFA:	*Journal of Field Archaeology*
JGS:	*Journal of Glass Studies*
JHS:	*Journal of Hellenic Studies*
JNES:	*Journal of Near Eastern Studies*
MMAB:	*Metropolitan Museum of Art Bulletin*
MMAJour:	*Metropolitan Museum Journal*
PEQ:	*Palestine Exploration Quarterly*

CATALOGUE

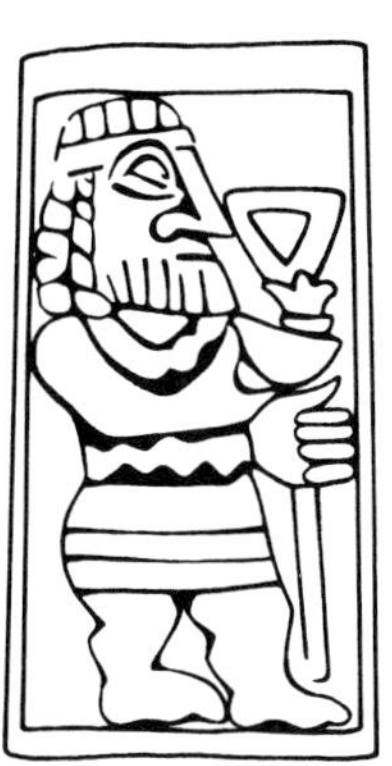

I

BATTLE SCENES

A: CHARIOT SCENES

1 BB31 **[1]** (8); 64-757; MMA 65.163.19; ht. 2.7, w. 9.5, th. .7; Muscarella 1966, fig. 11.
Fragment of a chariot and its two horses, right, with a nude enemy trampled beneath the horses; only the four legs—all touching the ground—and tail of one horse are preserved. The angle of the two legs at the far right suggests that they belong to the rear part of a cavalry horse preceding the chariot. The chariot box, tapered top to bottom, has vertical side markings and a buckle—presumably from a shield—projecting from the lower rear; wheels have six spokes and no linchpin (not depicted on any Hasanlu chariot). The nude man—his penis is distinct—lies on his left side facing down; he wears sandals, has small round eyes, a thin mouth and a large nose, a mustache and a beard. A guilloche pattern formed the lower border; the edge is intact, as is also the plain left edge; a dowel hole is at the lower left. The reverse has irregular scoring.

2 CC31 **[2]** (7); 64-888; T; ht. 2.8, w. 3.8, th. .6.
Fragment of a chariot horse, right, with a nude enemy, facing up, beneath the horse. A plain circular plaque or harness decoration is held by three straps. Body hair is depicted by neat triangular incisions; the back and belly are outlined with a linear herringbone pattern. The top edge is intact and the horses' heads, probably two, were on a separate plaque.

3 BB31 **[1]** (8); 64-781; T; ht. 1, w. 3.8, th. .8.
Extant are part of a chariot wheel followed by two horse's legs and the finger tips of an enemy. The legs could be from a chariot or cavalry horse. The bottom edge, part of a guilloche, is intact; the guilloche was probably completed on another plaque.

4 BB31/CC31 (8); 64-1076; T 25868; ht. 1.5, w. 3.3, th. .5.
A six-spoked chariot wheel and the rear legs and tail of a horse, right. The right hand of an enemy is seen at the right above a dowel *in situ*. The intact lower edge is a raised band. The axle is at the rear of the chariot box.

5 CC31 **[2]** (7); 64-890; T 25849; ht. 6, w. 6.
Part of a chariot horse, right. Its body is outlined by a thick, rope-like pattern, its mane by a thick herringbone; there are no body hair incisions. The horse is a stallion, as are all the horses represented on the ivories. A tassel (?) hangs below the body and a feathered headdress is worn (cf. nos. 26, 27). The reins pass through a rein ring at the neck and across the chest, and are held by both hands of the charioteer who also seems to hold a whip. The horse's front legs appear to be collapsing and the rear leg may be bent forward. Upper and lower edges are intact with narrow raised bands; the plain right edge is also intact and the horse was completed on a separate plaque.

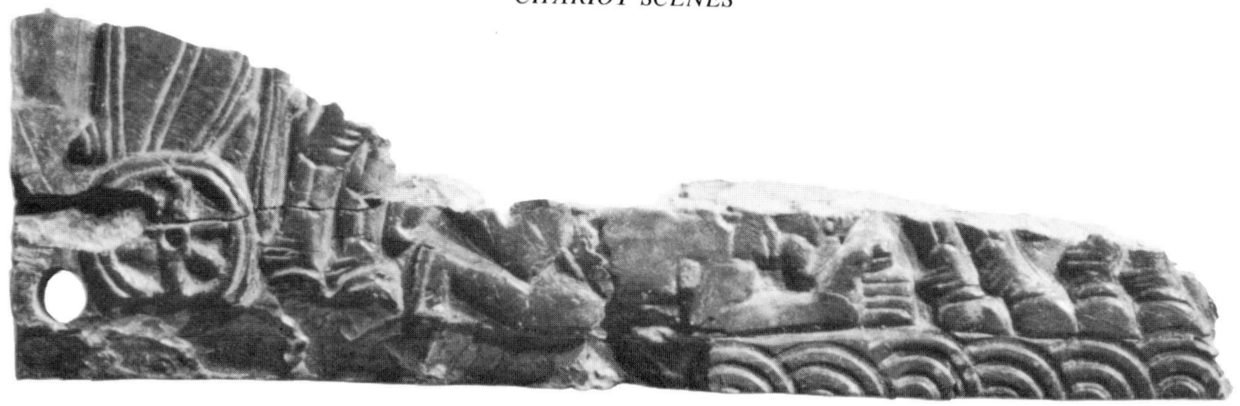

1

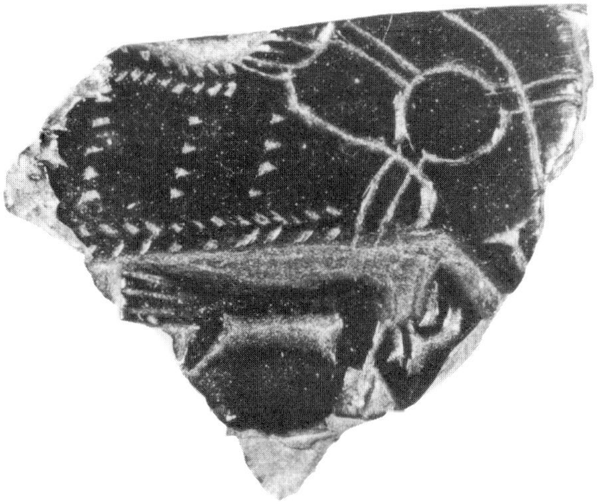

2

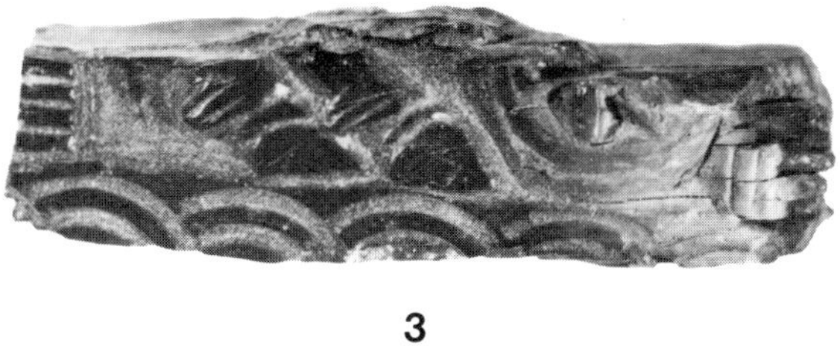

3

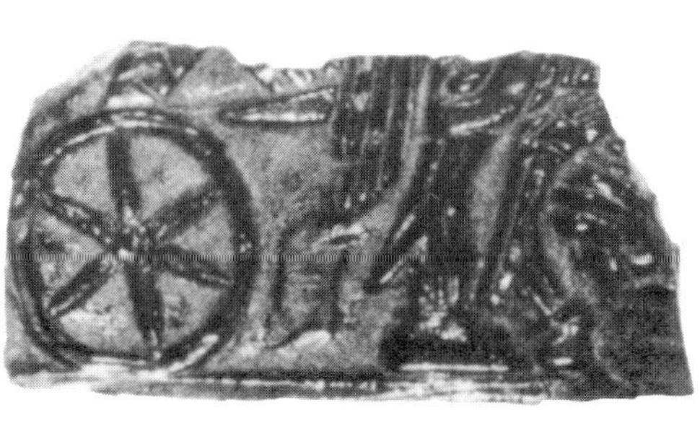

4

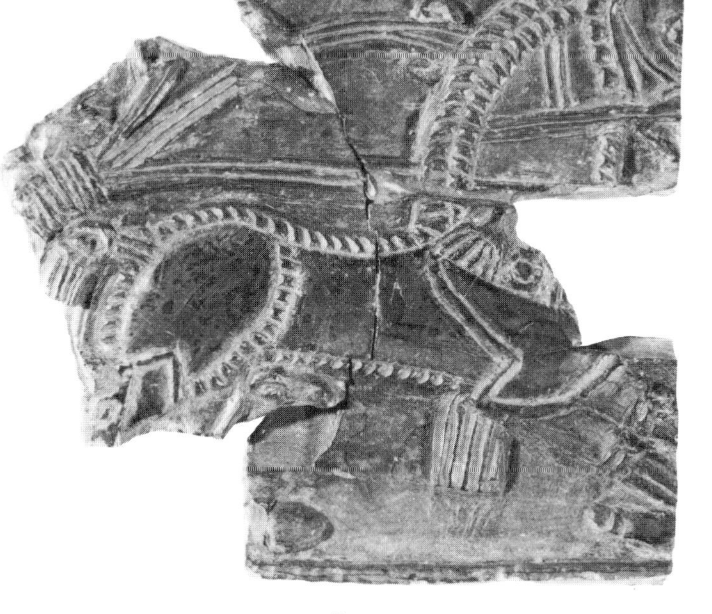

5

6 CC31 [1] (6); 64-919; T; ht. 2.1, w. 4.8, th. .4.
Part of two chariot horses, right; one body but two overlapping heads are depicted. Body and harness are like no. 2, but there is more plastic detail. No bits or cheek pieces are exhibited here, or on any horse represented on the ivories (cf. no. 17). A triangular object is pendent below the necks and is probably a bell (cf. nos. 29, 30, 34). The reverse is irregularly scored.

7 Wood; CC31 [1] (6); 64-927; UM 65-31-304; ht. 3, w. 2.6, th. .6.
Fragment depicting the rear part of a chariot horse and part of the box and yoke pole, as well as one hand of the charioteer holding the reins.

8 BB31 [1] (8); 64-790; T; ht. 2.1, w. 3.2, th. .9.
A charioteer, head missing, in a chariot box, left; both hands hold the reins. A hand holding a sword is seen at the right. The plain right edge is intact and there is a dowel in place.

9 BB31 [1] (8); 64-760; T; ht. 1.7, w. 4.6, th. .7.
Fragment of a horse, left, and part of a chariot box and yoke pole. The horse similar to nos. 2, 6, 10, 11.

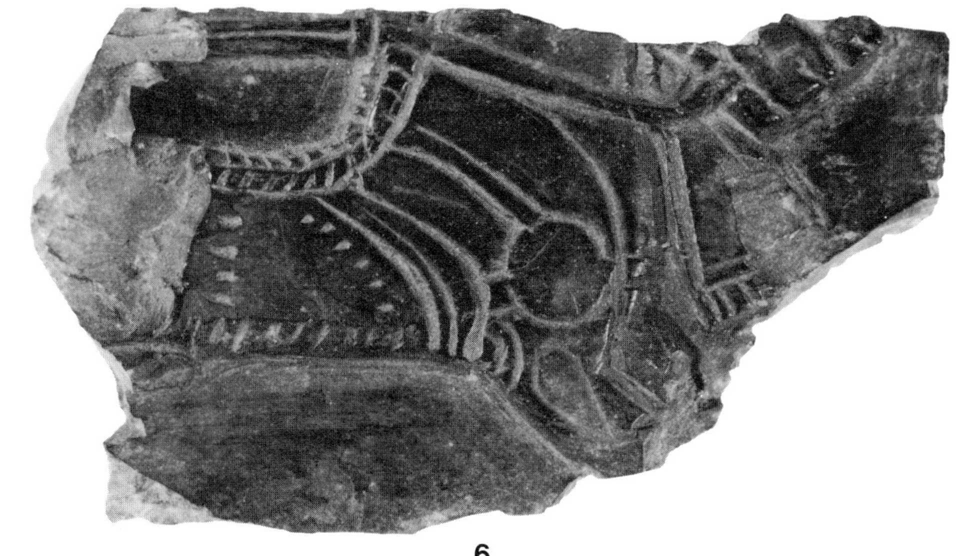

6

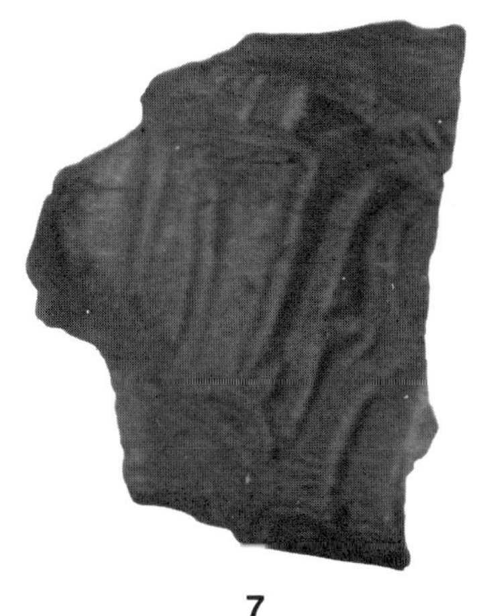

7

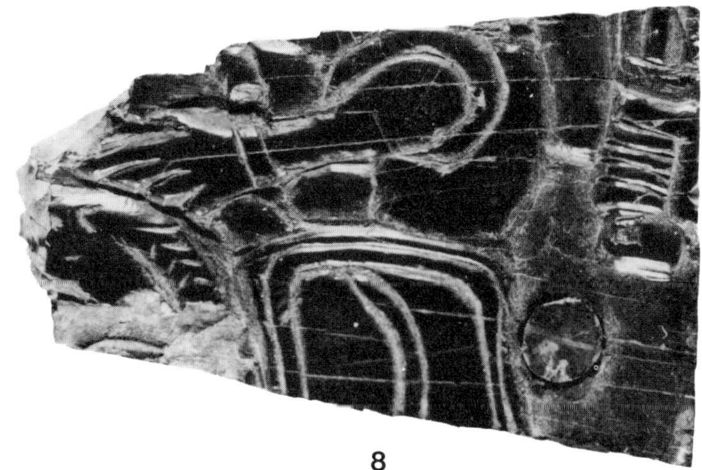

8

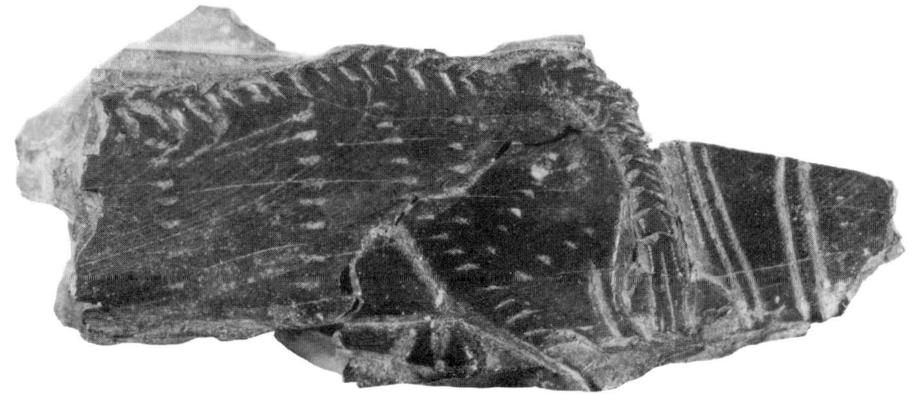

9

10 CC31 [1] (7); 64-909; T.
Part of the left rear leg of a horse, the yoke pole, and part of the chariot box, left. Reverse is irregularly scored.

11 BB31 [1] (8); 64-773; T. No photograph
Fragment like nos. 9, 10, right. Reverse scored irregularly.

12 BB31/CC31 (8); 64-   ; UM 65-31-477; ht. 1.5, w. 2.2, th. .3.
Part of a six-spoked chariot wheel and the box, with the rear buckle; a section of the horse's tail is evident.

13 CC31 [2] (7); 64-947; T 25851; ht. 2.2, w. 8.9, th. .6.
A six-spoked chariot wheel and part of the four legs and tail of a horse, left; all feet touch the ground. The bottom edge, a raised band, and the plain left edge are intact, with the scene completed on a separate plaque.

14 BB31 [1] (8); 64-788; T; ht. 1.6, w. 4.4, th. .8.
The lower part of a six-spoked chariot wheel and horse, right. Two more rear legs belong to another horse—a chariot horse?—overlapped by the foreground one. The raised bottom band and the plain right edges are intact, with the scene completed on a separate plaque. There is a dowel between the legs; the reverse is irregularly scratched.

15 BB31 [1] (8); 64-768; UM 65-31-364; ht. 2, w. 4.3, th. .7.
Part of a chariot box with yoke pole, six-spoked wheel, and horse, left. The legs are rather heavy. What appears to be the tip of another horse's hoof is at the lower right. The lower intact border is a raised band. The reverse has fine uniform scoring.

16 BB II; 64-   ; UM 65-31-574; ht. 2.3, w. 2, th. .4; Muscarella 1971a, pl. 63, fig. 2.
A chariot box and rear buckle, with a four-spoked wheel, right; a section of the horse's tail and yoke pole is at the right. The plain left border is intact.

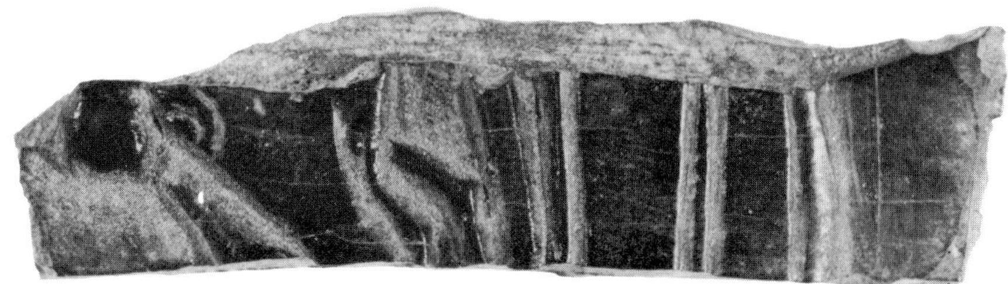

10

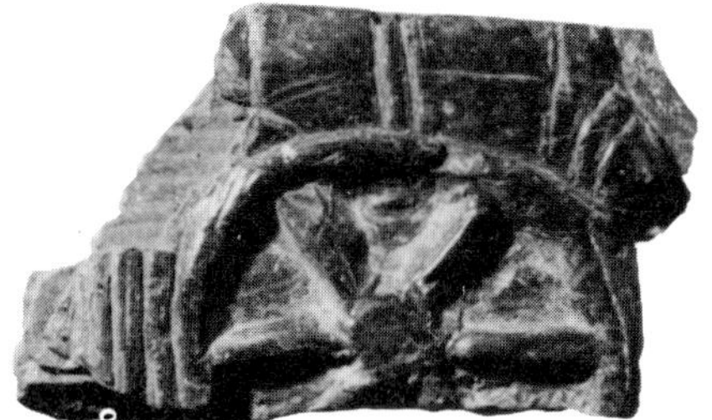

12

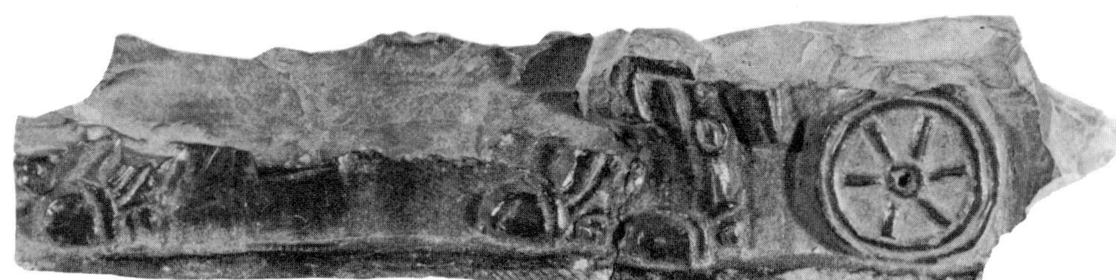

13

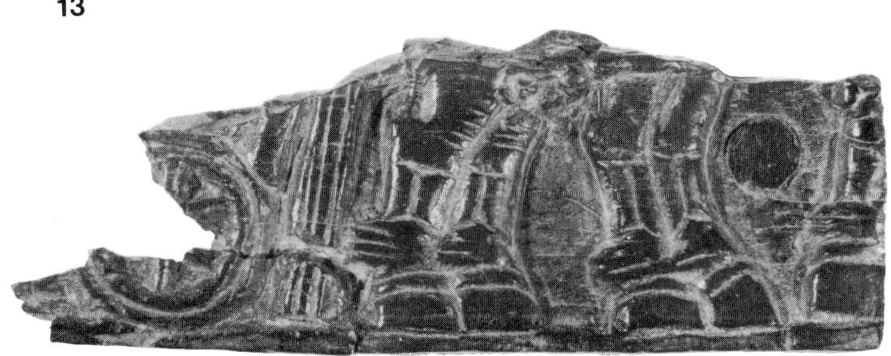

14

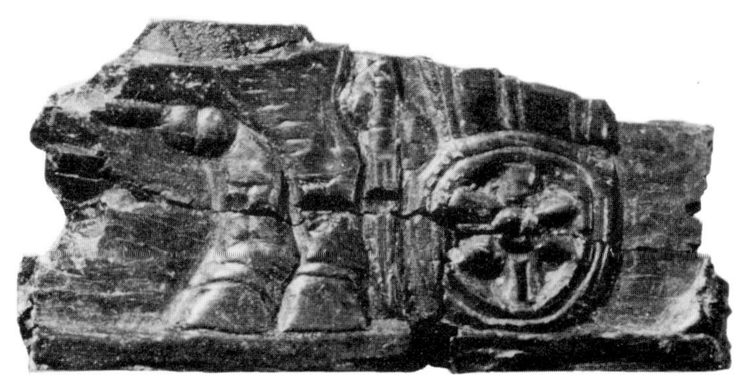

15

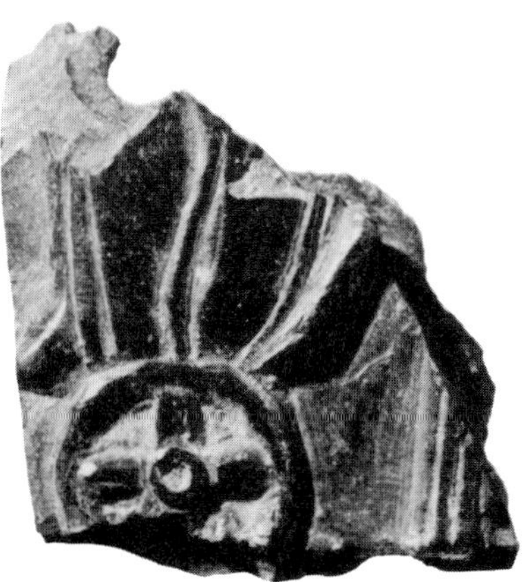

16

17 CC31 [2] (7); 64-885; T; ht. 1.9, w. 3.5, th. .75.
This fragment appears to depict a chariot box, the upper part of a wheel and a bit of the yoke pole, right. The box is decorated with a crossed motif in chunky-style relief. Above this there seems to be the outline of thick garments of the occupants. No other chariot box has the same crossed design. The plain upper edge is intact and the scene was completed on another plaque.

18 BB31 [1] (8); 64-782; UM 65-31-363; ht. 3.3, w. 3.5, th. .7.
Fragment with a six-spoked wheel and chariot-box buckle followed by a horse, of which only the lower legs are extant, left. Right and lower edges are intact, the latter showing the top part of a guilloche that, along with the horse, was completed on a separate plaque; a dowel hole exists behind the wheel. The reverse is irregularly scored.

19 BB31 (8); 64-1065; UM 65-31-344; ht. 1.5, w. 4.8.
Fragment depicting two overlapping chariot horses' heads, right. The mane is rendered by thick oblique and semicircular patterns; a herringbone motif is on the upper neck (a strap?); a curved thickness by the (broken away) mouth could be a bit. Before them is a warrior with a spear raised in his right hand. He wears a "feather" helmet (cf. nos. 55A, B, 57, 59, 61) with straight hair flaring out in the rear; his cloak has a scalloped border. The reverse is plain.

20 BB31 [1] (8); 64-774; MMA 65.163.21; ht. 1.5, w. 3.6, th. .8; Muscarella 1966, fig. 11.
Scene exactly like no. 19, but showing less of the warrior and preserving part of the upper guilloche border. Reverse has rocker scoring. The plain lower edge is intact and the scene was completed on a separate plaque.

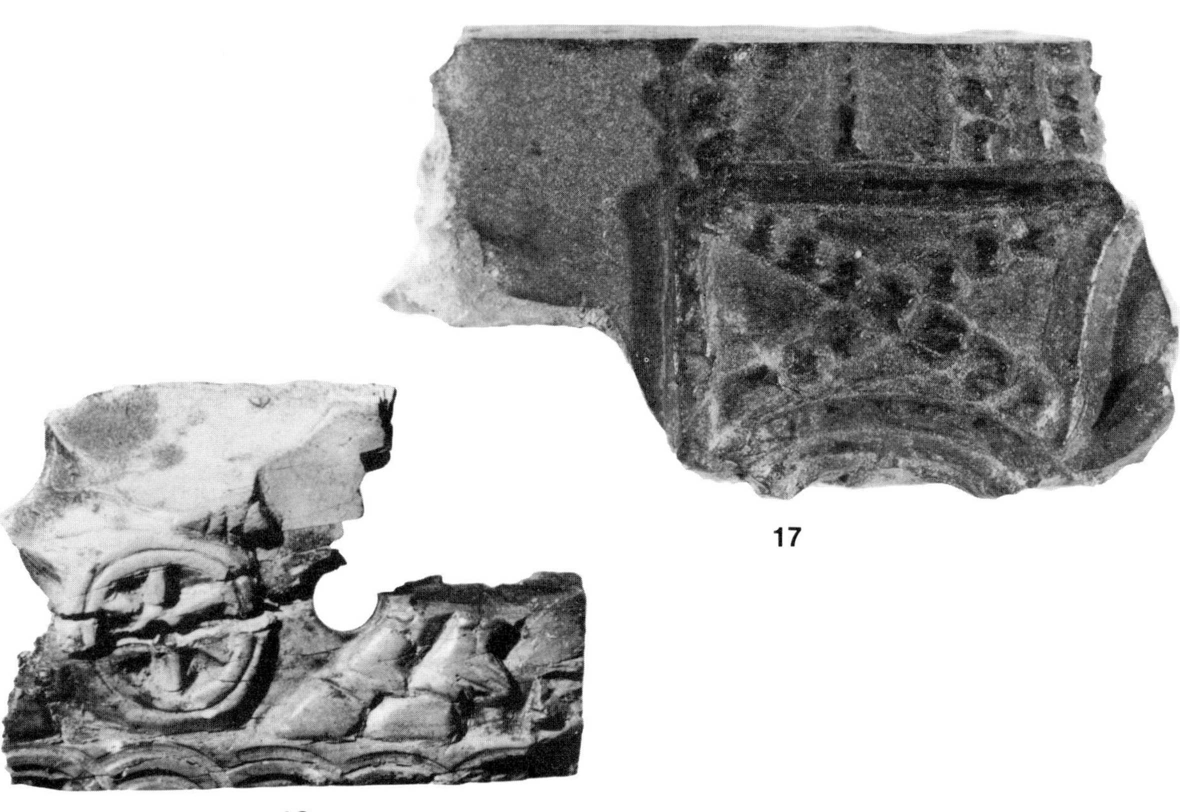

17

18

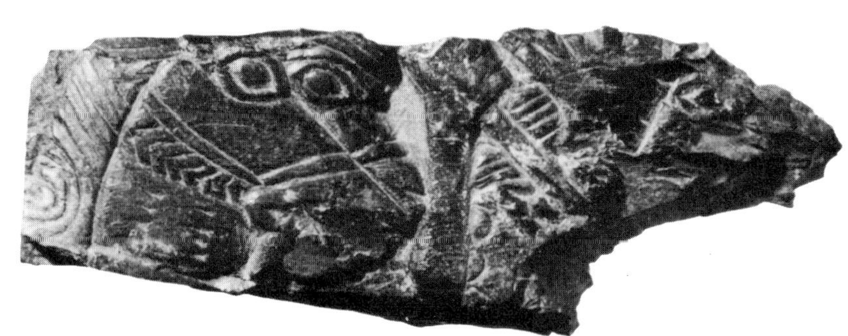

19

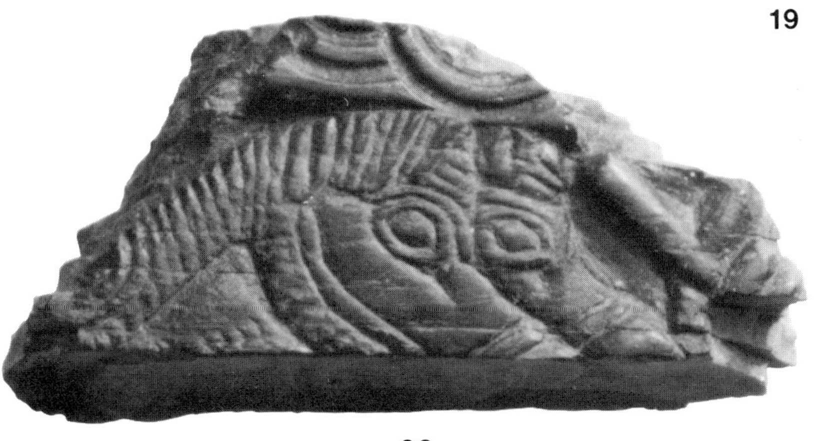

20

21 CC32 [1] [2] (area east of 7); 70-409; T; ht. 4; front and back views. Fragment with two chariot horses, heads overlapping, right; body decorations like nos. 2, 6, 9, 19, 20; cf. also nos. 28, 29, 171. To the right is a warrior with a large nose and prominent round eyes, who wields a spear against the horses. A complete guilloche pierced by a dowel hole forms the intact upper border; the lower edge seems also to be intact. Neat oblique scoring on the reverse along with two grooves; the top edge has neat rocker scoring.

22A CC32 [1] [2] (area east of 7); 70-411; UM 71-23-166; ht. 2.1, w. 4.8, th. .6.
B CC32 [1] [2]; 70-412; T.
C CC32 [1] [2]; 70-413; UM 71-23-167; ht. 1.7, w. 2.7, th. .6.

Three fragments depicting overlapping chariot horses' heads like no. 21, right. One has a guilloche upper border, one a narrow band, the other a slightly wider one, suggesting three different plaques. A small fragment with two horse's feet may belong to one of these plaques. The backs are irregularly scored like no. 21, as shown in back views.

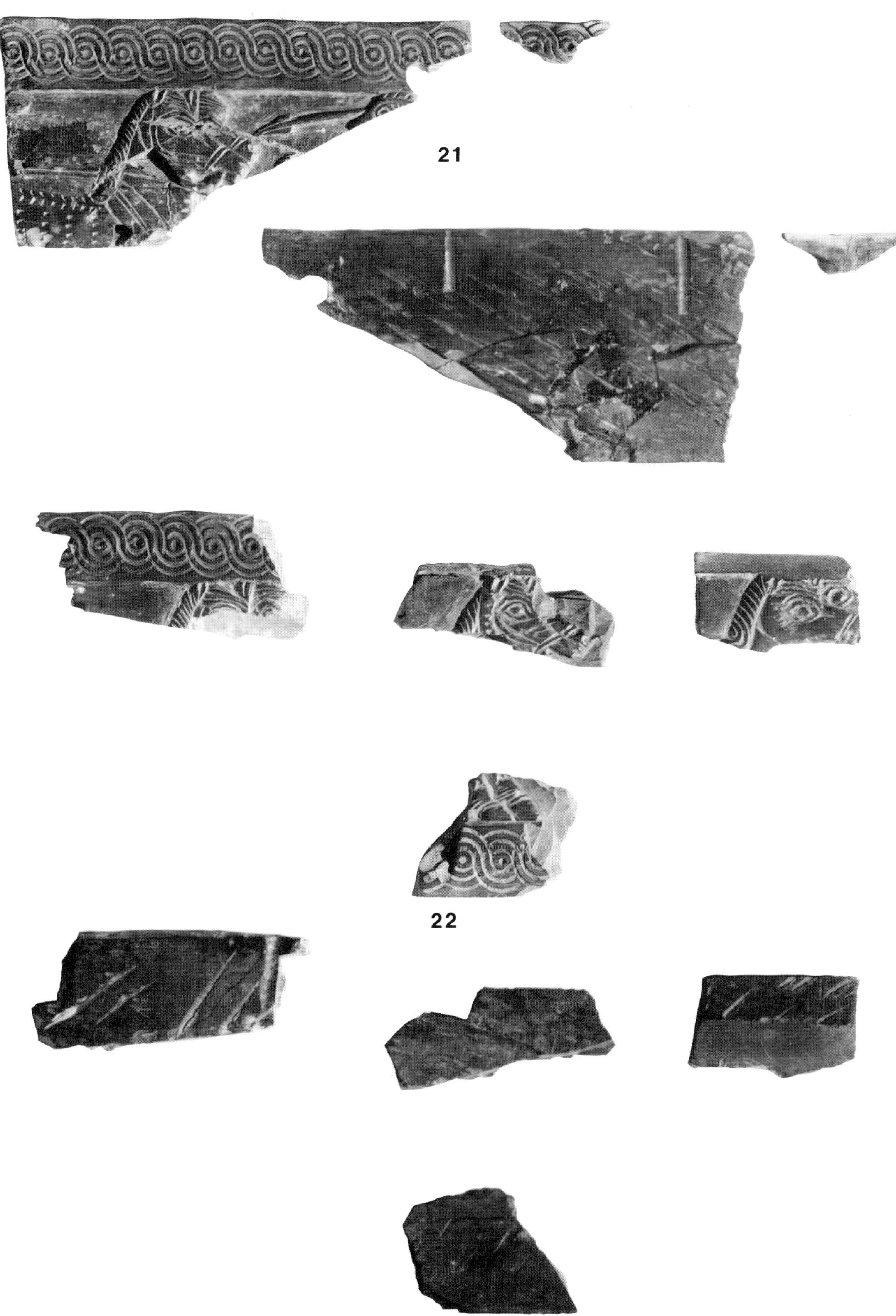

21

22

23 BB31 **[1]** (8); 64-767; T; ht. 2.1, w. 5.3, th. 1.1.
Two overlapping chariot horses' heads, left. The feathers of an arrow (note the notch) shot from the chariot, at the left. Upper intact border is a raised band; a dowel hole is at the left.

24 CC31 **[2]** (7); 64-1064; UM 65-31-344; ht. 1, w. 3.6, th. .9.
Two overlapping chariot horses' heads, left. A rocker scoring exists on the upper intact edge.

25 BB31/CC31 (8); 64- ; UM 65-31-542; ht. 1, w. 3.4, th. .8.
Upper part of two overlapping chariot horses' heads, left. The upper intact border is a raised band.

26 BB31/CC31 (8); 64-1076; T 25868; ht. 2, w. 3.4, th. .8.
Two overlapping chariot horses' heads, left. Both wear feathered headdresses. The upper intact border is a raised band.

27 BB31/CC31 (8); 64-1069; UM 65-31-346; w. 4, th. .8.
Apparently a horse's feathered headdress(?), but different from nos. 5 and 26. The upper guilloche border, completed on another plaque, and the sawed right edge are intact; an ivory dowel is *in situ*. The reverse has neat rocker scoring.

28 BB31/CC31 (8); 64- ; UM 65-31-562; ht. .5, w. 3.5, th. .6.
The necks of two overlapping horses; left. Compare for the mane nos. 19-22; the herringbone band, nos. 19, 20.

29 BB31/CC31 (8); 64- ; UM 65-31-561; ht. .7, w. 3.4, th. .7.
Part of a bell pendent from a horse's neck; chariot or cavalry, right. The reverse has relatively deep irregular scoring.

30 BB31/CC31 (8); 64- ; UM 65-31-568; ht. 1.6, w. 1.8, th. .4.
Part of a bell pendent from a horse's neck, right; cavalry or chariot.

31 BB31/CC31 (8); 64-1072; T 25866; ht. 1.6, w. 2.3, th. .6.
Part of a charioteer with reins held in both hands, right. His thick lips and beard are extant.

32 BB31 (8); 64-1065; UM 65-31-344; ht. of larger 2, w. 3.
Two fragments of hands of charioteers holding reins, left. Vertical scoring on the reverse.

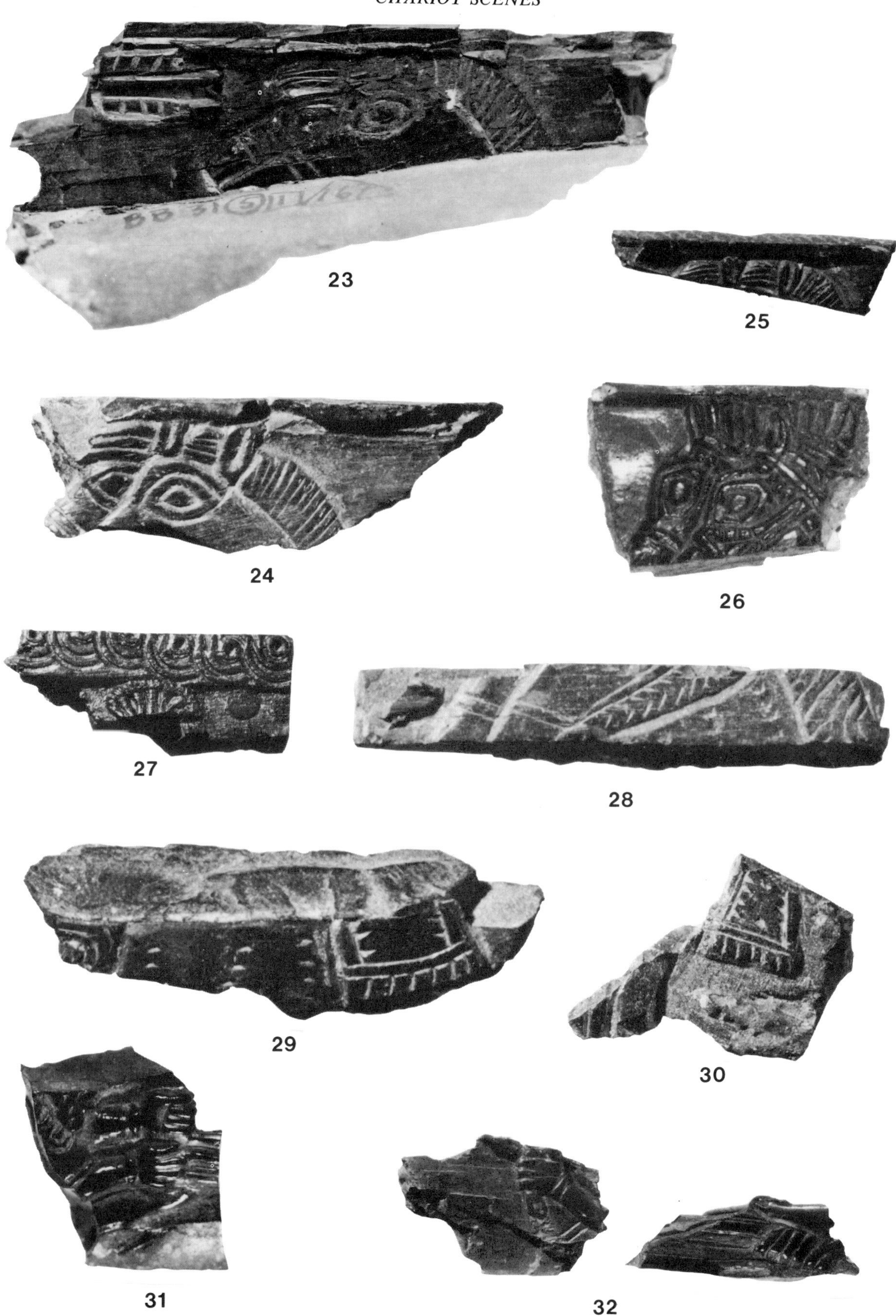
23
25
24
26
27
28
29
30
31
32

B: CAVALRY SCENES

33 BB31 [1] (8); 64-769; MMA 65.163.9; ht. 4.5, w. 7.1, th. .9; Muscarella 1966, fig. 12
A cavalryman holds a spear in his right hand while the left holds the reins close to the mane, right. The warrior wears a short-sleeved fringed garment, knee- or calf-length, with scalloped borders; he may be wearing boots. The horse is the same type as the chariot ones and is also not gelded; no saddle is depicted. A bearded nude enemy, with straight hair, wearing sandals, is under the horse. The plain right edge is intact and the scene was completed on another plaque.

34 AA30 (5,N); 60-950; T; ht. 6.2, w. 7.5, th. .8.
A single horse's head, and thus a cavalry horse, wearing a bell, right. The hand of a warrior, right, wielding a weapon, is obviously an ally of the cavalryman. This is our only evidence that cavalry horses also wore bells.

35 BB31/CC31 (8); 64-1076; T 25868; ht. 1.4, w. 2.5, th. .8.
Part of a single horse's head, and thus cavalry, right. The point of an enemy spear touches the nose.

36 AA30 (5,N); 60-950; T; ht. 1.9, w. 5, th. .8; drawing.
A cavalryman, only part of whose face and hand are extant, and the back of the horse's head, right. The plain lower edge is intact, the scene having been completed on another plaque.

37 BB II; 64-   ; UM 65-31-585; ht. .4, w. 3.4, th. .8.
A scene like no. 36, but less complete; left.

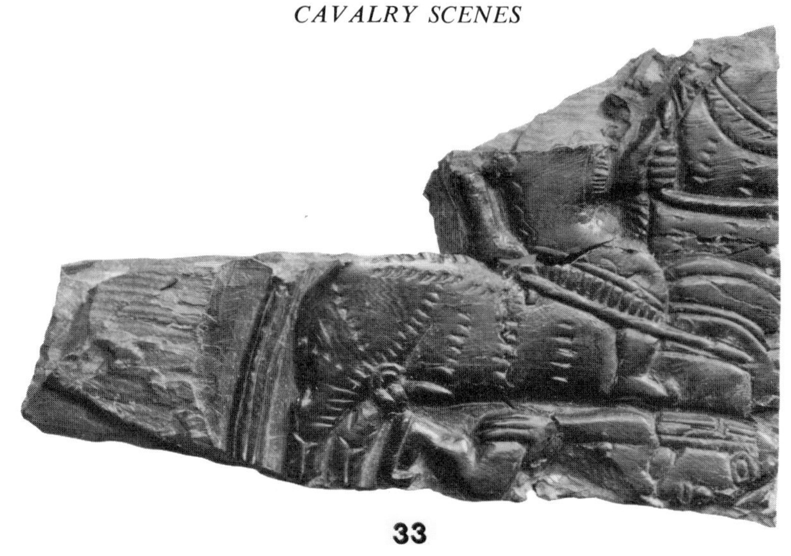

33

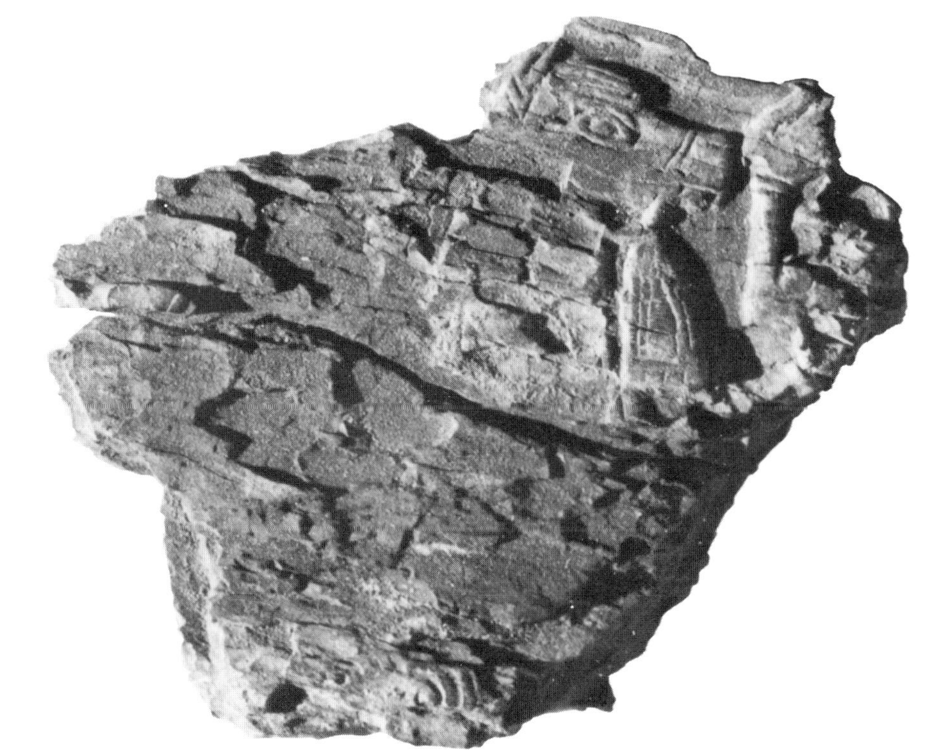

34

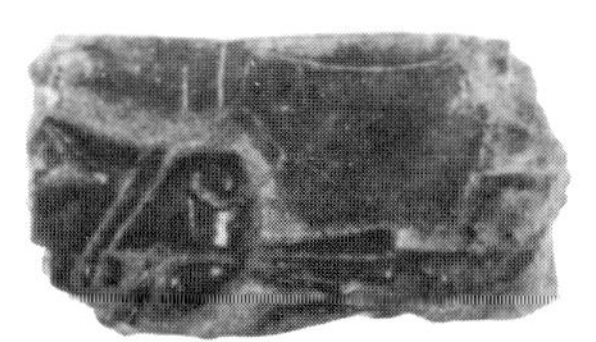

35

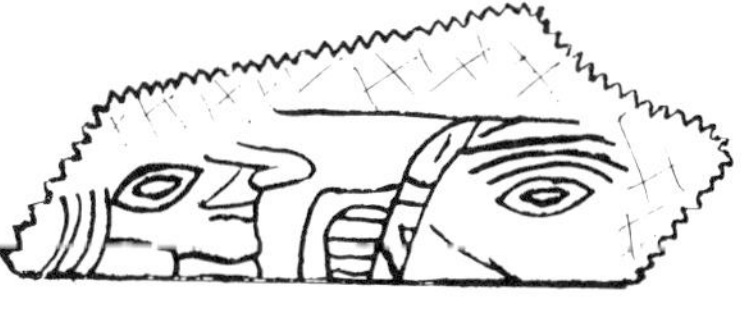

36

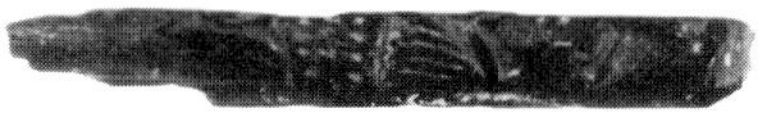

37

38 Wood; BB30 (5,C); 60-1007; T; ht. 10, w. 16, th. 3; Dyson 1961, fig. 13; 1964a, fig. 10.
Cut in high relief; charred so that no clothing or body details are preserved. A bearded man sits lightly on a horse; his right hand holds reins or the horse's mane, his left is held high. The horse is large with a thick tail; no sex seems indicated. A rectangular cutting exists on the horse's rump.

39 Wood; CC31 [1] (6); 64-928; MMA 65.163.43; ht. 2.5, w. 1.9, th. .25; Muscarella 1966, fig. 26.
Part of a horse's head, right. Top edge plain and intact. Note that this piece and the following pieces up to no. 47 could be from either chariot or cavalry scenes. The reverse is fairly smooth and has no scoring.

40 BB31 (8); 64-1066; UM 65-31-356; ht. 1.3, w. 6.4.
The lower part of a nude enemy under a horse. The lower border is intact with part of a guilloche, completed on another plaque; a dowel is *in situ* under the man.

41 AA30 (5,N); 60-950; T; ht. 2.2, w. 4.7, th. .9.
The left hand and arm of a nude enemy under a horse, only the front legs of which are extant, right. The rear legs of a preceding cavalry horse are extant. Lower edge plain and intact.

42 CC31 [1] (6); 64-908; UM 65-31-338; ht. 1.5, w. 4.4, th. .5.
The front legs of a horse, left; the hocks are prominent. Left and bottom edges plain and intact. The reverse has oblique irregular scoring.

43 CC31 [1] (6); 64-910; T; ht. 1.2, w. 1.9, th. .5.
Same as above, right.

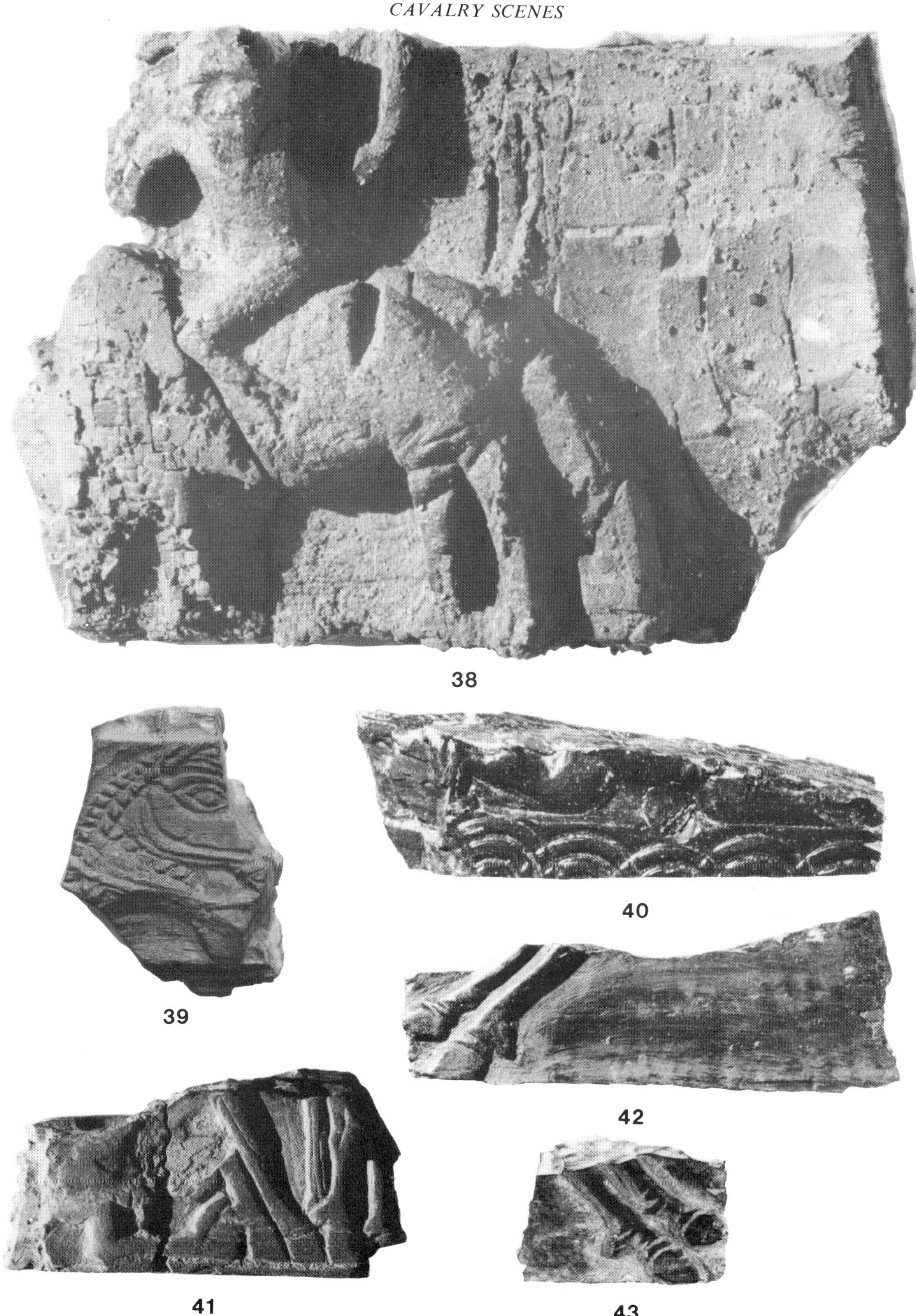

38

39

40

41

42

43

44 Wood; CC31 [1] (6); 64-925; T; ht. 2.3, w. 2.3, th. .7.
Same as no. 42, left. The damaged tip of the horse's mouth is barely preserved. Left and bottom edges are plain and intact.

45 Wood; CC31 [2] (7); 64-1003; UM 65-31-305A; ht. 3.3, w. 4.5, th. 1.2.
Same as above, left. A damaged motif appears at the left. The lower border is decorated with triangular cut-outs.

46 Wood; BB31/CC31 (8); 64-   ; UM 65-31-303A.
The tip of a spear, left or right, not clear. Spears are usually carried by foot warriors and cavalrymen.

47 BB31/CC31 (8); 64-   ; UM 65-31-492; ht. .7, w. 2.7. UM 65-31-505; ht. .6, w. 1.9, th. .7. UM-65-31-510; ht. 1, w. 3.2, th. .7. UM-65-31-555; ht. .7, w. 3.4, th. .9.
Four fragments of horses' hooves, right and left; two have lower guilloche borders, at least one of which was completed on a separate plaque.

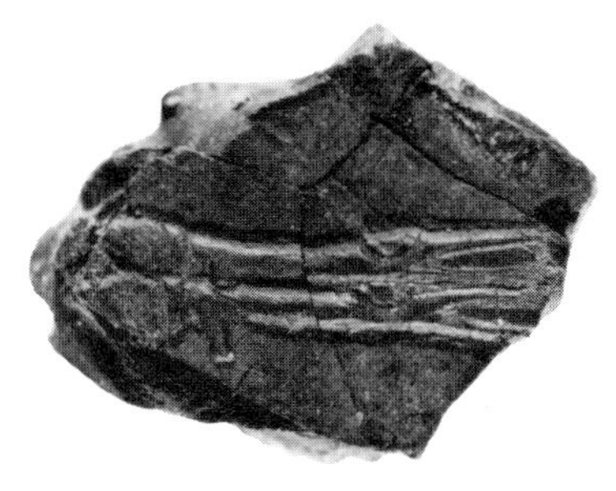

44

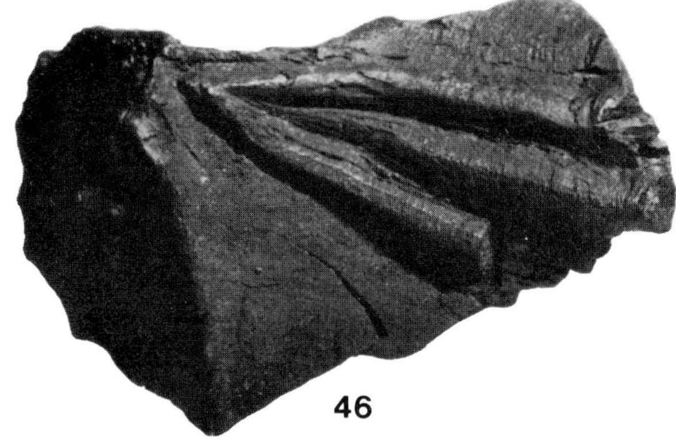

46

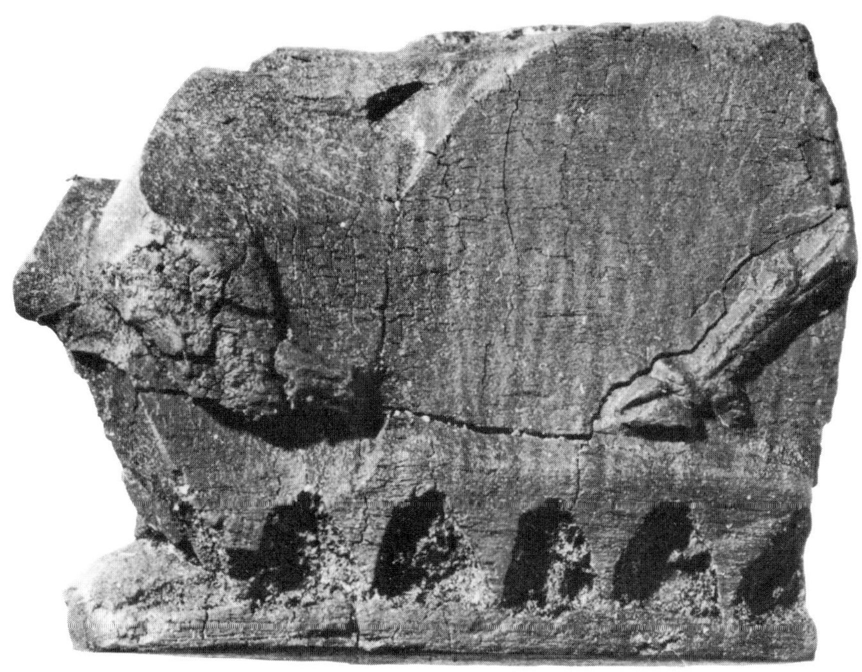

45

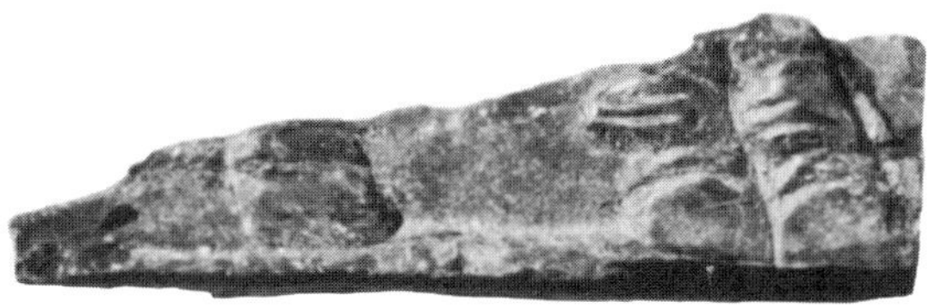

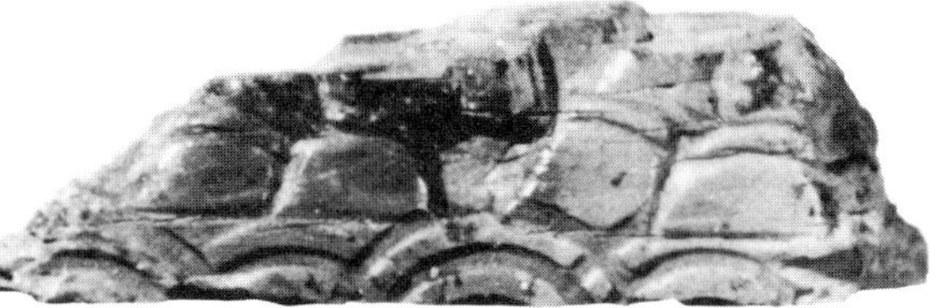

47

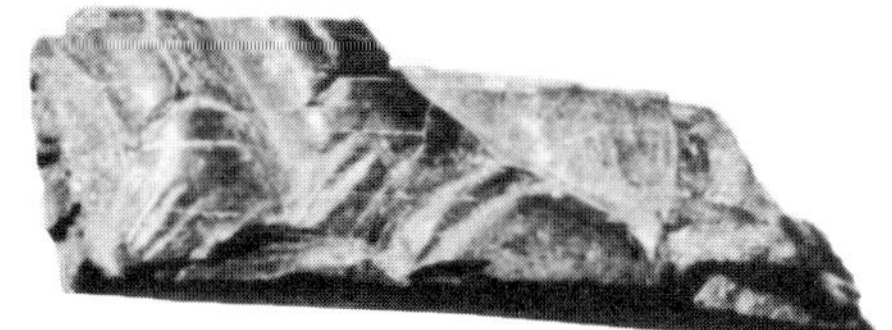

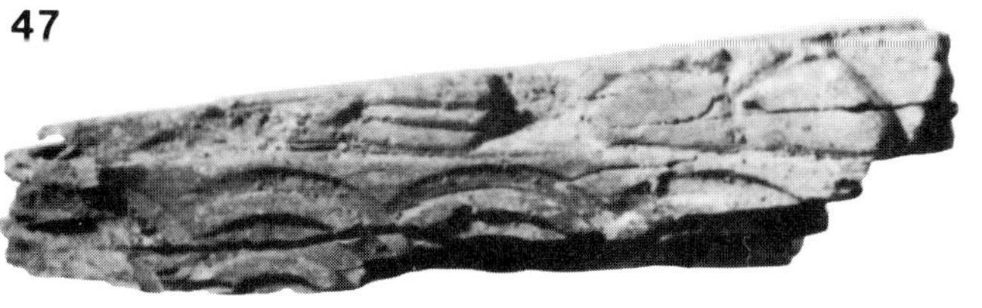

C: WARRIORS

48 CC31 [2] (7); 64-893; UM 65-31-361; ht. 2, w. 4.9, th. .4.
Fragment from a chariot scene depicting a charioteer, background, and an archer, foreground, right The warriors have thick lips, prominent noses, S-shaped ears; hair and beard rendered in thick, squarish chunks; they seem to wear "feather" helmets without earflaps (cf. nos. 59, 61). Garments are V-necked, with heavy, chunky, bandoliers and thick belts. Neither the end of the arrow shaft nor the bow string is depicted. The reverse is smooth.

49 BB31 [1] (8); 64-776; T; ht. 2.4, w. 3.9, th. .6.
Apparently a charioteer and an archer but the positions of the hands are not clear. The man in the foreground seems to hold reins in his left hand —a bit of the reins is below the hand—and his right hand is raised—to hold a weapon? The rear man seems to hold a bow in both hands. Hair is rendered as spiral curls (cf. nos. 61, 174); noses are prominent. The belted garments are fringed at the short sleeves and neck. The plain left edge is intact; the reverse has rocker scoring.

50 Wood; CC31 [1] (6); 64-926; T 25873; ht. 2.3, w. 3.5, th. .7; front view and drawing.
Front half of face and left arm of an archer, right. It is not clear if a helmet is worn; thick bow string visible up to the face but not crossing it. A dowel is *in situ* at the right.

51 BB31 (8); 64-1065; MMA 65.163.25; ht. 1.4, w. 2.7, th. .5; Muscarella 1966, fig. 15.
Two overlapping figures, the foreground one holding a bow and arrow, right. Hair is straight and thick; belt and fringe of short sleeves rendered in chunky style. The arrow and bow string cross over the figure (cf. no. 50). Whether the background figure is another archer or a charioteer is not known. Plain left and lower borders are intact. No scoring on the reverse.

52 BB31 (8); 64-1072; T 25866; ht. 1.8, w. 4.2, th. 1.6.
Extant are the left arm and part of a bow and arrow aimed right. An unidentified object is visible in the center. A second small fragment of another hand and the tip of an arrow comes from the same provenience.

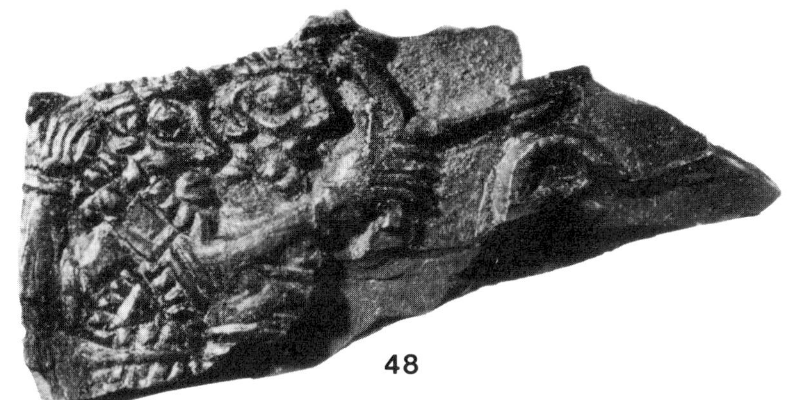

48

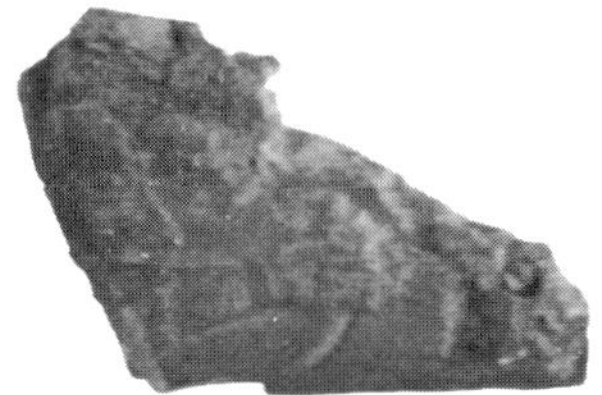

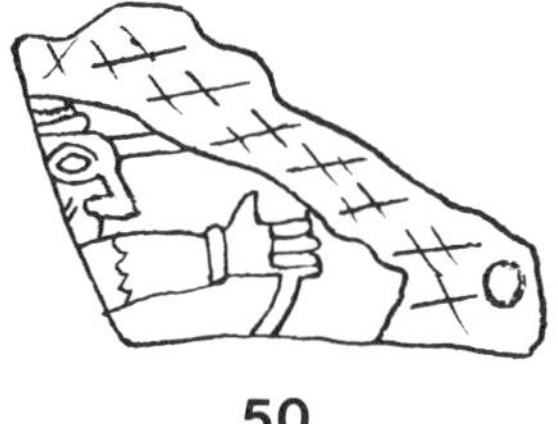

50

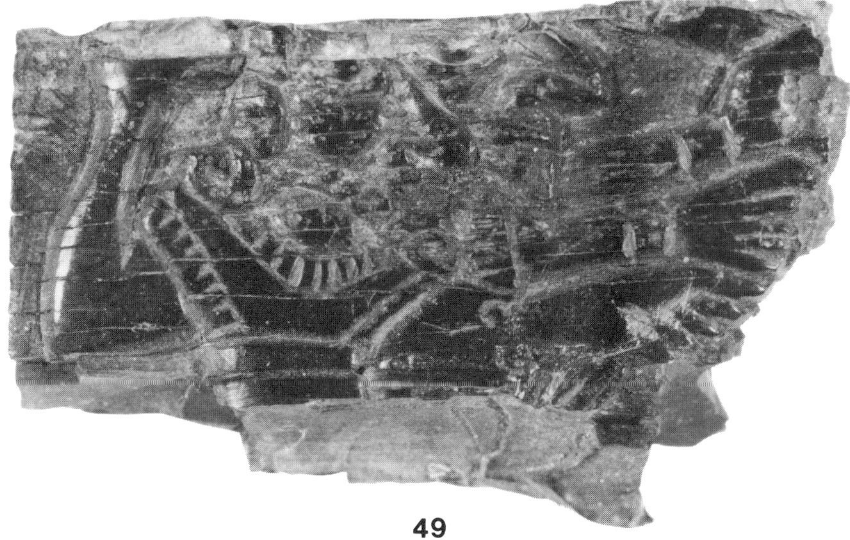

49

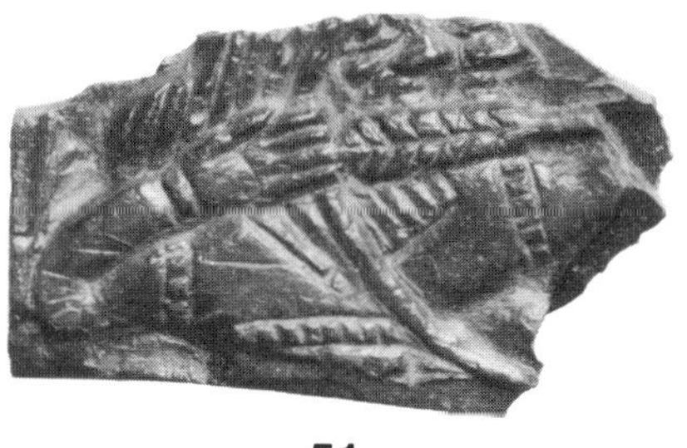

51

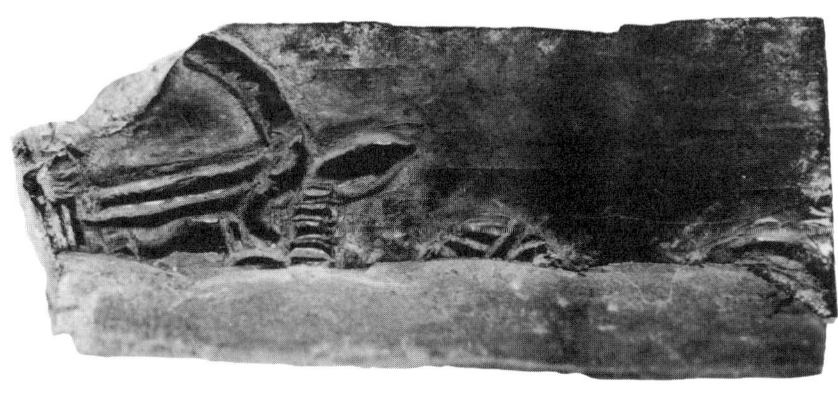

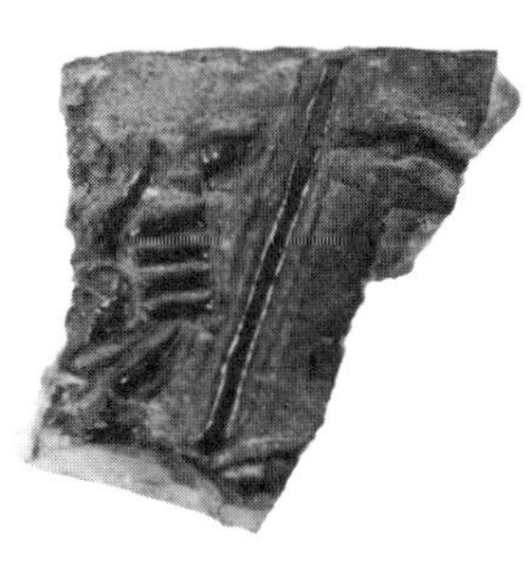

52

53 CC31 [2] (7); 64-892; MMA 65.163.17; ht. 1.6, w. 5.2, th. .8; Baer 1971, fig. 1.
Parts of two archers, back to back and shooting in opposite directions. Each wears a quiver; the bowstrings pass over their faces. Hair is rendered in chunky style and is held by a fillet; traces of an ear are present. This is the only evidence for quivers on the archer scenes. Top border, a narrow band, is complete. Irregular scoring on the reverse.

54 BB31 [1] (8); 64-793; T; ht. 2.5, w. 4.9, th. .8.
Striding warrior, right, wielding a spear in his right hand, a small round shield in his left; the spear shaft does not pass across his body. The nose of a horse (not clear if there are two horses) is extant at the left. The warrior wears a short-sleeved, knee-length garment with a plain narrow belt; borders are scalloped and fringed. His helmet is like nos. 55A, 57, with a leather earflap incised with a V-shaped tool. The beard is rendered in incised oblique straight lines; lips are thick. The plain right and bottom edges are intact, the scene being completed on another plaque. The reverse has rocker scoring.

55A BB31 [1] (8); 64-791; MMA 65.163.8; ht. 3.4, w. 6.6, th. .8; Muscarella 1966, fig. 14.
Warrior, like no. 54, right. Here, however, the spear is pointed down and the shaft crosses over the body; the garment is scalloped and without fringes. Hair, projecting at right angles from the head, and beard are rendered in incised lines; lips are barely depicted. The helmet is flat at the top with triangular cut-outs, which may be decoration or an attempt to depict a "feather" motif; leather earflaps protect the face. Thrust at the warrior from the right are two spears. The plain left edge is intact, as is the upper, decorated with a guilloche; a dowel hole is preserved. Reverse irregularly scored.

55B BB31 [1] (8); 64-789; MMA 65.123.18; ht. 2.7, w. 4.7, th. .9; Muscarella 1966, fig. 14.
The bare right foot of a warrior advancing from the left, whose spear touches the bare left foot of an opponent. It is possible that this fragment is part of no. 55A; at least it belongs to a similar scene. The drawing of the spear supports the former conclusion, and the reverse has the same scoring; it also has a shallow vertical groove.

56 BB31/CC31 (8); 64-   ; UM 65-31-469; ht. 1.7, w. 3.1, th. .4.
A fragment of a warrior in a scene like the previous two examples, right. The spear shaft is visible below the chest. His clothing is like no. 54.

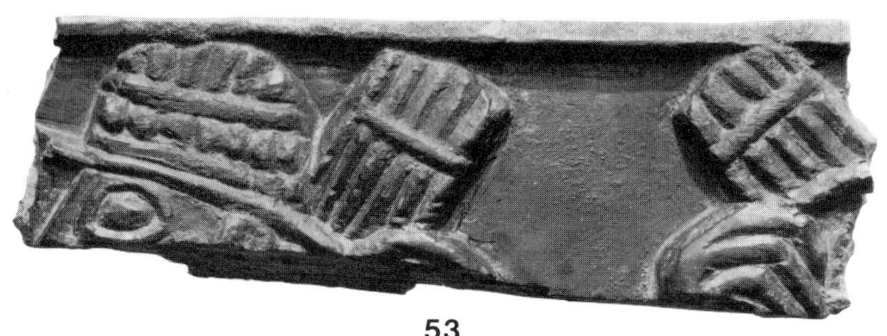

53

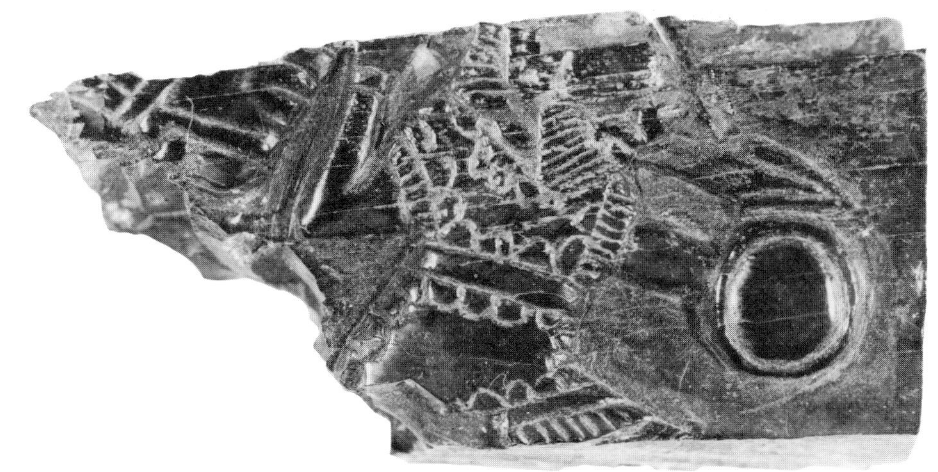

54

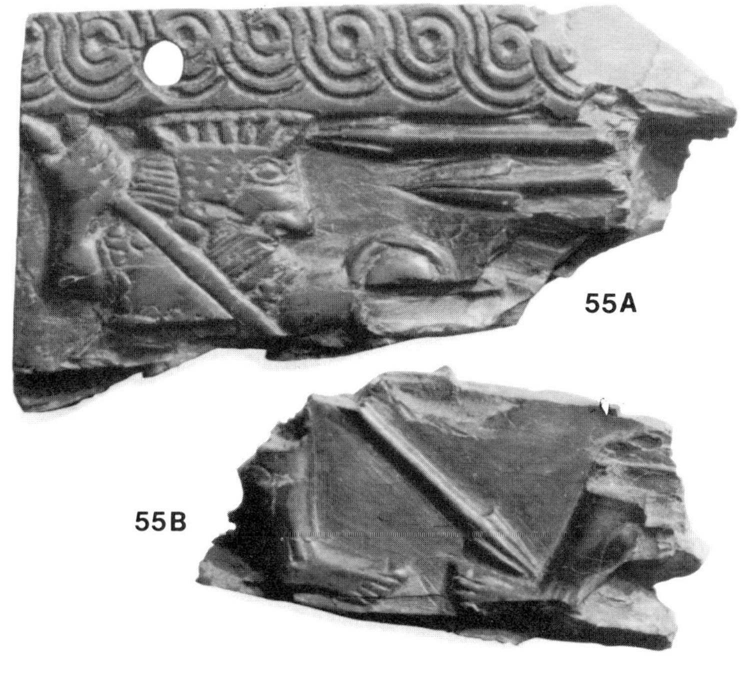

55A

55B

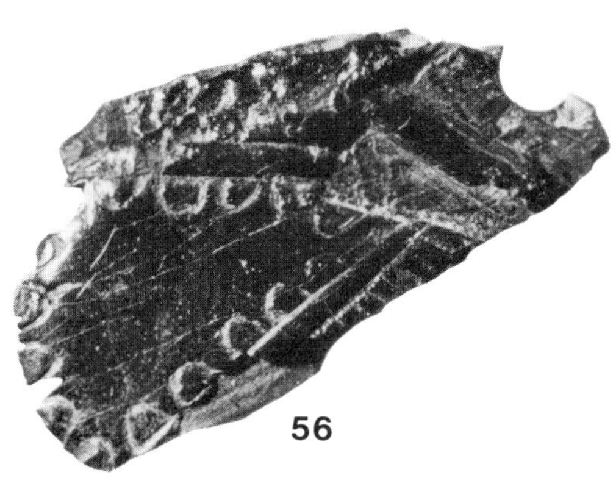

56

57 BB31/CC31 (8); 64-1069; UM 65-31-346; ht. 1.4, w. 5.8, th. 1.
The head of a warrior like the preceding examples, right. The top of the feathered helmet is not fully carved. The upper border has a guilloche pattern. The reverse has neat scoring.

58 CC32 [1] [2] (area east of 7); 70-414; T; ht. 2.1, w. 4.7; front and back views.
Warrior with prominent nose and pointed incised beard holds a spear in his left hand, a round shield in his right, left. A horse's tail is extant at the left. The warrior's belted garment is scalloped and fringed. The reverse has rocker scoring.

59 CC31 [2] (7); 64-895; T; ht. 2.4, w. 4.2, th. .6.
Parts of two warriors, right. The front one wields a sword, the other a spear and shield. Their noses are long and thin; ears are S-shaped; mouths are thick; the hair flares back from the head. Note that the shield is depicted as if held awkwardly around the rim (cf. nos. 62, 64). The helmet has no earflaps and is of the "feather" type. The plain upper edge is intact.

60 BB31 [1] (8); 64-997; UM 65-31-326; ht. 2.7, w. 3.
A warrior dressed in a scalloped garment, right; his right arm is raised, his left seems straight. A thick curved object that turns down frames the man; it is not clear what this scene represents—perhaps he is seated?

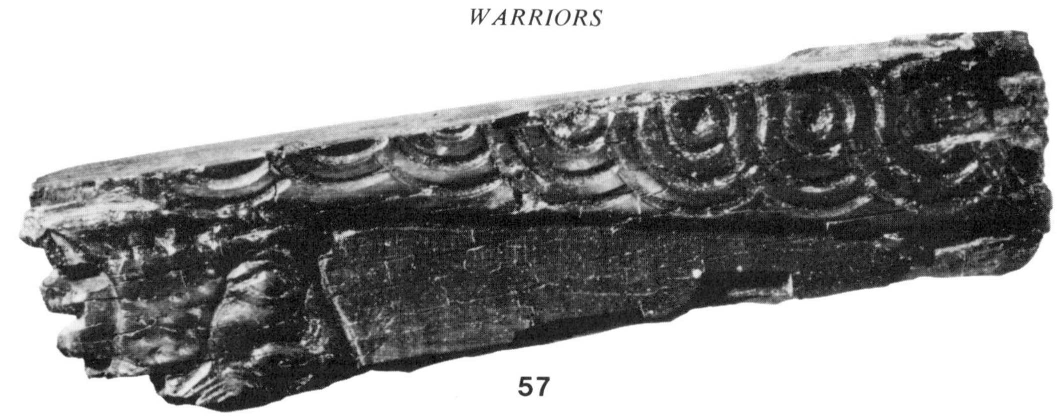

57

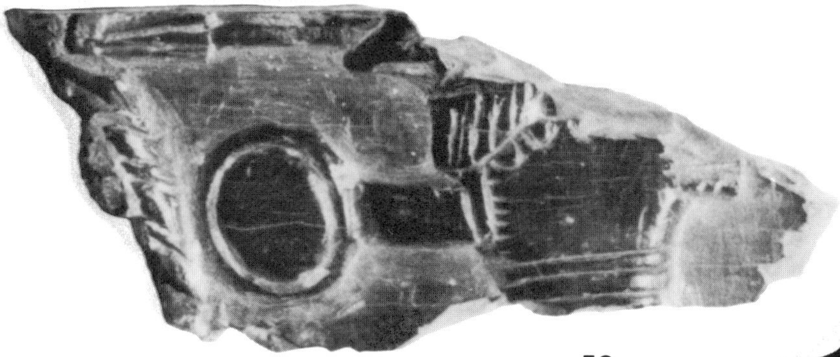

58

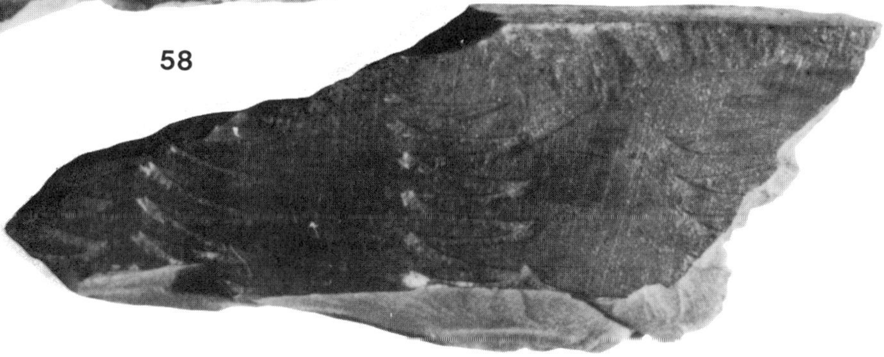

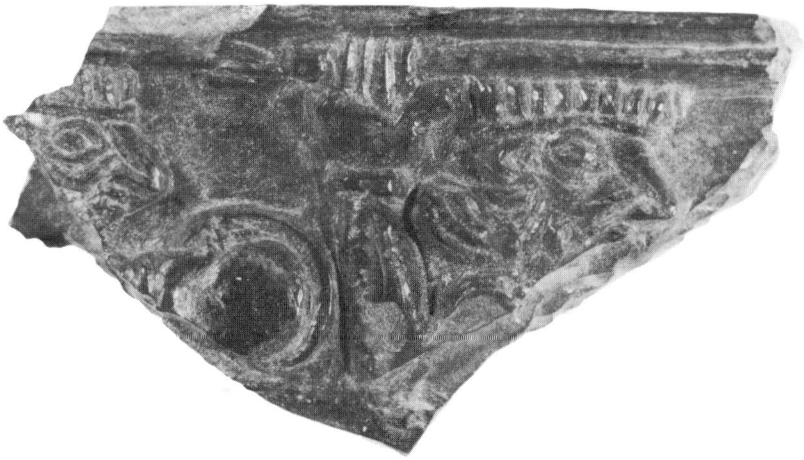

59

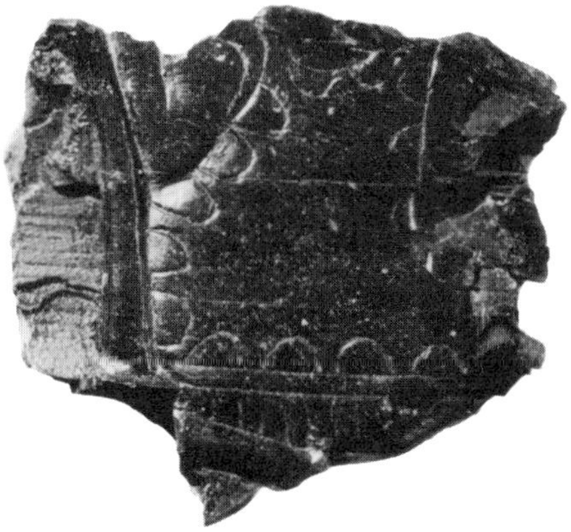

60

61 CC31 [2] (7); 64-891; T; ht. 2.7, w. 4, th. .7.
A warrior with a "feather" helmet, and no earflaps, strides right. Behind him is the tip of a horse's mouth (?). The warrior carries an unidentifiable weapon, probably a mace (?); the end of an oval object at his chest may be a shield. Eyes are oval, nose sharp, hair is rendered in thick spirals (cf. nos. 49, 174); his elbow is outlined in parallel curves (cf. nos. 65, 105). The garment is V-necked and seems to be bordered by a chunky design. The plain left edge is intact, as is the top, which is a narrow band.

63 Z26 (BB I West); 58-431; UM 59-4-147; ht. 1.5, w. 1.4; Dyson 1964a, fig. 2.
Two small fragments, one depicting a warrior with a "feather" type helmet, left. He holds a weapon in a raised hand, seen behind his head; two shields are visible, one held by the rim by an opposing warrior, the other probably his. Straight hair projects upward from the head; eyes are lozenge-shaped. The other fragment preserves just the head, and is exactly like the first fragment; no ears are depicted. Upper border of each, a narrow band, is intact.

63 Z26 (BB I West); 58-431; UM 59-4-147; ht. 1.5, w. 1.4; Dyson 1964a, fig. 2.
A bearded man with sharp nose, thick lips, lozenge-shaped eyes, and flaring hair held by a fillet; no ears are depicted; left. He holds a curved object in his right hand; it may be a free-swinging mace head.

64 CC31 [2] (7); 64-899; UM 65-31-302; ht. 1.9, w. 2.6, th. .6.
Extant are a hand at the left holding a shield by the rim (cf. nos. 59, 62) and at the right, apparently in opposition, a hand holding a spear vertically.

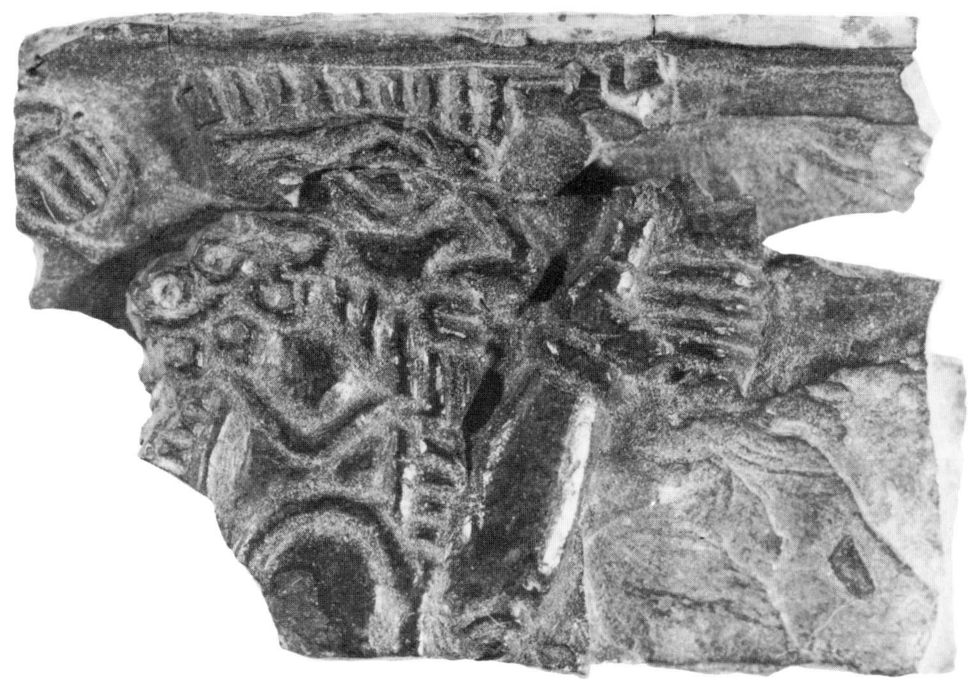

61

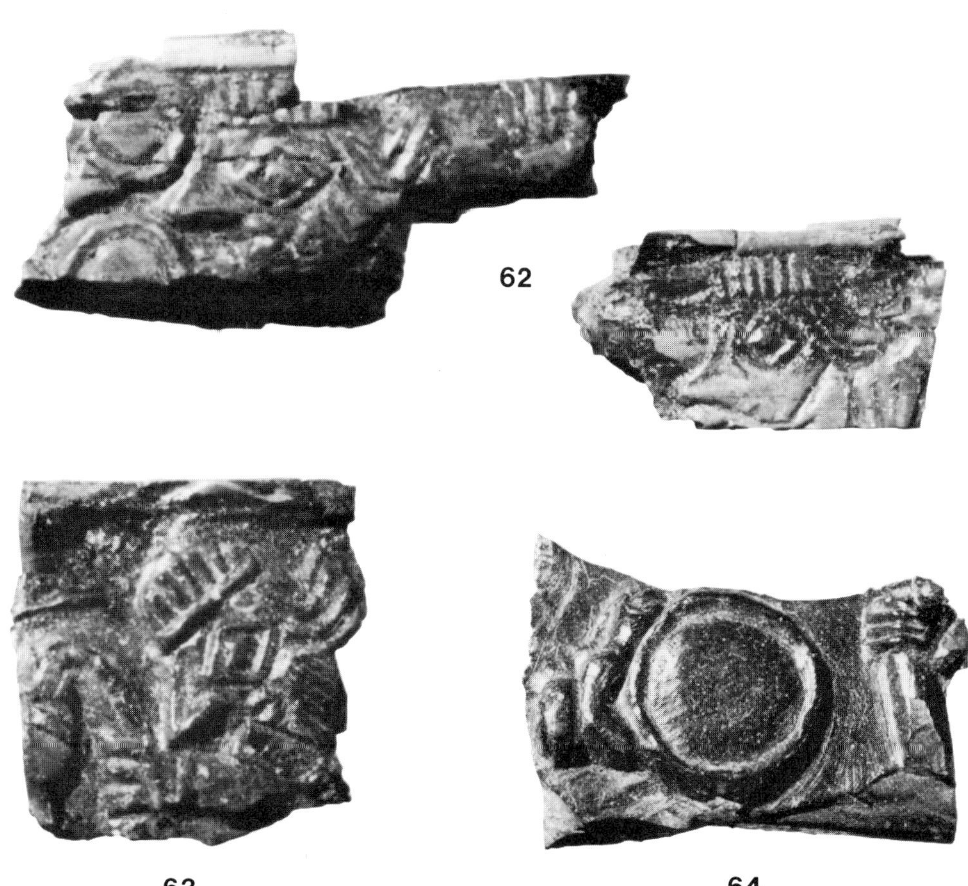

62

63

64

65 BB31 [1] (7); 64-756; T; ht. 1.7, w. 4, th. .9.
The lower part of a barefoot man in a fringed garment, right. The calves and knees are outlined in parallel curves. Bottom and right plain edges are intact; a dowel is at the right.

66 BB31 (8); 64-1073; T 25867; ht. 1.1, w. 3.8, th. .8.
Lower part of a barefoot warrior in a fringed knee-length garment, left. The right border, a thick band, and the bottom, a narrow band, are intact; a dowel hole at the right.

67 BB31 (8); 64-1066; UM 65-31-356; ht. 1.5, w. 3.6, th. .25.
Extant are one bare foot, right, followed by a horse's foot. The lower edge, a narrow band, is intact. The reverse has two short vertical grooves.

68 BB31 (8); 64-1066; UM 65-31-356; ht. 1.6, w. 3.8, th. .6.
Extant are three human feet at the left, and a horse's hoof at the right. Two feet facing right belong to one man, the other facing left belongs to another. Bottom edge, a band, is intact.

69 BB31 [1] (8); 64-765; MMA 65.163.24; ht. 3, w. 3.6, th. .8; Muscarella 1966, fig. 16.
A fragment apparently from a city under siege. A female (?), facing right, holds her head in despair. Directly behind her is a turret or tower into which an arrow or spear is stuck. Plain left, and upper border, a band, are intact; a dowel hole partly preserved by the hand at right. The reverse is smooth but has a shallow vertical groove.

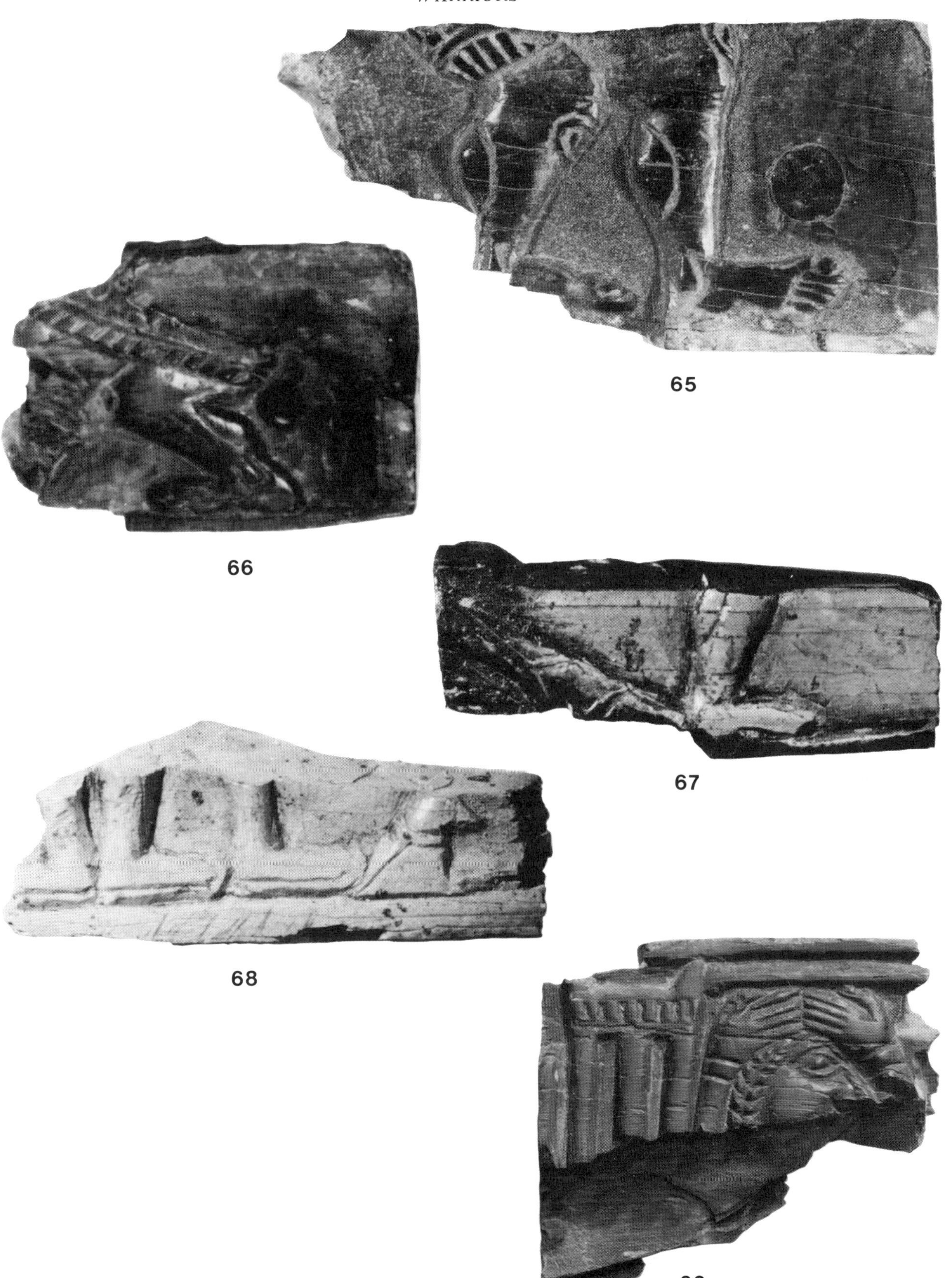

65

66

67

68

69

70 AA30 (5,N); 60-950; T; ht. 3.7, w. 6; Dyson 1961, fig. 15.
Fragment of a siege scene. The architecture seems to depict two piers/ turrets, or towers, flanking a gate. They have a grooved top and beaded vertical borders. Defending warriors—only the feet are extant—stand on the piers. At the right a defending warrior's shield touches that of an attacker mounting a ladder. A horse's head is seen between the fortress and the ladder.

71 BB31 [1] (8); 64-981; T 25858; ht. 4.4, w. 3, th. 1.1.
On the left are two figures, sex not clear, clasping each other. They have sharp prominent noses and hair held by fillets. At the right is a ladder and to its right are a series of horizontal lines, unidentified. This is undoubtedly a siege scene. The reverse has rocker scoring, and is slightly concave; the upper left edge is intact.

72 CC31 [1] (6); 64-1075; T 25862; ht. 8, w. 4.1.
A fragment in the round preserving part of three city towers or turrets of the same type as depicted on no. 70. Above are a row of chevrons inlaid with wood. Three small dowel holes are extant. The original function of this piece is not clear.

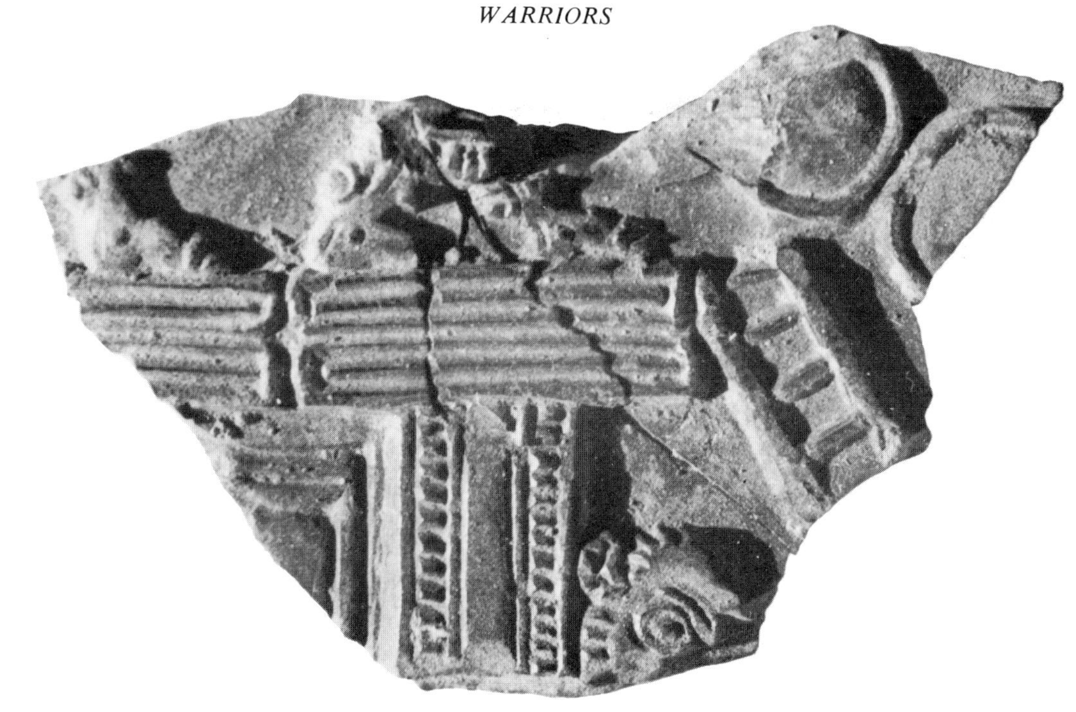

70

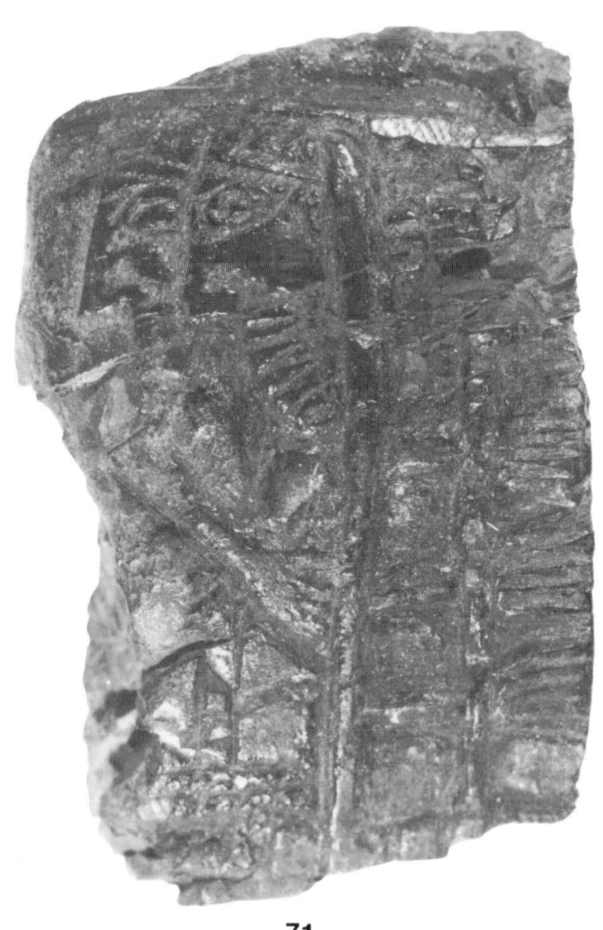

71

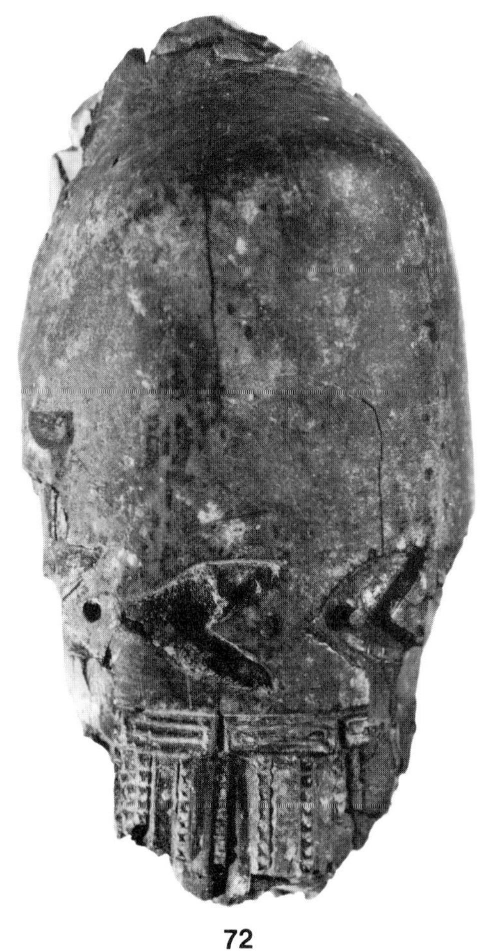

72

II

HUMAN HEADS AND BODIES: DRINKING AND PROCESSION SCENES

73 Bone; AA31 (5,E); 62-436; T; ht. 8.3; Dyson, *Archaeology* 16,2 (1963), 132; 1964a, fig. 1; 1964b, figs. 14-17; views of all four sides.
Cosmetic container, open at both ends, rectangular in section, tapering slightly toward the grooved top. Each side is decorated with two panels. The lower four depict animals: one a bearded and apparently human-headed goat, one a goat, another a calf (?), the fourth a couchant bull; one of the upper panels has a couchant goat. The other three upper panels depict two standing and one seated man. All are bareheaded, with shoulder-length herringbone-patterned hair, apparently held by a fillet, largely fleshy noses straight-bridged from the forehead, and lozenge or oval eyes. All carry staffs in the left hand, cups in the right. The standing men have short-sleeved (?) knee-length belted garments with fringes; the seated man wears a beltless, slightly longer garment, and he alone wears a bracelet and apparently sandals.

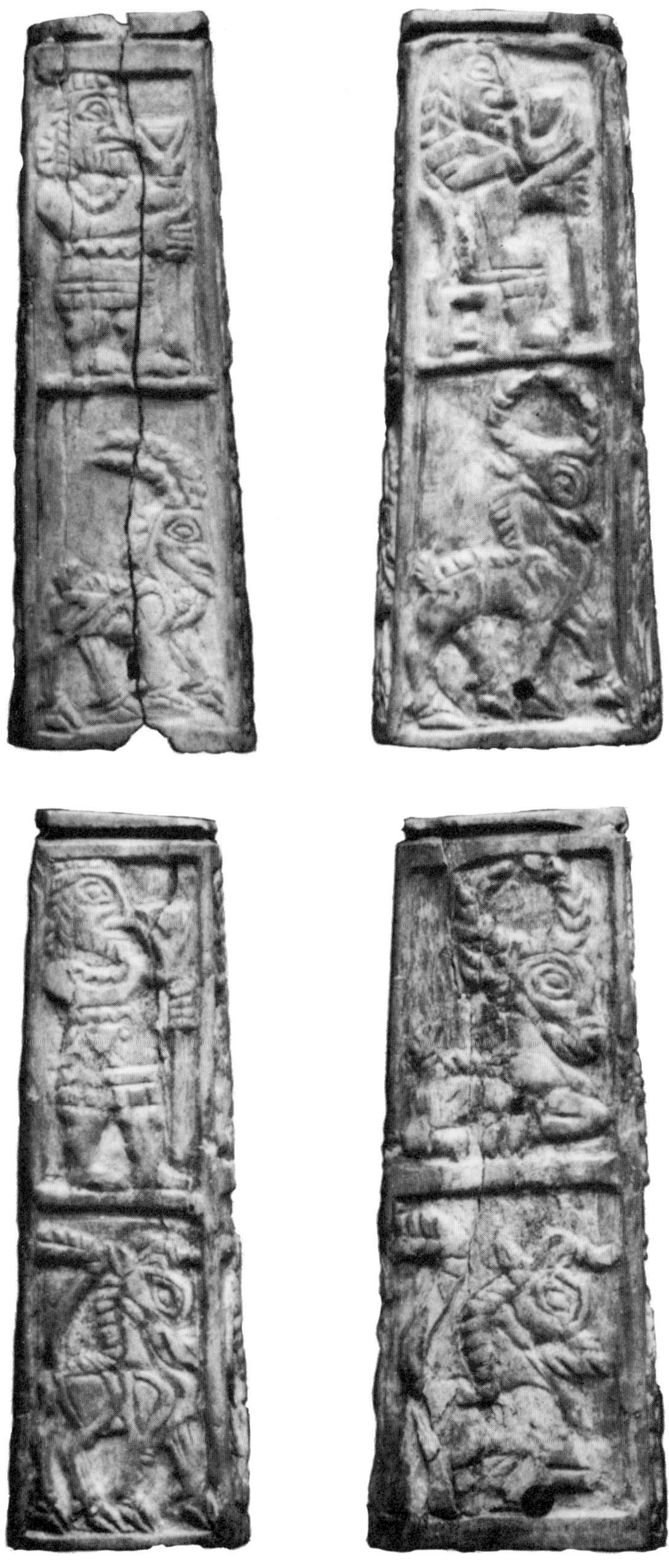

73

74 BB31 [1] (8); 64-780; MMA 65.163.27; ht. 3.3, w. 1.7, th. .4.
A figure like the preceding examples, holding a staff in his left, a cup in his right hand. His garment is full-sleeved and fringed. We do not know whether he was seated. The reverse is smooth and slightly concave.

75 CC31 [1] (6); 64-920; MMA 65.163.16; ht. 2.9, w. 2.2, th. .3; Muscarella 1966, fig. 8.
A man facing right holding to his mouth a thin vessel (?) the bottom of which projects below his right hand. His shoulder-length hair is held by a fillet: a heavy brow frames the oval eye; ears are not depicted; the nose is very fleshy and straight-bridged from the forehead; beard hair is not marked off. The garment seems to end at the shoulder. An almost imperceptible oval swelling on the bracelet might be decoration. The back is slightly concave, like no. 74, and has rocker scoring.

76 BB31/CC31 (8); 64-1069; UM 65-31-346; ht. 1.5, w. 1.9, th. .4.
Extant is part of the head of a man holding a vessel to his mouth with his right hand, right. Straight hair like that of nos. 62, 63, 106 flares out from his head. His beard is scraggy.

77 BB31 (8); 64-1065; UM 65-31-344; ht. 1.7.
Scene similar to no. 76. Extant are the lower part of the face, the bare arm and the right hand, which is thick. The beard is scraggy, like nos. 76, 78.

78 BB31/CC31 (8); 64- ; UM 65-31-503; ht. 1.4, w. 1.2, th. .3.
Like the preceding two examples. Extant are a sharp prominent nose, scraggy beard, and a right hand.

79 BB31 [1] (8); 64-778; MMA 65.163.15; ht. 2.5, w. 2, th. .5; Muscarella 1966, fig. 9.
Head of a man facing right. His hair is straight, held by a fillet, and projects obliquely downward; his beard has unique horizontal incisions. The nose is fleshy and prominent, the ears S-shaped; a dowel originally formed the eye, above which is a brow; the mouth is thick and closed. Upper edge is an intact band. The reverse is broken. This piece has been burned to a grey color.

80 CC31 [2] (7); 64-896; MMA 65.163.23; ht. 2.6, w. 1.9, th. .4.
The head of a man facing right. His hair is rendered in a chunky style, his short beard by three thick units; he has a long drooping mustache. Eyebrows and ears are not depicted. He apparently wears a plain necklace above a V-necked garment outlined in chunky style. The plain bottom edge is intact so that the rest of the body was carved on a separate plaque. Reverse is irregularly scored.

81 BB31/CC31 (8); 64-1069; UM 65-31-346; ht. 1.5.
Part of a human head, left. The face is similar to nos. 76-78.

82 BB31/CC31 (8); 64-1069; UM 65-31-346; ht. 1.4.
Part of a human head, right. Face like the above.

83 BB31 (8); 64- ; UM 65-31-613; ht. 1.8, w. 2, th. .3.
A badly damaged fragment depicting a human head, left, similar in style to nos. 76-78, 81-82.

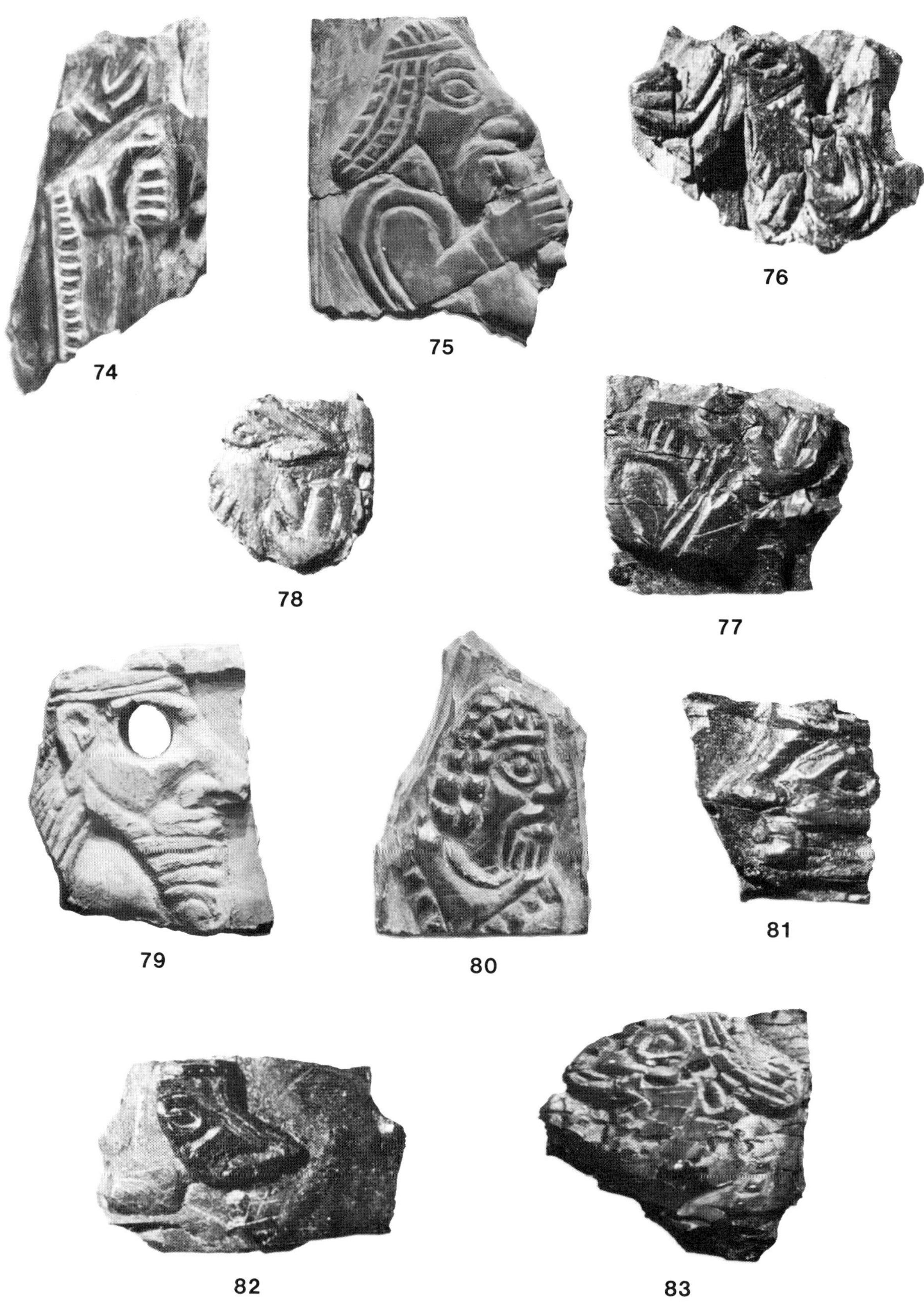
74
75
76
78
77
79
80
81
82
83

84 BB31 [1] (8); 64-786; UM 65-31-341; ht. 2.2, w. 2.8, th. .5.
Human head, left. The eye is oval, nose sharp and prominent, with nostrils represented; ears S-shaped, hair—or a hat—is flat and not delineated at top except for horizontal lines, and hangs thinly at the rear, decorated in a herringbone or braided pattern. Plain top and right edges are intact. The top border is beveled and has a horizontal groove; a dowel hole at the left.

85 BB31 [1] (8); 64-787; T; ht. 2.2, w. 1.9, th. .5.
Fragment of a head, left, similar to no. 84; the lips are thick. The plain left edge is intact as is the upper edge, a narrow band.

86 BB31/CC31 (8); 64-   ; UM 65-31-507; ht. 3.1, w. 2.2, th. .8.
Human head, left, as above. The eye was filled with a dowel.

87 BB31 [1] (8); 64-783; T; ht. 2.3, w. 3.8, th. .6.
Head like above, right. Here the mouth is a slit, the hair straight. A hand holds an unidentified object before the face. The plain upper edge is intact.

88 BB31 [1] (8); 64-763; T; ht. 4, w. 2.8.
The face of one and the back of the head of another figure are preserved, right. The eyes of both were filled with round dowels; the nose is fleshy and prominent, with nostrils represented; the mouth is a thin slit, ears S-shaped, and the chin long (no hair is represented to indicate that this is a beard). Top hair is flat, the rear falls in a thin herringbone braid probably to the feet (*infra*). The figure at the left wears a gorget. The heads are similar in style to the preceding four examples.

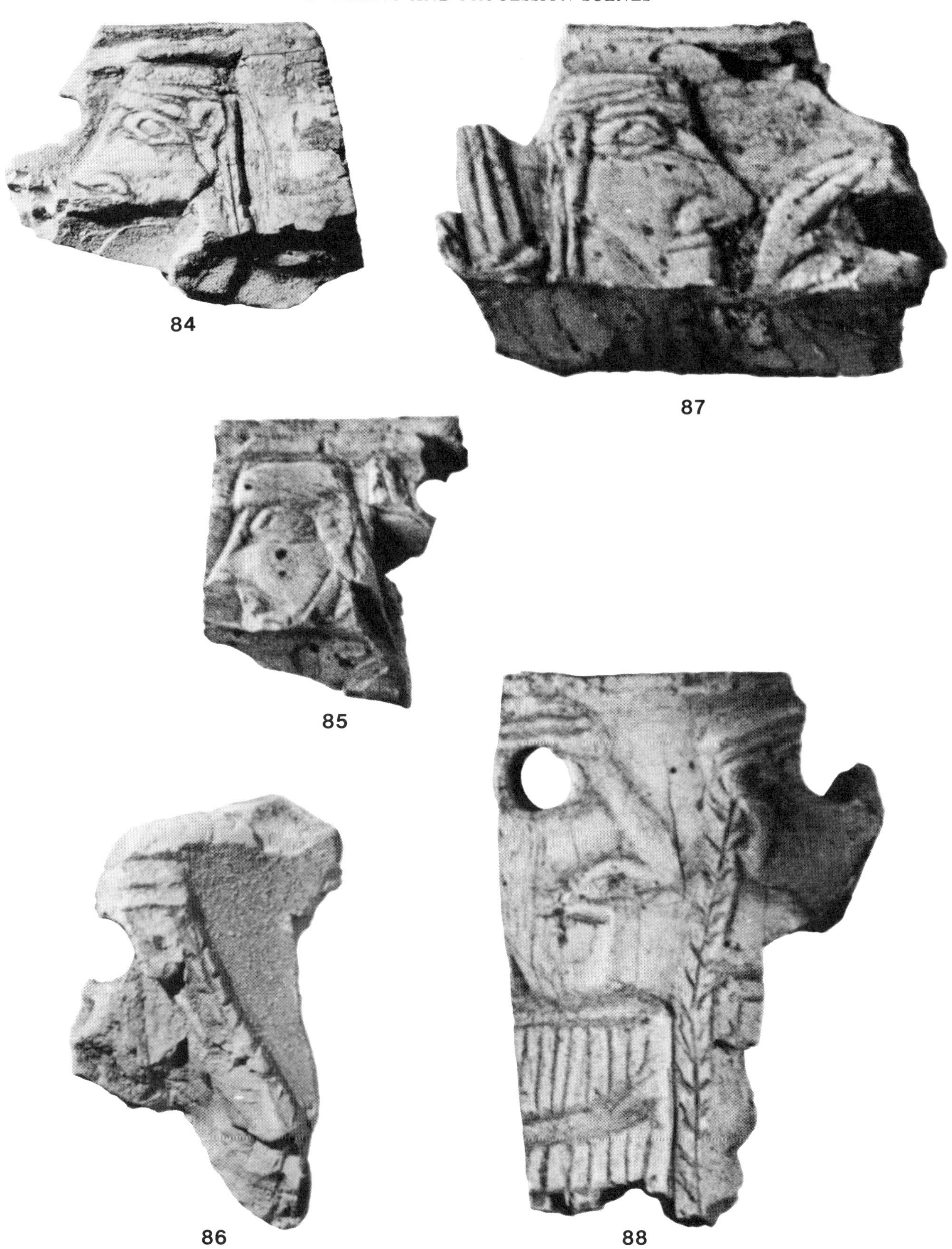

84

87

85

86

88

89 BB31 [1] (8); 64-983; UM 65-31-366; ht. 6.7, w. 2.2, th. .9.
Fragment that formed a corner of a panel. Extant is the rear half of a figure with long braided hair that reaches to the feet, S-shaped ears, eye formed by a round dowel, and a long, thickly belted (?) garment. Hands are apparently held in front. The figure is similar to the preceding examples but the top hair is divided vertically, not horizontally.

90 BB31 [1] (8); 64-784; MMA 65.163.26; ht. 3.9, w. 2.3, th. .8.
Preserved is the right leg of a figure with sandal, right. Behind the leg is the lower part of the braided herringbone hair, like that of the preceding figures. The left border is a scored raised band. The reverse has gouge marks and irregular scoring.

91A BB31 (8); 64-1065; UM 65-31-344; ht. 3.5, w. 2.4, th. .7.
B BB31 (8); 64-1072; T 25866 (three fragments).

Four fragments preserving figures, right, with long floor-length braided hair. In all examples crudely carved hands are preserved; in at least three examples the hands hold an unidentifiable rectangular (?) object at the sides. One fragment preserves the long hair of a second figure at the right, suggesting a procession or group activity.

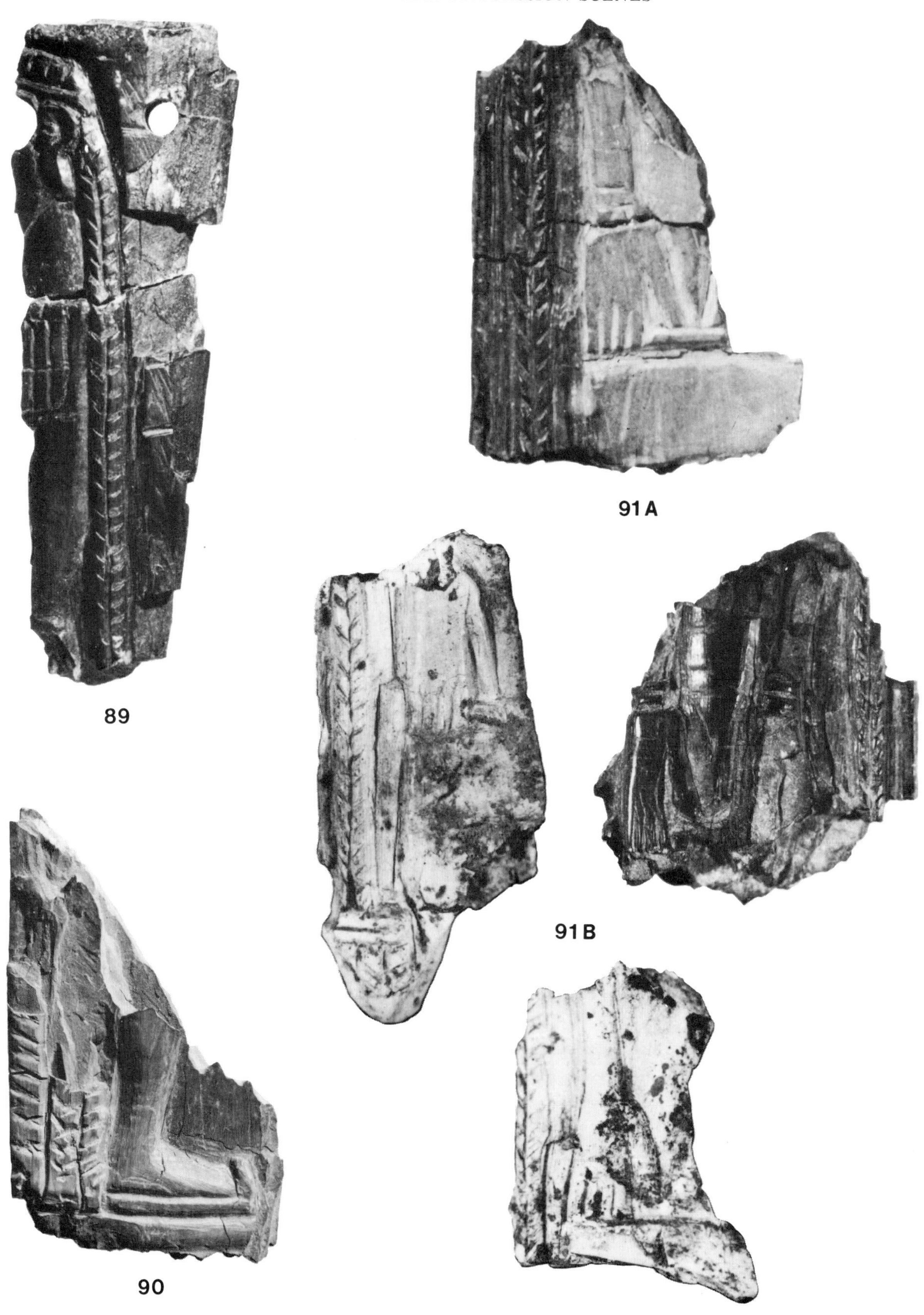

89

91 A

91 B

90

92 CC31 [2] (7); 64-930, 935; MMA 65.163.1a, b, c; ht. 25; Muscarella 1966, fig. 7; Porada 1975, 394, Abb. 311a, b; front and side views.
The object is divided into four zones: the upper consisting of a deity standing on a lion, all in the round; a now-missing unit that masked a tang holding two parts together; a cylindrical section with relief carvings; and the lowest preserved section, not readily identifiable but probably the base, with relief decoration.

The deity and lion were cut from one piece, the cylindrical unit and part of the base from another, and the remainder of the base from a third. A cylindrical tang, carved with the relief section, was fitted into a socket at the base of the lion; a bronze nail, placed between the lion's paws, secures the tang. Just below the relief section, on the base, a bronze nail held this part to the remainder of the base.

Of the deity, only the bare feet remain. (See no. 123, possibly the head belonging to this piece.) The lion, couchant, is quite foreshortened (probably determined by the size of the ivory to be worked). His tail rests along one flank having passed under the leg; his shoulders are outlined in relief with rectangles, his ruff with triangles. The gable-like head is very plastically rendered with thick muzzle and nose wrinkles, small pointed ears, "warts" above the round eyes that once held inlays; the menacing open mouth has bared fangs and a non-protruding tongue.

The relief scene consists of three men, two walking right, facing a third. The man to the left is the same type as nos. 88-90, 93: long chin without beard, thin mouth, braided long hair, round S-shaped ears; and he wears a gorget. The figure at the right, less preserved, is the same physical type, and he too wears a gorget. Both have the head and legs in profile and torso in front view. Both wear mini-skirts and sandals with turned-up toes, and have a thin object or article of clothing resting along one thigh. The figure in the center has a beard and hair of a different type, depicted here with straight incisions and held by a fillet (cf. no. 96). He alone drinks from a vessel, which is held in his right hand. He is also slightly larger that his neighbors and wears a longer garment, one that is pleated, reaching to his thighs. Moreover, he is placed directly below the head of the lion, in front view and he is no doubt the major figure. Between him and the figure at the right is a mace, held head down either by the center figure in his left hand or by the figure at the right. In either case it might be assumed that the mace held head down is a sign of peaceful intent.

The lowest section is shattered and it is not possible to know whether it was free standing, functioning perhaps as a handle, or whether it functioned as an attachment or as part of furniture. Cf. no. 93.

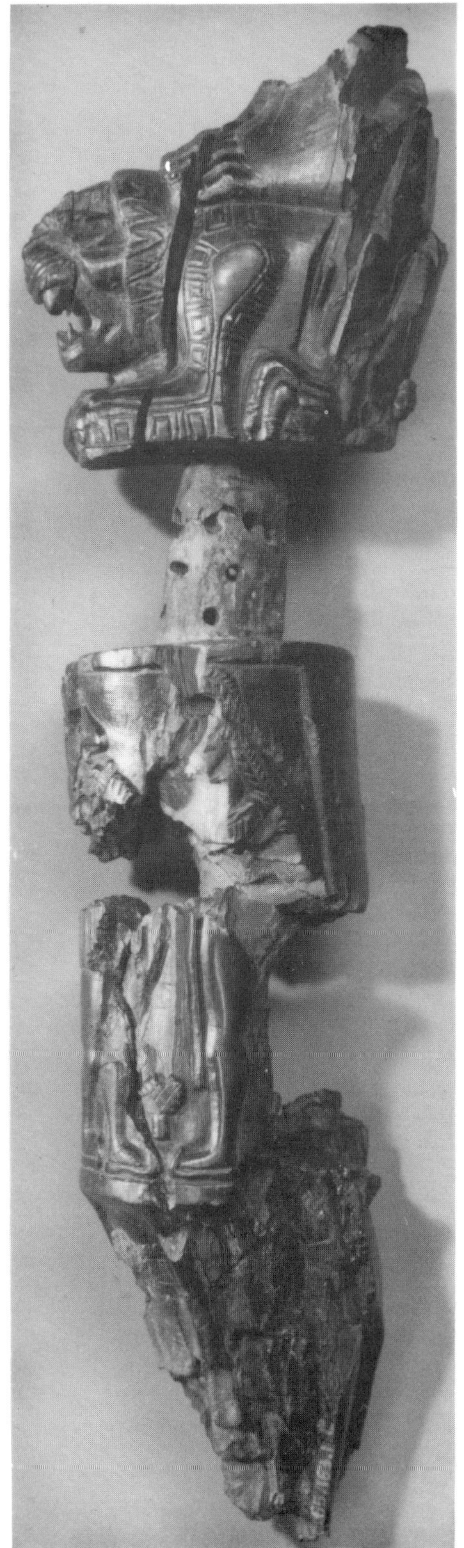
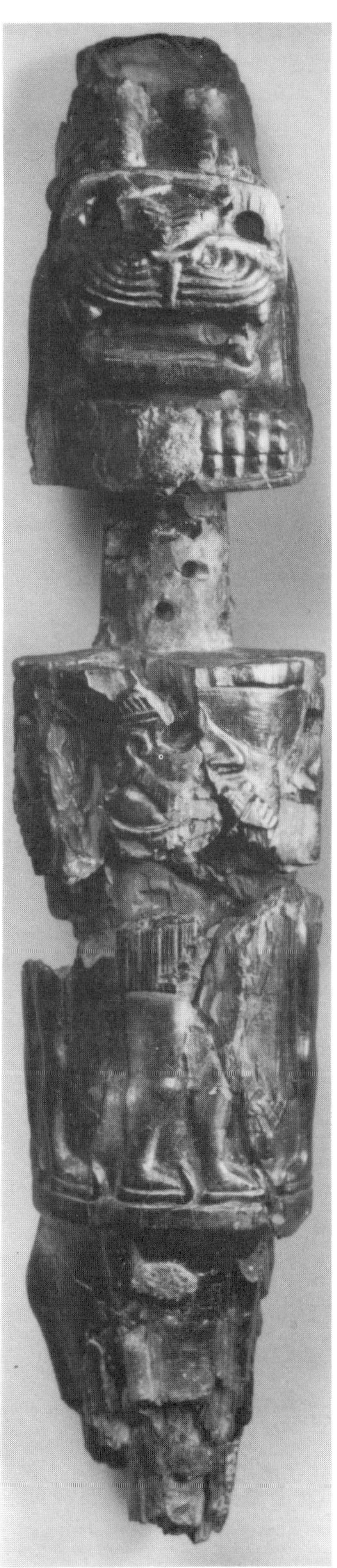
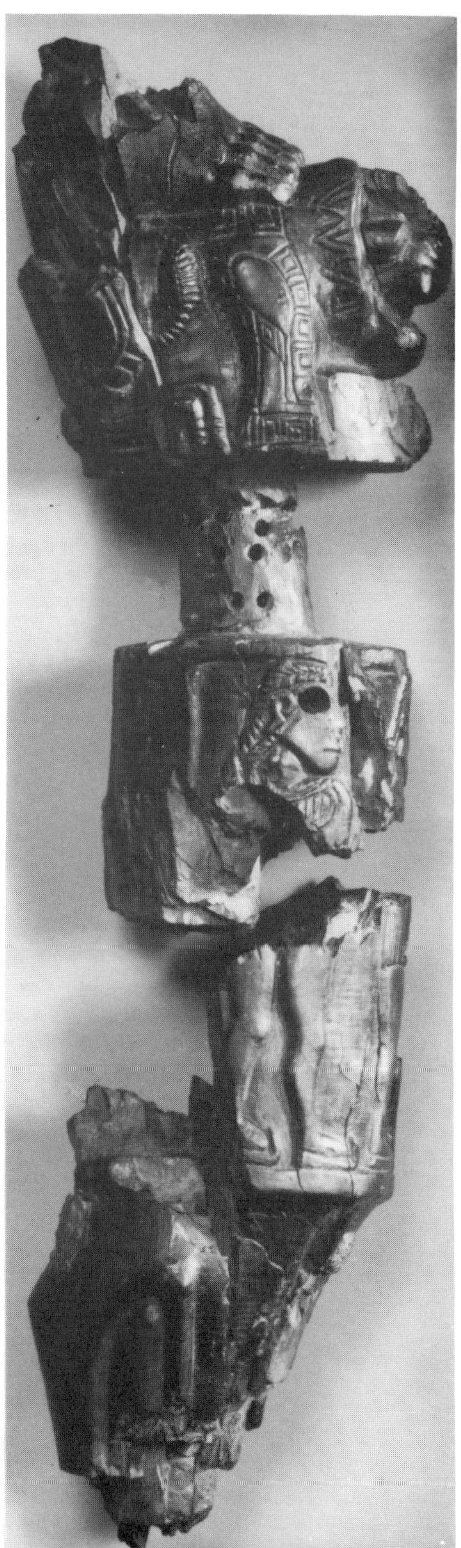

92

93 CC32 (area east of 7); 70-408; T; front, side, and back views of main fragment group and front views of additional fragments.

(Known to me only from photographs.) An object apparently like no. 92, but more fragmentary. Extant are a section of the cylindrical unit with part of the tang still present, and fragments of the lower base. The cylindrical relief section was made in two halves, only one of which survives; a dowel, *in situ* in the gorget, helped hold the two halves together.

The relief preserves parts of two men facing each other. The left one is the same type as the two side figures on no. 92: braided long hair, long beardless chin, S-shaped ear, thin mouth; the gorget is worn, here complete. Both arms are at the sides. The neighboring figure is a different type. He has straight hair, the rear part missing, S-shaped ears, thick lips, and a short beard; his long garment is belted and is stitched at the side. His right hand, executed thinly, perhaps because of limited space, rests apparently on the shoulder of his neighbor. The other half of this relief could have accommodated one or more figures.

We do not know of course if this object also supported a deity standing on a lion, but I think it may be assumed. The execution of the relief suggests a different artist's hand from the one who made no. 92. The fact that it was found in an area close to no. 92 suggests that it may have been juxtaposed to the latter piece; it may even have been part of the same object—but there is no independent evidence to support this suggestion.

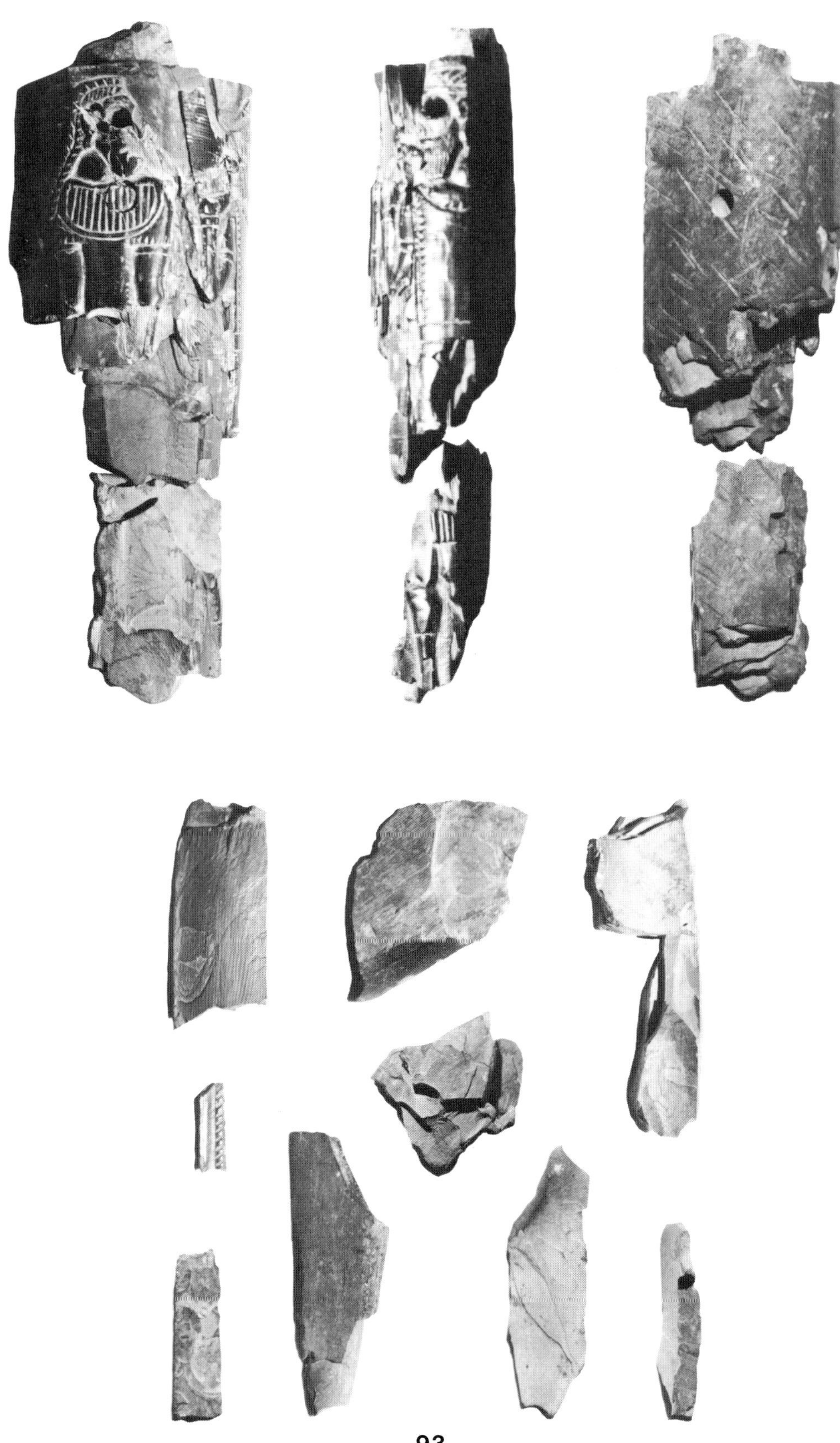

93

94 BB31/CC31 (8); 64- ; UM 65-31-482; ht. 1.9, w. 1.8, th. .7.
A fragment with part of a winged man, left. He wears a thick belt over a fleece-like garment that covers his left thigh; the right thigh is exposed. Part of a wing curves down before flaring out; it is possible that the man had more than one wing represented. This is the only preserved example of a winged figure on a plaque. Unfortunately, we do not know whether the head was human or that of a griffin.

95 Wood; CC31 [2] (7); 64-980; MMA 65.163.42; ht. 2.4, w. 3; Muscarella 1966, fig. 25.
A fragment preserving the upper part of a lion's head, on the top of which are the toes of a human right foot. This piece therefore originally consisted of a deity on a lion. Although we cannot say for sure that it was an object like the preceding two examples, the possibility exists that it was.

The lion is open-mouthed with six teeth and bared fangs; nose wrinkles are thick; the ruff is depicted in chunky style, the mane by a neat triangular pattern. Between the ruff and the round eyes that once held inlays is an area decorated with small raised dots.

96 AA30 (5,N); 60-950; T; ht. 3, w. 3.2, th. 1.7; Dyson 1964a, fig. 8.
The obverse of this fragment is convex, the reverse flat, allowing us to conclude that it is not part of a panel; it may in fact be part of a cylindrical object similar, at least in part, to nos. 92, 93.

Extant is part of a human head, left, with S-shaped ears, oval eye that once held an inlay, a beard, and long straight hair continuing down the shoulders, held by a fillet. He is the same type as the central figure on no. 92. Behind this figure is the sharp, prominent nose of another. A dowel hole is partly preserved. The upper intact edge is a raised band.

97 CC31 [2] (7); 64-900; UM 65-31-352; ht. 7.1, w. 3.1, th. .5.
A barefoot figure dressed in an ankle-length garment, right. Shoulder-length hair, held by a fillet, is rendered in chunky style; the eye is oval, the nose fleshy and straight-bridged from the forehead, the mouth thick, the chin broken away; a swelling above the mouth may be a mustache. The garment has a V-neck, a fringed hem, and a vertical decoration joined at the left by a horizontal one, all rendered in chunky style. The figure carries an unidentified object—antler/branch ?—in the left hand; the right is missing. The plain top edge is intact; the right and bottom edges are narrow bands and intact.

98 AA30 (5,N); 60-950; T; ht. 3.8, w. 2.5, th. 1; Dyson 1964a, fig. 12.
A figure wearing what appears to be a "feather" crown or hat, left. He wears a belted, sleeveless, knee-length garment fringed at the hem. His hair is shoulder-length and appears not to be incised; ears are S-shaped, eye an oval; the biceps muscle is incised. Behind are two hands. The right holds a staff (?) but it is not clear if the left also holds it. A dowel hole exists behind the head. The piece seems crudely executed. The plain upper border is intact. A fragment of a human head of the same type, and from the same provenience, is probably from the same object as the larger fragment (not illustrated).

99 BB31 (8); 64-1072; T 25866.
A small fragment preserving a figure holding a staff in both hands, right. The head and most of the body are missing.

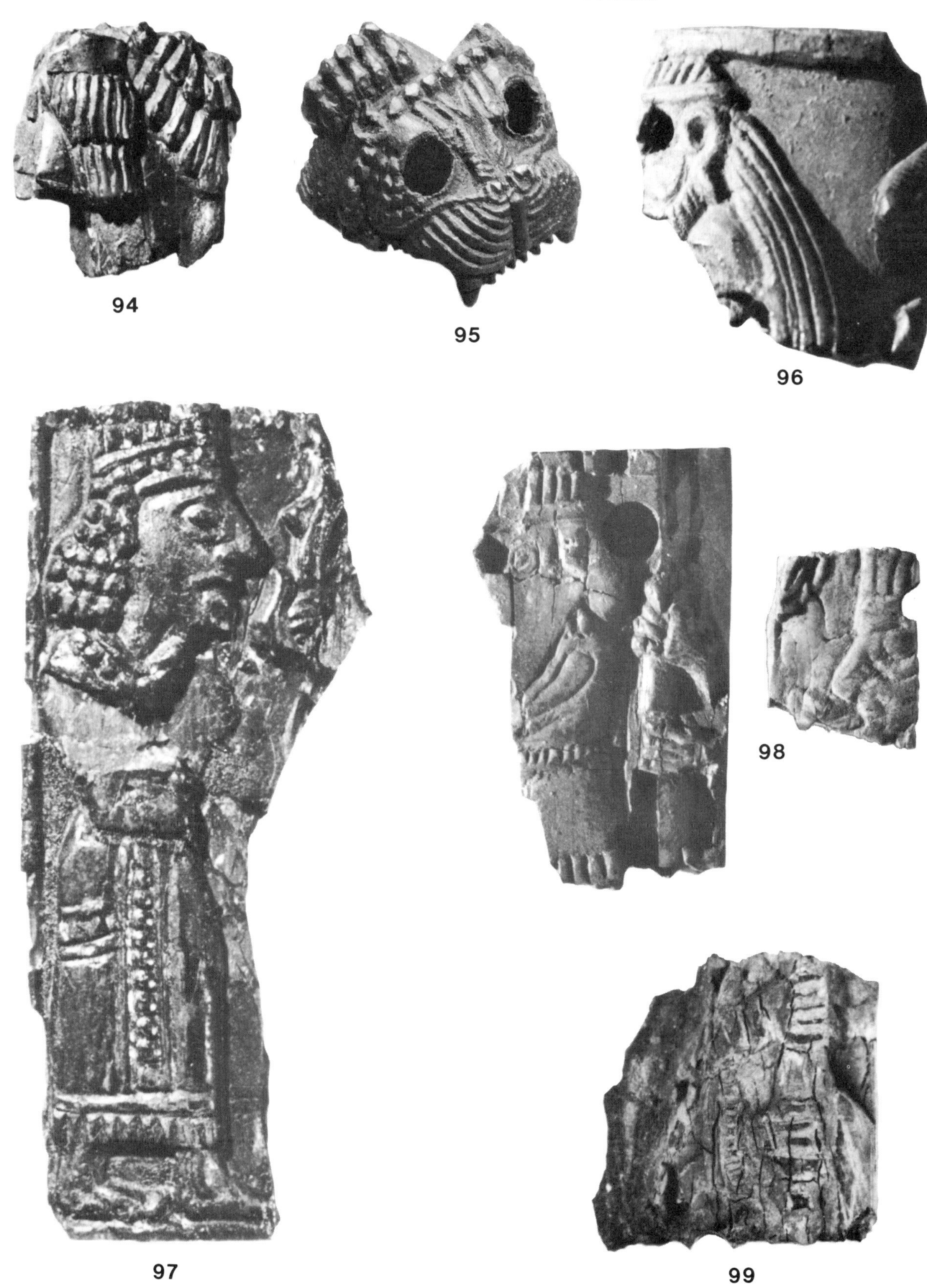
94
95
96
97
98
99

100 BB31 (8); 64-1065; UM 65-31-344; ht. 2.
A small fragment of a hand holding a staff. The fragment has burned white.

101 BB31 (8); 64-1065; UM 65-31-344; ht. 2.8, w. 1.3, th. .5.
A small fragment preserving the right hand of a figure holding a staff, and the tip of his nose. The reverse has irregular scoring.

102 BB31 **[1]** (8); 64-785; T; ht. 4.9, w. 1.3, th. .7.
The rear part of a figure wearing a "feather" helmet or crown, or a fillet below vertically incised hair, left. His sleeved garment is long, knee length (?), with incisions down the back. He is bearded and has flaring shoulder-length hair; no ear is depicted. The left arm is forward—carrying a staff? The plain top and right edges are intact.

103 BB31 **[1]** (8); 64-779; T; ht. 3.9, w. 2.8, th. .4.
Lower part of a figure, right. His garment is knee-length, with incised (crease?) marks front and back, and has a fringed hem. The right arm holds an unidentifiable rectangular (?) object; low boots are worn. The plain left edge is intact.

104 BB31 (8); 64-1072; T 25866.
Preserved are the left shoulder, bent arm and hand of a human figure, left.

105 CC31 **[2]** (7); 64-897; T; ht. 1.5, w. 3.5, th. .7.
Preserved is part of a human figure, left. His right arm is held before his face; the elbow is outlined in parellel curves. The garment is short-sleeved, and is decorated in chunky style. The beard reminds us of no. 80.

106 BB II; 64- ; UM 65-31-486; ht. 3.1, w. 1.7, th. .5.
Part of a human figure, right. His hair and beard are like nos. 76-78, 102. The right hand may hold an object—a vessel? The intact left border is a band.

107 BB31 (8); 64-1066; UM 65-31-356; ht. 2, w. 1.7.
Small fragment preserving the lower rear part of a figure, left. The rear and hem fringes of the garment are rendered in chunky style; the foot is bare

108 BB31 (8); 64-1066; UM 65-31-356; ht. 3.8, w. 1.8, th. .5.
Fragment with a barefoot figure similar to no. 107 above. Here a ground line in the form of a raised band separates the figure from another scene, indistinct, in a lower panel. The left edge is a raised band and is intact.

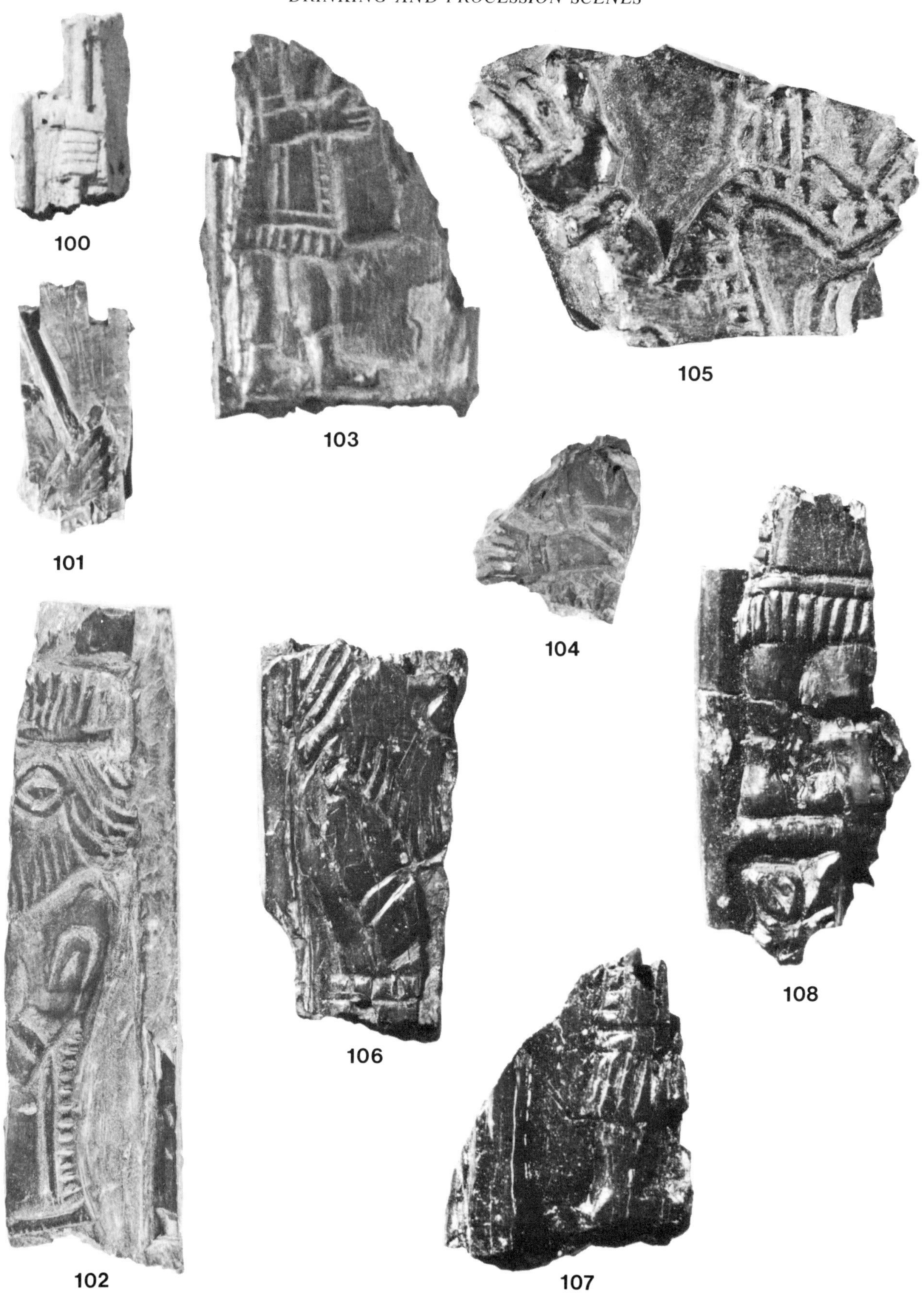
100
101
102
103
104
105
106
107
108

109 BB31 (8); 64-1073; T 25867; ht. 2.6, w. 2.8, th. .4, and ht. 2.3, w. 1.5, th. .4.
Two fragments like nos. 107, 108, left. Here both wear sandals.

110 BB31 (8); 64-1066; UM 65-31-356; 4 by 2.1.
A surface-damaged fragment depicting a nude male wearing sandals. His straight legs and the raised intact edge at his back make it impossible to decide whether he is standing or is an enemy lying under a horse. The plain right (or upper) edge is also intact.

111 BB31/CC31 (8); 64-1069; UM 65-31-346; ht. 2.2, w. 4.1.
A damaged fragment that preserves part of the heads of two figures, right. The left figure has straight hair held by a fillet, an oval eye, and a prominent nose. He carries two unidentified objects, a sistrum or a branch, or, more probably, arrows. In front is a larger figure (cf. no. 92), also with straight long hair. He has typical thick lips and a dowel formed the eye. Something seems to touch the back of his head—fingers? The reverse has thin cross-hatched scoring.

112 BB31/CC31 (8); 64- ; UM 65-31-545; ht. 1.1, w. 3.8, th. 1.
Small fragment preserving the back of a head like no. 111, and perhaps part of the same panel or scene. An object barely touches the back of the head. The upper intact border is a raised band.

113 CC31 **[1]** (6); 64-911; UM 65-31-349; ht. 2.5, w. 1.5, th. .4.
Extant is the right hand of a figure holding two stalks of wheat (?), or arrows (?), right. A small curved object is also held in the hand. The reverse has neat rocker scoring.

114 BB31 (8); 64-1065; UM 65-31-344; ht. 1.7, w. 1.8, th. .7.
Extant is a right arm with hand holding two stalks of wheat (?), apparently like no. 113; the plain belt of the figure's garment is also preserved.

115 BB31 (8); 64-1065; UM 65-31-344; ht. 1.7, w. 3.
Extant is the thin bent arm of a figure holding a palm (?) or a stalk of wheat (?), right. Two vertical bands exist at the right.

116 BB31 (8); 64-1068; MMA 65.163.14; ht. 2.5, w. 3.3, th. .7.
A figure in a long gown and wearing sandals sits on a chair, left. The gown's thick fringe is in the form of a zig-zag; arm and buttock fringes are incised. A staff or spear is held in the left hand; the arm is crude and cylindrical. The chair is armless and has rectangular feet with square joints at the seat and mid-point of the legs, the latter connected by a cross-piece; a slightly curved back is just visible. The plain right and narrow-banded lower edges are intact.

117 BB31 **[1]** (8); 64-766; T; ht. 2.5, w. 3.8, th. .7.
A small fragment preserving the thick legs and sandaled feet of a figure, right. He holds a spear, point down. In front of the spear is the back of a chair, of the same type as no. 116. The scene probably depicts a guard standing behind an important person's chair or throne. The lower border is intact and preserves part of a guilloche, completed on a separate panel.

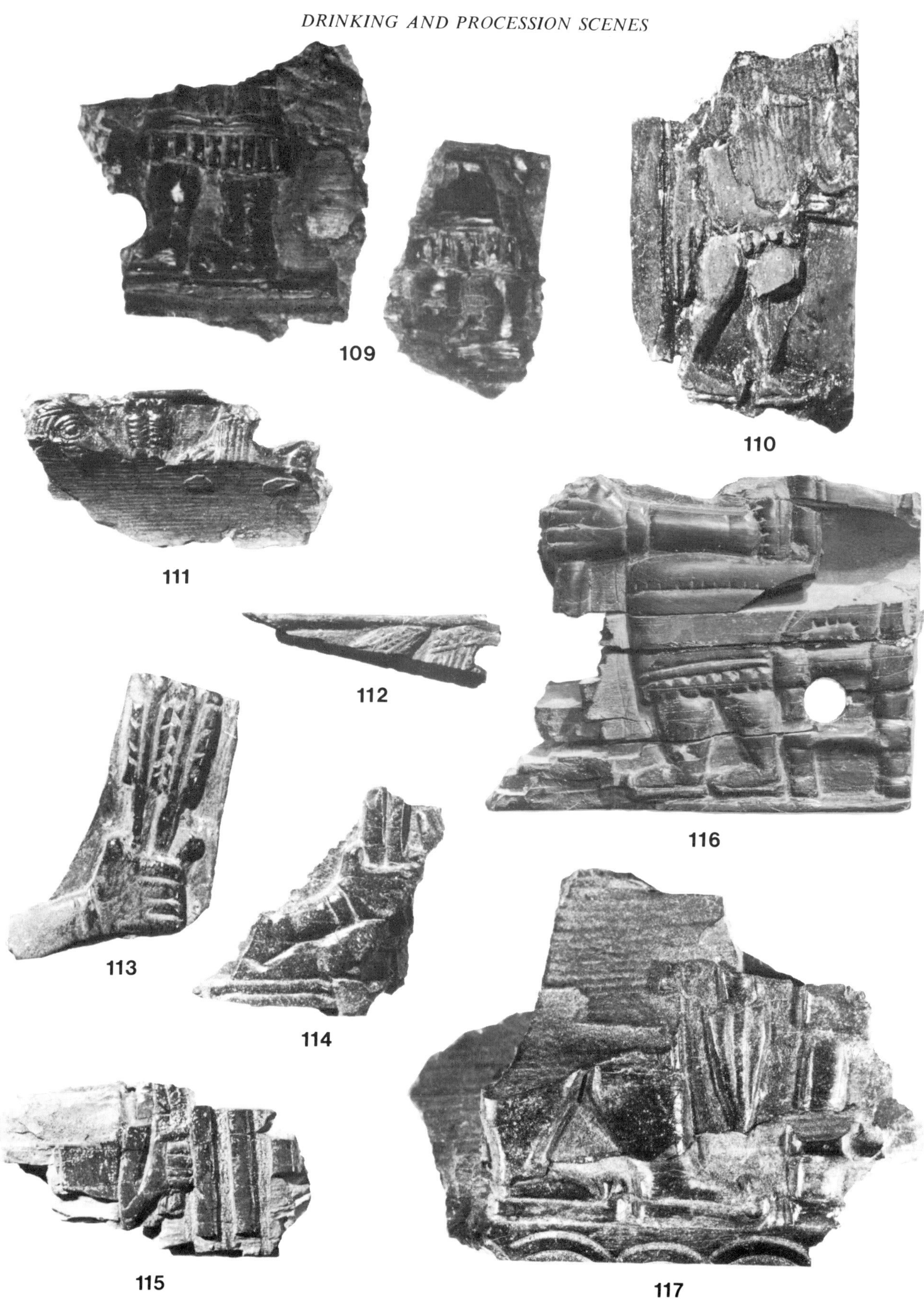
109
110
111
112
113
114
115
116
117

118 BB31 [1] (8); 64-775; UM 65-31-360; ht. 2.9, w. 4.7, th. .9; Muscarella 1971a, fig. 2.
Preserved is a figure seated on the edge of a chair, of the same type as those above, nos. 116, 117. Vertical incisions above the arm seem to indicate a beard. The man wears a garment with fringe at the hem and side indicated by incision, and at the lap by plastic zig-zags. His rather large left hand rests on his lap, while the right holds a vessel to his mouth. His sandaled feet rest on a lion's head, the body of which is apparently resting under the chair's legs. A small object, perhaps a tripod, is at the right. The reverse has neatly incised scoring.

119 BB31 [1] (6); 64-996; T; ht. 1.9, w. 3.5, th. 1.5.
A damaged fragment. What is clear are two cleft animal feet at the left, joined by a strut—a tripod or tetrapod with the upper section vertically grooved. To the right is an unidentified object, which could be a chair: a leg with a horizontal strut seems to be visible; below this are vertical incisions, perhaps tassels or fringe. What might be the outline of a human foot is visible between the "chair" and the tripod, but the instep would then be under the latter's leg. The scene face is convex, the reverse flat with crosshatched scoring. Compare no. 169 for another possible tripod.

120 BB31 [1] (8); 64-777; UM 65-31-358; ht. 2.3, w. 2.9, th. .4.
Part of a panel depicting a man facing right. He has straight hair held by a fillet, lozenge-oval eyes, S-shaped ears, thick lips, prominent sharp nose, and apparently a beard. An object in front of the face appears to be a bull's foot; if so, this must be a bull-man. The plain lower and the left and right edges, raised bands, are intact; there is also a raised band that marked off an upper section, mostly missing. The body of the man was completed on a separate panel. A small dowel hole exists above the horizontal band and two larger ones flank the head. The surface is worn from use.

121 BB31/CC31 (8); 64- ; UM 65-31-478; ht. 1.8, w. 1.5.
Apparently a fragment of a head, left. Extant are a lozenge eye surrounded by thick radiating lines that might be hair, and typically thick lips; hair seems also to fall behind the head. This could be a mythical creature; it does not resemble any human head in the repertory.

122 BB31/CC31 (8); 64-1069; UM 65-31-346; ht. 2.2, w. 3.
Apparently a fragment of a human head or a mythical creature, right; similar in some respects to no. 121. Extant are an oval eye, thick scraggy hair and a long neck. The upper border is a thick band; two dowel holes to the right.

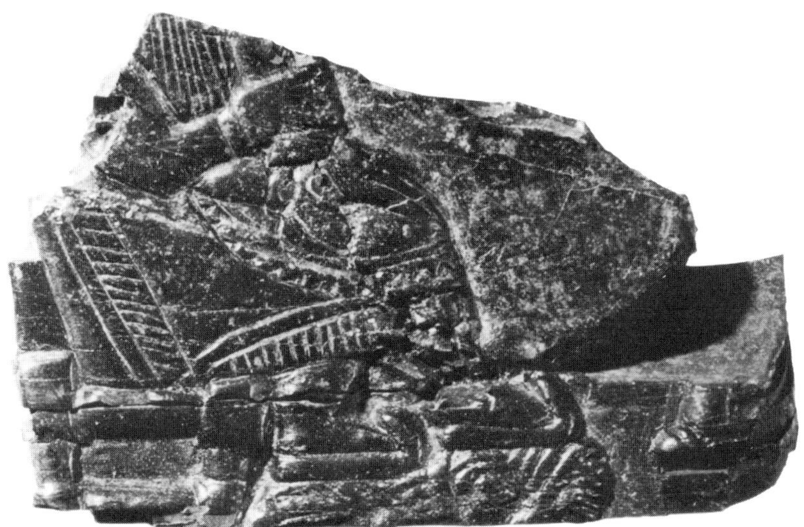
118

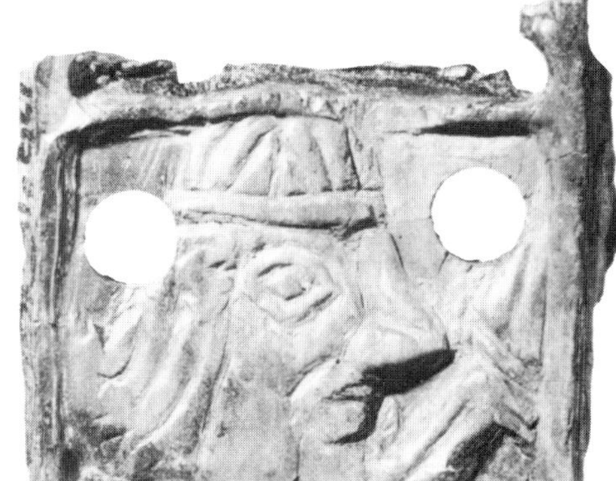
120

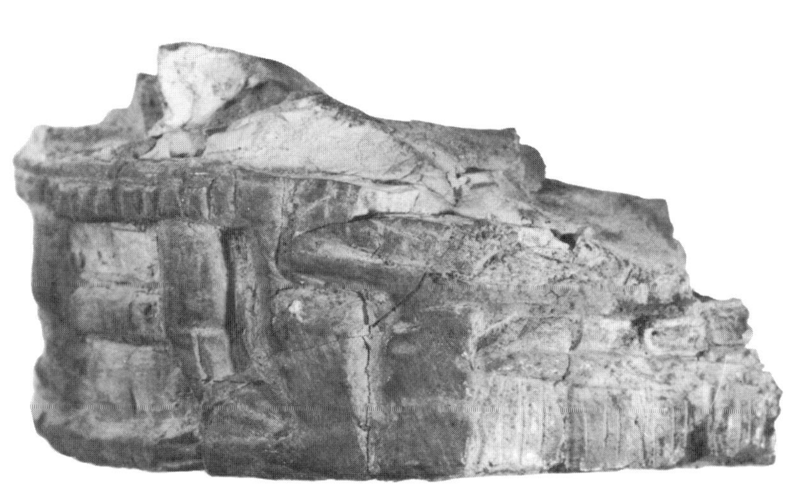
119

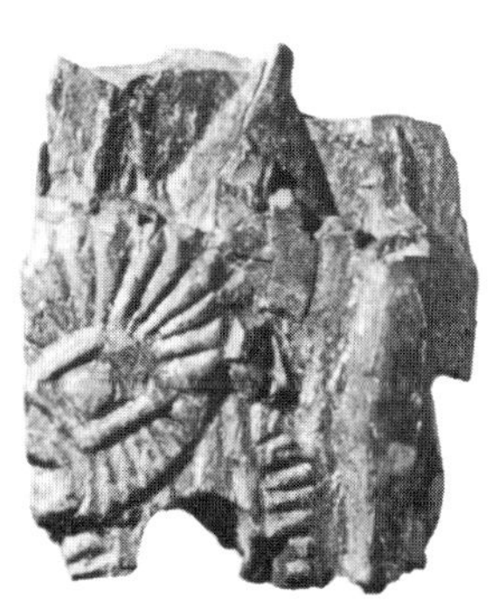
121

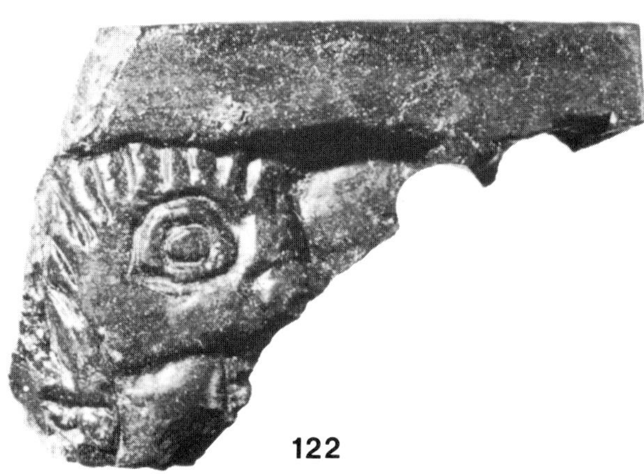
122

III

HUMAN SCULPTURE IN THE ROUND

123 CC31 [2] (7); 64-939; MMA 65.163.6; ht. 4.5, w. 2.9, th. 2; Muscarella 1966, fig. 22; front and side views.

Lower half of a human head in the round, missing the area above the base of the eye socket and the back; the nose is broken. The characteristics are high cheek bones tapering to a long prominent chin, cleft at the center; mouth full but thin lipped, the upper part projecting slightly over the lower; eyes large and oval, cut out to hold inlays. The neck is long and without an "Adam's apple." This feature plus the lack of a beard suggests that the figure is a female, strong features notwithstanding (see no. 92). The masterful execution of the sculptor is obvious. The back is broken away but at the mid-nose position is preserved the bottom of a drilling; it is not clear from which direction it was cut.

124 BB31 [1] (8); 64-764; UM 65-31-355; ht. 5.5, with tang 8; w. 3.9; front and side views.

Greater part of a human head in the round; part of the right side and the back are missing, and the nose and part of the upper lip are broken away. The head is similar to no. 123 but not so finely executed: here the long chin is wide and without a cleft, the mouth is wider, and instead of a neck there is a rectangular peg for insertion into a separately made body or other unit. Eyes are oval with traces of a black substance within, probably a glue; heavy brows in relief meet over the eyes; the ear is large and S-shaped as on the reliefs, and pierced for an earring. Two electrum earrings found in Room 6 still contained ivory which indicates that they belonged to a statuette like this: Muscarella 1966, fig. 36. (Note that an earring of exactly the same type was found in 1970 in CC32.) A circular hole, 3.3 cm. in depth and ca. 2 cm. in diameter was cut into the top, no doubt to hold a headdress; above the forehead the head is inset and was probably covered by the headdress.

The lack of a beard suggests that this head is that of a female.

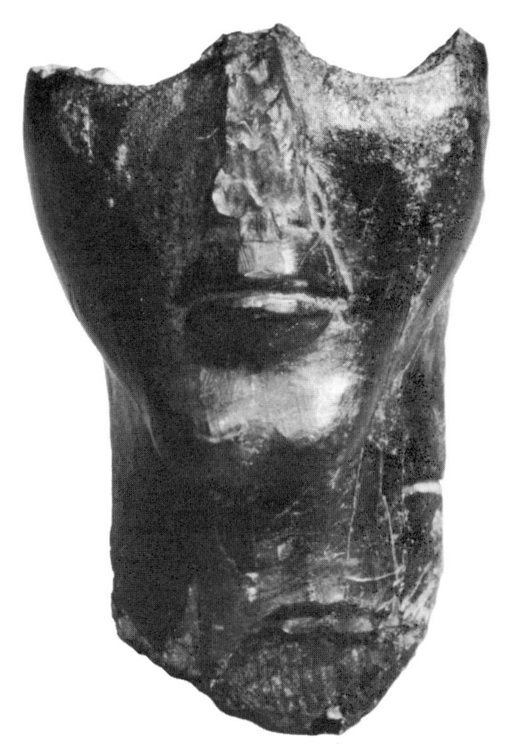

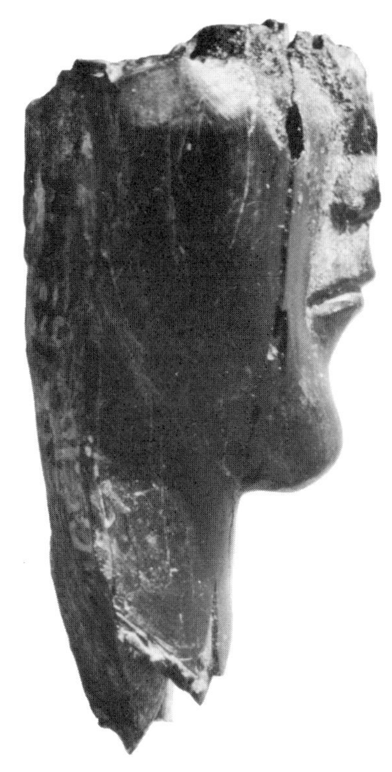

123

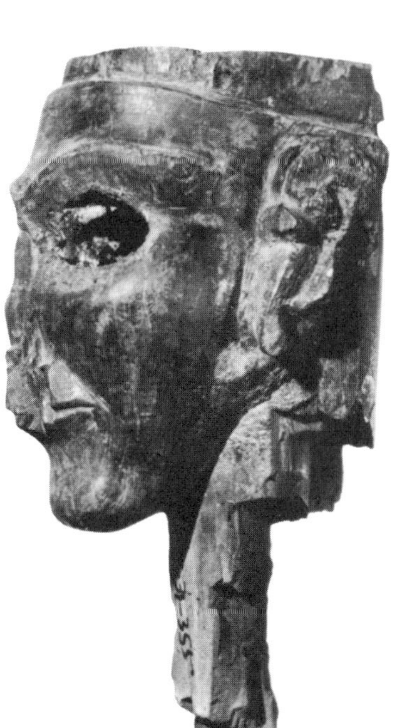

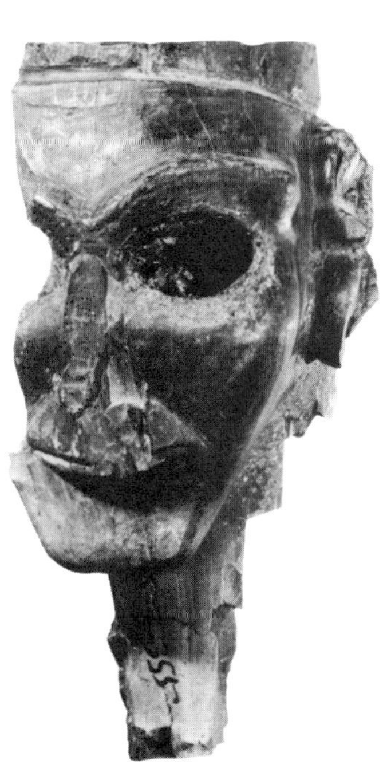

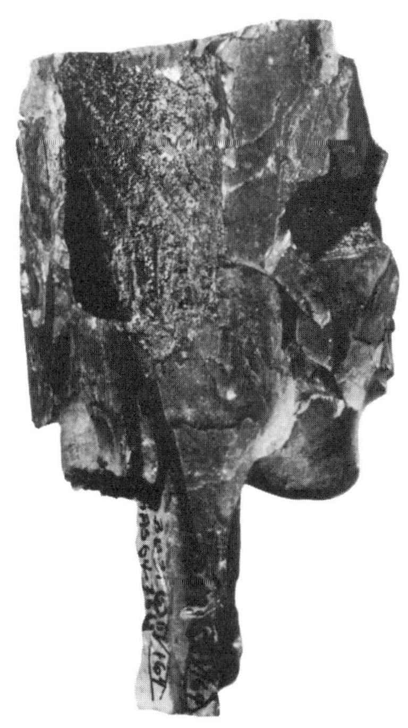

124

125 CC31 **[2]** (7); 64-938; MMA 65.163.7; ht. 7.1, w. 5.2, th. .4; Muscarella 1966, fig. 24; side, front, and back views.

A very much damaged head almost in the round, originally similar to nos. 123, 124. It has large oval, deeply cut eyes that once held inlays; the right eye preserves a drill pit. Prominent eyebrows join over the eyes and held inlay; ten drill holes are still visible. The chin was long and narrow and is not undercut and there is no neck. The mouth area is broken away but two drill holes are extant in the remaining ivory, which suggests that they were dowel holes to hold a separately made mouth section, and which further suggests that a repair existed here. The nose and ears are broken away but the thick base—the lower chin and neck area—is intact. This thick unbroken base means that the head was not part of a statue but is complete as is.

On both sides is a cut-out from the plain flat top to the mouth level, where it widens; two small dowel holes are preserved in each cut-out; perhaps this area held part of a wig or headdress. The back of the head is flat and has a vertical groove widening at the bottom, and three dowel holes arranged in a triangle; one preserves burnt wood, probably from a dowel that attached the head to a backing.

126 BB31 (8); 64-1074; T.

A very badly damaged head similar to no. 125. Its eyes and brows also once held inlays. (I do not know what exists at the back.)

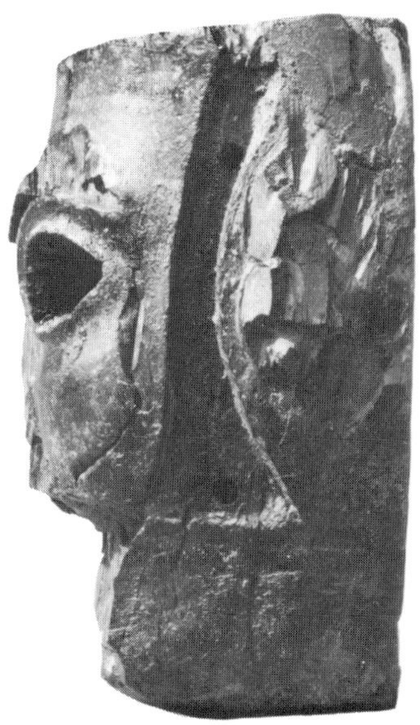
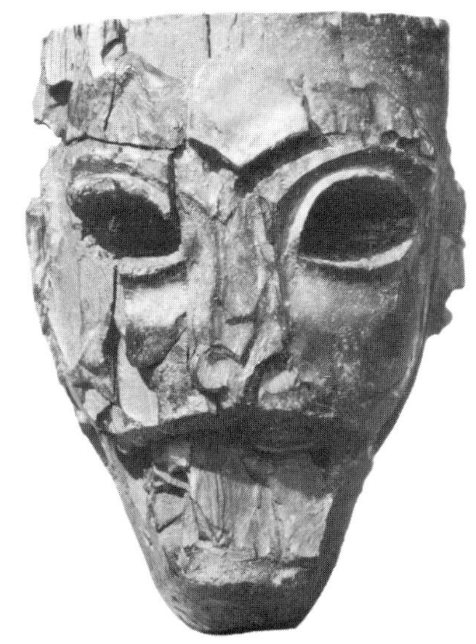
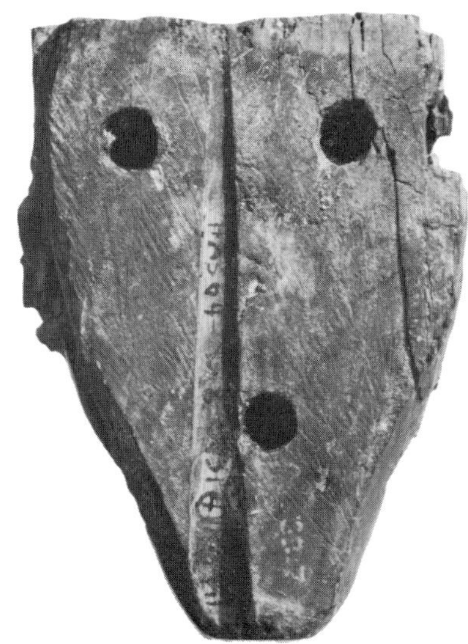

125

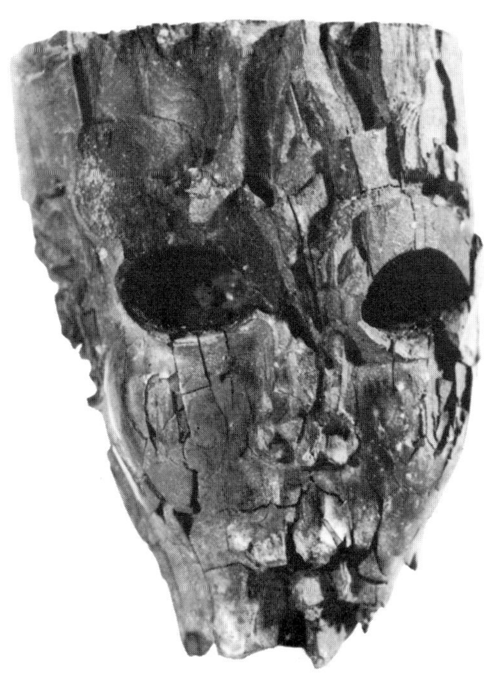

126

127 Wood; CC31 [1] (6); 64-931; T; ht. 8.2, w. 4.3; Dyson 1965, fig. 6A; 1968, pl. XXXVIII; front, back, and side views.

A human head in the round preserving the neck and part of the chest and headdress. This fragment was probably from a statuette. The face is very long and narrow, tapering from top to bottom. The relatively large oval eyes once held inlays, below thick eyebrows that met over the thin nose and were also inlaid. The mouth is small and thin, the cheeks quite hollow, and the rounded chin long. The headdress passes over the large ears—one of which is now missing—and down the neck; it is broken away at the top but a dowel hole is still extant. A necklace consisting of three strands of beads is worn above a wide V-necked garment fastened with a rosette-shaped brooch on the left shoulder.

In the form of the eyes, brows, and in particular the hollow cheeks and long chin, the head is clearly related to the previous ones. Nevertheless, it is unique in expression and in facial measurements, not to mention the presence of the headdress. This head too seems to be female.

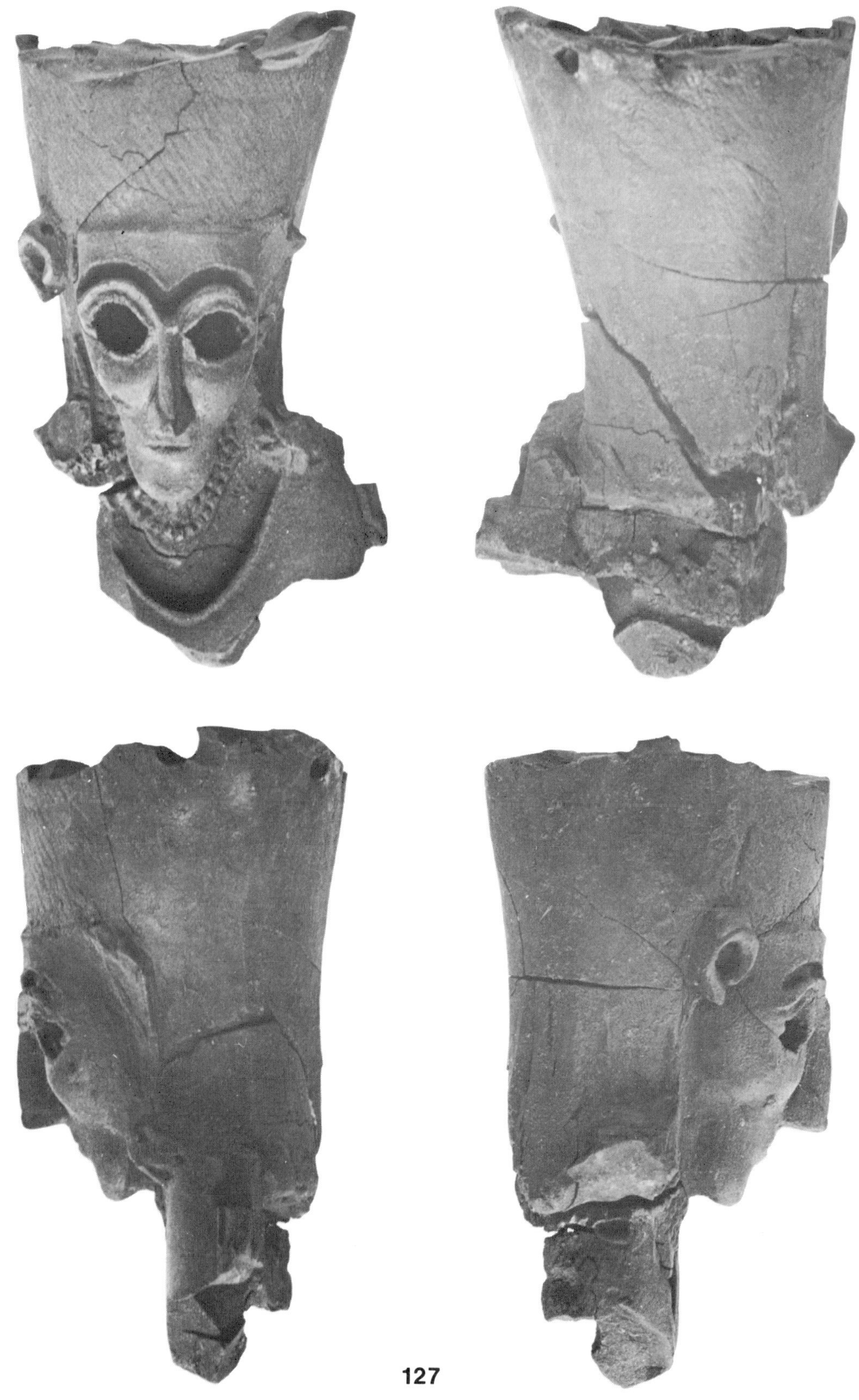

127

128 BB31 (8); 64-1067; UM 65-31-331; ht. 6.7, w. 3.4, th. 1.6.
A very much damaged fragment of a human head and upper torso not completely in the round. Preserved are only the general form and the bottom of the deep eye sockets; at the top are traces of what may be hair incisions. The reverse is flat and irregularly scored.

129 BB II; 60-489; T.
A badly damaged human head and torso in the round preserving in detail only one inlaid eye and socket. The top is flat and plain; it has a round hole for attachment. The back is partly hollowed out with five dowel holes, three arranged in a triangle.

130 CC31 [1] (6); 64-903; UM 65-31-368; ht. 5.3, w. 3.1, th. 1.4; front and back views.
A fragmentary figure carved at the front only; the back is flat with two dowel holes. Missing are the top of the head, the right side, and the lower part of the body. The face is badly damaged, preserving only the eye sockets and one eyebrow in relief; a beard seems evident. Thick herring-bone-pattern hair falls to the shoulder; ears are not depicted.

The figure holds a round object against his body—a shield/tambourine? The garment is V-necked, decorated by a band of reciprocal triangles, with a short sleeve bordered by rosettes. Multiple plain bracelets are worn on the wrist of the foreshortened arm.

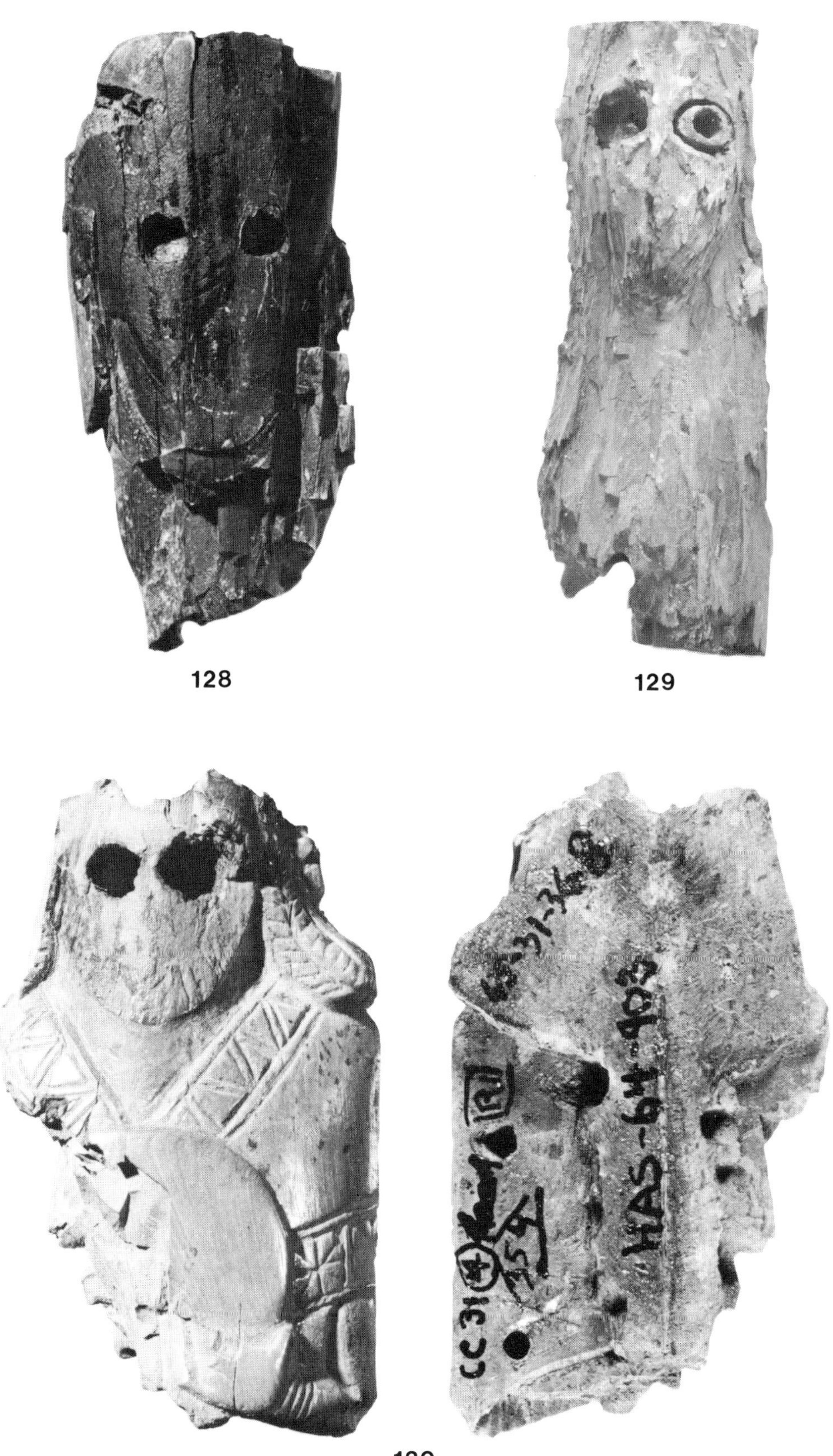

128

129

130

131 AA30 (5,N); 60-950; T; ht. with tang 8, l. 7; side view and drawings of front and side.
The left foot of a human in the round with sandal straps across the instep and around the big toe; the sole appears bare. Below the foot and carved with it is a tapering tang pierced twice to secure the statuette to a base.

132 BB31 (8); 64-1079; T 25863.
Three small fragments of human feet in the round, two right, one left. One right foot has a thick base.

133 BB30 (5,C); 64- ; UM 65-31-548; ht. 3.5.
Fragment of a right foot in the round.

134 BB II; 64- ; UM 65-31-303H; ht. 1.7, w. 2.5.
Fragment of a left foot in the round.

135 CC31 (BB II); 64-1077; T.
Two human feet from a sculpture in the round, on a pedestal consisting of a low platform over a lobed base–probably a floral motif. The base should be compared with the palm capital no. 272.

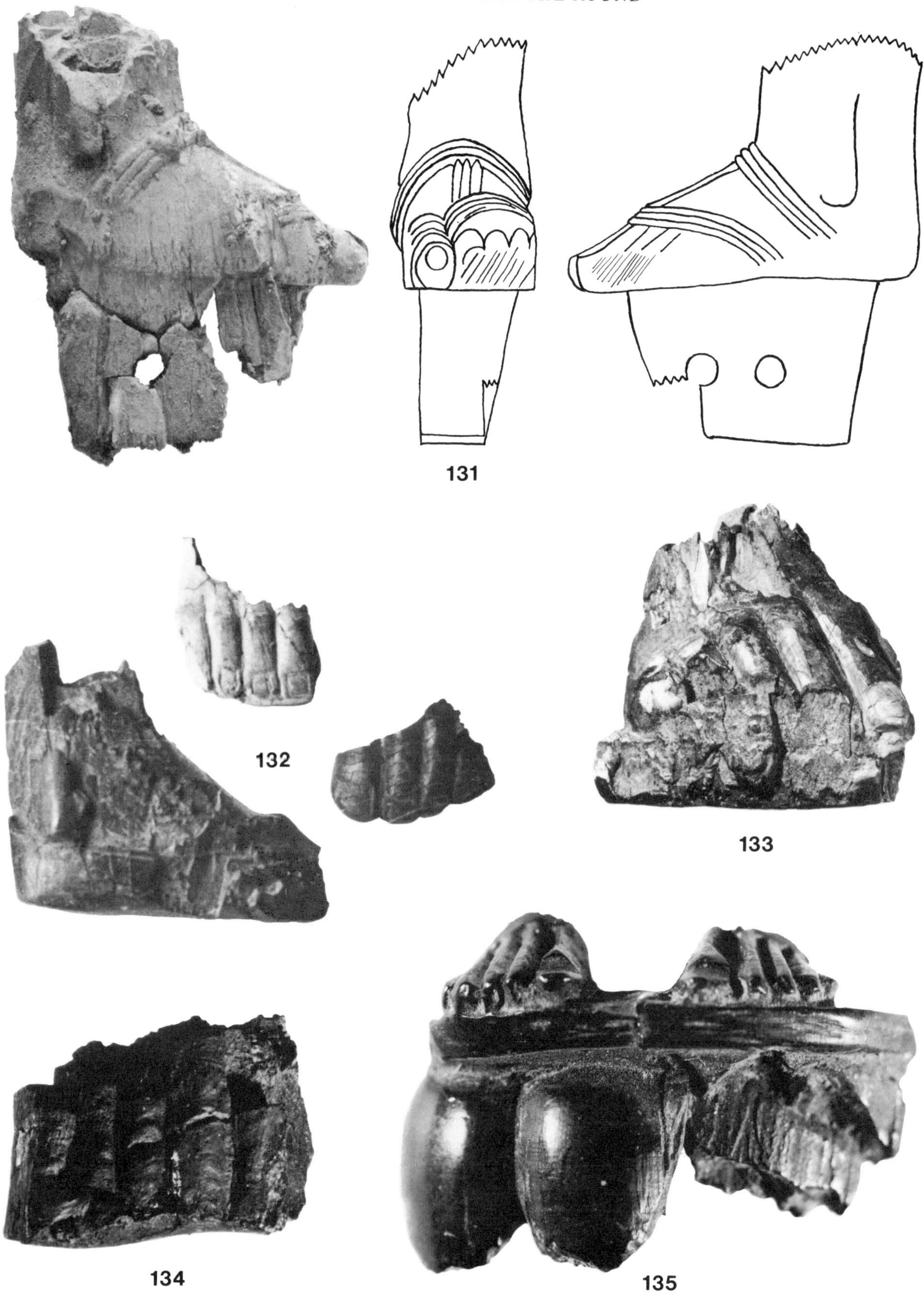

131

132

133

134

135

136 CC31 [2] (7); 64-934; T; ht. 5.4, w. 5.5, th. 3.5; front and back views.
A fragment in the round preserving two hands holding the rim of a long oval object; the thumbs touch. Herringbone-decorated wings are seen on the front, sides and rear. At the rear is also a raised button and a reserved area decorated with vertical incisions. The flat bottom has a broken tang for insertion into another piece that completed the figure.

137 Y33 [2] (BB V 3, SE corner); 74N-594e; UM 75-29-388; l. 2.9, w. .9, th. .4, and l. 2.5, w. .8, th. .4.
Two small fragmentary curved wings in the round, deeply carved on both sides in a thick herringbone pattern. There is a groove on the concave side for attachment.

138 Wood; CC31 [2] (7); 64-946; T; l. 11.6, w. 2.7, th. .6.
A single complete wing decorated on all sides in a herringbone pattern in relief bordered by rectangular panel sections. A tang cut with the wing is on the curved edge; another, along with a dowel hole, exists on the straight edge. Thus the wing was attached to a figure but also apparently joined a frame. The borders of the wings once held inlays. A small fragment of the wing's mate was also found.

139 BB II; 64- ; UM 65-31-578; ht. 3.5, w. 2.1, th. 1.
The tip of a wing in the round decorated on both sides with a thick herringbone pattern.

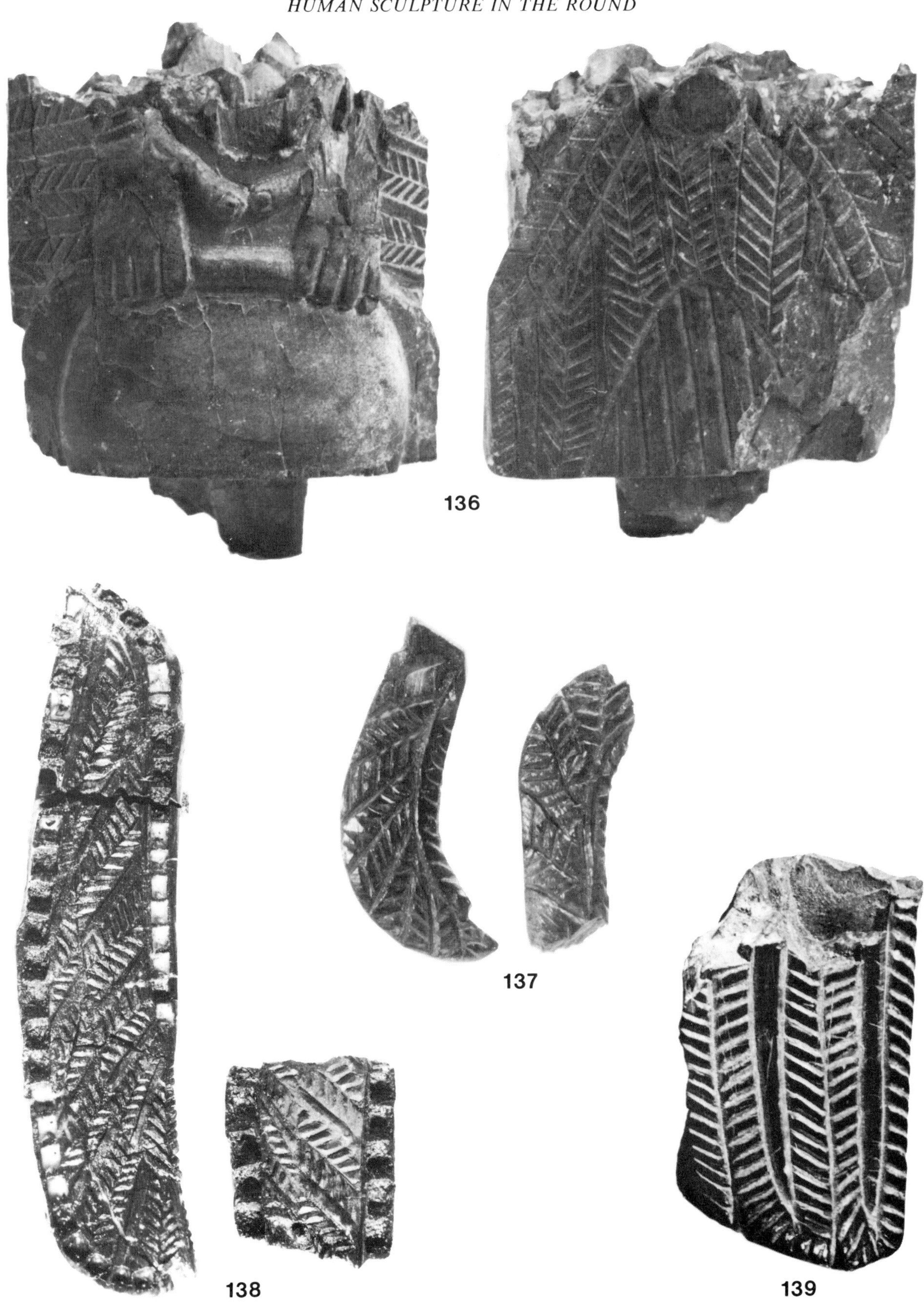
136
137
138
139

140 BB II; 64- ; UM 65-31-578; l. of largest 7.1.
Seven wing fragments belonging to figures in the round (there are actually twenty-two more fragments from the same provenience). Three wings have plastically rendered herringbone patterns, four have incised herringbone patterns.

141 CC32 **[1] [2]** (area east of 7); 70-428, 432; T.
Twenty-six fragments of wings from figures in the round, like no. 140. One small fragment catalogued here preserves a flame pattern and may not be part of a wing.

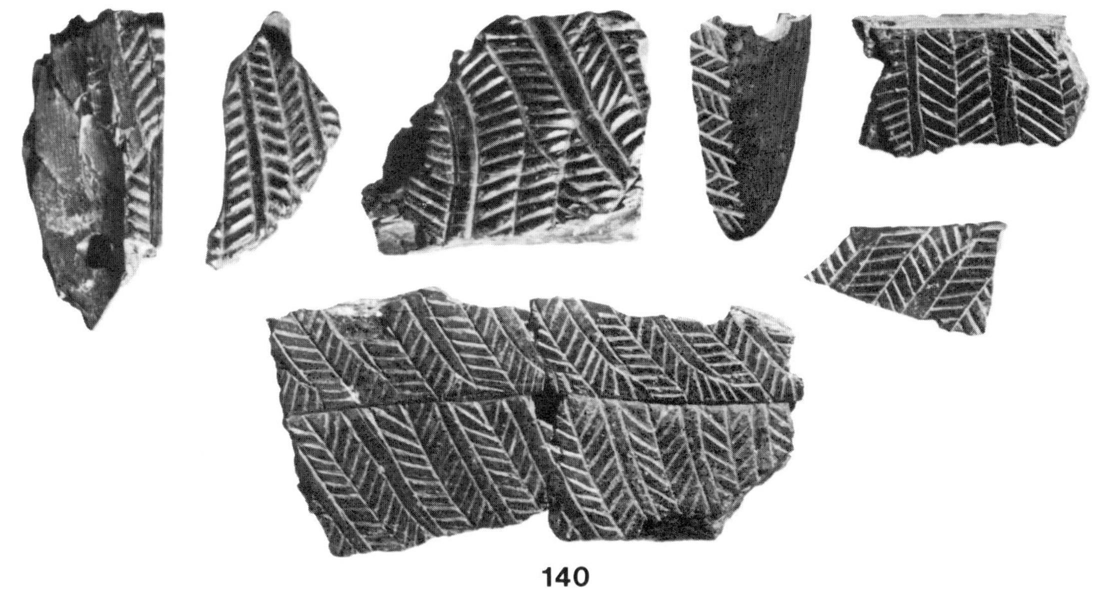

140

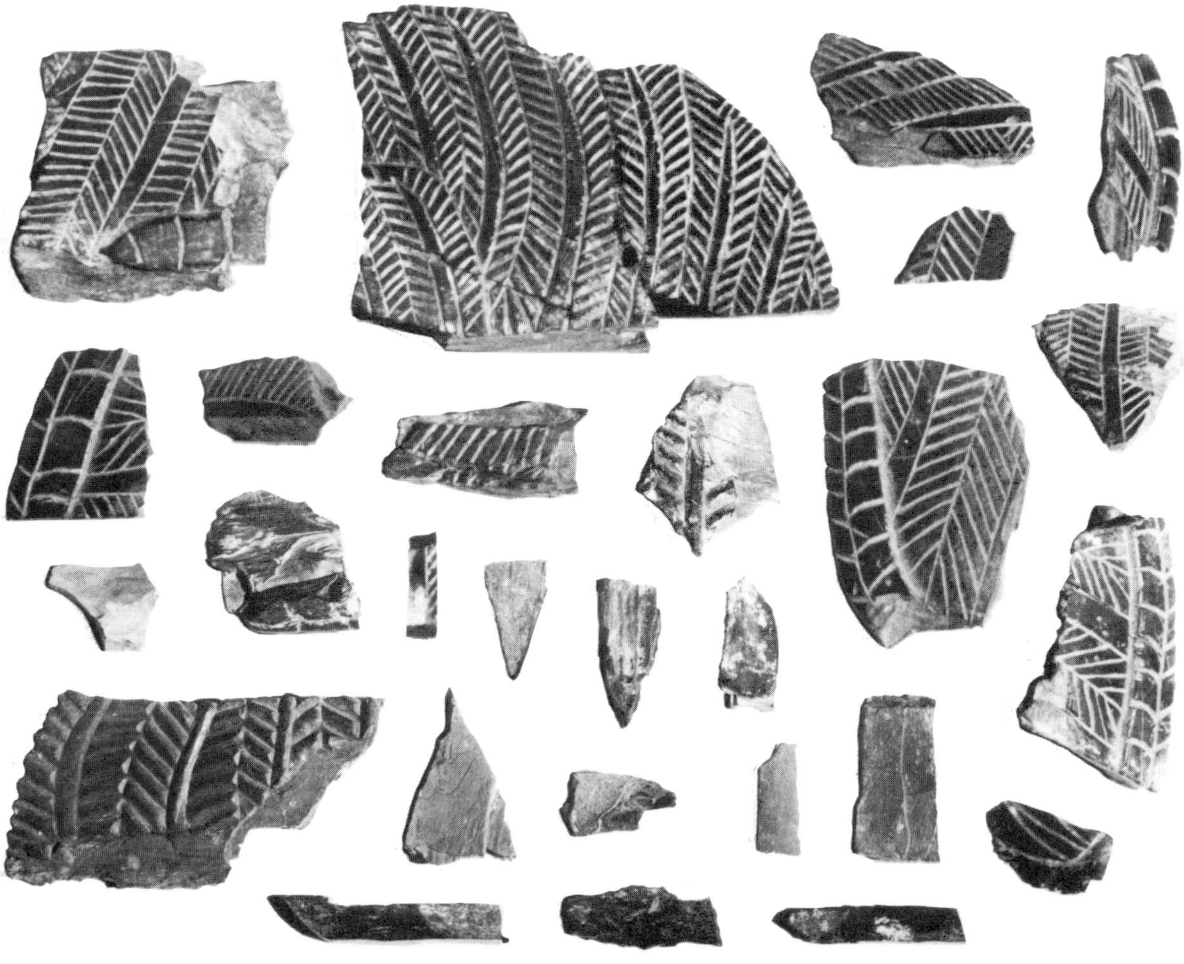

141

IV

ANIMALS, BIRDS, HUNTING SCENES

142 BB31 [1] (8); 64-738; T; ht. 6.6, w. 2.2, th. .4.
An animal—probably a bull, but the horns are missing—apparently stands on one foot while the other three may confront an adversary (cf. nos. 183, 184, 185)—or, he walks on three feet and raises one, left. The back and stomach are decorated with incisions; the shoulder is outlined by a groove. The left, right and bottom edges are intact; the lower is broad and decorated with incised concentric circles. The relief is low.

143 Wood; CC31 [1] (6); 64-924; UM 65-31-307; ht. 2.6, w. 3.2, th. 1.1.
The rear part of a stallion, left. The back and tail are decorated in herringbone pattern. Plain bottom and right edges are intact.

144 CC31 [1] (6); 64-922; T.
Extant is the body of an animal—a horse or bull; no sex is indicated—lacking the head, left. One or both front legs are bent back as if the animal were collapsing. An unidentified object is on the animal's back—an animal head?

145 CC31 [2] (7); 64-1064; UM 65-31-344; ht. 1.4, w. 5, th. .7.
Fragment preserving the rear part of an animal galloping (?) right. A thick herringbone pattern decorates the back. An unidentified object touches the back; it may be a spear head.

146 CC31 [2] (7); 64-1064; UM 65-31-344; ht. 2.1, w. 2.2, th. .4.
Apparently an animal moving left. Its body is outlined in thick incisions and what appears to be the tip of a tail is seen below its body.

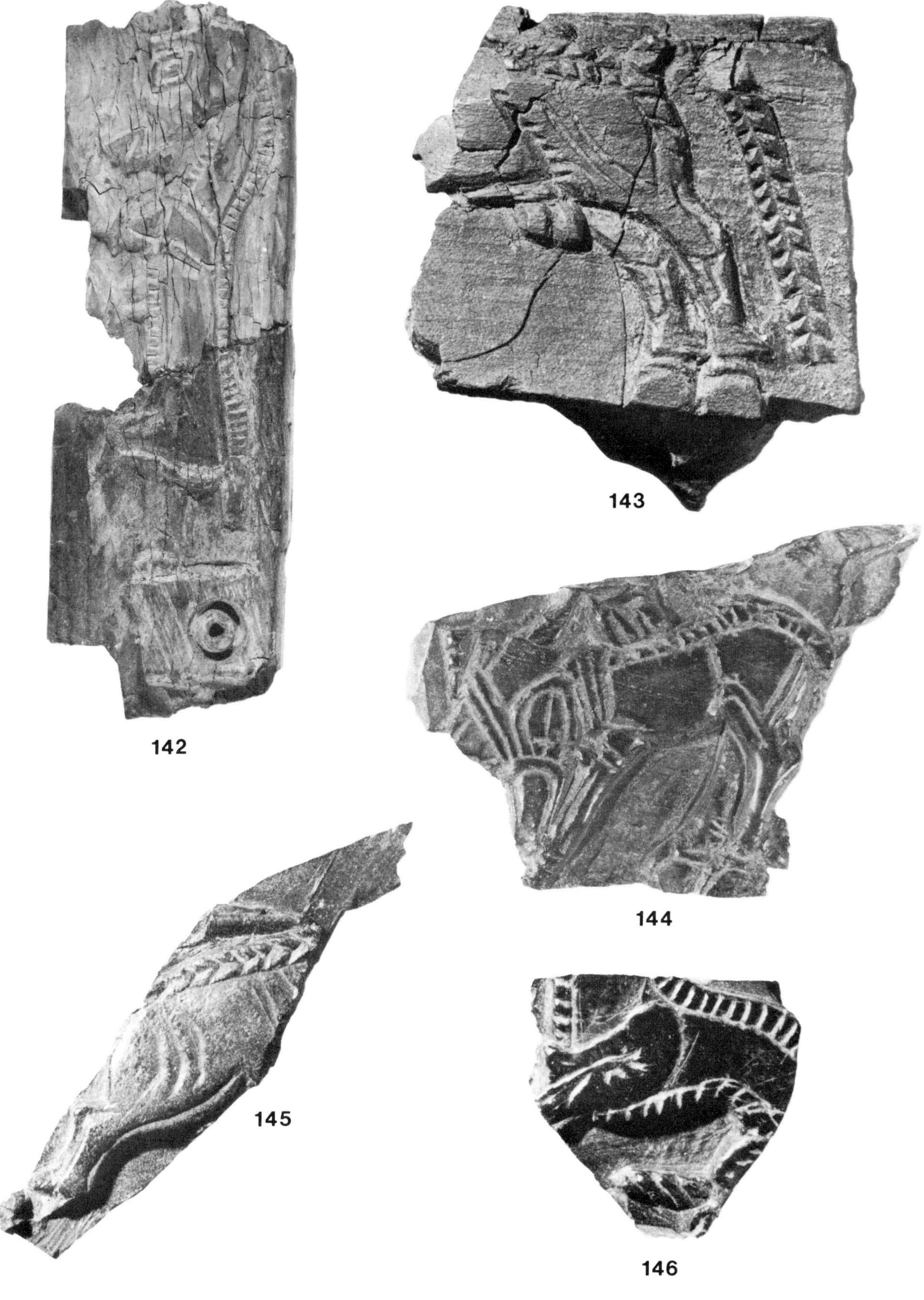

142

143

144

145

146

147 CC31 **[2]** (7); 64-1060; MMA 65.163.12; ht. 2.8, w. 1.5, th. .6.
A horned animal, probably a goat, leaping right, the front feet tucked back against the body. The body is outlined with incisions, as is the shoulder. Horns are divided right and left; an ear sticks out; eyes are incised ovals. The reverse is irregularly scored with deep cuts.

148 CC31 **[2]** (7); 64-1064; UM 65-31-344; ht. 3.7, w. 2.6, th. .6.
At the left is a leaping animal, right, similar to no. 147 in form, although only one horn is depicted and the body is not outlined. The mouth and eye are in relief. A small dowel hole is below the legs; another is at the right edge. The right part of the relief was left rough and has rocker scoring. This part was probably set into a slot in a separate piece. The plain upper and right edges are complete.

149 BB31/CC31 (8); 64-1076; T 25868; ht. 1.6, w. 2.1, th. .6.
The rear part of an animal, right. Extant is the right haunch with a distinctive incised zig-zag pattern. The body hair is depicted as long.

150 BB31 **[1]** (6); 64-759; T; ht. 2.5, w. 2.9, th. .5.
A small fragment preserving part of a bull's head, left. The horn seems to be placed rather low on the forehead. A groove at the left delineated some unknown object.

151 BB31/CC31 (8); 64-1076; T 25868.
Part of a bull's head, right; a section of the tail is extant. The preserved upper border is a raised band.

152 CC31 **[2]** (7); 64-1064; UM 65-31-344; ht. 2, w. 2.6, th. .5.
Small fragment preserving part of the horned head of an animal, left. Part of the ear and a section of the back decorated in herringbone pattern in relief are extant. (Cf. no. 153.) The top edge, a narrow band, is intact.

153 BB31/CC31 (8); 64-   ; UM 65-31-489; ht. 1.5, w. 2.9, th. .5.
Part of the head of a horned animal like no. 152, right.

154 CC31 **[2]** (7); 64-1064; UM 65-31-344; ht. 1.7, w. 2.5, th. .5.
Part of a horned animal, right. The horn, in relief and incised, curves around to touch the back of the neck. This area as well as a pattern on the neck is in relief. The plain left border is intact.

155 BB31/CC31 (8); 64-   ; UM 65-31-532; ht. 1.4, w. 1.4, th. .4.
A small fragment preserving part of the head of a horned animal left, like nos. 152-154.

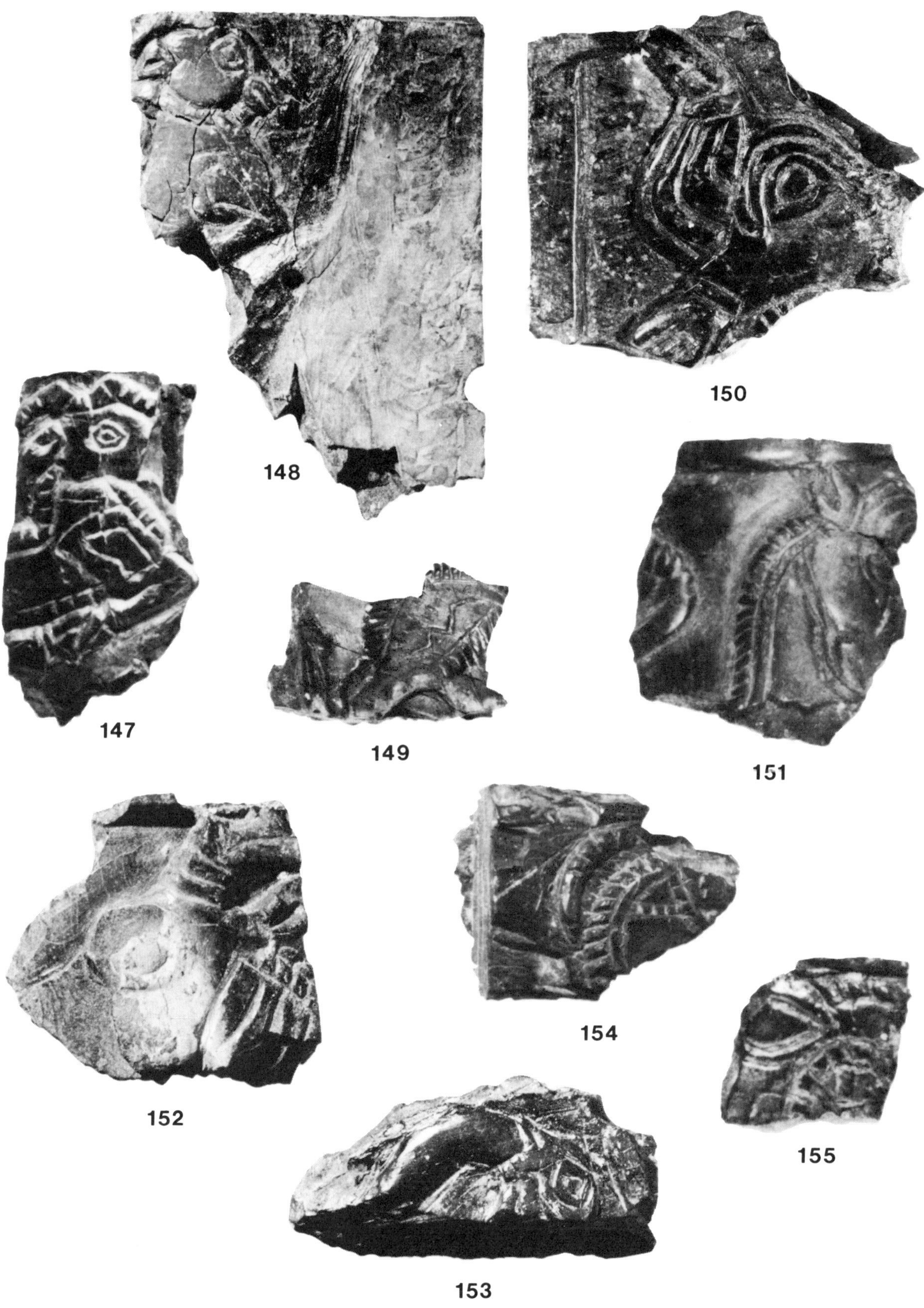
148
150
147
149
151
152
154
155
153

156 CC31 [1] (6); 64-921; T; ht. 3.1, w. 2.9, th. .4.
A stag either standing with a foot raised, or walking with its head lowered right. The antlers are decorated in thick sections, the back with a herringbone pattern, and the leg and shoulder are outlined. A prominent hock exists at the cleft foot. Upper, left, and right edges are intact; a dowel *in situ* is behind the stag. Rocker scoring on the reverse.

157 BB31/CC31 (8); 64-1076; T 25868; ht. 1.9, w. 2.8, th. .8.
The front half of an animal with lowered head, right; the cleft front feet are extant; one ear, but no horn is evident. The eye has no pupil or border. The head and feet ar disproportionately short. Both the lower and upper intact edges are narrow bands. An unidentified vertical object is at the right.

158 BB31/CC31 (8); 64-1076; T 25868; ht. 2.1, w. 2.2, th. .4.
Part of an animal with lowered head, right; one thin foot rests on a narrow ridge, the lower intact border.

159 Z26 (BB I West); 58-431; UM 59-4-137; ht. 1.3, w. 3.5, th. .4.
A small fragment preserving the cleft rear feet of an animal, right, followed by part of the head of an animal grazing: both deer? Incised lines radiate from the oval eye, which is in relief. The scene probably consisted of at least two grazing deer. Plain lower edge is intact.

160 CC31 [2] (7); 64-1064; UM 65-31-344; ht. 1.3, w. 2.2, th. .5.
A bird with a sharp beak, a squat body, and short legs, left. A tail flares out behind. The plain upper and left, and the raised bottom, edges are intact.

161 CC31 [2] (7); 64-1064; MMA 65.163.63; ht. 1.5, w. 2.2, th. .5.
A bird like no. 160, right; here legs are longer. The lower raised edge is intact; a dowel hole is at the right. The reverse has irregular scoring and is concave. A third bird of exactly the same type was found in BB II (64-1076; T 25868).

162 BB31 (8); 64-1064; MMA 65.163.11; ht. 4.1, w. 2.5, th. .5; Muscarella 1966, fig. 18.
Two confronting snarling lions, their front paws touching, and their rear legs no doubt on the ground. Teeth as well as fangs are depicted. All body detailing is deeply incised, creating a plastic image. The reverse is slightly concave.

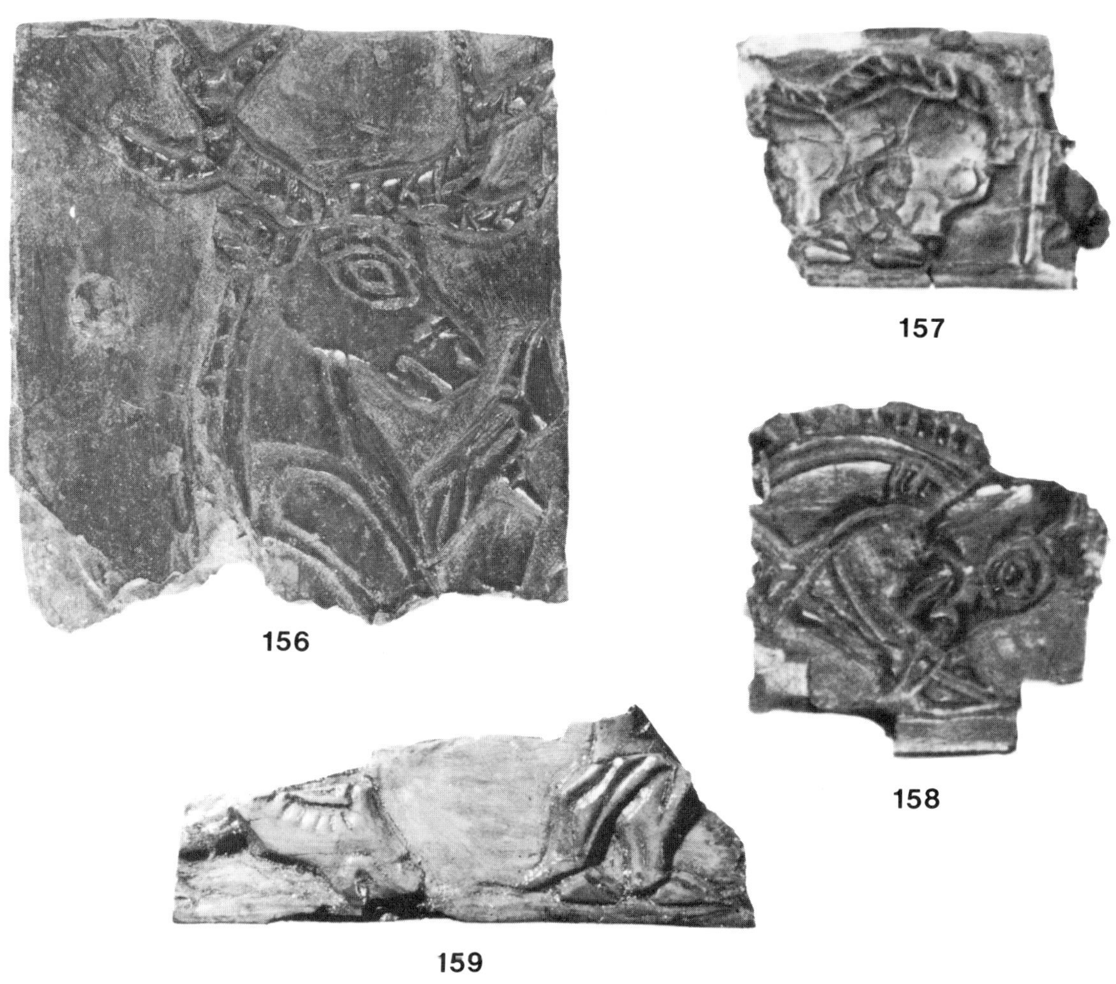

156

157

158

159

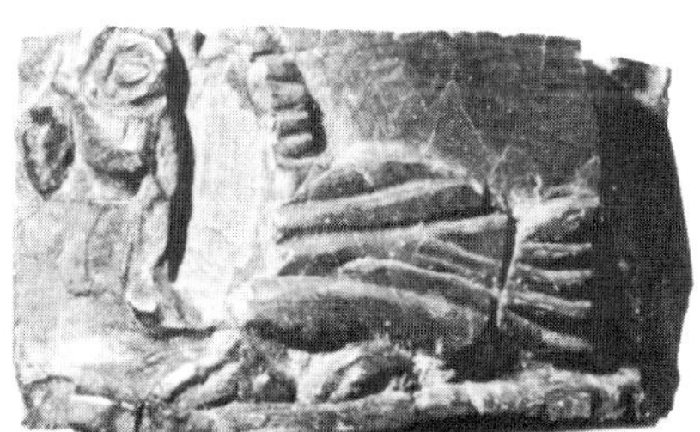

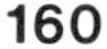

160

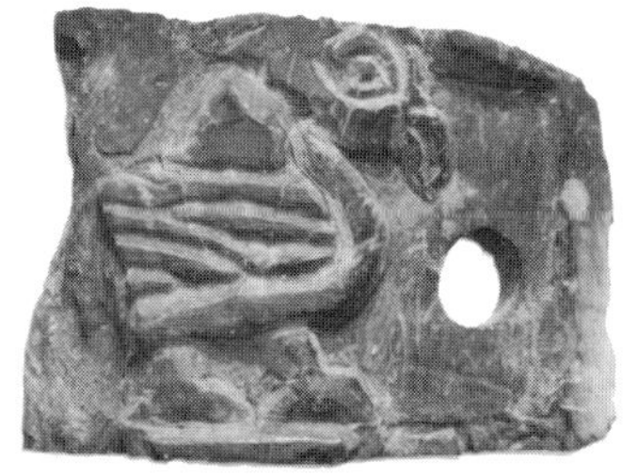

161

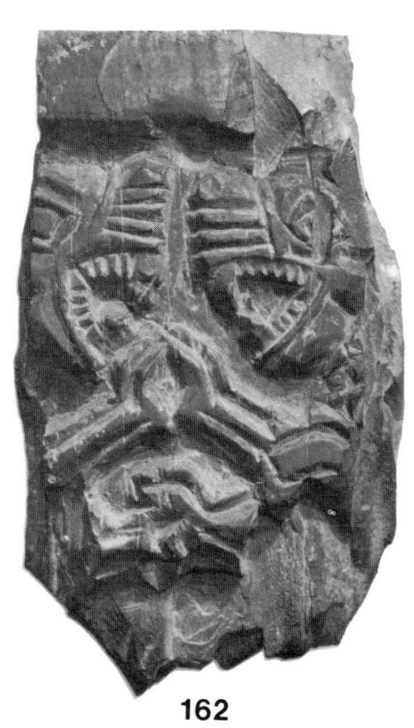

162

163 CC31 **[1]** (6); 64-918; MMA 65.163.10; ht. 3.4, w. 4.8, th. .7; Muscarella 1966, fig. 21.
Two seated winged lions (not griffins as there are no horns) with their muzzles and raised paws touching. Extant are most of the left lion and the tip of the right lion's muzzle. Two wings are depicted, each terminating in a squared tip; the right flares up, the left down along the back. The mane is rendered in triangular tufts, the ruff and tail in chunky fashion; the back and stomach are outlined in chunky herringbone pattern, as are also the wings. The tail tip is not complete and may have ended in a scorpion's sting. There is a dowel *in situ* at the lower left; the plain left edge is intact. The reverse is crudely scored with deep incisions and gouge marks.

164 CC31 **[1]** (6); 64-915; UM 65-31-367; ht. 2.7, w. 3.2, th. .6; Dyson 1972, fig. 3; front and back views.
Same type of lion as no. 163, left. A dowel hole is at the right. The plain upper and right edges are intact; the reverse has rocker scoring.

165 CC31 **[1]** (6); 64-912; MMA 65.163.22; ht. 2.3, w. 3.1, th. .45.
Same lion type as above, right. Plain top, right, and left edges are intact; a dowel hole is at the upper left. The reverse has rocker scoring.

166 CC31 **[1]** (6); 64-913; T; ht. 1.2, w. 3.2, th. .6.
Same lion type as above, left. Plain upper and right edges are intact; irregular scoring on the reverse.

167 CC31 **[1]** (6); 64-916; UM 65-31-365a; ht. 3, w. 2.7, th. .4.
Same type of lion as above four examples, right. Minor differences are: legs with more musculature and a pointed tuft, an ear projecting backward behind the mane, wing decoration that is less neat. Note also the solid hair tuft on the lower back. This lion has both legs raised and is therefore standing or attacking. Rocker scoring on the reverse.

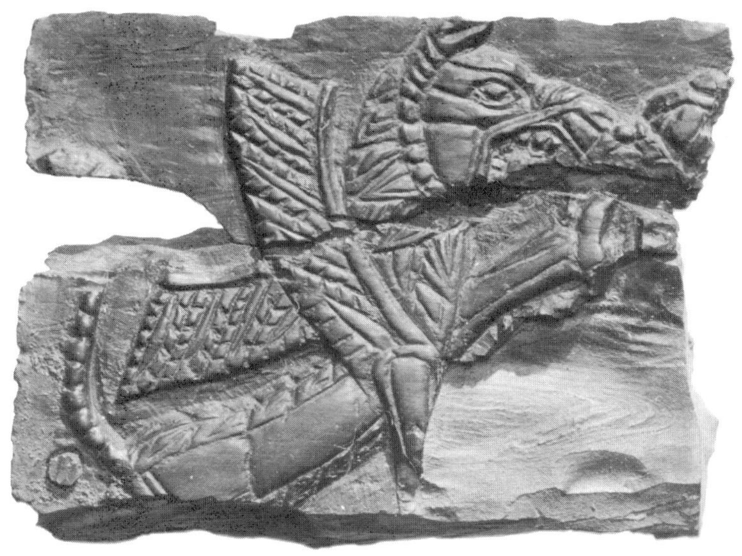

163

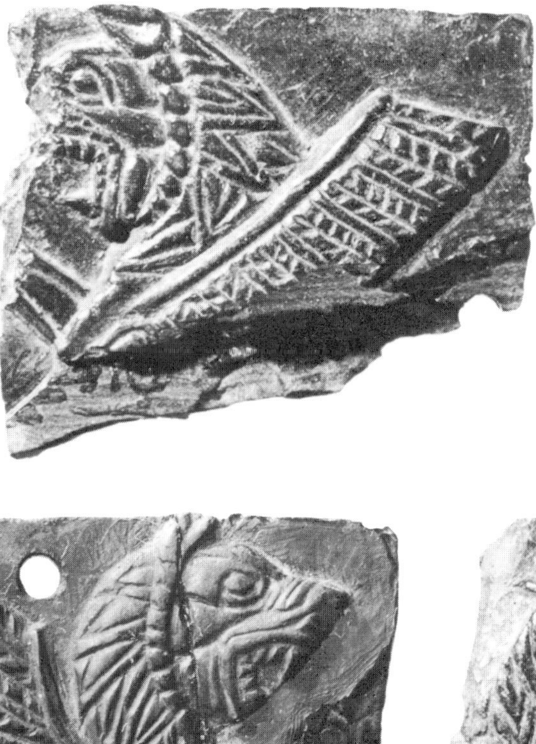

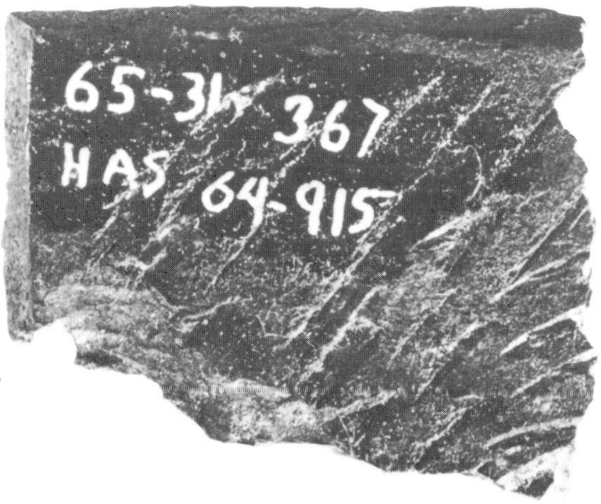

164

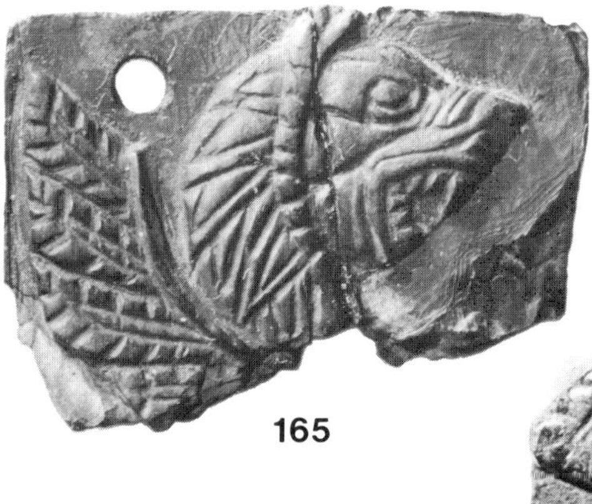

165

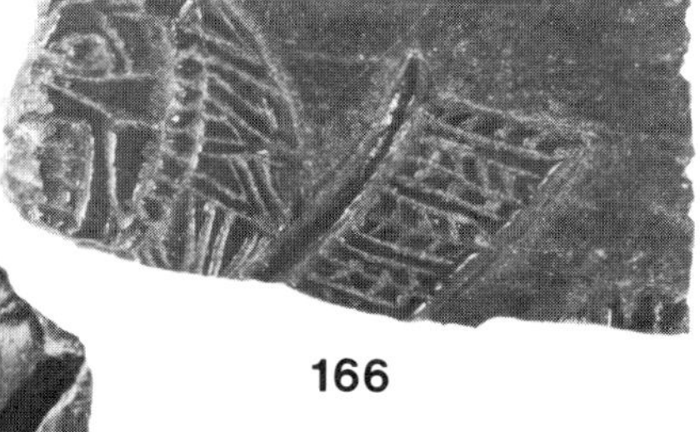

166

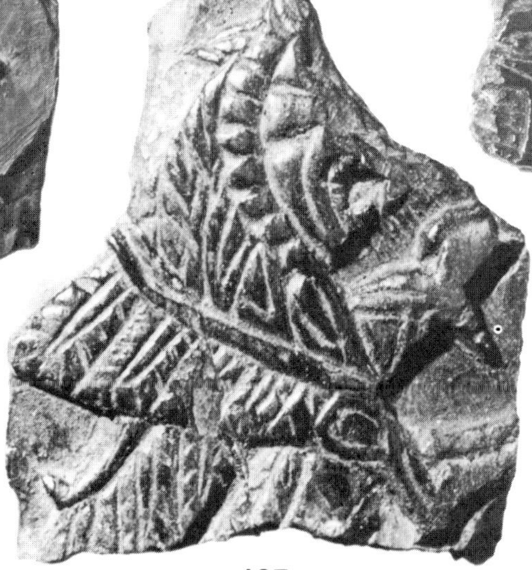

167

168 BB31 [1] (8); 64-792; UM 65-31-362; ht. 2.7, w. 5.7, th. .9; front and back views.
Lion similar to the previous examples but neater in execution and with slight differences in details. Extant are the chest and part of the body, part of the front legs, each with pointed tufts, part of both wings. Wings are decorated with neat tongue-like patterns, the back and probably the stomach with a thick herringbone outline, and the chest conventionally with tufts (cf. no. 178). The area in front of the lion is empty. The reverse has linear scoring and two vertical grooves.

169 AA30 (5,N); 60-950; T.
Preserved is the forepart of a snarling lion with prominent fangs, reclining, right. His feet are distinctly claw-like, resembling others in the ivory repertory (nos. 175-178), and the body is rendered very plastically. Above is what appear to be the feet of a tripod/tetrapod, with long animal's feet and a strut. This object has no groundline and it is not clear what its relationship is to the lion (cf. no. 119 for a tripod/tetrapod).

170 CC31 [2] (7); 64-899; T; ht. 4.7, w. 6.8, th. .7.
Fragment of a scene depicting a chariot involved in a lion hunt. Moving left are the horses, of which only one head is in part visible, with the head-harness. Their front feet are raised off the ground and overlap a twisted lion. The lion's snarling head and front paw confront the horses while its rear part appears to be touching the ground. The lion's mane is depicted typically in triangular tufts, while the back and stomach of the horse have a thick herringbone pattern. The lion's leg has a figure-eight pattern (cf. no. 187). The plain right edge is intact.

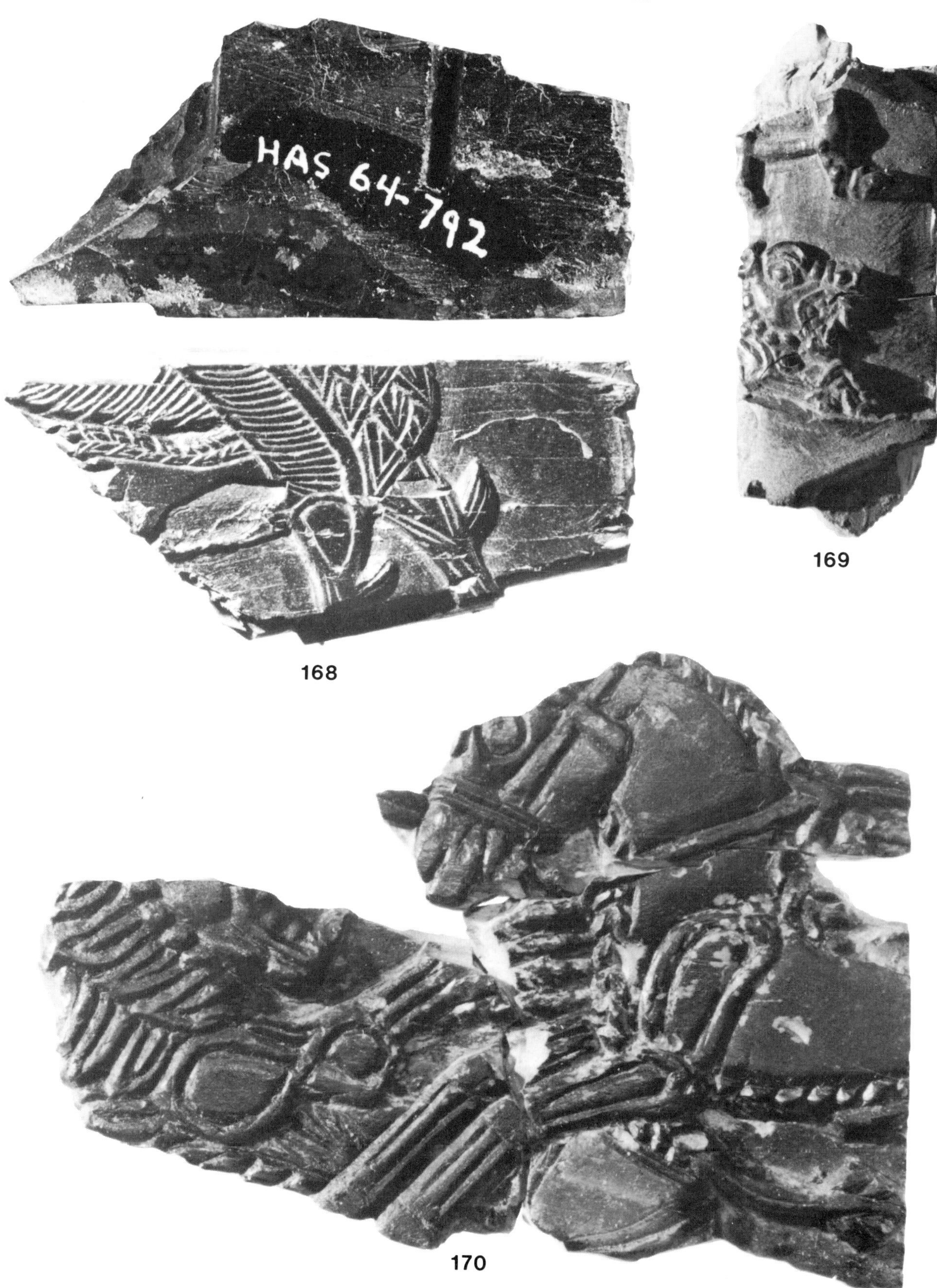

168

169

170

171 BB31 [2] (corridor east of 8); 64-761; MMA 65.123.20; ht. 2.9, w. 5.1, th. .9.
Fragment of a horse involved in a lion hunt. Extant are the head of the lion facing left but whose body probably moved right, and the neck and tip of the nose of a horse. The horse is like nos. 20 ff. in style. The plain left edge and the upper edge, a narrow band, are intact. The upper edge has rocker scoring; the reverse is fragmented but preserves two vertical grooves.

172 BB31 [1] (8); 64-770; T 25853; ht. 2.6, w. 4.4, th. .8.
A lion like no. 171, its body moving right but the head turned facing a hunter whose hand in relief is at the left with an incised arrow. The plain right edge and the upper band are intact. The top edge has a rocker pattern and the reverse has hatching.

173 BB31/CC31 (8); 64-1076; T 25868.
The head of a snarling lion facing left probably from a scene similar to no. 172.

174 BB31 [1] (8); 64-762; T; ht. 1.6, w. 5.2, th. 1.
A small fragment preserving the upper part of a hunting scene. Two men stand back to back, one facing a snarling lion at the left. The figure at the right has what appears to be a "feather" hat and his hair is made up of small spirals (cf. nos. 49, 61). The other figure has straight flaring hair held by a fillet (cf. no. 63). Probably different ranks are represented. The upper border is intact and has a guilloche pattern completed on a separate plaque.

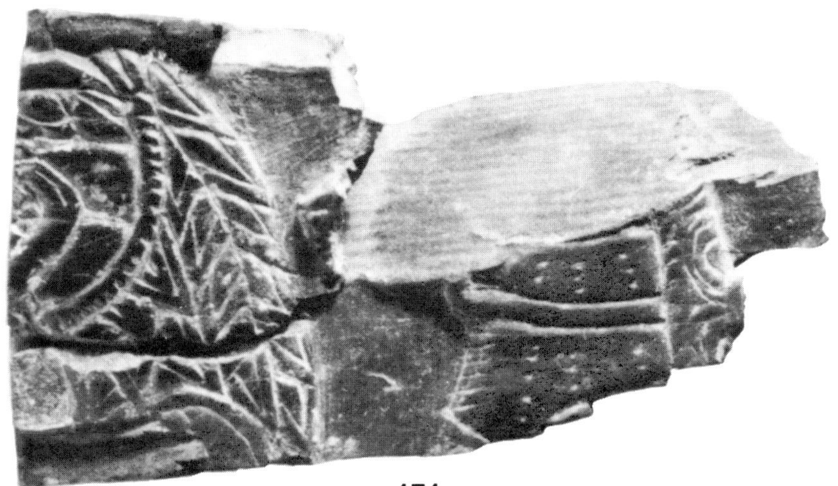

171

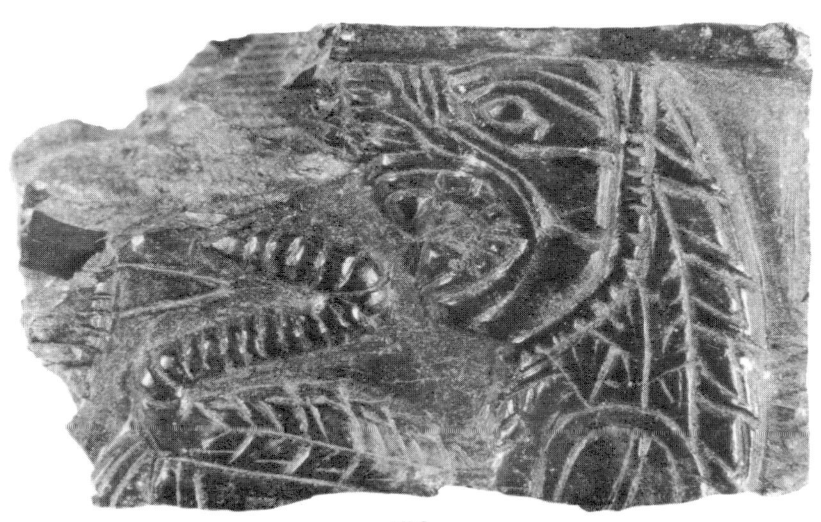

172

173

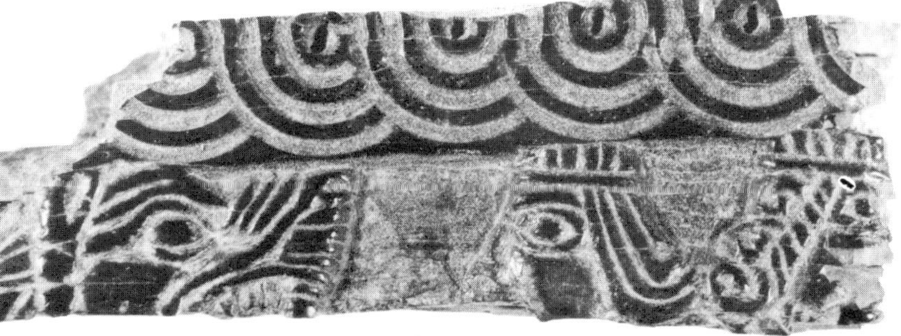

174

175 CC31 [2] (7); 64-933; T; ht. 7.5; l. of gold strip, 18, w. 3.5, th. .05; Dyson 1972, fig. 4; two views and drawing.
Placed around a fragment of ivory and held by three gold studs is a gold band decorated in repoussé. The surface of the ivory is grooved vertically and has a narrow vertical herringbone zone. The fragment could be from the head of a statuette (?), judging by the grooves that could be hair. The scene represented consists of two snarling lions and a standing archer who shoots at the lion to the left; no string or arrow is shown. The archer wears a calf-length, belted, short-sleeved garment fringed at the bottom and sleeves; he seems to be barefoot. The lions have claw-like feet with tufts similar to other Hasanlu lions (cf. nos. 176-181). Body decoration consists of simple incised dashes; the shoulders are fully outlined and well angulated. The scene is bordered by narrow bands. The execution is rather crude.

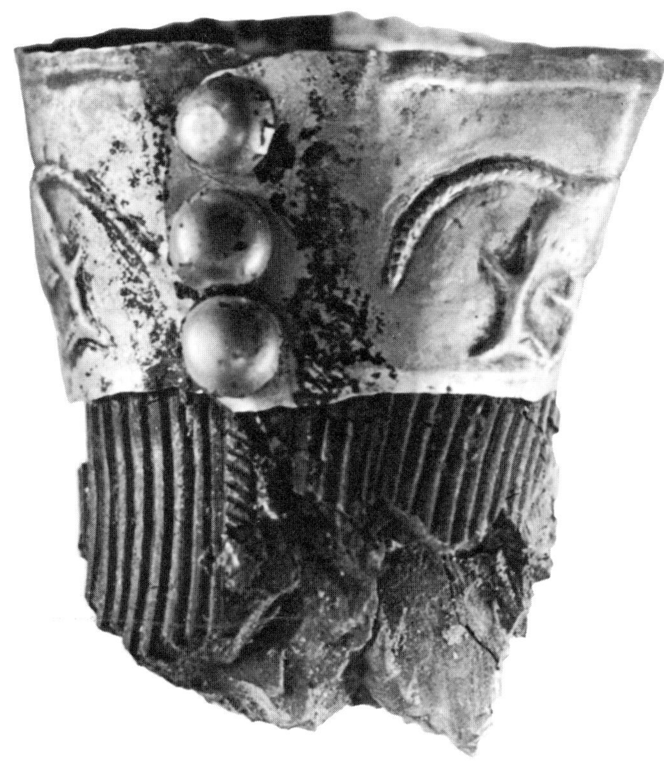

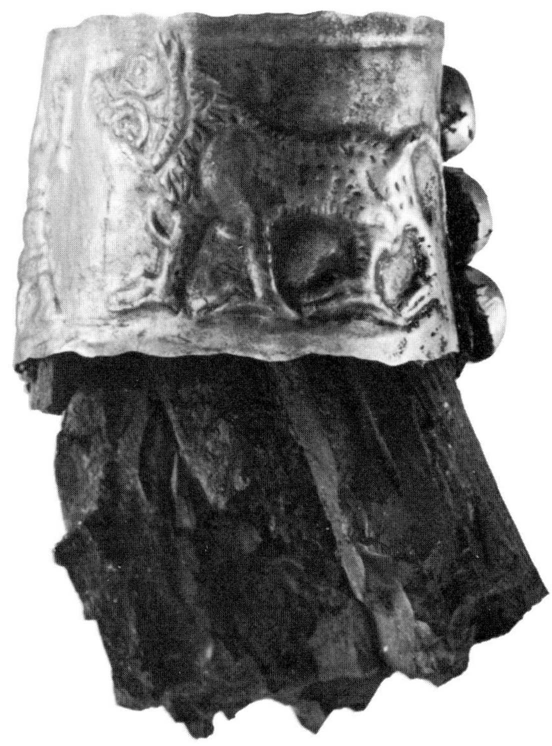

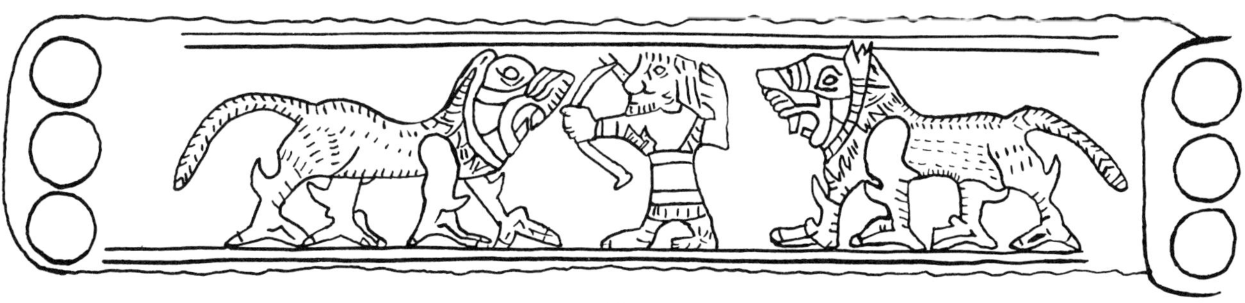

175

176 BB31 (8); 64-   ; UM 65-31-577; ht. .8, w. 3.6, th. .8.
Extant are two claw-like feet of a lion confronting a human foot at right. Probably a lion and hunter. The plain left and narrow banded lower edges are intact; the scene was completed on another plaque.

177 CC31 [2] (7); 64-1064; UM 65-31-344; ht. 2.8, w. 4.8, th. .8; front and back views.
Extant are two claw-like rear feet of a lion; no tufts are shown. A section of the stomach is visible at the right. The plain right edge is intact; the intact lower edge has the top part of a guilloche completed on a separate plaque. The reverse has many neat scoring marks, vertical and horizontal.

178 CC32 [1] [2] (area east of 7); 70-410; T; ht. 4.5; front and back views.
Preserved at the left is a lion with claw-like feet and tufts, right. Its body is plain but back and stomach have herringbone borders, the mane has triangular tufts, and the shoulders are outlined (cf. no. 168). Confronting him is a hunter with a round shield in his right hand and a weapon (missing) in his raised left hand. He wears sandals, a knee-length, short sleeved garment, scalloped at the neck (cf. nos. 33, 54, 55A, 56, 60). A guilloche border forms the intact lower edge; the plain upper and right edges are also intact; the heads of the hunter and lion were carved on a separate plaque. The reverse is irregularly scored.

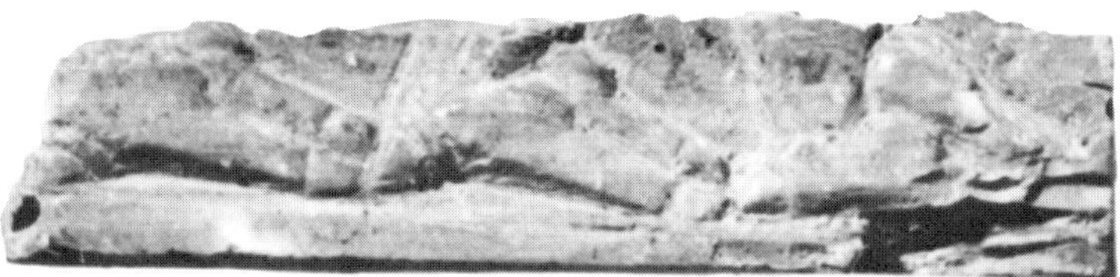

176

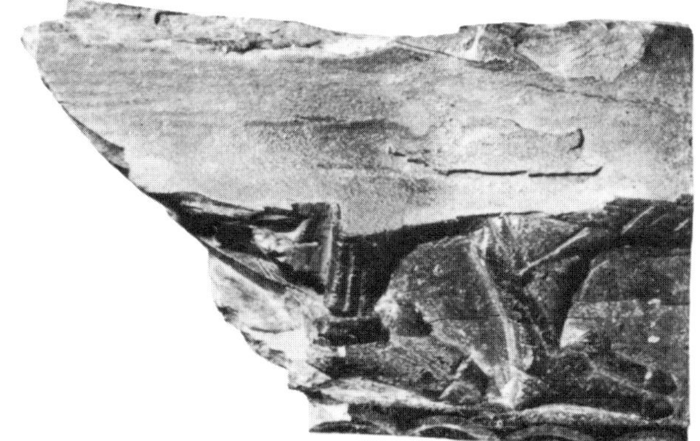

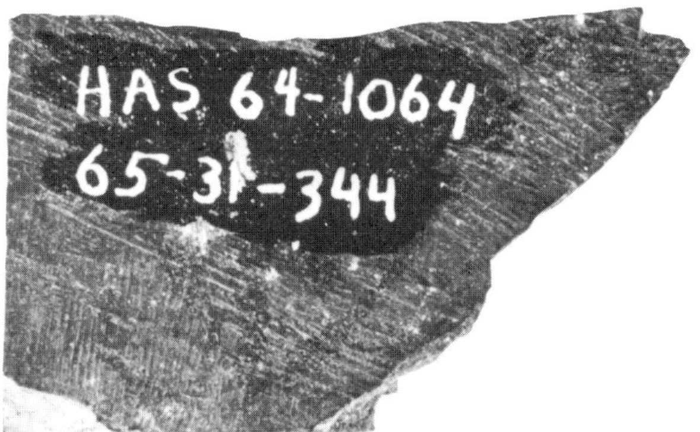

177

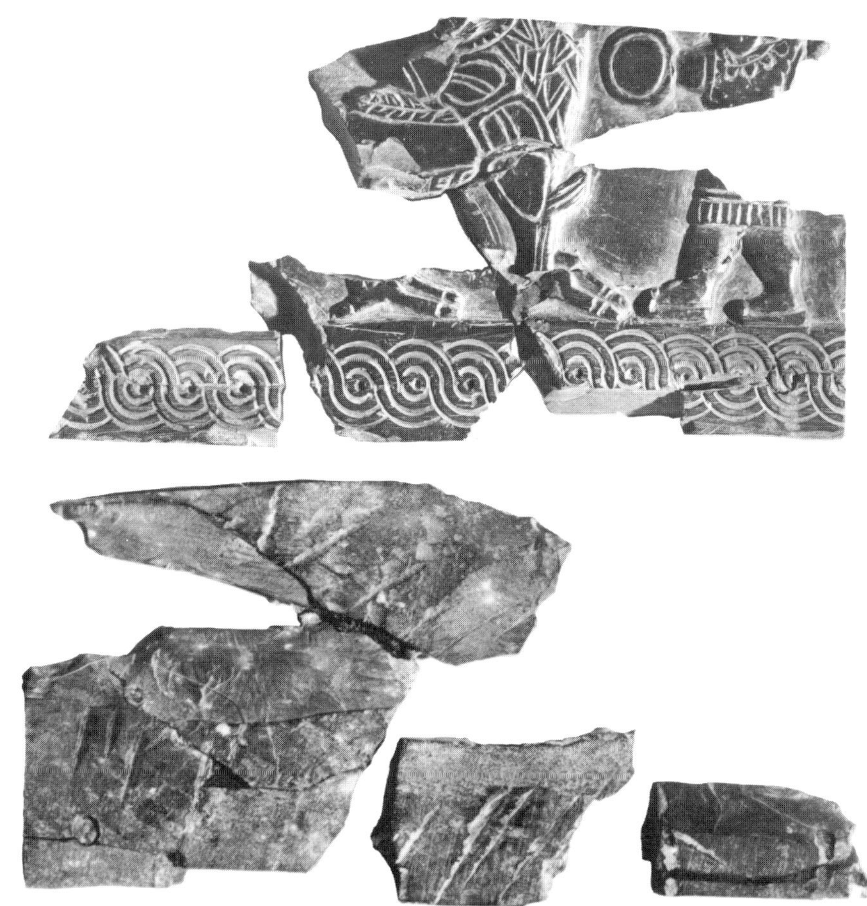

178

179 BB II; 64- ; UM 65-31-597; ht. 1.3, w. 3.4, th. .8.
A small fragment preserving a claw-like foot of a lion, right.

180 BB31/CC31 (8); 64- ; UM 65-31-479; ht. 1.6, w. 3.5, th. .8.
Extant are the damaged claw-like foot of a lion, left, another damaged one to its right, and the tip of a spear coming from the upper left.

181 BB31/CC31 (8); 64- ; UM 65-31-483; ht. 1.7, w. 3.2, th. .7.
Extant are two claw-like feet, right, one resting on the leg of a cleft foot, probably a bull or stag.

182 CC31 [1] (6); 64-914; UM 65-31-312; ht. 2.7, w. 5.1, th. 1.
Preserved at the left is part of an upright lion with one paw extended to touch a winged creature facing it. The creature's decorated chest, hatched wing, upper leg, and lower part of a hair curl are preserved. It may be standing on two legs, which, if true, means that the creature is a siren, rather than a sphinx. The reverse has rocker scoring.

183 CC31 [1] (6); 64-917; UM 65-31-357; ht. 1.4, w. 4.3, th. .6.
Small fragment preserving part of a bull's head, right, the horns of which are held by a human hand. The scene could be similar in form to nos. 184, 185. A fragment of an object behind the bull could be remains of a wing. The reverse has rocker scoring.

184 BB31 [1] (8); 64-982; UM 65-31-359; ht. 3.3, w. 4.3, th. .6.
Preserved is part of a battle between a hero at the left and an animal, apparently a lion. The hero wears a belted garment decorated at the sides and fringed at the bottom. With his right hand he attacks the animal with a short dagger; a protuberance at the top seems to be the hero's large nose. The animal stands on its right leg and touches the hero with the remaining ones. The upper edge is complete, the heads completed on a separate plaque. Piercing both bodies are dowel holes. The reverse is irregularly scored.

185 BB31 [1] (8); 64-772; UM 65-31-351; ht. 6.8, w. 3.9, th. .5.
At the left is an upright winged lion on one rear foot confronting a sphinx. The lion's other feet touch those of the sphinx; its wings–only one is shown—are small and curve down behind the waist; a short tail is visible below the dowel hole. The sphinx, also on one leg, touches both legs and the muzzle of the lion. His face is almost all nose; he has short flaring hair; there may be a short beard. His wing is small and has one thick border like the lion's, but curves up behind the waist, perhaps symbolically; a short tail exists. Three incised circles decorate the upper border (cf. no. 142) above which there seems to have been another panel. The plain bottom edge, and the narrow bands at the right and left edge are intact. The reverse has irregular scoring.

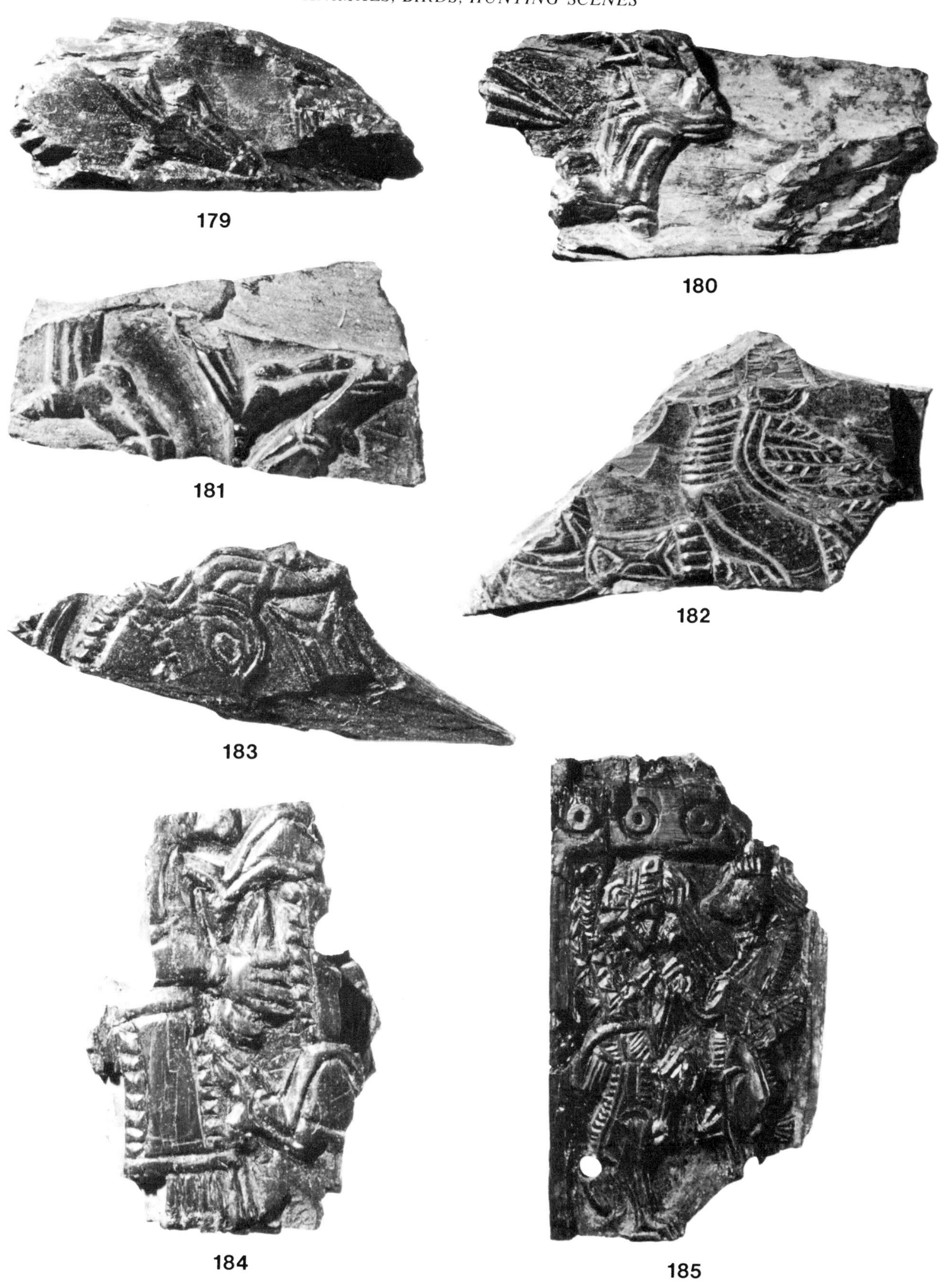

179

180

181

182

183

184

185

V

ANIMAL SCULPTURE

186 BB31 [1] (8); 64-998; UM 65-31-353; ht. 2.1, w. 1.4, l. 3.8; two views. The forepart of a crouching lion, with most of the left and part of the right foot extant. The body is in the round and is free of decoration but for an incised tulip design on the legs. Whiskers and nose wrinkles are in relief; the deep-set eyes are hollowed out to hold inlays. The interior of the open mouth is solid and the teeth are carved in relief; the lower jaw is missing. Ears, round knobs set within a crescent, are placed above the thick ruff, at the base of a slightly gabled head.

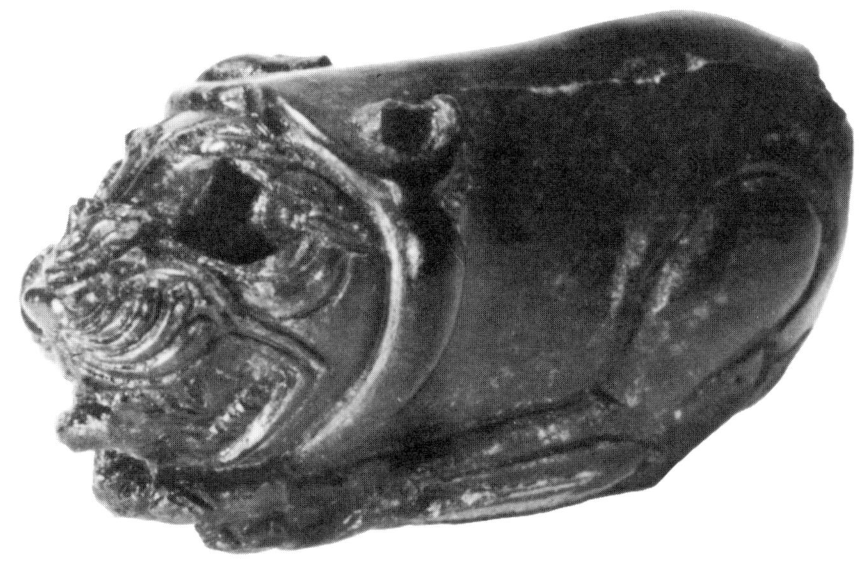

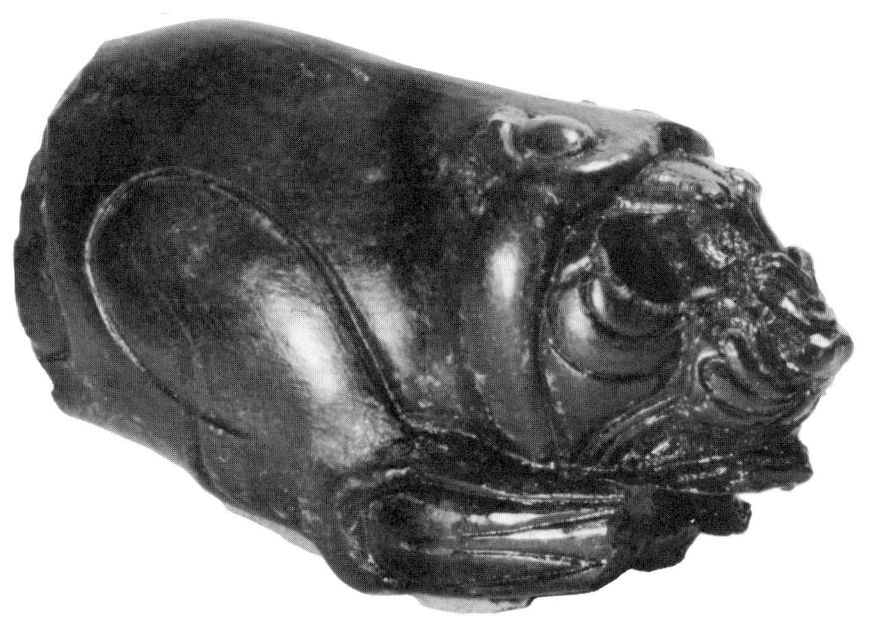

186

187 CC31 [1] (7); 64-901; T; ht. 1.6, w. 1.5, l. 4.1; side view and drawing.
A compact crouching open-mouthed lion in the round, with a flat base containing two dowel holes for attachment (to a lid? cf. nos. 242-245). Missing are parts of the head and the right side. The body is highly decorated in relief and there were inlays of green frit set in gold on both shoulders. Both flanks and the eyes also once held inlays. The forelegs have a figure-eight pattern (cf. no. 170).

188 CC31 [2] (7); 64-1063A; MMA 65.163.28; ht. 2.1, l. 3.9.
Fragment of an open-mouthed lion, preserving half of the upper jaw and head, part of the back, and part of the left leg. The ruff has a zig-zag pattern; the flat ear is behind the ruff. The leg is in high relief.

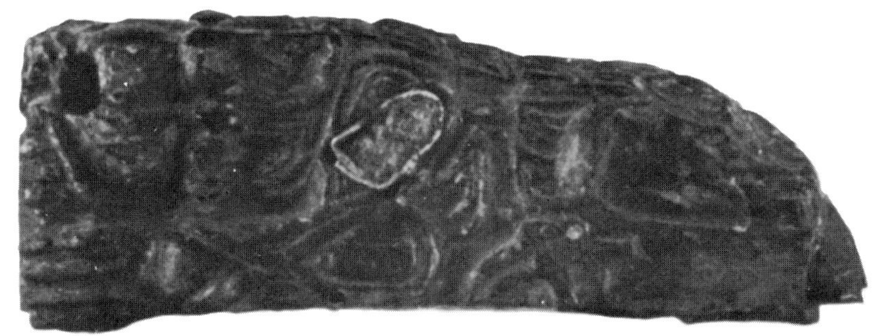

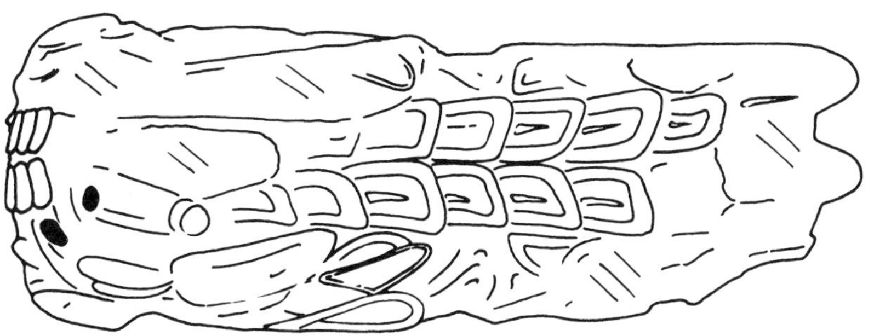

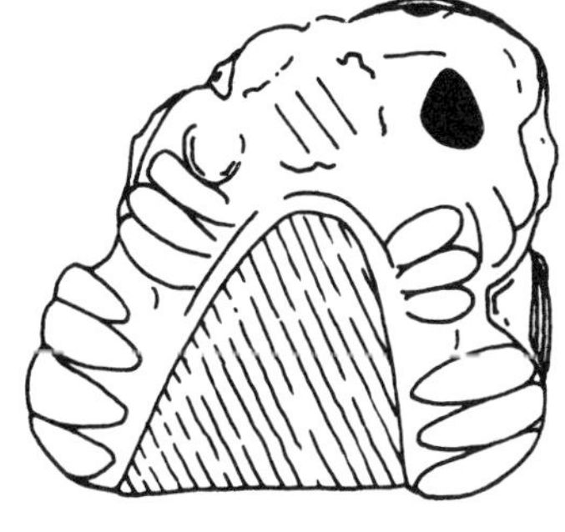

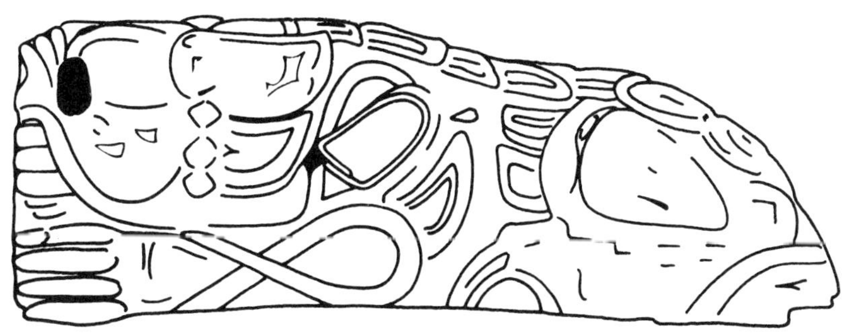

187

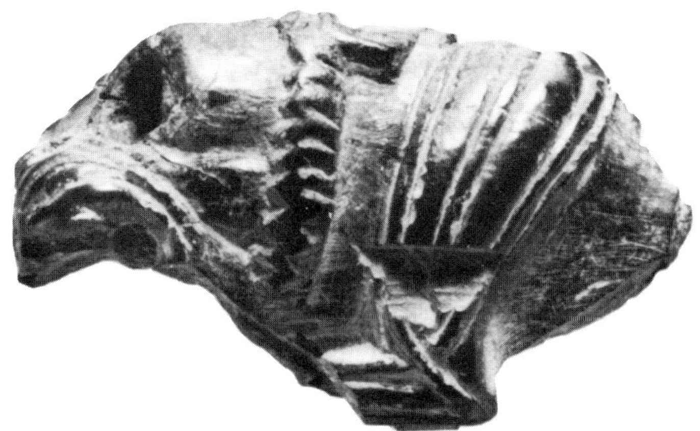

188

189 CC31 [1] (6); 64-902; T; ht. 3.7, w. 3.3, l. 5.2; two views.
A complete lion head in the round carved together with a rectangular base and a square tang for insertion. The mouth is open and the four fangs touch; no tongue protrudes. Eyes once held inlays; two ridges on the forehead terminate in holes for wart inlays. The mane has typical triangular tufts; the nose wrinkles and whiskers are in typical relief. At the bottom of the rectangular base are the crudely carved toes of the feet, meant to be seen from the front. Whether this object was a protome or handle is not clear. Fragments of the mate to this piece were found nearby.

190 Wood; BB II; 64-980A; MMA 65.163.44; ht. 4.7, w. 4.6.
A small fragment preserving a right foot resting on a base, below which is an undercut section with a dowel *in situ*. The foot has thongs (?) that criss-cross. It is not altogether clear if this foot is animal or human; the thongs, if that is what they are, would make it human.

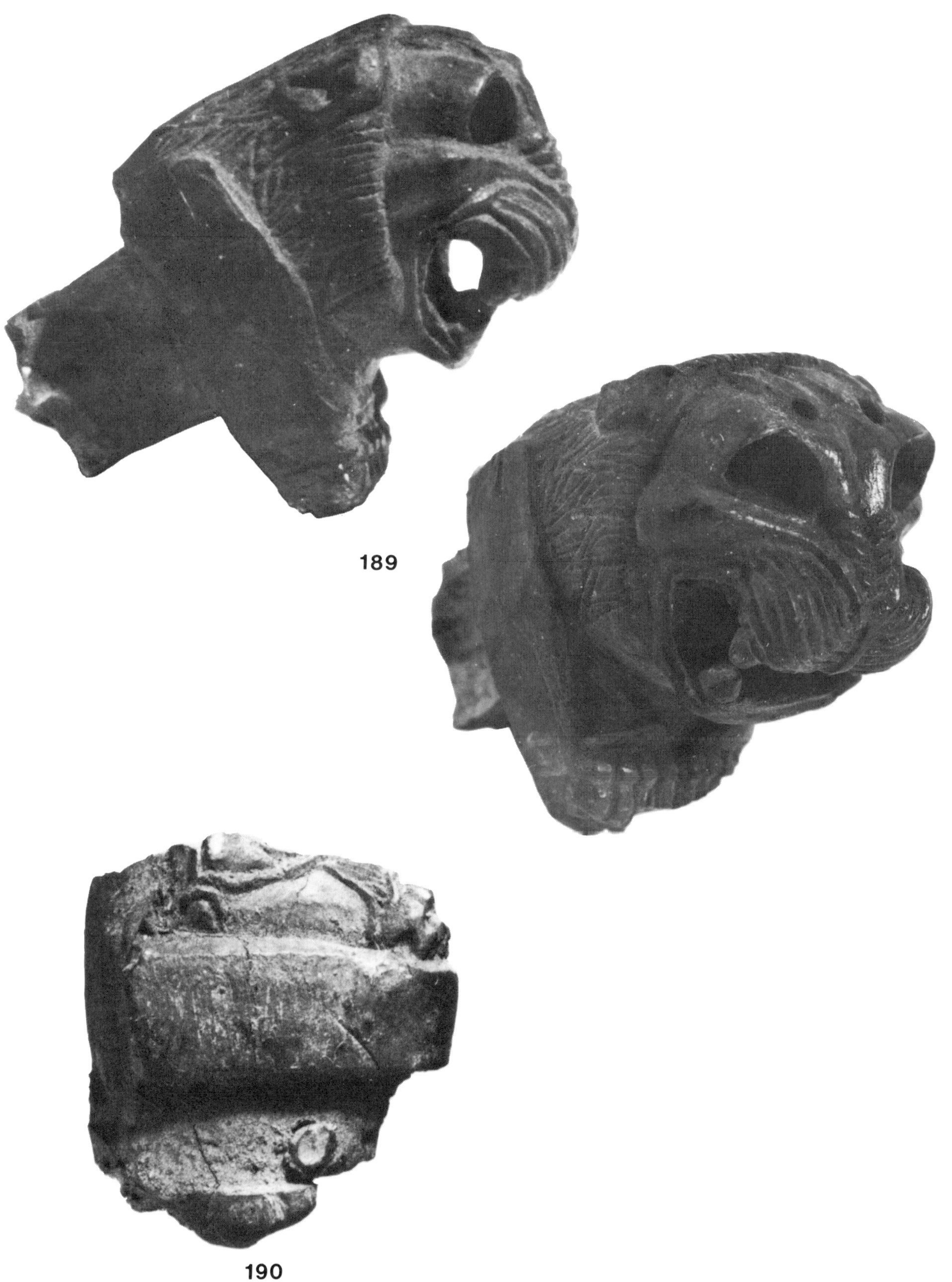

189

190

VI

TREES, PLANTS, MISCELLANEOUS

191 CC31 [1] (7); 64-907; MMA 65.163.32; ht. 3.9, w. 2.5, th. .2.
Thin plaque preserving the upper part of a stylized tree. Five grooved leaves symmetrically arranged project at the top from a grooved rectangular base. Below, extending from each side of the trunk, is a branch with a three-petaled flower, one petal of which extends under the base. The reverse is irregularly scored. A dowel hole is extant at the top.

192 BB II; 64- ; UM 65-31-612; T.
Five fragments of plaques, as above. One has a dowel hole preserved.

193 BB31 [1] (8); 64-907; UM 65-31-343.
Three fragments like the above.

194 Wood; CC31 [1] (6); 64-932; UM 65-31-306a; ht. 2.3, w. 1.7, th. .4.
Two fragments, like the above except that the leaves are plain, not incised.

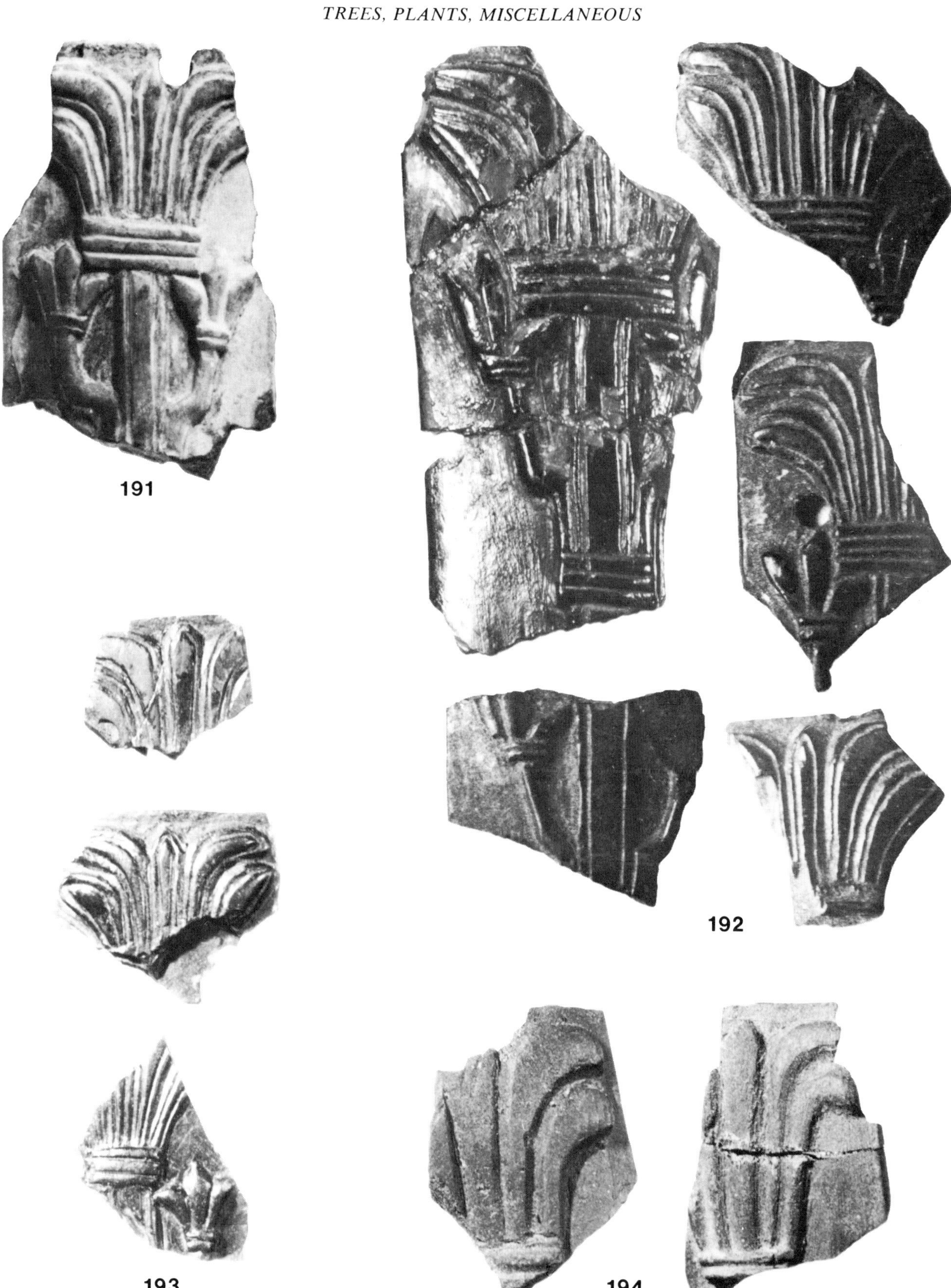
191
192
193
194

195 CC31 [1] (6); 64-904; MMA 65.163.31; ht. 3.7, w. 2, th. .25; Baer 1971, fig. 1, left (upside down).
Fragment of a stylized tree, as above. The base of the tree is squared with two spiralled volutes, one on each side; a dowel is *in situ*. The reverse is smooth.

196 CC31 [1] (6); 64-905; UM 65-31-336; ht. 2.7, w. 2.5, th. .25; front and back views.
Same as above, except for an incised triangle in the base and a more compact volute. The reverse has rocker scoring..

197 BB II; 64- ; T; MMA 65.163.45a, b.
Four fragments like no. 196; two have dowel holes, one at the base, the other above a volute. The two Metropolitan Museum examples (illustrated) have rocker scoring on the reverse.

198 BB31/CC31 (8); 64- ; UM 65-31-500; l. 2, .8, and 1.2.
Three fragments of a narrow panel with a row of lotus buds. One has above the row an object that appears in the photograph to be a human foot, but which is actually a flaked fragment of a unit above the lotus. The other two fragments have a serrated upper edge.

199 BB31/CC31 (8); 64- ; UM 65-31-488; ht. 3.1, w. 1.7, th. .5.
Fragment of a plaque preserving parts of two superimposed registers. The upper is indistinct, the lower has a tree, three branches of which have flowers; only two are preserved.

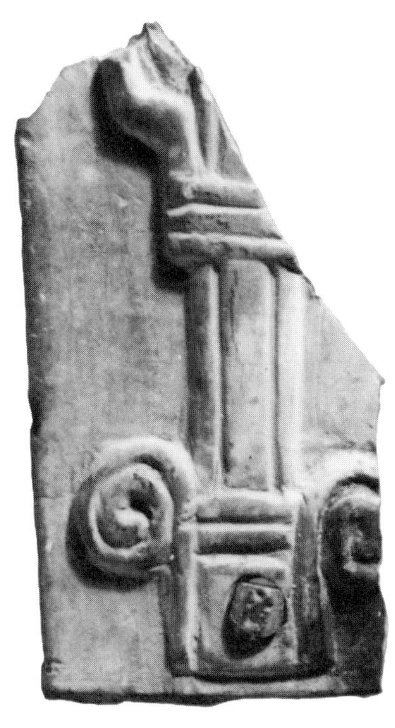

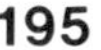

195

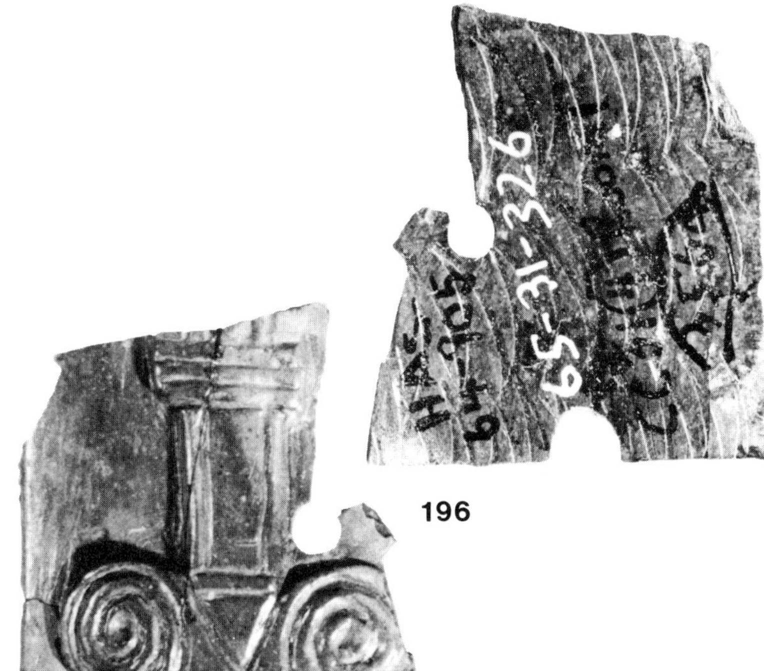

196

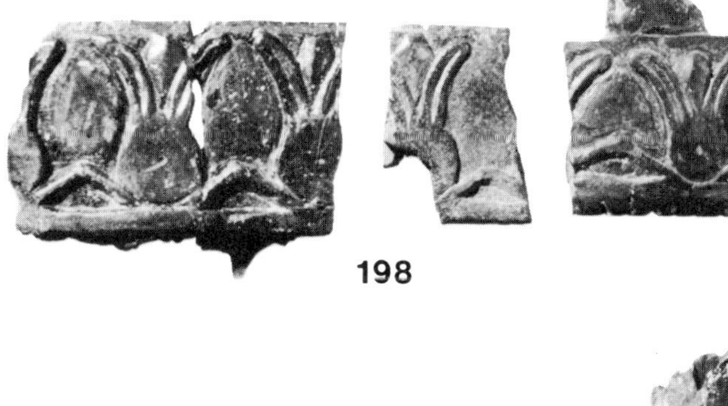

198

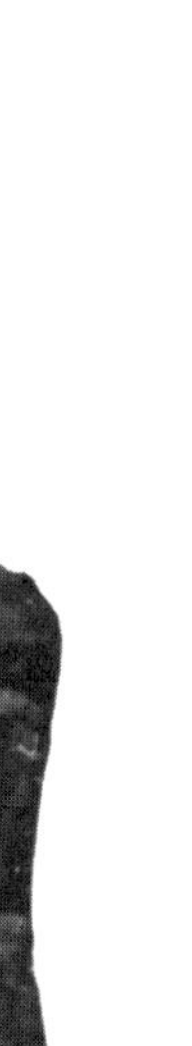

197

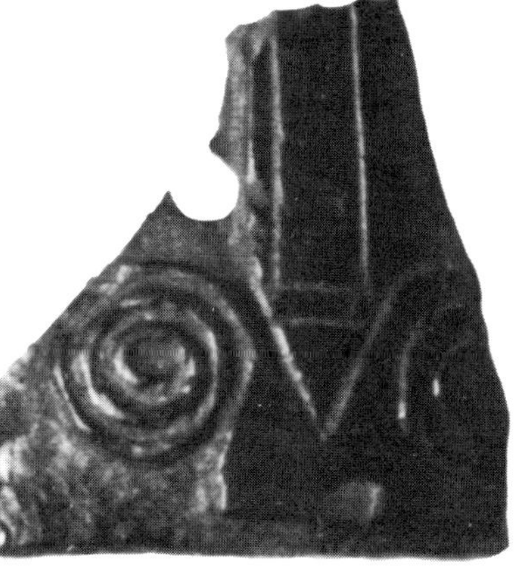

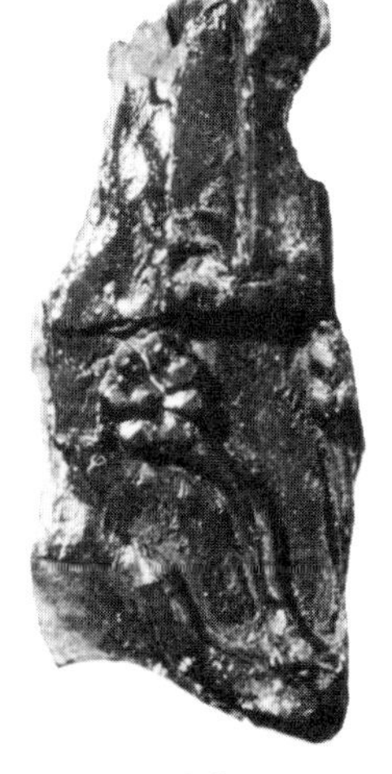

199

200 BB II; 64- ; UM 65-31-572; ht. 2.4, w. 2.9.
A bulging, flattened knob with rectangular projections on three sides; one is broken. Nine other similar fragments were found in AA30 (GH, N) (60-476). They may be too small for furniture pieces.

201 Z26 (BB I West); 58-425; UM 59-4-68; l. 3.5, w. 2.9, th. .6.
Rectangular flat lid (?) with a bronze knob for a handle.

202 Z26 (BB I West); 58- ; UM 59-4-68.
Three fragments of a lid, like no. 201.

203 BB31/CC31 (8); 64- ; UM 65-31-558; ht. 7.3.
Fragment preserving the neatly squared corner of a box or handle; undecorated. A row of four holes—two large, two small—are at the top of one face.

204 Bone; BB29 (5,W); 60-912; UM 61-5-64; ht. 2.1, w. 4.5, th. .5.
A solid crescent-shaped object with a hole, probably a sword- or dagger-hilt pommel; one side is polished, the other left rough. Several similar examples in stone, without the hole, have been found in BB II.

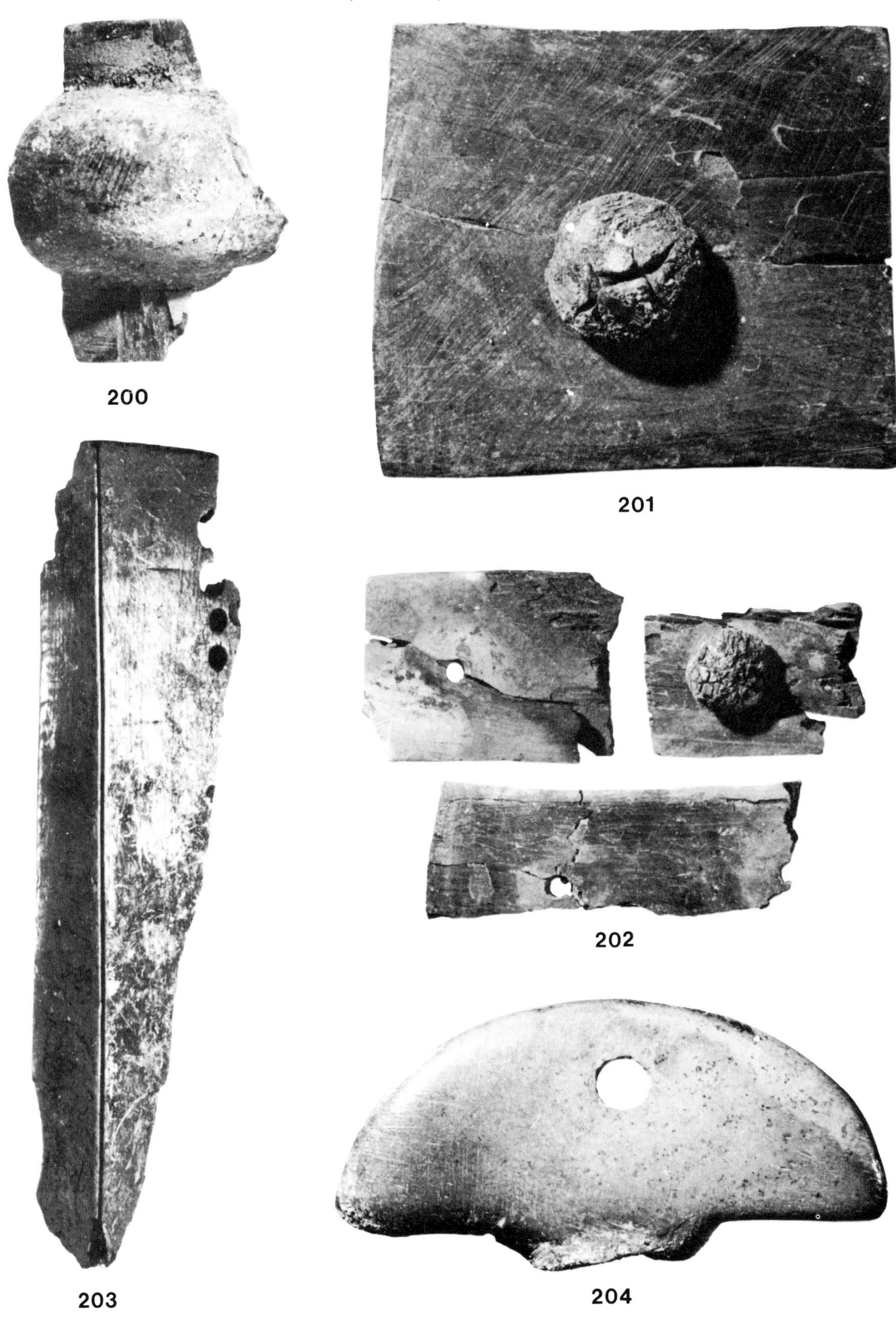

200

201

202

203

204

205 Bone; AA30 [3] (5,N); 60-899; UM 65-5-205; l. 3.3.
An eye-shaped object with a perforation for the pupil. Probably from a statuette.

206 Bone; CC31 (8); 64-515; UM 65-31-339; l. 4.5.
Same as above but larger.

207 BB31 [1] (8); 64-734; UM 65-31-327; diam. 1.6, th. .4.
Sixteen discs decorated with incised rosettes or six- and seven-spoked wheel designs; some of the outer edges are irregular.

208 BB31 [1] (8); 64-731; T; ht. 2, w. 3.3, th. .4, and ht. 3.3, w. 5.2, th. .9; no photograph of larger plaque.
Rectangular plaques with incised rosettes or spoked-wheel designs framing a hole.

209 BB31 [1] (8); 64-732; UM 65-31-316; l. 2.6.
Three sides of a plaque that has part of an incised rosette design, the rest of which was completed on neighboring plaques; pierced.

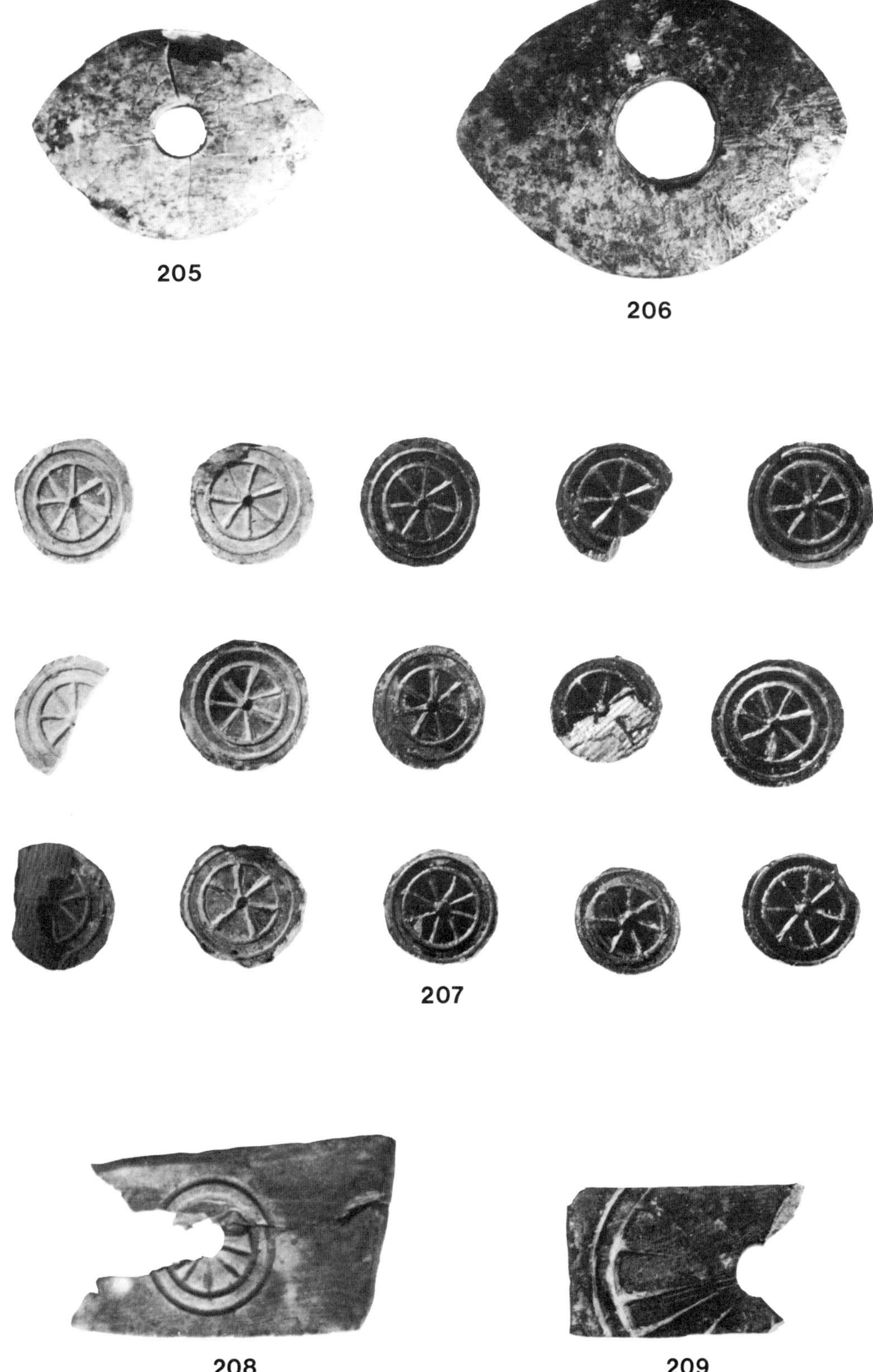
205
206
207
208
209

210A BB31 [1] (8); 64- ; UM 65-31-571; l. of largest 6.1.
B AA30 (5,N); 60-476; UM 61-5-336; l. of largest 4.3.

Assorted small pieces and fragments of inlays: chevrons, rectangles, points. Some are rocker scored on the reverse.

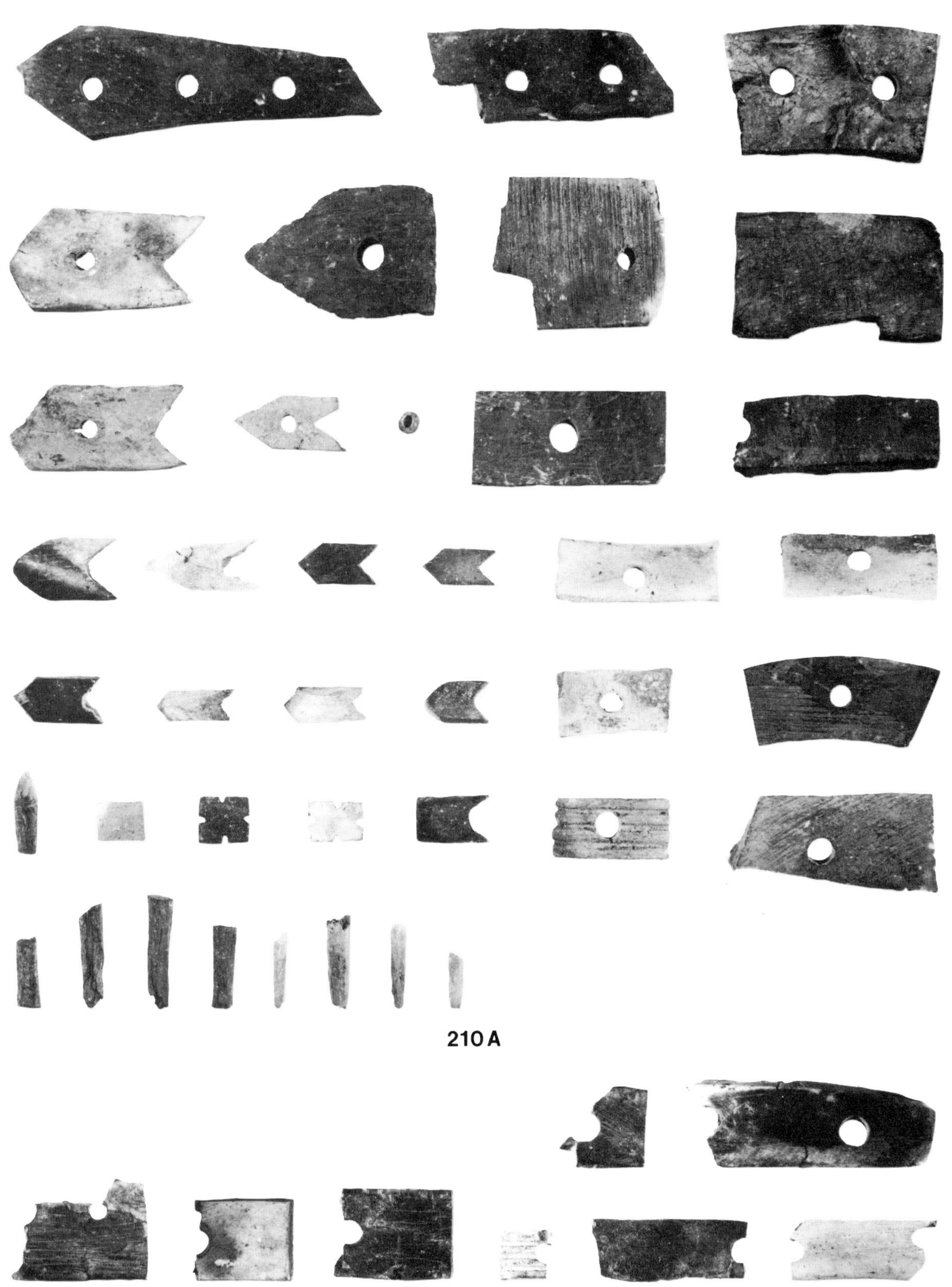

210A

210B

211 BB31 [1] (8); 64-729; UM 65-31-30; ht. 2.2, w. 2.1, th. .7; front and back views.
Three-pronged object set on a grooved base; broken below. The front of each prong is hollowed out, probably for inlays; the reverse is smooth except for grooves. Perhaps a representation of an architectural unit. A prong from a second example was also found.

212 BB II; 64-   ; UM 65-31-493, 575, 472; ht. 1-1.5.
Fragments of strips decorated with guilloche bands, oriented both right to left and left to right. In AA30 (GHN), in 1960, several similar strips were found.

213 CC32 [1] [2] (area east of 7); 70-433; T.
A lunate shape decorated with incised circles around the border and one in the center. The reverse has irregular scoring.

213 bis BB II; 64-   ; UM 65-31-579; ht. of largest fragment 4.5.
Several fragments of round (?) bases (?) decorated by vertical and oblique incisions and by herringbone pattern, all in high relief. On the largest piece the bottom is flat and intact; the flat top has the barest remains of a projection, suggesting that something once continued above.

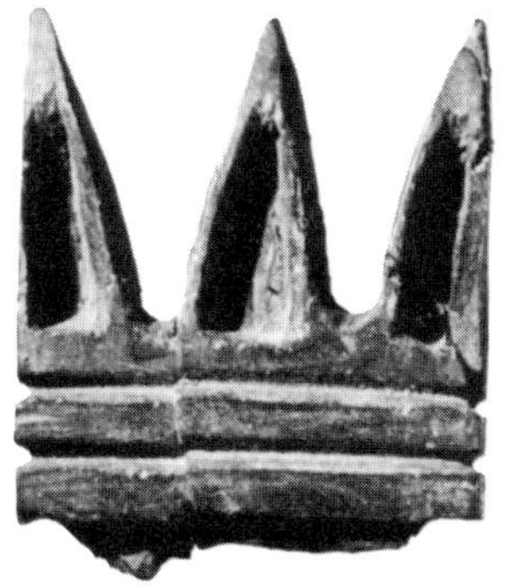
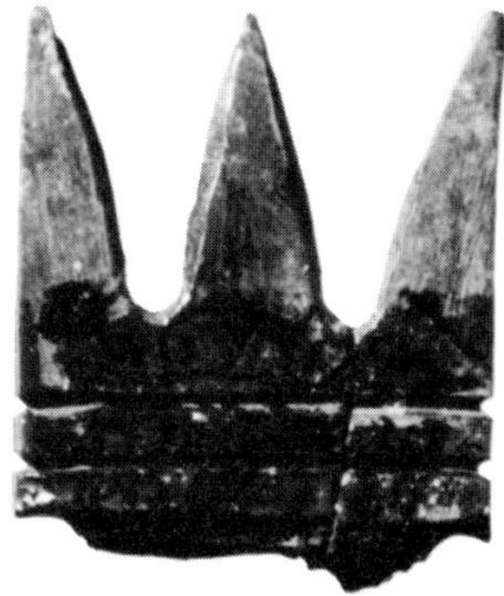

211

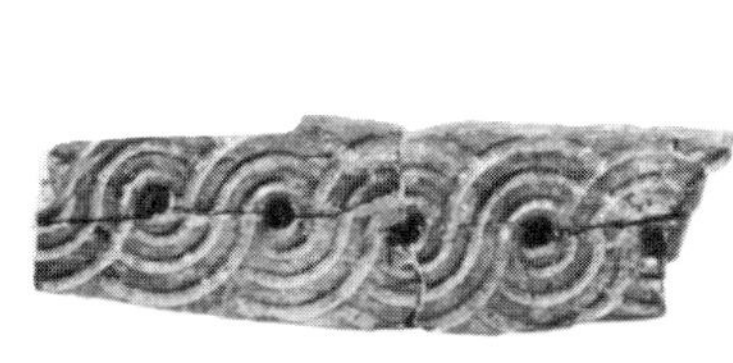
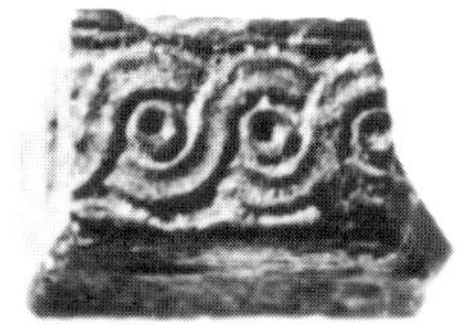
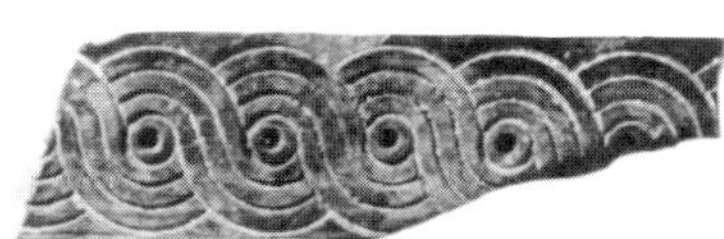
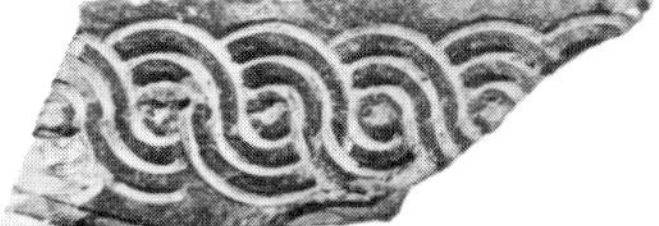
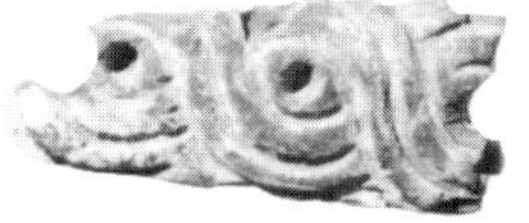

212

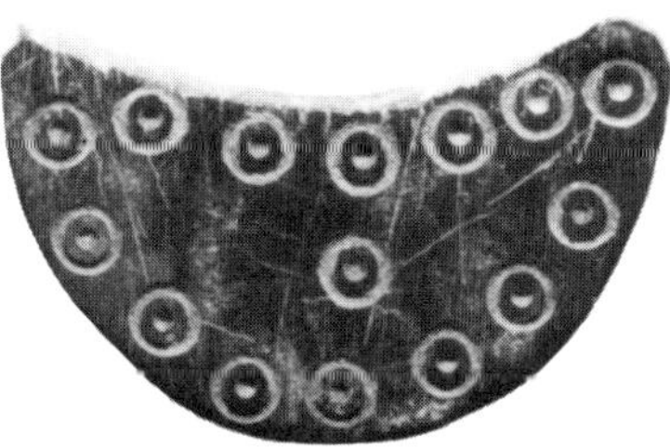

213

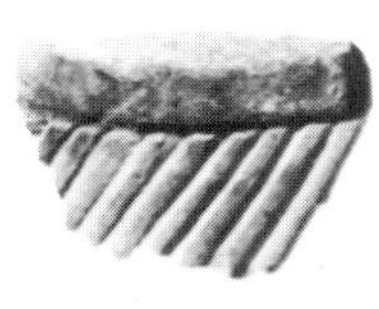
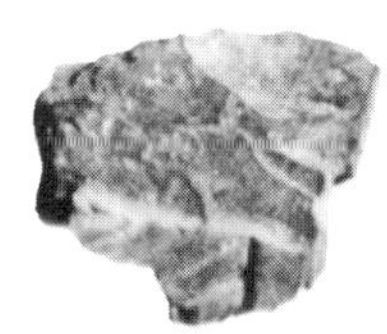
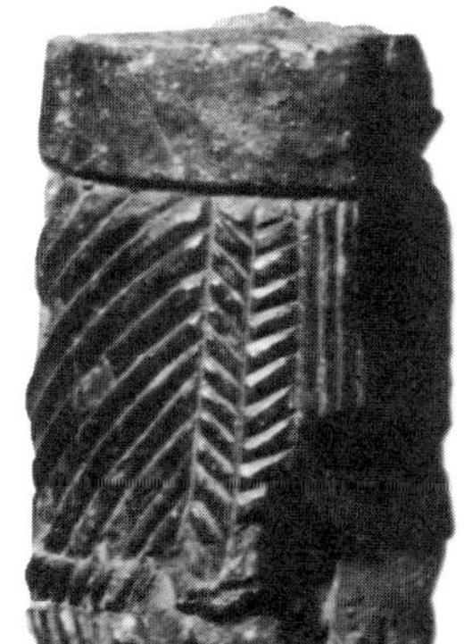
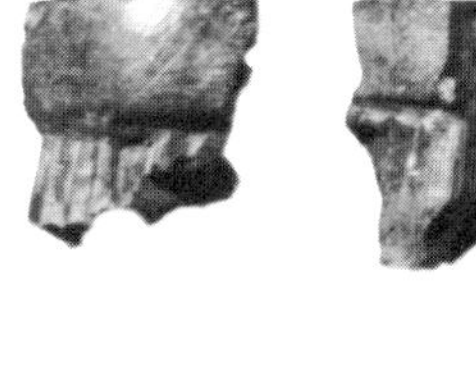
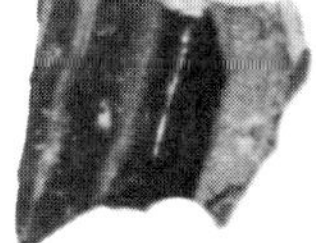

213 bis

VII

IRANIAN IVORIES

214 BB32 **[1]** (10); 64-999; T; ht. 8.3, w. 9.7, th. (damaged) .7; front view and drawing.

A winged bull strides right. Extant are much of the body and front legs, and a rear leg. Surface much pock-marked and only traces of body decoration are visible, but all is neatly incised: spiral curls below the ears, neck and chest, and projecting from the forehead and legs. A wing stands away from the body and is decorated with a herringbone feather pattern, divided into two zones, and terminating in round units. The thick, short horn curves up and out in front of two overlapping ears; a thick brow overlies a round eye, which is a dowel hole. The tail curves down close to the body. The execution is in low relief.

In front of and behind the bull are incised rosettes that are the flowers of trees or plants. A second dowel hole is by the left upper foreleg. The plain upper and right edges are intact, the right tree being completed on a separate plaque. Nos. 214-217 are of the same style and in spite of their damaged state one may see that they are superbly executed.

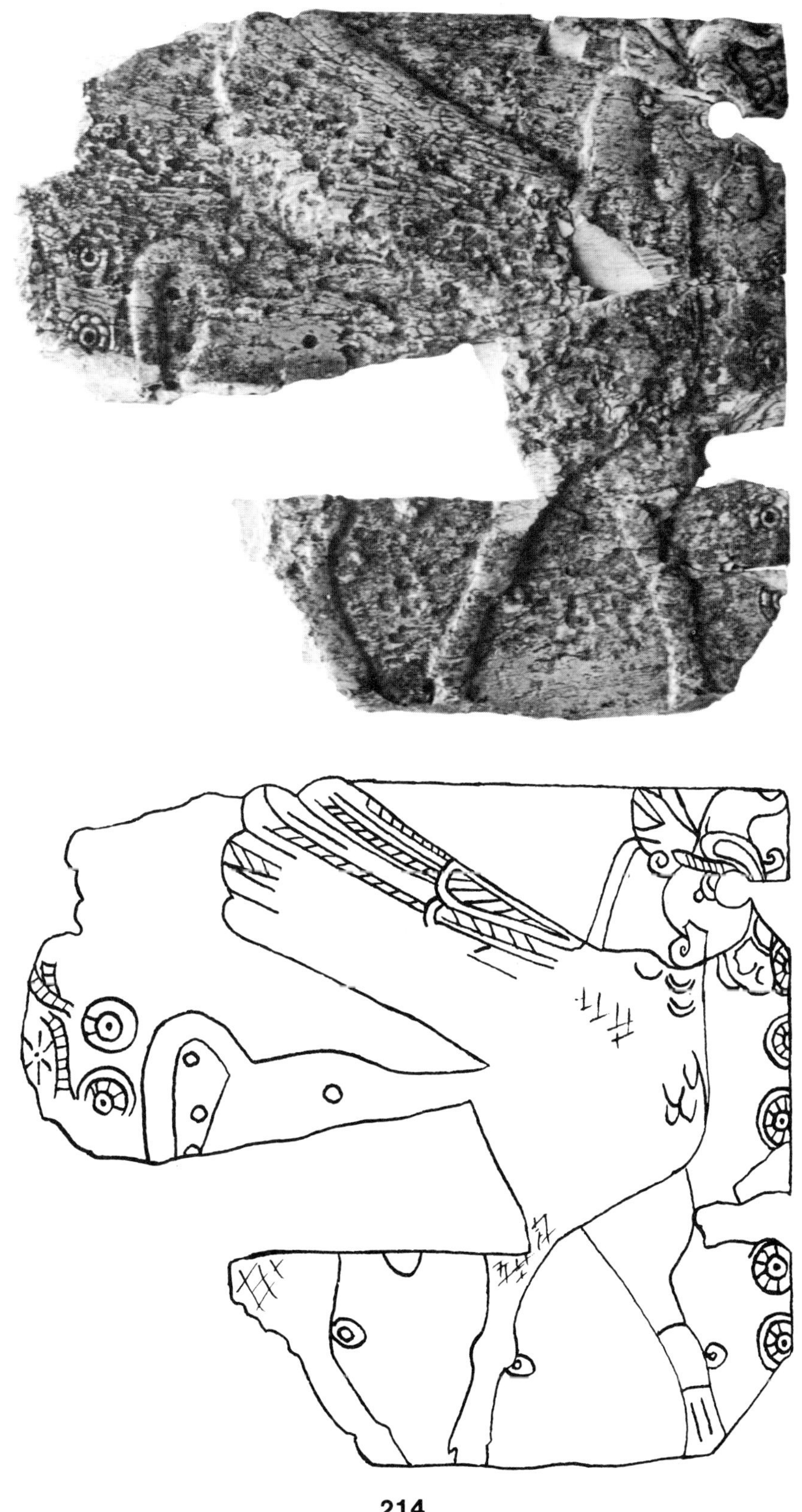

214

215 BB32 **[1]** (10); 64-1000; UM 65-31-347; ht. 6.4, w. 13.7, th. .6; front view and drawing.
Badly damaged and pockmarked fragment of a bull exactly like no. 214, right. Here we see that the belly and the base of the tail have spiral curls, and the rump has incised circles; the eye is oval. This bull seems to have a wing placed horizontally across its body and another above, also placed horizontally rather than flaring up. The head of the bull touches a tree whose flowers are depicted as incised rosettes, as above. To the right of the tree is the wing tip of another winged bull striding right: thus the bulls and trees alternated. Plain top and left edges are intact: no dowel holes are extant. Irregular scoring on the reverse.

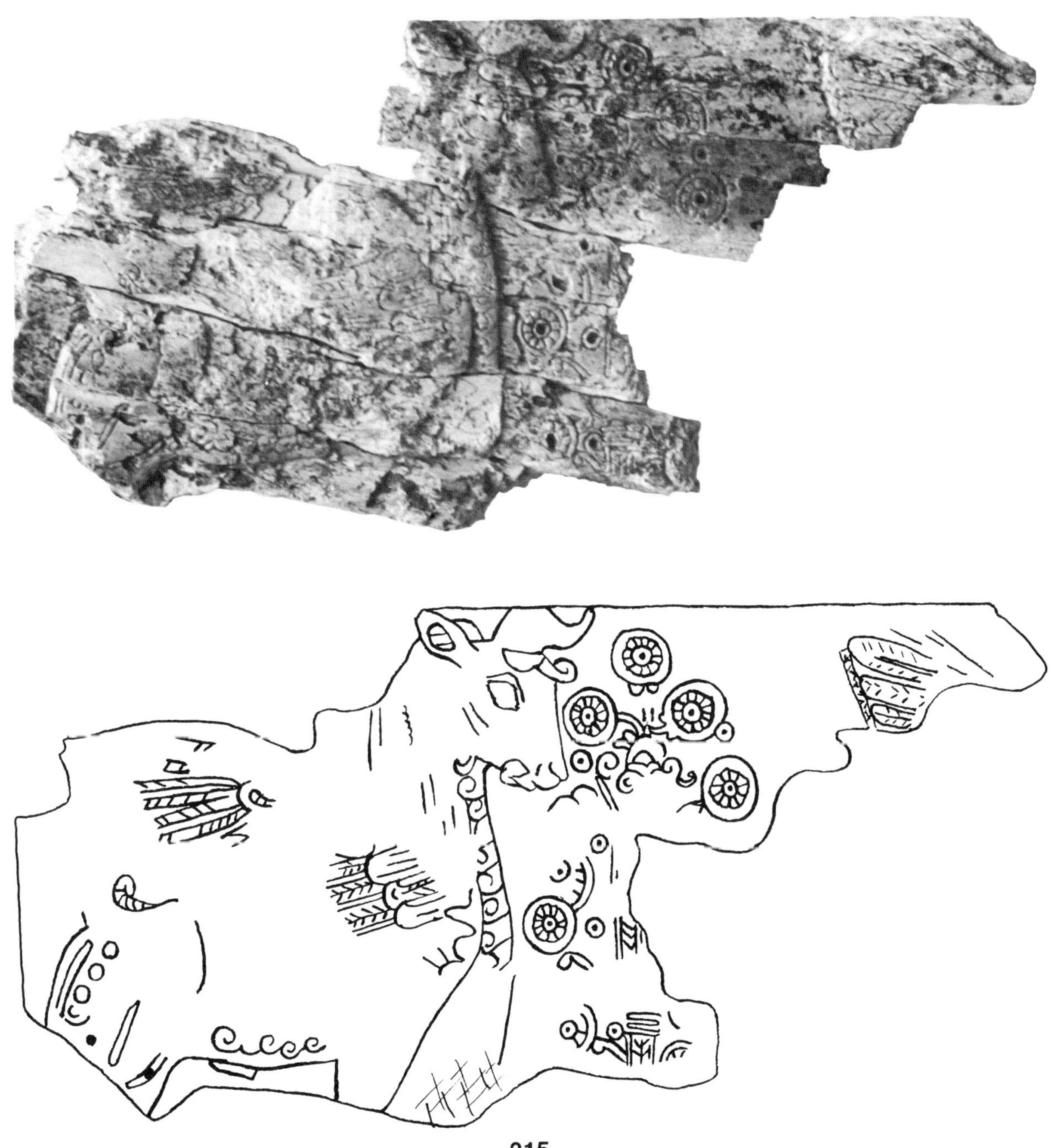

215

216 BB32 [1] (10); 64-1080; T; ht. 1.8, w. 4.9, th. 1.1.
A damaged, pockmarked fragment of a bull exactly like the previous two examples, right. Part of the tree is at the right. A dowel hole overlaps one of the flowers. The plain right edge is intact, the tree completed on a separate plaque.

217 BB32 [1] (10); 64-1000; UM 65-31-347; ht. of largest fragment: 2.8, w. 12.
Damaged, pockmarked fragments of a bull like the previous examples, right. To its right is a typical tree with rosettes; between it and the bull are visible three small wings, two projecting up, one down, which could be from a four-winged genius (?), the body part of which is now damaged.

218 BB31 (8/9); 64-1071; UM 65-31-334; ht. 4.2, w. 5, th. .7, and ht. 1.8, w. 5.1, th. 1.
Fragment of a winged bull in high relief, right. Extant are the middle and rear of the body, most of the wing, part of the neck and head.

The wings are sharply cut, decorated with incised lines terminating in points; there is no herringbone pattern. The neck folds are indicated by neatly cut thin grooves separated from the head by a thicker fold, and separated from the wings by curls. The stomach is outlined and decorated by incised dashes; vertical rib incisions are visible above the stomach. Legs have incised outlines and chevron decoration. The plain left edge and the upper, a narrow band, are intact. Another fragment shows the base of a tree trunk with horizontal incisions on either side of a vertical line.

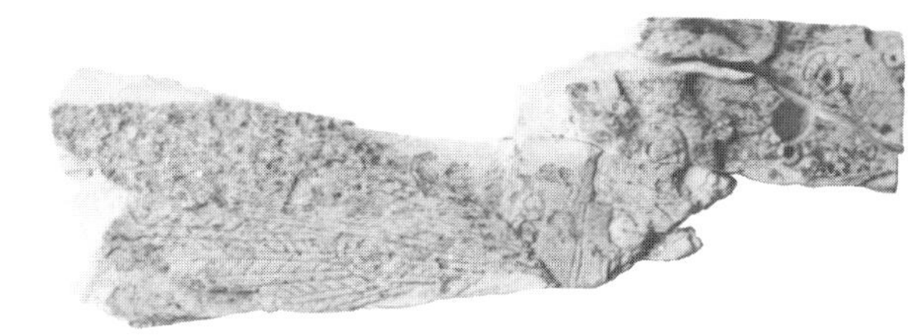

216

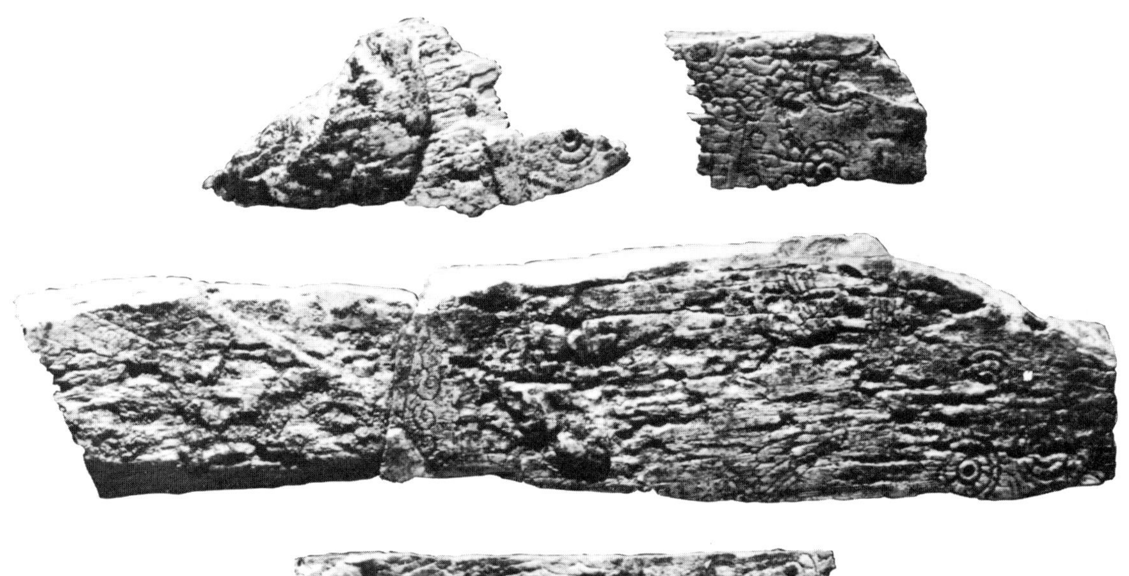

217

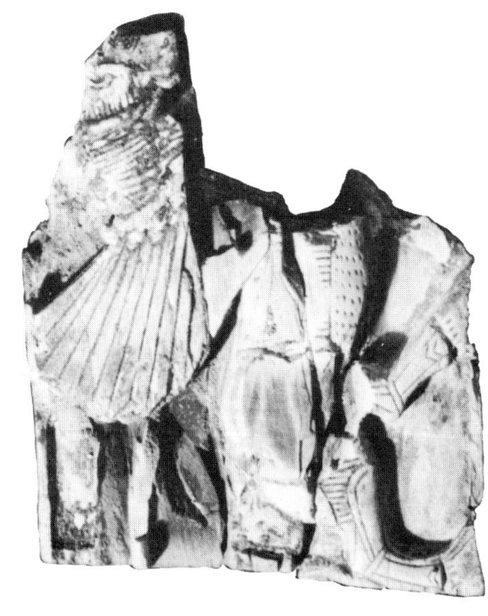

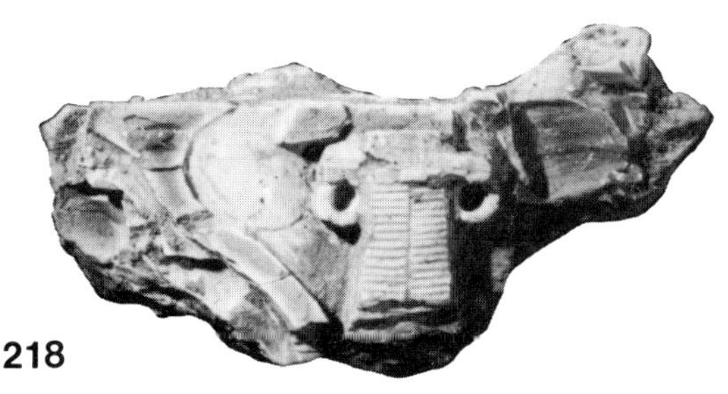

218

219 BB31 **[1]** (8); 64-771; T; ht. 3.6, w. 5.6, th. .8.
Winged bull like that above, left. Undamaged parts reveal that the rump and head are also decorated with incised dashes; the muzzle is close to the chest, which has a wavy contour. This piece and no. 218 are the most finely executed pieces in the Hasanlu repertory.

220 BB32 **[1]** (10); 64-1050; T.
Fragments of a bull like no. 219, right. The right front leg seems to be bent back close to the body, and the bull may be kneeling or collapsing. Note that a fragment of the haunch and part of a bull's head were found near this fragment. It is not clear if wings were present.

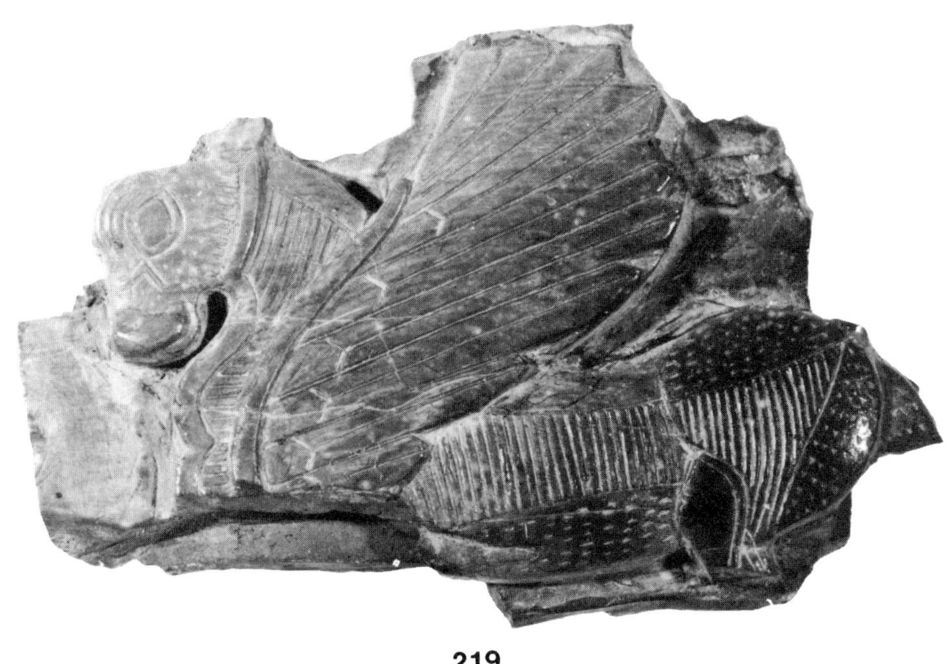

219

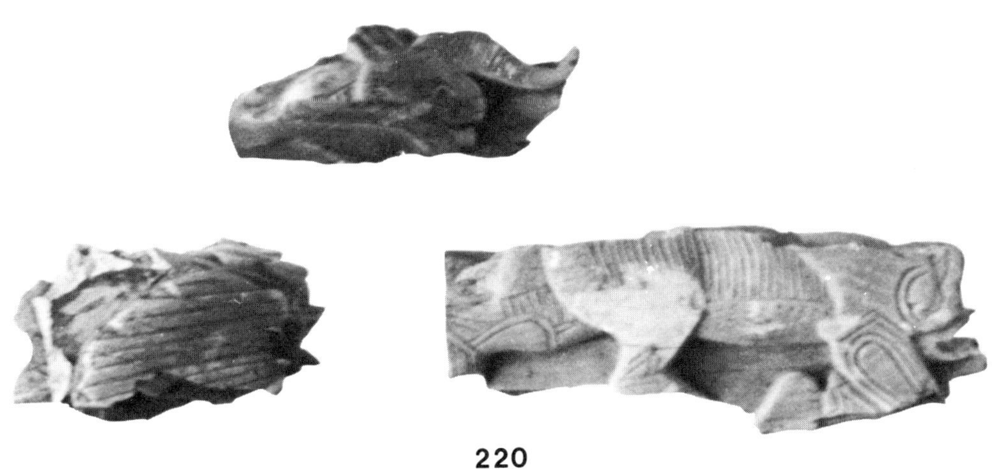

220

221 BB32 [1] (10); 64-1051A; UM 65-31-348; ht. of largest 6.8.
Miscellaneous fragments of the same bull-and-tree types as nos. 214-217. Extant are parts of a bull's leg and parts of a tree. One fragment shows legs moving right, another a horn, right, and part of a tree.

221 bis Shell (?); CC31 [2] (7); 64-1082; T 25876.
Fragment of a small dish or buckle. The convex surface has two heraldic stylized horned animals in relief flanking a series of vertical bands that form a panel, probably one arm of a cross. A smaller fragment was also found.

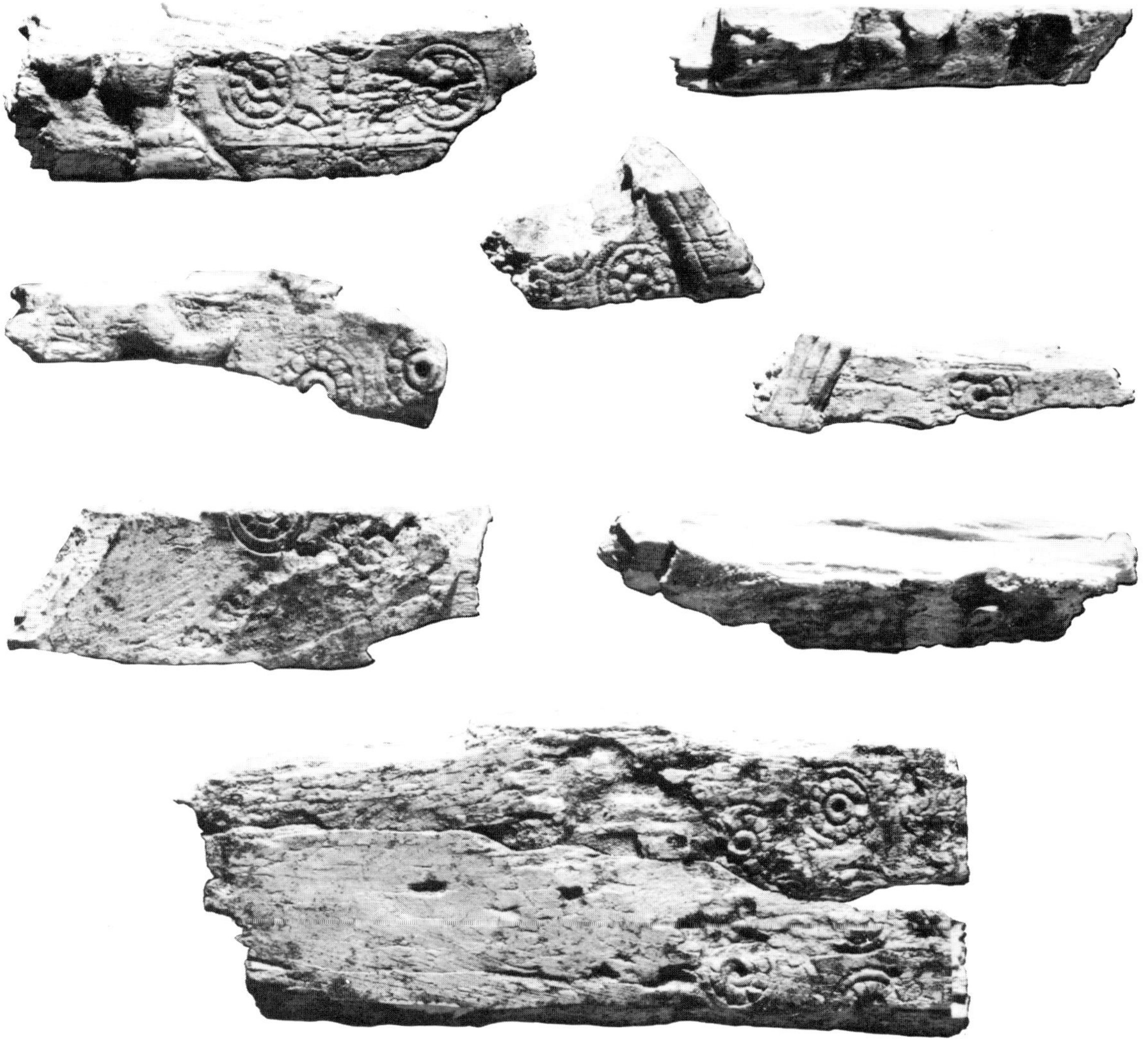

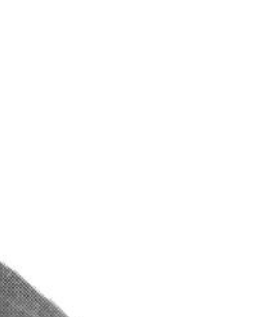

221

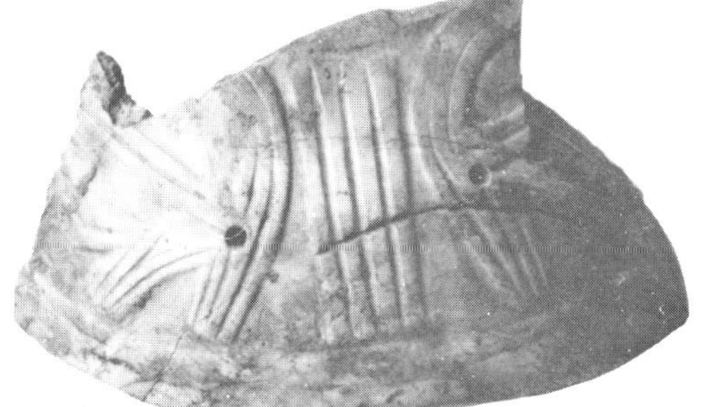

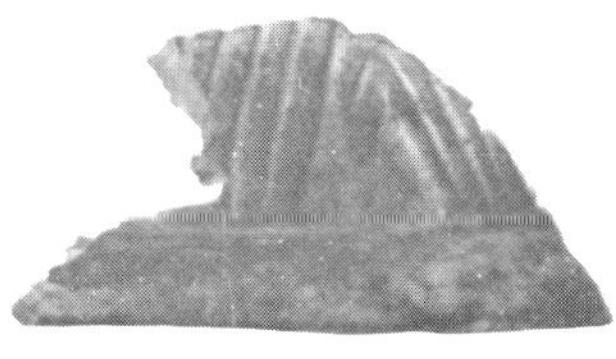

221 bis

VIII

NORTH SYRIAN IVORIES

A: LION BOWLS

222 BB II; 64- ; UM 65-31-602, 604; l. of larger 4.4; original outer diam. ca. 10; front and side views of smaller fragment.
Two rim fragments from a bowl with two winged creatures facing outward carved in relief on the side of the vessel opposite that clasped by a lion; extant are the claws of the lion and two wings. See Muscarella 1974 for a fuller discussion and reconstruction of these fragments as a lion bowl.

223 Y33 [2] (BB V 3, SE corner); 74N-491; UM 75-29-368; l. 4.4, ht. 2.1, th. .7; original inner diam. ca. 7.
A small fragment of a lion bowl preserving in relief the left wing of one creature and the right of a second, both facing outward. Two small grooves, apparently intentional, exist between the wings.

224 Y33 [2] (BB V 3, SE corner); 74N-501; UM 75-29-375; l. 2.1, ht. 2.
A small fragment of a lion bowl preserving only part of the lion's left claws and the tail of a bird; the interior has flaked away. This fragment is apparently not from the same bowl as no. 223 but this is not certain.

225 Y33 [5] (BB V 8, SW corner); 74N-633; UM 75-29-402; l. 3.2, ht. 1.5, th. .55; original upper diam. ca. 7.
A small fragment of a lion bowl preserving part of the lion's left claws and part—the tip—of a bird's tail. This fragment is not from the same object as no. 224.

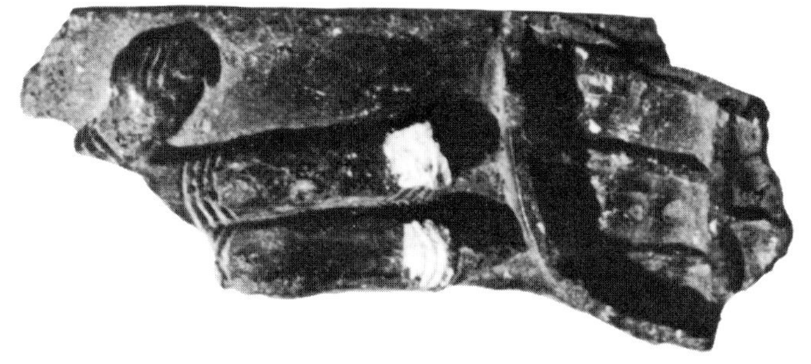

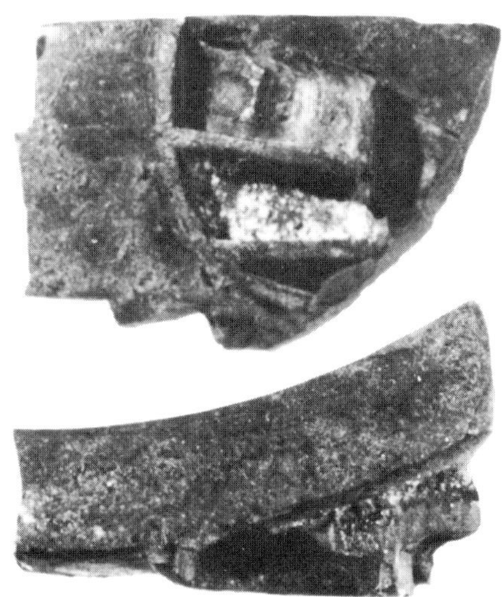

222

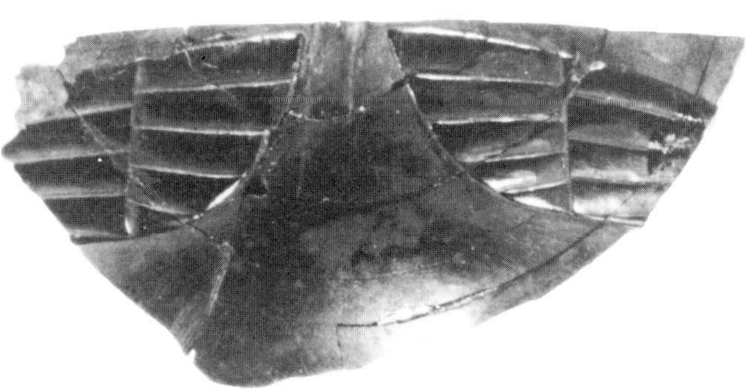

223

224

225

B: PYXIDES

226 CC31 [2] (7); 64-976; UM 65-31-400; original outer diam. ca. 12-13, ht. 5.6, ht. of design 2.5, w. 8.4, th. 1; Dyson 1972, fig. 2; Muscarella 1974b, fig. 4; front and back views.
Three joining fragments of a damaged pyxis that form a complete original height. In heraldic position are two couchant sphinxes wearing soft pointed hats. The one preserved has its right wing extended forward touching a palm frond, the other rests along its body; the left wing of the other sphinx touches the other side of the palm. The wings have sections cut out to receive inlays; small drill holes are extant. A small hole drilled within the incised eye once held another inlay. The scene is framed by a zig-zag border above, a plain banded one below. Both exterior and interior are highly polished. At the base of the interior is a narrow inset to receive the separately made bottom held by dowels, of which the hole for one is preserved.

227 CC31 [2] (7); 64-894b; MMA 65.163.5; original inner diam. at base ca. 11, ht. 4.8, ht. of design 2.5, w. 4.2, th. 1; Muscarella 1966, fig. 6; Dyson 1972, fig. 2.
Fragment of a pyxis like no. 226. Extant are the head and part of the left wing of a couchant sphinx, left. A trace of gold foil remains in the wing. A dowel is *in situ* at the same position as the hole in no. 226. The lower edge is preserved but there is no inset in the interior (cf. nos. 226, 229, 231, 234). The exterior is highly polished but the interior seems to have the natural grain of the tusk (damaged?).

228 Y33 [5] (BB V 8, SW corner); 74N-634; UM 75-29-403; ht. 2.7, w. 2.2, th. .25.
A small fragment of a very thin pyxis. Preserved is the tip of a sphinx's wing, with cut-outs for inlay, that touches the remains of a palm frond in relief; another sphinx's wings would have been to the right. The interior is smoothed. This fragment must have been a pyxis similar to nos. 226, 227.

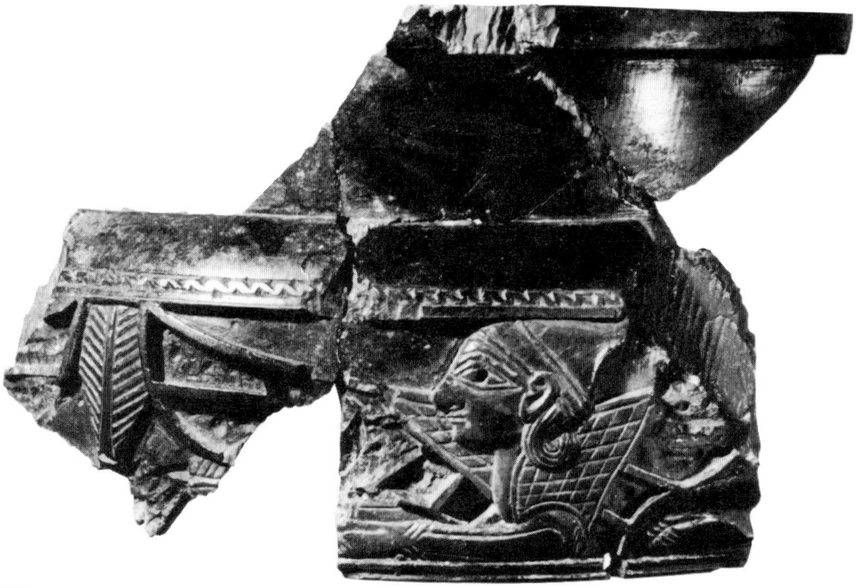

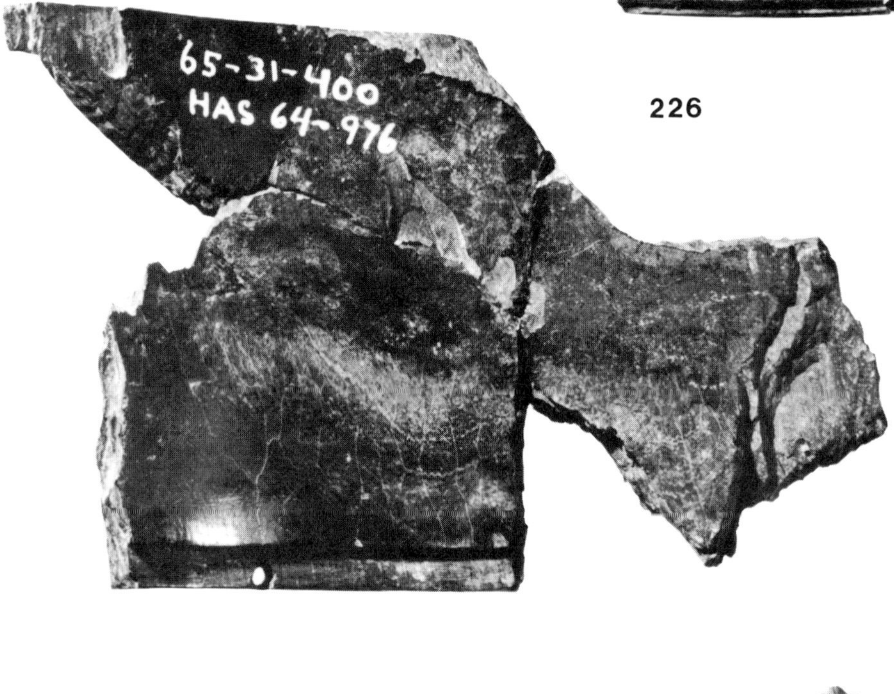

226

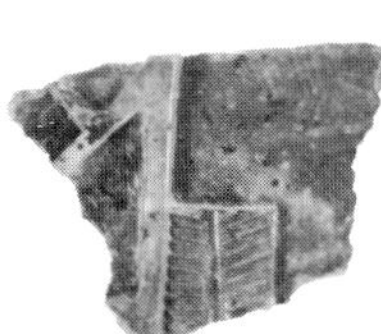

227

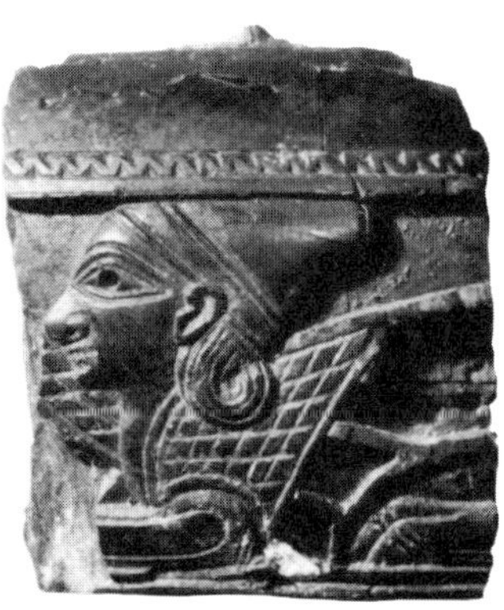

228

229 CC31 [2] (7); 64-894c; MMA 65.163.81; ht. 4, w. 2.7, th. .9; Muscarella 1966, fig. 6.
Damaged pyxis fragment preserving the rear part of a couchant sphinx, left. The flame pattern is neatly incised on the rump and there is a small section of neatly incised hair just behind. A white substance is still *in situ* in one wing hollow and is partly overlaid with gold foil. The interior is polished smooth and has an inset at the base for setting in the separately made bottom.

230 CC31 [1] (6); 64-905; UM 65-31-336; ht. 3, w. 2.2, th. .8.
Pyxis fragment preserving part of the head and neck of a sphinx, right. A beaded necklace is worn, not found on the other sphinxes.

231 CC31 [2] (7); 64-894a; MMA 65.163.80; ht. 5.8, ht. of design 2.6, original inner diam. ca. 12, th. 1.4.
Pyxis fragment preserving the rear parts of two couchant sphinxes. Their tails are raised framing a now-missing section that may have contained three fronds. A drilling that does not pierce the ivory is in the plain upper band. The height of this pyxis is complete. The interior is polished smooth and has an inset close to the base for the insertion of the separately made bottom; a dowel hole is preserved at the base, which held the separately made bottom in place.

232 CC31 [2] (7); 64-845; MMA 65.163.82; ht. 4, w. 3.5, th. 1.
Pyxis fragment preserving only the tail of a couchant sphinx, right, part of the upper border, and an element that separated the rear of one sphinx from the other. The interior is polished smooth; the base and top are broken away.

233 CC32 (area east of 7); 70-423; T; no photograph.
A very small fragment of a pyxis preserving part of the right wing of a sphinx and part of the zig-zag border. This fragment could belong to one of the pyxides from the adjacent Room 6 or Room 7.

234 CC31 [2] (7); 64-977; T; ht. 4.1, ht. of design ca. 2.5, w. 7.2, original outer diam. ca. 10, th. 1.1.
Pyxis fragment preserving a couchant sphinx, right. The sphinx is of a type different from the preceding examples in the face, curly hair, fillet and in having no hat. A zig-zag border exists both above and below the scene; two dowel holes are at the base. Traces of gold foil are extant on the wings, body, and base. The interior is polished and there is an inset at the base.

235A CC31 [2] (7); 64-977; T 25846; ht. 3.2, w. 3.3, th. .3.
The head and part of a wing of a sphinx like no. 234, left. It is not from the same pyxis as no. 234; cf. no. 235B. The interior is polished smooth.

235B CC31 [2] (7); 64-977; T 25846.
A fragment of a head like no. 235A, and possibly from the same pyxis. The interior is polished smooth.

236 CC31 [2] (7); 64-977; T 25846; ht. 5.1, w. 6.1, th. .8.
Pyxis fragment preserving the front feet of two couchant sphinxes; the palm area in between is damaged. The lower border has a zig-zag pattern, with a trace of gold foil, and two small dowel holes.

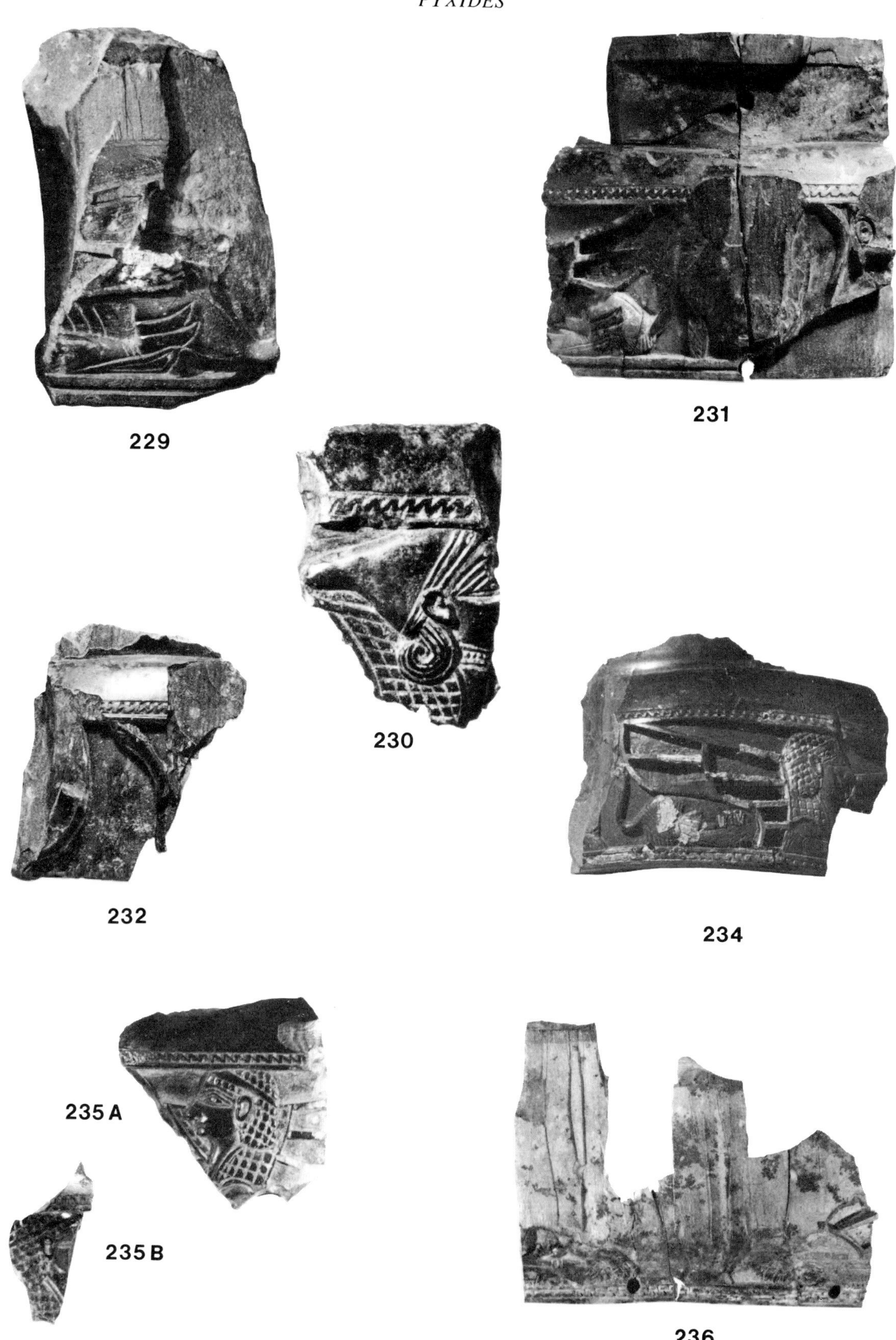
229
231
230
232
234
235 A
235 B
236

237 Y33 [2] (BB V 3, SE corner); 74N-502; UM 75-29- ; ht. 2.7, w. 2, th. at rim .3.
A small fragment from a thin pyxis, preserving in relatively high relief the slightly overlapping legs of a standing sphinx over a guilloche border, which is the intact base. The details are very neatly executed. Both the interior and exterior are highly polished; the ivory has turned brown from heat.

238 Y33 [6] (BB V 8); 74N-592; UM 75-29-383; ht. 2.4, w. 5.5, th. .5, original outer diam. at base 14.
Fragment of a pyxis preserving the flaked-off leg of a bull and part of its stomach and testicles, right. The decorated scene is inset from the area below, which has an incomplete but fully preserved guilloche at the intact base. The interior is roughly smoothed.

239 BB II; 64- ; UM 65-31-314a; ht. 1.2, w. 1, th. .4.
A small fragment preserving only the forepart of the wing decorated in lozenge pattern like nos. 226, 227, and what seems to be the lower part of hair curls; the hair is not the same as that of the sphinxes on the other pyxides. Gold foil is preserved.

240 BB II; 64- ; UM 65-31-517; ht. 2.9, w. 1, th. .3, and ht. 3.1, w. 1, th. .3.
Two small fragments from what appears to be the sides of a plain pyxis with a lower border consisting of a guilloche pattern; one fragment preserves a dowel hole, apparently to hold a bottom. The interior is smooth but tool marks are visible.

241 Y33 [2] (BB V 3, SE corner); 74N-535; UM 75-29-379; ht. 5.3, w. 4, th. .5.
A fragment of a plain pyxis with a lower guilloche border, like no. 240; here too, a dowel hole is preserved at the base, in the guilloche itself.

242 CC31 [2] (7); 64-898; T; ht. 1.6, w. 2.5, l. 4.6.
A couchant calf with its head turned back to rest against the body. Hair consists of elaborately carved curls on the back, rump, head and neck; incised triangular tufts form the stomach hair. There is an incised flame pattern on the flank. Eyes are hollow for inlays. The base has a dowel hole at each end of a narrow slot, for attachment to a pyxis lid.

243 CC31 [2] (7); 64-941; UM 65-31-345; ht. 1.6, w. 2.1, l. 4.8; top, side, and bottom views.
A fragment of a couchant calf, as above, no. 242. Extant is part of the body and neck. The base has two dowel holes and a slot.

244 CC31 [2] (7); 64-942; MMA 65.163.29; l. 3.6.
A fragment of a couchant calf similar to the above examples but with slight differences: the knee is more rounded; the ribbing is straight rather than curved; and there is less body decoration. The piece has been burned to a fine brown color.

245 Y33 [5] (BB V 8, SW corner); 74N-635; UM 75-29-404; l. 5.1.
A badly preserved fragment of a couchant calf, as above. The flat base has part of a rectangular or perhaps a bottle-shaped slot preserved for attachment, within which small drill holes are visible.

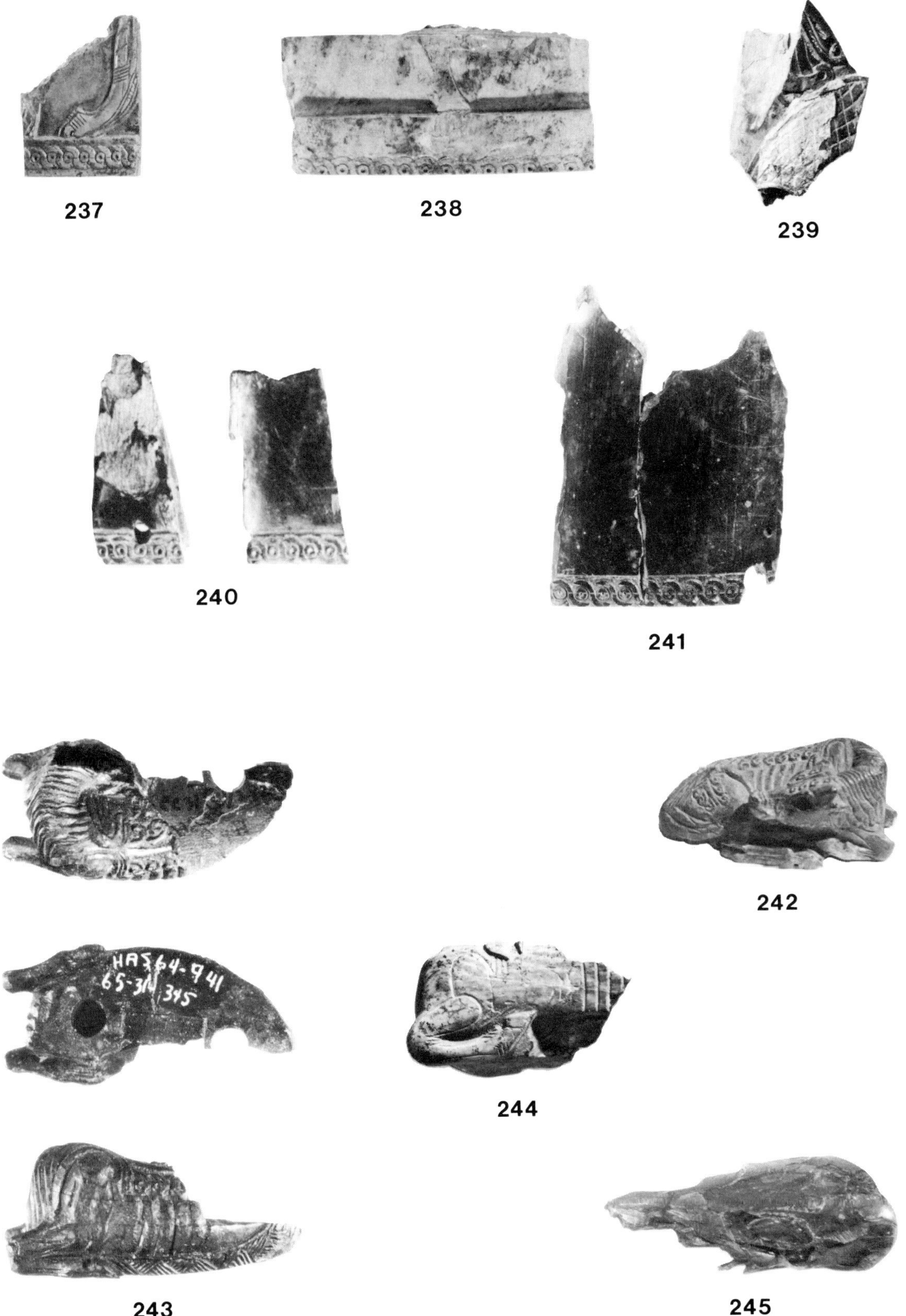

237 238 239

240 241

242

244

243 245

246A BB31/CC31 (8); 64- ; UM 65-31-522; original diam. 11, th. .5; front and back views.

Fragment of a round "lid" of a pyxis. Both sides are decorated by a linear-incised zone framing a guilloche pattern which frames the main field. This field consists of six-petaled rosettes, the petals of each shared by the neighboring rosettes; each petal has a double incised line. The rosettes of one side are larger than those on the other. A small fragment of a similar lid from BB V, found in 1974, 74N-495, UM 75-29-371, has a plain back and a dowel *in situ* through its thickness (.3).

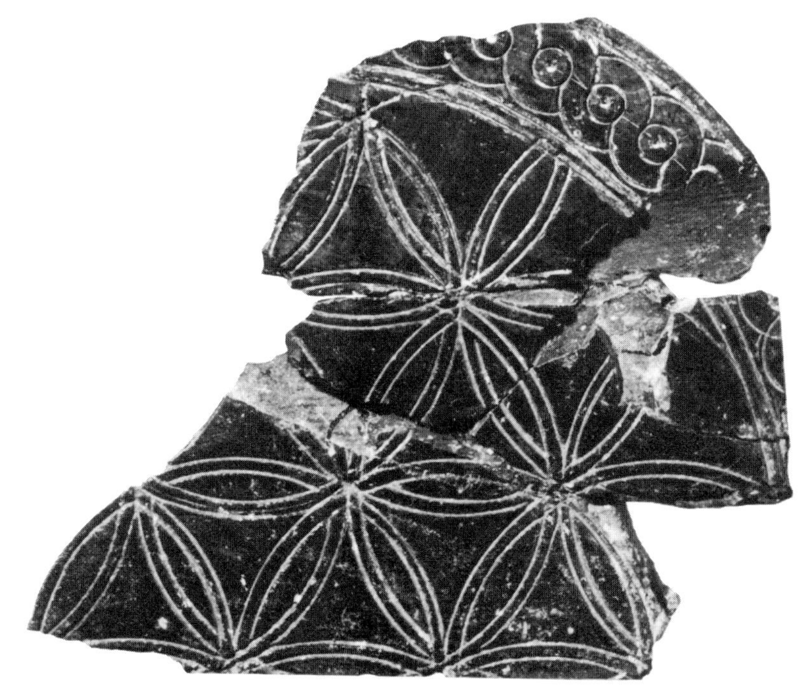

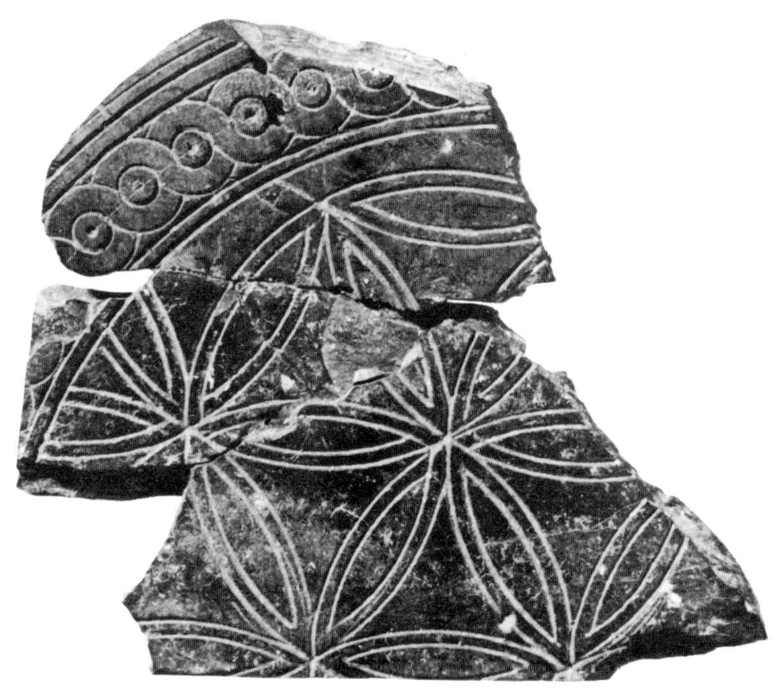

246 A

246B BB31/CC31; (8); 64- ; UM 65-31-521, 519, 518, 520 (L to R); th. .3-.5; front and back views.
Fragments of pyxis "lids." Several have double guilloche borders; one has a row of concentric circles covered with gold foil; one fragment has no rosette pattern on either side. Another fragment also has gold foil traces; the edges are grooved.

247 BB II; 64- ; UM 65-31-603; original diam. 11, th. .4, and original diam. 10, th. .4; edge, front, and back views of both fragments.
Two fragments of pyxis "lids." On one side are guilloches; on the reverse, one fragment has a border of concentric circles and the other a larger drill hole in every other circle. Both fragments have dowel holes preserved in the edge, which is also grooved. Traces of gold foil exist on the edge of one fragment. Several fragments of lids exactly like these were found in BB V in 1974: 74N-507, 74N-624, 74N-628. This last piece has five dowel holes (with two dowels *in situ*) in the edge, traces of gold foil, and white material preserved in the drilled holes on the surface.

248 BB II; 64- ; UM 65-31-601; original outer diam. ca. 11, th. .6; edge and front views.
Fragment of a pyxis lid different from the above types. The obverse has a row of small twelve-petaled rosettes, some of which were not completed. A large drilled hole at the left may have been for the attachment of a couchant calf; a smaller hole is at the right, in a space between two rosettes. The edge has a neat guilloche pattern still covered with gold foil. The reverse is plain.

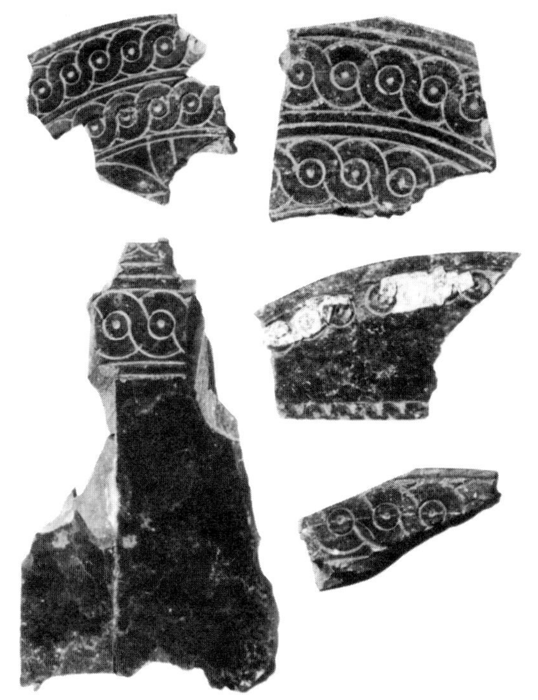

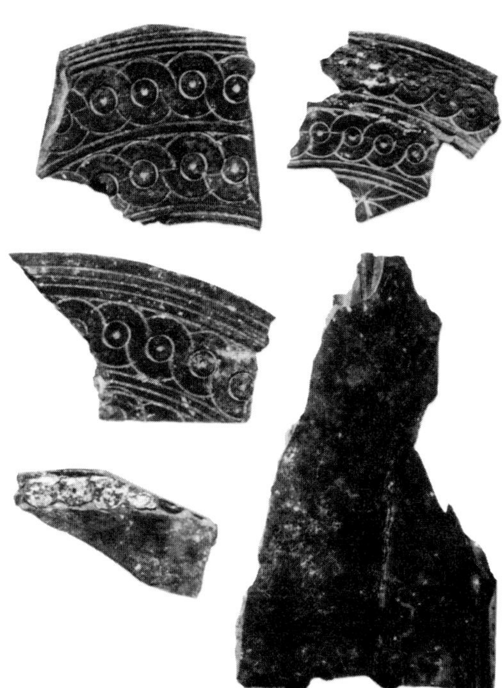

246B

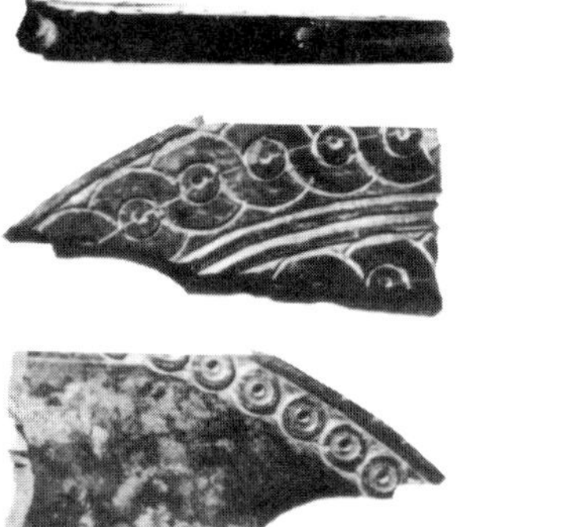

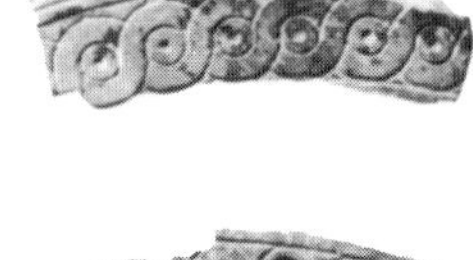

247

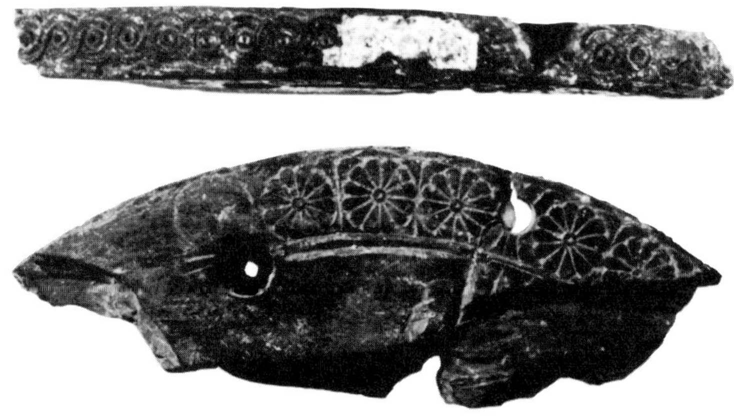

248

C: HEADS, STATUETTES, ANIMALS

249 CC31 [2] (7); 64-923; T; ht. 5.9, w. 3.3; Dyson 1965a, 158, fig. lower left; 1968, fig. 108; top, side, and front views.

A human head in the round complete but for the nose and lower part at the back. It wears a high polos decorated by vertical panels framed by narrow bands. Strands of wavy hair, represented by zig-zags in relief, curve around the face from a center part and hang down in back. Oval eyes are incised, with shallow pupils that held inlays; the left still contains a black substance. Eyebrows are deeply cut to hold inlays; they do not meet over the nose. The mouth is thin-lipped and small; the chin prominent. Ears are in relief, and are now damaged.

The flat top of the polos has a rectangular hole, and at the bottom of the head is a round one. The head has a blue coloring probably resulting from fire in the destruction.

The head is that of a female and has many parallels at Nimrud, *infra.*

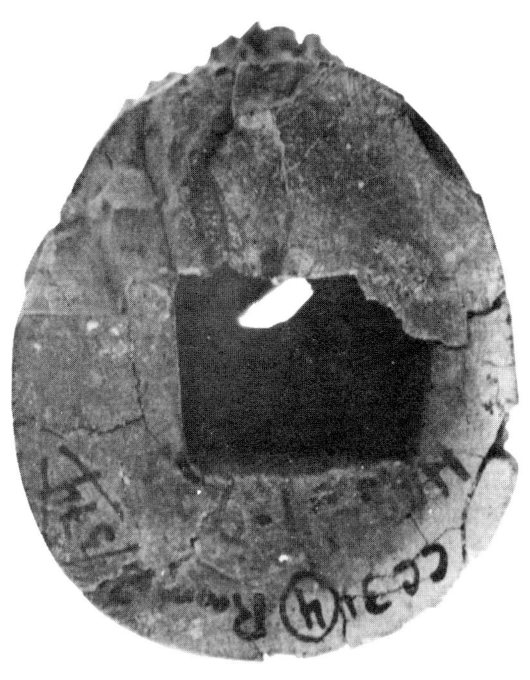

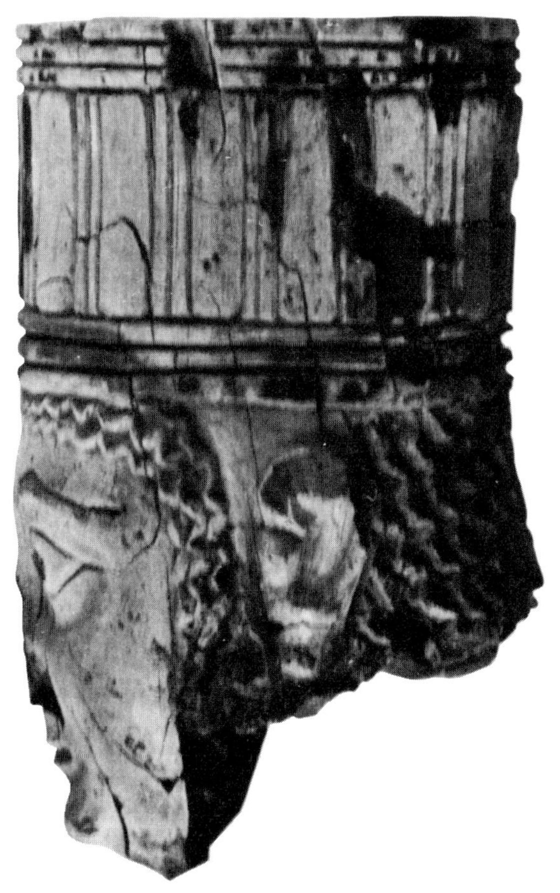

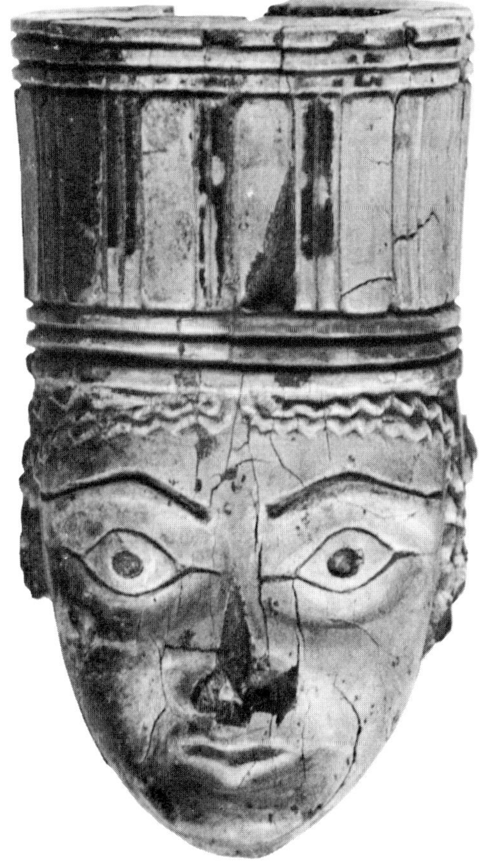

249

250 Y33 [2] (BB V 3, SE corner); 74-311; T; ht. 2.4, w. 1.65; front and side views.
A human head in the round, broken away at the neck. It is of the same type as no. 249, but smaller and different in small details: a low polos divided uniformly in vertical bands; hair represented in strands that are straight rather than wavy, and pulled upward from the forehead; eyes that once held inlays. The back of the head is concave and there are holes above the ears—for dowels?

251 BB31/CC31 (8); 64- ; UM 65-31-496; ht. 2.3, w. 1.4, th. .9. UM 65-31-498; ht. 2.6, w. 1.3, th. .3.
Two small fragments of statuettes, each preserving a hand in relief held at the side of the body. They are clearly not from the same statuette.

252A Y33 [5] (BB V 8, SW corner); 74N-640; UM 75-29-409; ht. 2.5, w. .8.
B Y33 [2] (BB V 3, SE corner); 74N-497; ht. 4.7, w. 2, and ht. 5.5, w. 1.8.
C Y33 [5] (BB V 8, SW corner); 74N-638; UM 75-29-407; ht. 2, w. 1.2.

These four fragments were found in adjacent areas. One could be a human arm bent at the elbow; two of the others could be thighs and legs of a human figure—but could also be handles or parts of furniture (?). One could be the ankles, with three-strand anklets, of a standing figure.

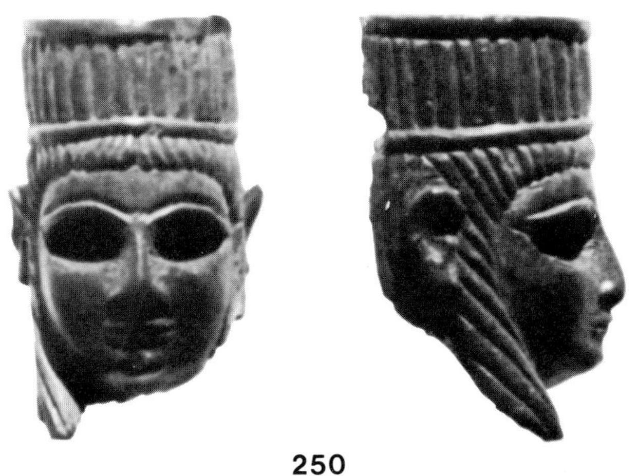

250

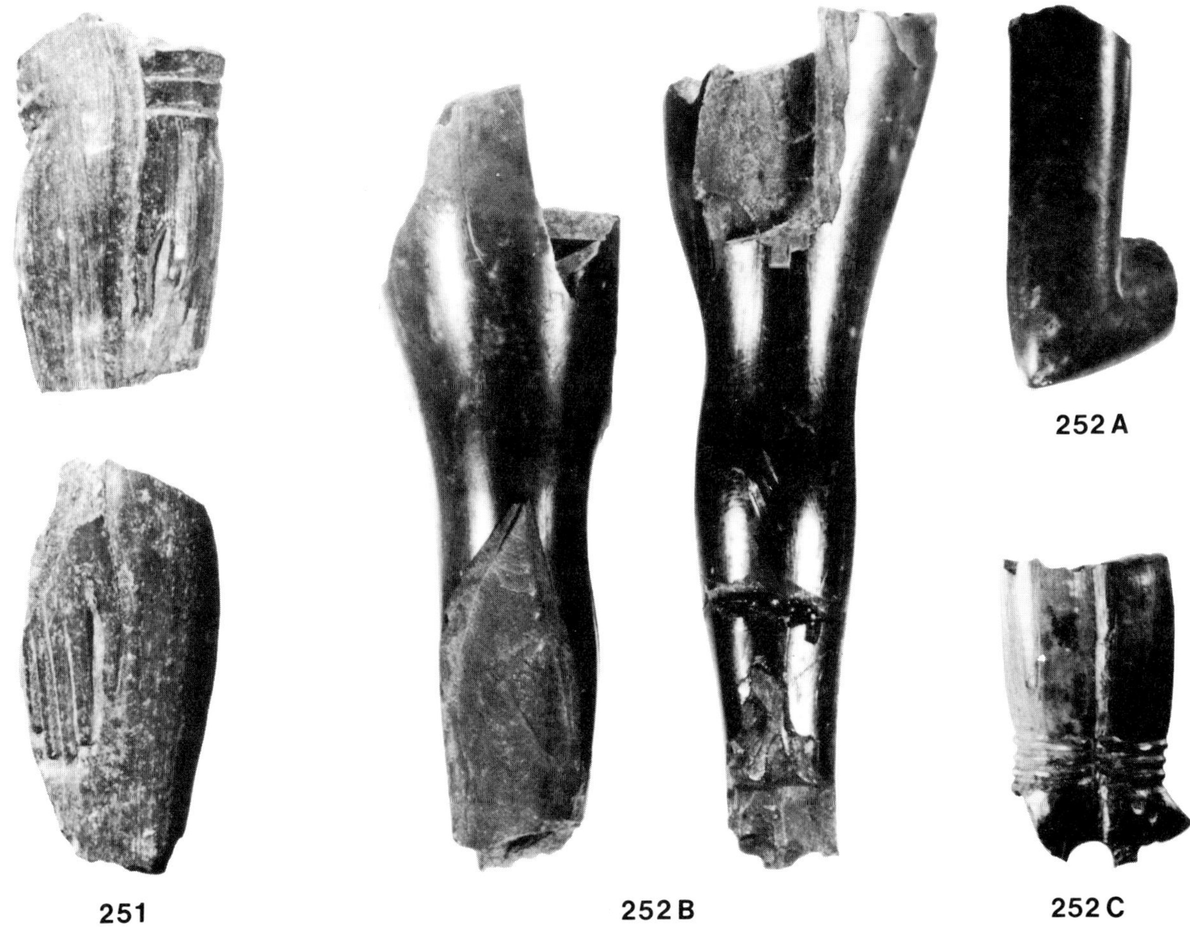

251

252 A

252 B

252 C

253 CC31 [2] (7); 64-1062; UM 65-31-325; ht. of largest fragment ca. 11.4; back, front, and side views of main fragment group, front and back views of two additional fragments.
Fragments of a composite sculpture in the round. The remains are too fragmentary to allow for a satisfactory interpretation beyond the following suggestion: on one side there is relief that appears to be the kilted thigh and part of an exposed leg of an individual; the "kilt" has a panel motif at the base and waist (?). To the side of the kilt is a wing decorated in herringbone pattern. Two dowel holes exist in a flat area at one side and another exists above the kilt: perhaps they held part of the body and arms made of separate pieces of ivory. Above the uppermost of the two peg holes are curls that seem to be the ends of hair. Two small fragments have the panel motif and are part of the kilt. The figure seems to have been a sculpture of a winged figure.

254 BB31/CC31 (8); 64- ; UM 65-31-485; ht. 4.5, w. 1.9, th. 1.1.
Fragment of a sculpture in the round. Extant is part of the left thigh of a male facing left, along with the left section of his kilt, which is decorated with incised lozenges, each of them filled with four lozenges; the mid-point of the kilt tapered to a point.

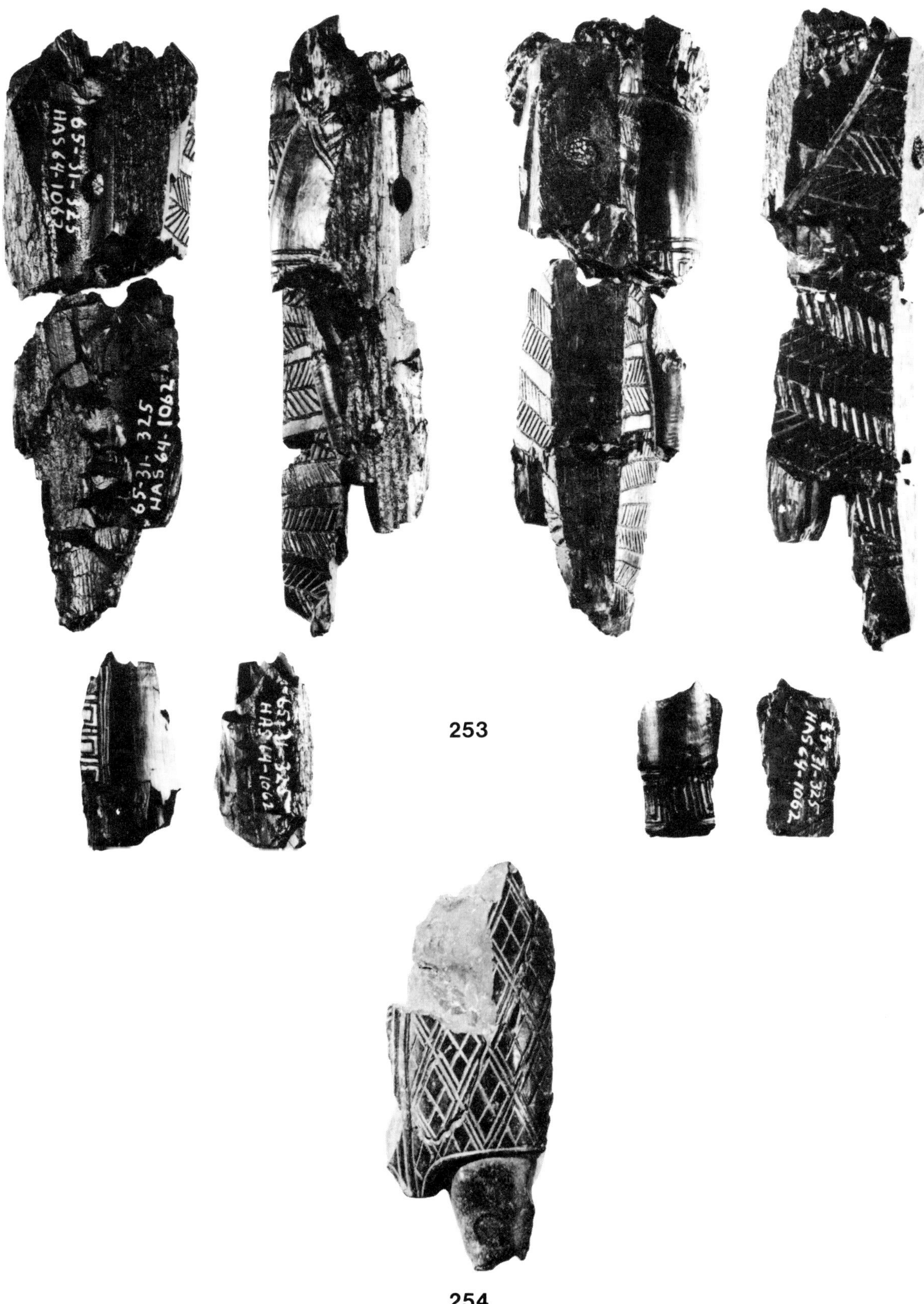

253

254

255 CC31 [1] (6); 64-1070; T; ht. 2.4, w. 6.5, l. 6.2.
Fragment of a lion's head. Extant are the top of the head and neck. Eyes are oval and preserve drill holes; gold foil is extant in the left eye. Ears, now missing, were separately made, and fitted into prepared slots. The top of the head has trianglar cut-outs for now-missing inlays. A neatly incised lozenge pattern depicts the mane.

256 Y33 [5] (BB V 8, SW corner); 74N-624; UM 75-29-395; l. of larger piece 5.6, w. 2.7, th. 2.2.
Two fragments of the right and left sides of a lion's head, from a section which when complete included only the top of the head, the upper muzzle and incised upper teeth; the base is flat and has a bottle-shaped groove for attachment. Most of the muzzle has broken away but neatly drilled dots are still evident (cf. no. 258). The oval eyes once held inlays; the ears were separately made and set into deep flat-rimmed holes, with deep cut-outs between them for inlays (cf. no. 255). The mane is exquisitely carved in low relief and consists of typical trianglar tufts. The neck is cut squarely. The object may have been part of a lion's head carved in the round but made in two units–the lower section now entirely missing–or it may have been attached as a half head to serve as a handle or decoration on another object.

257 CC31 [2] (7); 64-940; UM 65-31-323; l. 7.6; top, side, and bottom views.
Fragment of the body of a lion, lacking the legs, head and rear section. The mane and stomach hair are extant and consist of neatly carved triangular locks. On each side of the body is an incised rectangular area with interior vertical incisions, and the back is decorated with two incised lines with a "stitching" pattern.

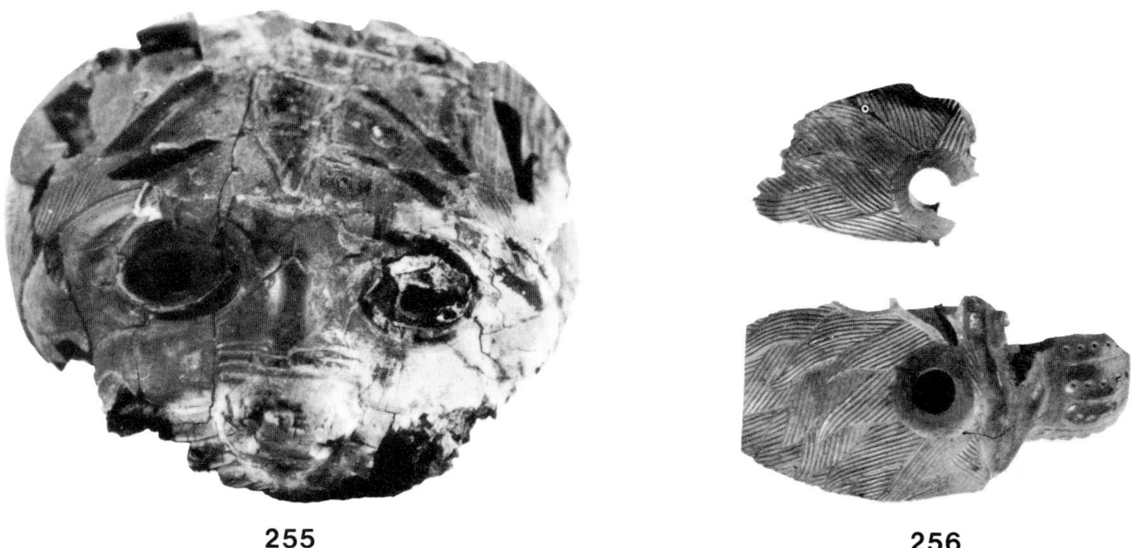

255

256

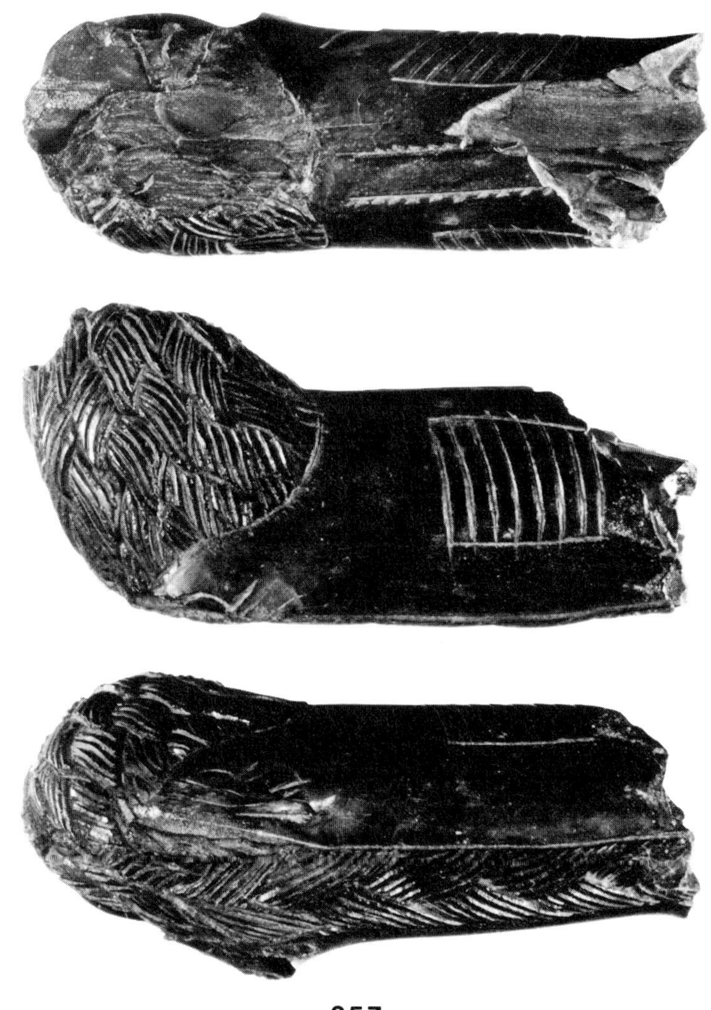

257

258 BB II; 64- ; UM 65-31-605; l. 7.1; front, top, and side views.
Fragment of the body of a lion. Extant are only part of the upper lip and muzzle decorated with drilled dots, and at the other end a small section that preserves a neat triangular tuft pattern. The interior of the fragment is concave. A dowel hole exists in the rear section, which slopes toward a smoothed rim. Perhaps this object was a handle.

259 Y33 [2] (BB V 3, SE corner); 74N-492; UM 75-29-369; ht. 3.5, w. 2.2.
A small fragment preserving a foot of a bull (?) standing on a guilloche. At the right is a raised border. The back is flaked away; it is not clear what object this piece came from.

260 BB31 (8); 64-1064; UM 65-31-344; ht. head, right, 2.7.
Fragments with representations of lions; there are at least three heads. The fragment at the left preserves the ear and part of the triangle-incised mane; the central one preserves the top part of the head; the right preserves the top of a head. Other fragments preserve the chest and front leg, part of a mane, and a neatly incised flame pattern from a haunch. All the intact upper borders have a grooved ridge. It is not clear whether these fragments were parts of plaques or of a vessel.

261 Y33 [5] (BB V 8, SW corner); 74N-636; UM 75-29-405; ht. 2.7, w. 2.2, th. .3.
A small, thin fragment preserving the hindquarters of a lion (or sphinx?) with a neatly incised flame pattern, cross-hatched hair below, and oblique lines at the base of the tail. A dowel hole is preserved in the flame pattern.

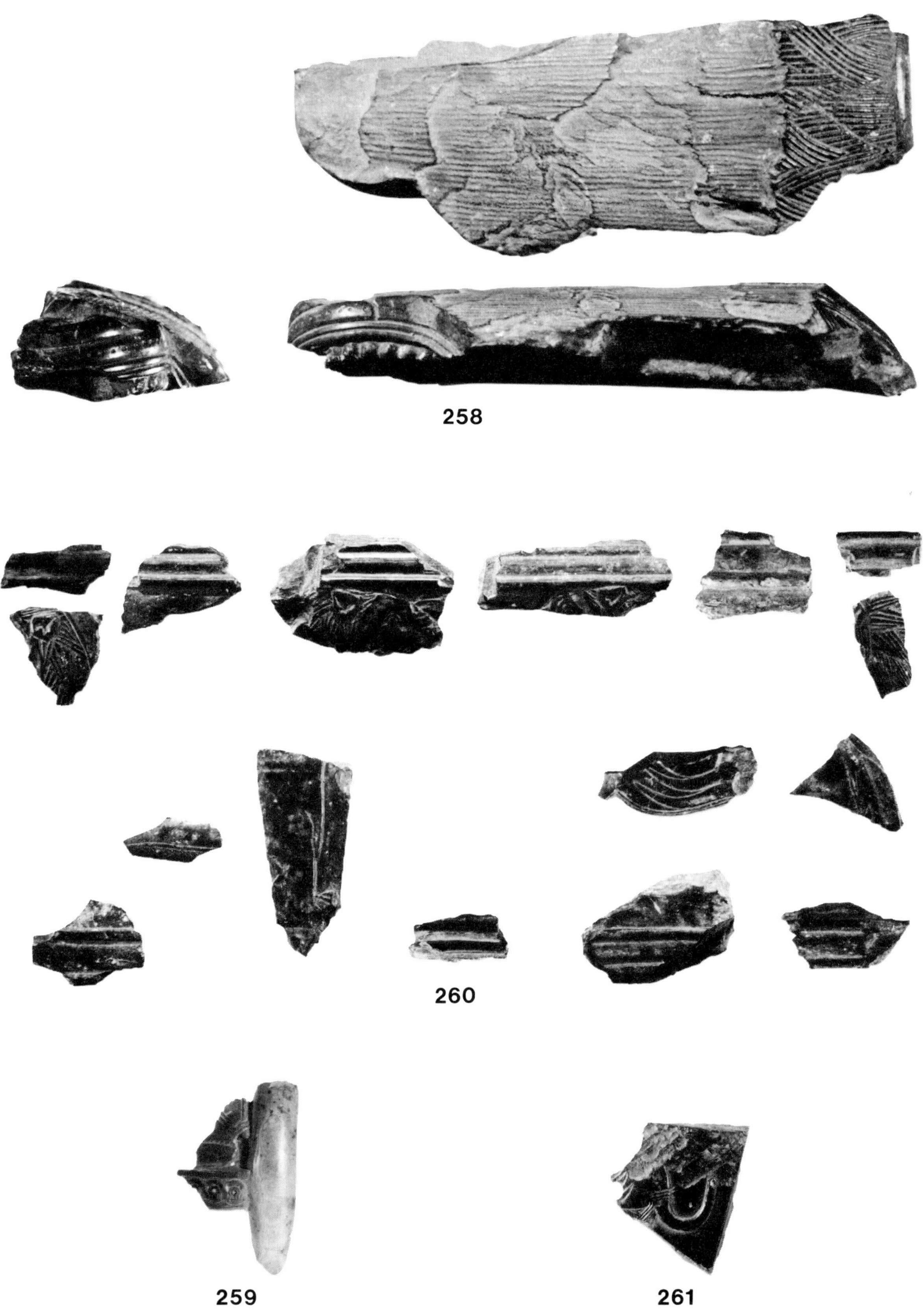

258

260

259

261

D: BOXES, HANDLES, MISCELLANEOUS

262 CC31 **[2]** (7); 64-944; T 25850; ht. of larger 5.7, w. 4, th. .4.
Two fragments of oval-shaped boxes or handles, a little more than one-half preserved. At one side of the larger fragment is a flattened duck's head in relief, the neck of which is in very low relief at both sides. A guilloche pattern framed by narrow bands forms the upper and lower borders. There is no evidence of holes for attachment. These objects may be bone, rather than ivory.

263 Bone; CC32 **[1]** **[2]** (area east of 7); 70-429; UM 71-23-75; ht. largest fragment (complete) 5.2, th. .4; front and back views.
Four fragments of an object just like no. 262. Here the guilloche border is framed by narrow bands.

264 Bone; CC31 **[2]** (7); 64-945; UM 65-31-322; ht. 4.6, w. 2.8, th. .4.
Fragment of an oval box-shaped handle preserving a bulge at the extant side and a plain body but for guilloche borders top and bottom. Faint traces of rocker scorings exist below the bulge; irregular scoring exists in the interior.

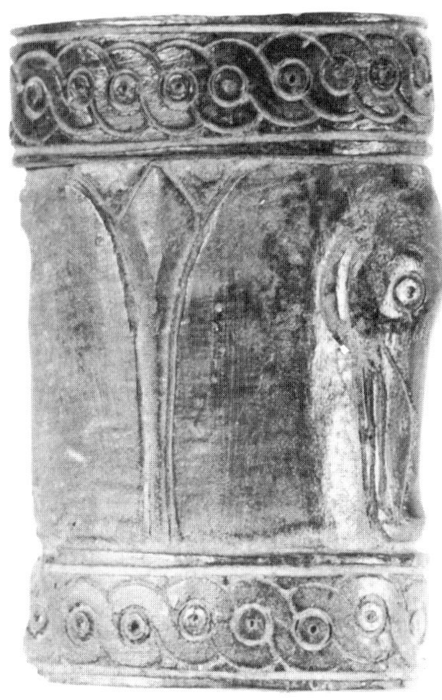

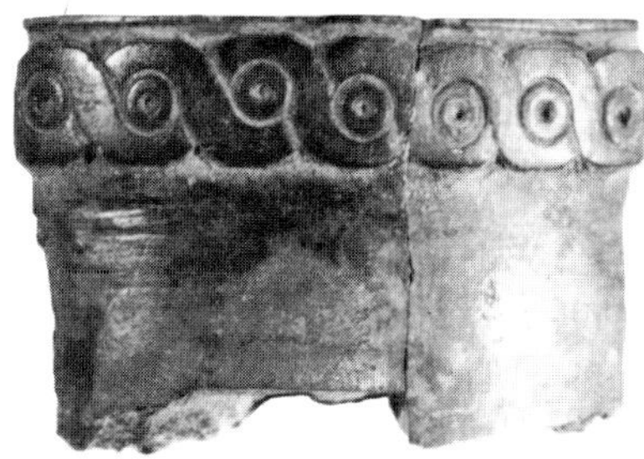

262

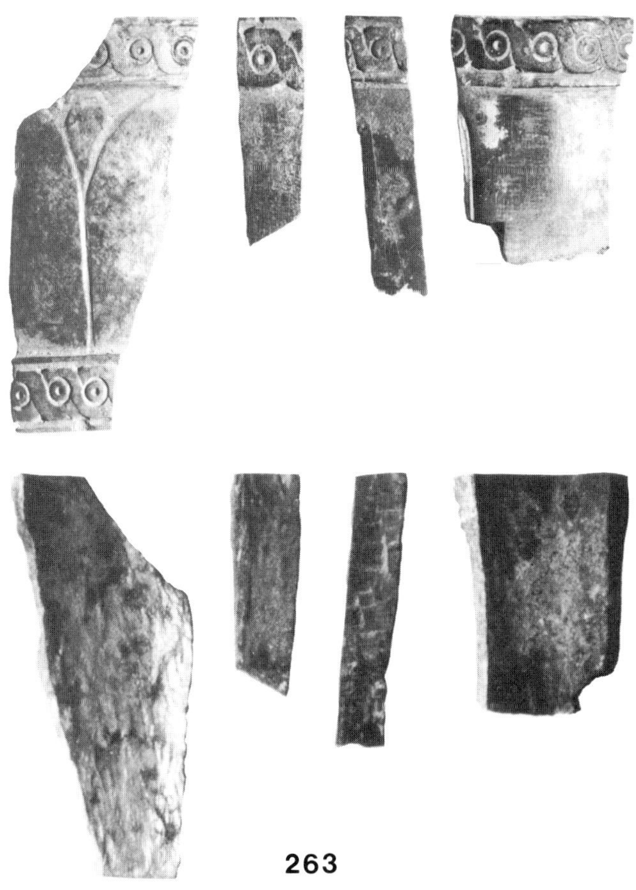

263

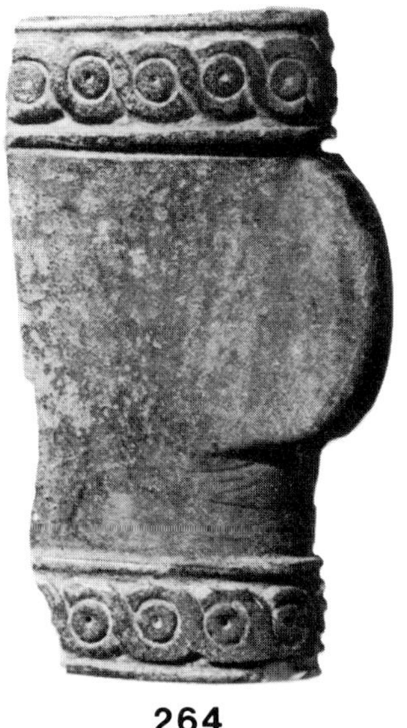

264

265 CC31 [2] (7); 64-943; T; ht. 6, w. 3; drawing, showing contour of upper edge.
Corner fragment of an oval box-shaped handle preserving the bodies of two creatures, probably bulls, standing and facing each other; part of the head of one creature is preserved. A guilloche border exists at top and bottom.

266 CC31 [2] (7); 64-945; UM 65-31-330; ht. 4.2, w. 1.9, th. .2.
Fragment of a box/handle apparently similar to no. 265. Preserved are only an ear—a bull's?—and part of the upper guilloche border.

267 BB31 [1] (8); 64-995; T; ht. 2.8, w. 1.4, th. .8; drawing.
Small neatly squared fragment from a corner of a box (?). On each long side is a rosette with six champlevé petals inlaid with "frit" inlays and bordered with silver (?); the center is a bronze stud; below are two champlevé triangles, one still with a frit inlay. On the extant short side are two champlevé triangles, one above the other, inlays now missing.

268 Purchased at Nagadeh; MMA 69.65; ht. 3.5.
A small broken fragment that gives no indication about its original shape or function. Preserved are a rosette, and part of another, with eight champlevé petals inlaid with a white material.

269 BB II; 64- ; UM 65-31-472; ht. 5.2, w. 1.5, th. .8; front and back views.
A squared corner fragment of a box or handle. On one side is an incised scroll pattern, on the other an incised tree over a twelve-petaled rosette band of the same type as no. 248; a dowel hole exists above the tree and a slot passes through the width.

270 Bone; CC31 [2] (7); 64-937; MMA 65.163.30; ht. 7, top diam. 3, top opening 1.8 x 2.2, bottom diam. 2.4, bottom opening 1.5 x 1.2; Muscarella 1966, fig. 3; three views.
Neatly incised and polished hollow handle or support, "lotus capital," tapering from top to bottom. The surface has an incised lotus leaf motif. The bottom edge has a border of narrow bands and a dowel hole; the upper edge is plain and has a wood dowel *in situ* (at right angles to the lower one) that holds a wooden plug in place. The upper opening is round-oval, the bottom rectangular, with rounded corners. A fragment of another example was found in the same area.

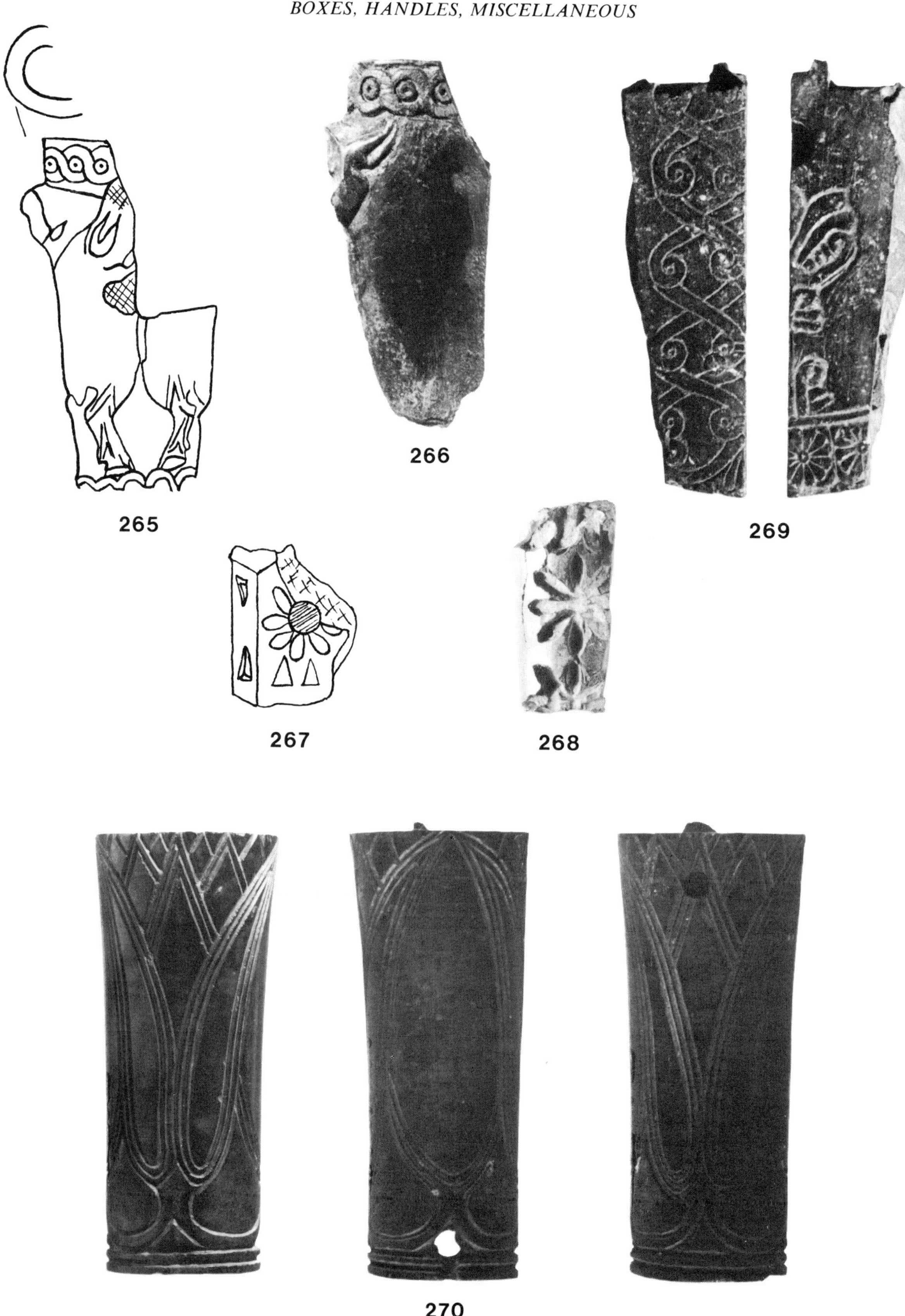
265
266
267
268
269
270

271A Y33 [5] (BB V 8, SW corner); 74N-625; UM 75-29-396; ht. 5.9.
B Y33 [2] [5] (BB V 3, SE corner, and 8, SW corner); 74N 627; MMA 1976.233.4; ht. 4.1.
C Y33 [5] (BB V 8, SW corner); 74N-637; UM 75-29-406; ht. 2.2.

Fragments of three handles/supports, like no. 270. Fragment B was recovered in two pieces, one from Room 3 and the other from Room 8, with fragments A and C.

272 CC31 [2] (7); 64-936; T; ht. 4.3, diam. top 2.5, bottom 2.3.
A hollow handle or support carved with an apparent lobed floral pattern in high relief; "palm capital"; no linear decoration (cf. no. 135). The upper border is a squared band with two dowel holes, the lower border is rounded and framed by bands; two dowels hold a wood plug *in situ*. The openings are rectangular with rounded corners.

273 CC31 [1] (6); 64-906; UM 65-31-369; l. 3.2, diam. ca. 1.3; top and side views.
Half of a hollow handle (?) carved in the form of a stylized horned animal's head. A narrow herringbone pattern forms the mane, and two relief bands, one a zig-zag, the other a rope pattern, define the neck.

274 BB31 [1] (8); 64-728; T; diam. 3.3.
Fragments of buttons or horses' harness attachments (?) carved in the form of multi-petaled rosettes and with a central perforation for attachment.

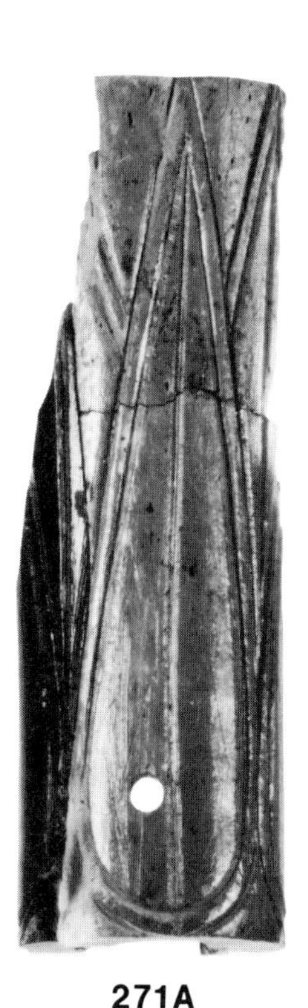

271A

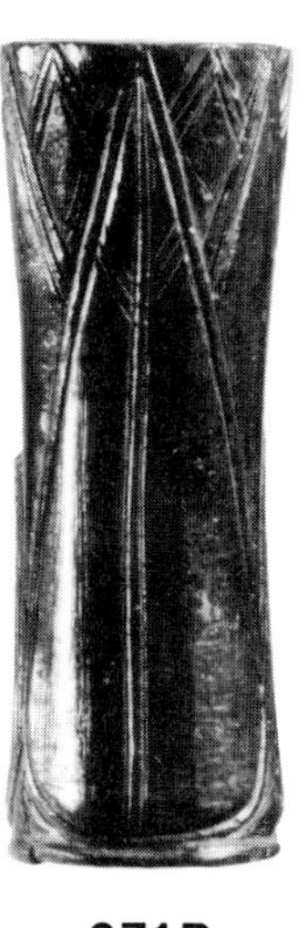

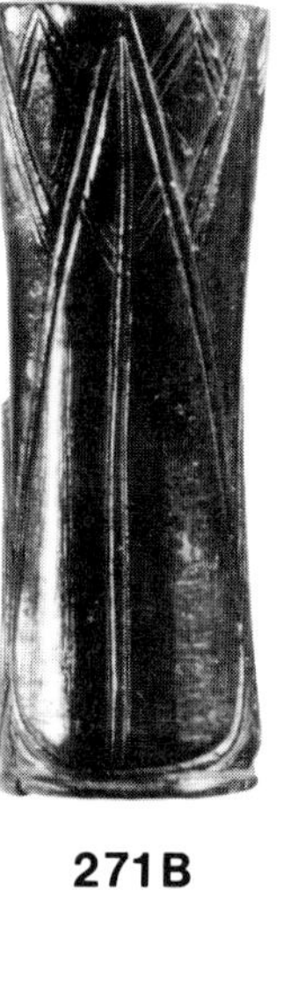

271B

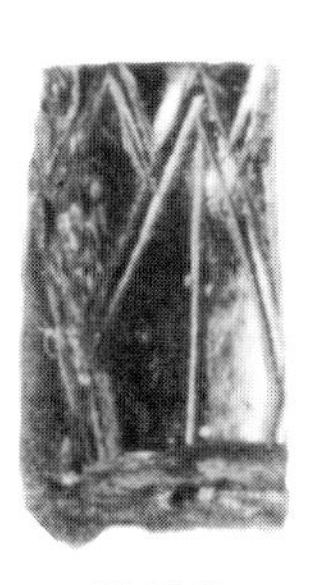

271C

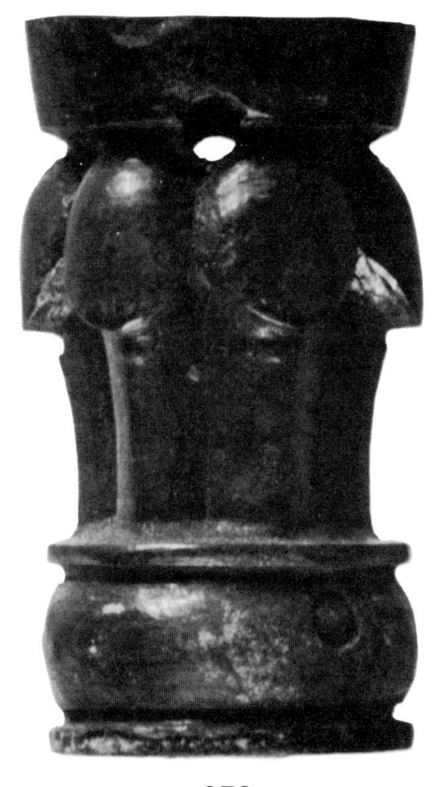

272

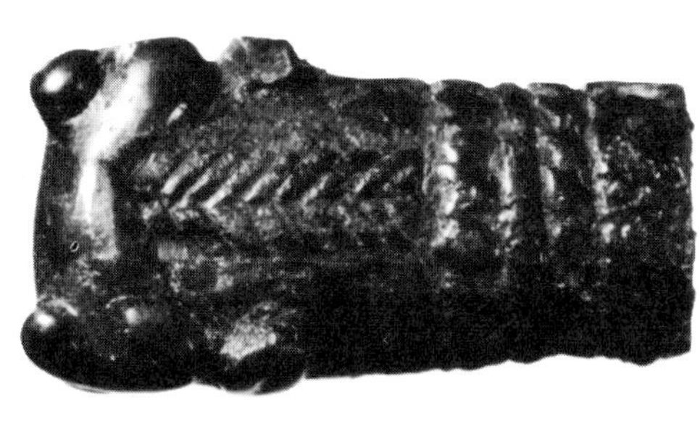

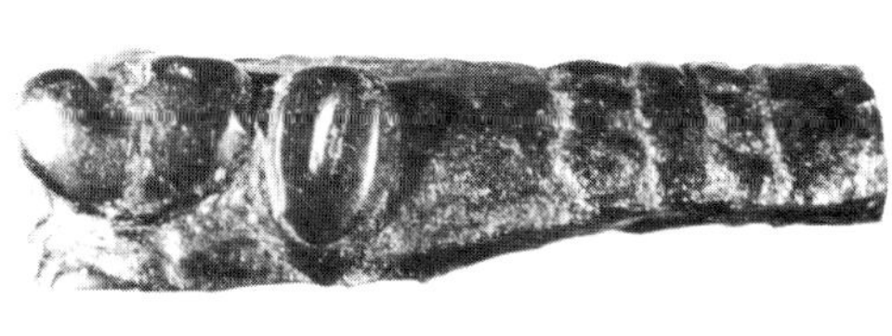

273

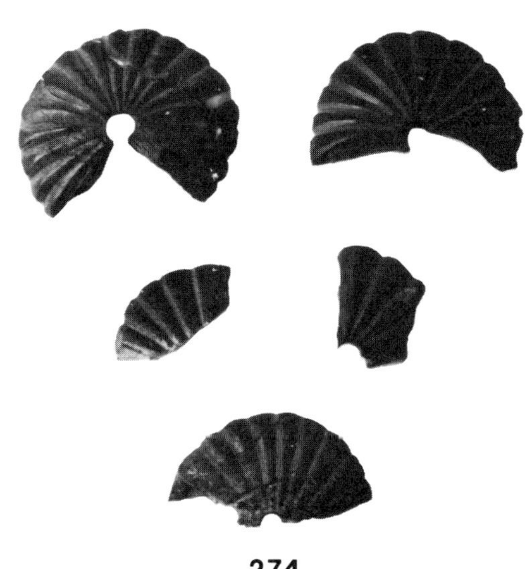

274

275 CC31 [4] (5,S); 64-118; UM 65-31-333; 3.8 x 3.8, ht. 1.8; front and side views.
Fragment of a small dish (?) with a flat interior ledge and an outer surface that is fluted. Several small fragments were also found in BB30 (GH, C).

276 CC31 [4] (5,S); 64-112; T; diam. 8.1 x 5.2, th. .6; front and back views.
Fragment of a small dish or buckle, possibly of shell rather than ivory. The exterior has champlevé six-petaled rosettes; the center is pierced.

277 AA30 (5,N); 60-491; T; diam. 4; no photograph.
Five small fragments of a dish or buckle like no. 276, with champlevé rosettes and a central hole.

278 Y33 [2] (BB V 3, SE corner); 74-317a, b; T; no photograph.
Two fragments of the same type of object as nos. 267, 277.

279 CC31 [4] (5,S); 64-325; UM 65-31-321; maximum w. 2.8.
Fragments of a small dish or buckle. The exterior is decorated with incised concentric circles.

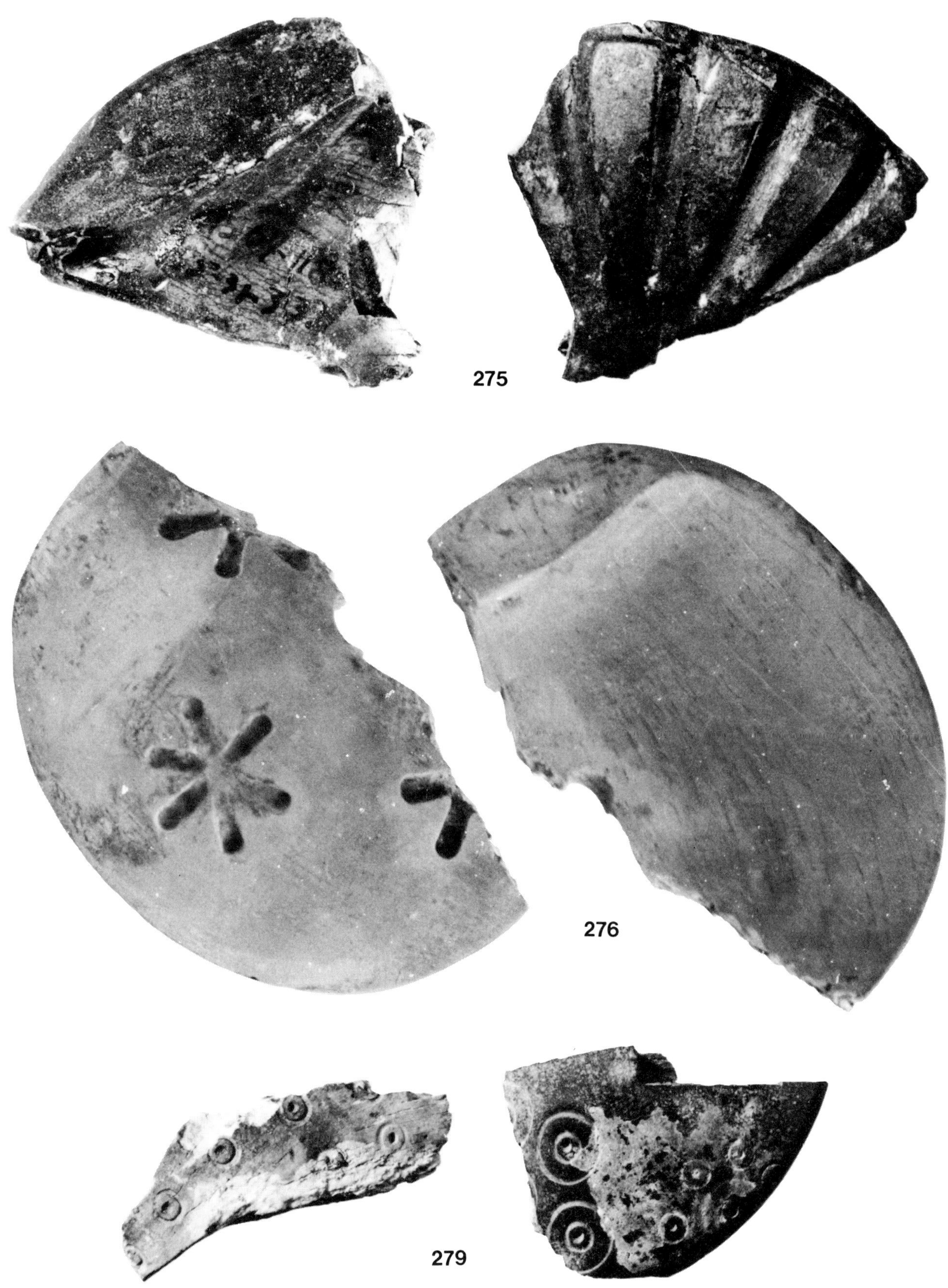
275
276
279

IX

ASSYRIAN IVORIES

280 BB32 [1] (10); 64-1047; MMA 65.163.2a, b; 3a-c; ht. as reconstructed ca. 22, th. 1.1; Muscarella 1966, fig. 2 and p. 125.

Eight fragments are extant from this plaque, which is straight at the top and may have been rounded at the bottom (cf. nos. 281, 282), but this is not certain. A bearded male carries an animal cradled in his left arm and a knob-headed staff or mace, which is held down, in his right. A row of tassels are pendent from the raised upper border; a dowel hole is at the upper left. The man's wavy hair, neatly incised, is held by a thick fillet, perhaps a braided band. The fillet (also the head in general) is smoothly worn from use, but there is no clear indication how it was decorated; scratching, apparently fortuitous, may be seen. A double swelling does exist, however, at the front of the band, and may have been a rosette in relief. A curly sideburn continues into the beard, framing the face. The beard, much worn, is curly at the chin, falling in straight tufts ending in neat curls for three layers; below the last row of tufted curls is a narrow row of small curls.

The outlined oval eye is covered by a thick brow decorated by a small incised triangle; below the mustache, the mouth is relatively thin. Jewellery is represented by a simple crescent earring—if there was a pendant it is now missing–and bracelets, which are so much worn that one does not know if they were originally decorated. The garment is short-sleeved and decorated, as far as may be seen, by fringe and a border of lines and small circles. The relief is relatively high. The reverse of the plaque is smooth; the top edge is scratched.

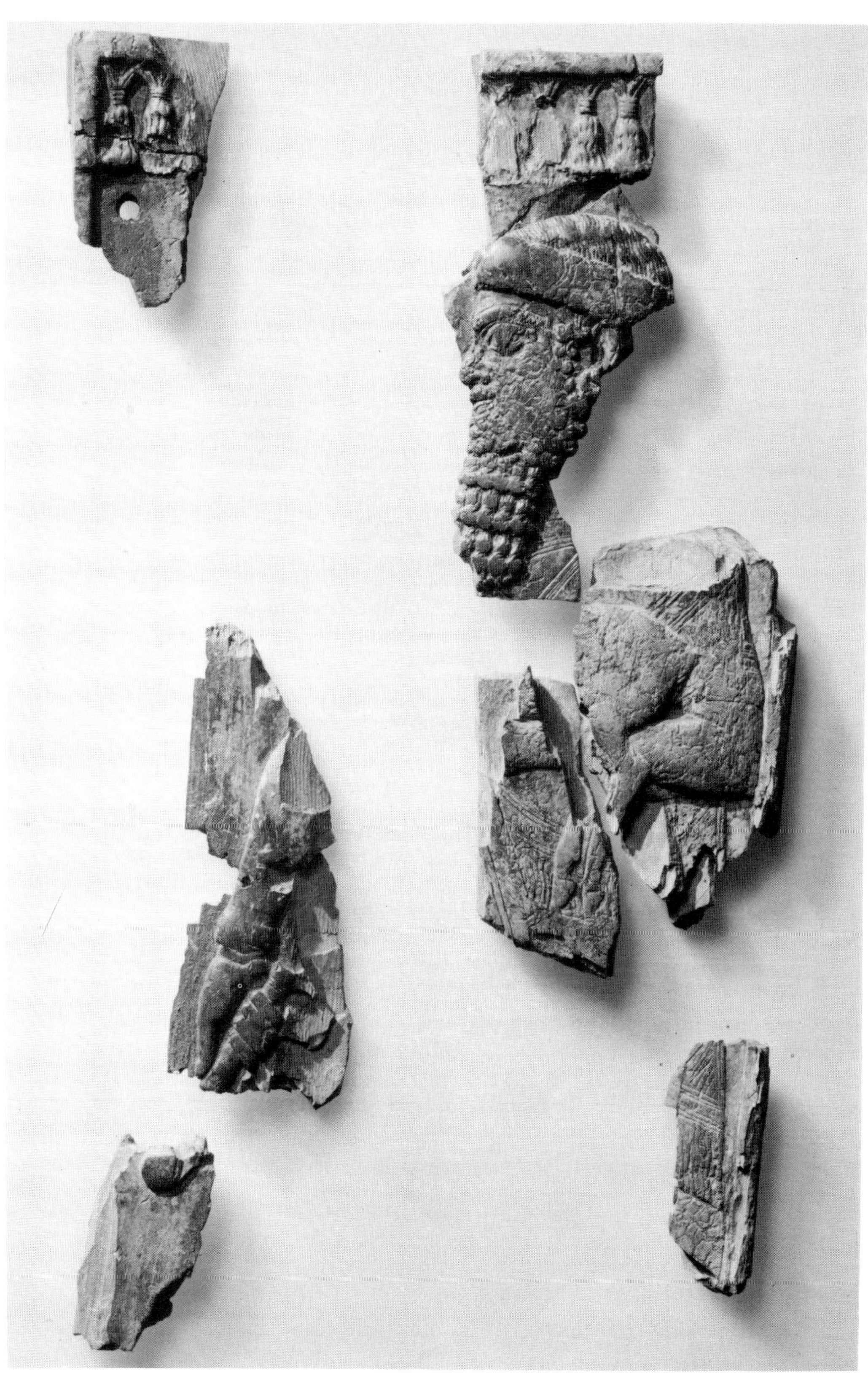

280

281 W31E [2] (BB IV East, 3); 72-112; T; ht. 10, w. 4.3; front view and drawing.
A fragmentary plaque straight at the top, rounded at the bottom. The field is divided into two decorated incised zones. The upper has a winged man striding left. He carries a kid cradled in his left arm and a bouquet of flowers, blossoms held down, in his right hand. Each wrist has a decorated bracelet, probably with a rosette; the man is barefoot but apparently has an anklet on the left leg. He stands on a mountain motif, itself placed over a guilloche pattern, moving right to left, that serves to separate the zones. His beard has typical tufted curls that terminate in a single curl. The head is almost completely missing, but it is clear that no hat was worn; we cannot state that a fillet existed. Four wings are shown indicating that the man is a genius. No upper-border decoration exists. The lower zone consists of a kneeling goat or ibex. There are two dowel holes, one in the mountain pattern, one below the animal.

282 W31E [2] (BB IV East, 3); 72-112; T; ht. of largest fragment 3; front view and drawing.
Fragments of a plaque like no. 281 in shape and probably also consisting of two zones. Extant is a bearded man with a fillet in his hair, right. His right hand is held forward, palm up; his left holds a mace with a lanyard held straight out from his body. He too stands on a mountain motif set upon a guilloche pattern like no. 281. The lower zone has a kneeling goat or ibex facing the same direction. It is not clear if the other fragments belong to this plaque: a rosette and part of a tree.

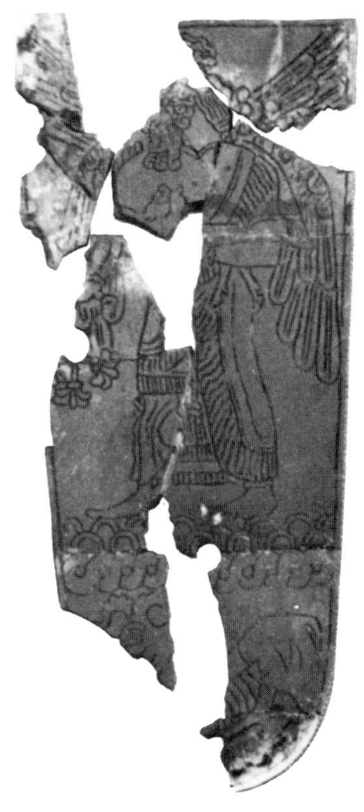

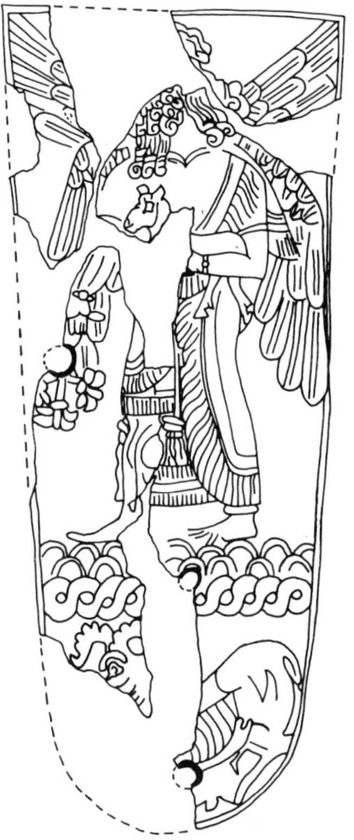

281

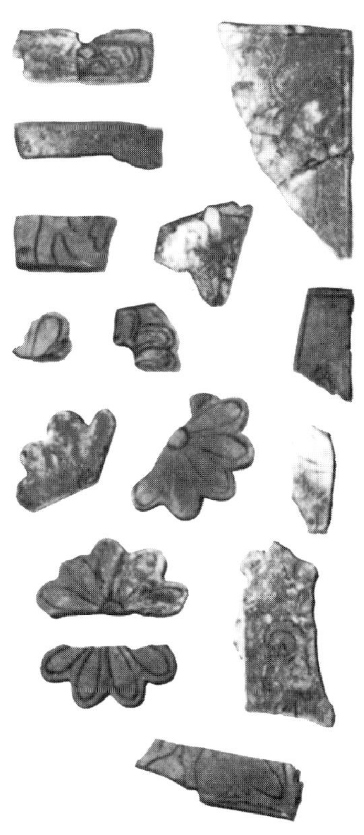

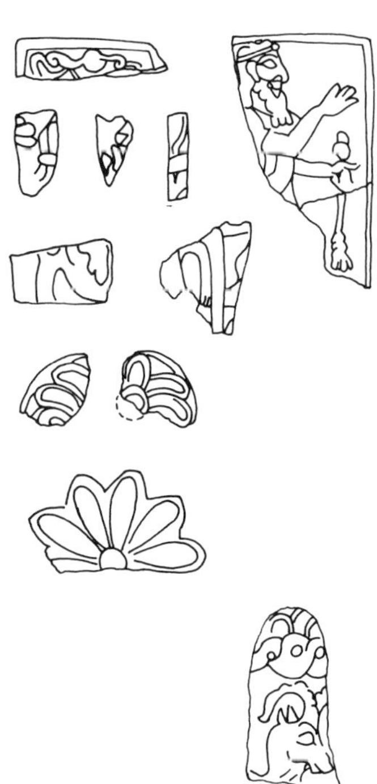

282

283 V31E [5] (BB IV East, 3); 74N-225; UM 75-29-366; ht. 3.1, th. 2; front view and drawing.
A small, thin fragment, badly burnt, preserving part of an incised kneeling animal placed below a guilloche band, right; a dowel hole is below the stomach. This is a fragment from a third object exactly like nos. 281 and 282.

284 BB32 [1] (10); 64-1046; T 25848; restored ht. ca. 8.2, w. ca. 18.3; front view and drawing.
Fragments of a plaque with two heraldic standing winged sphinxes. Each wears a low polos. The right sphinx has long hair and a multiple-strand necklace. On each side is one half of a tree that has curved branches with flowers or pine cones. It is possible that additional plaques on either side completed the scene but no other fragments were found. The relief, which is low, shows signs of wear. In the reconstruction of the fragments illustrated in the photograph and field drawing the only pieces that are in their correct relative positions are the heads and legs; in the drawing the head of the left figure is placed too far to the left. I am not sure that the two flower fragments are placed correctly, especially that on the right.

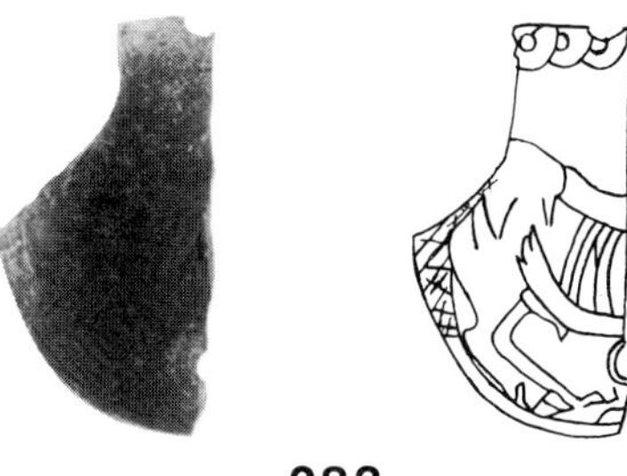

283

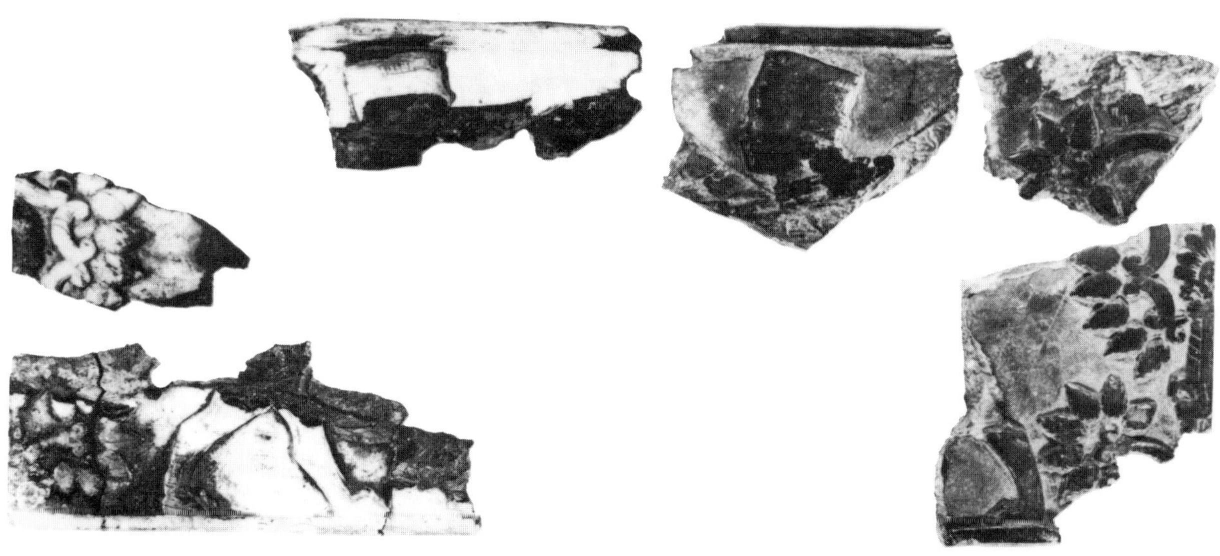

284

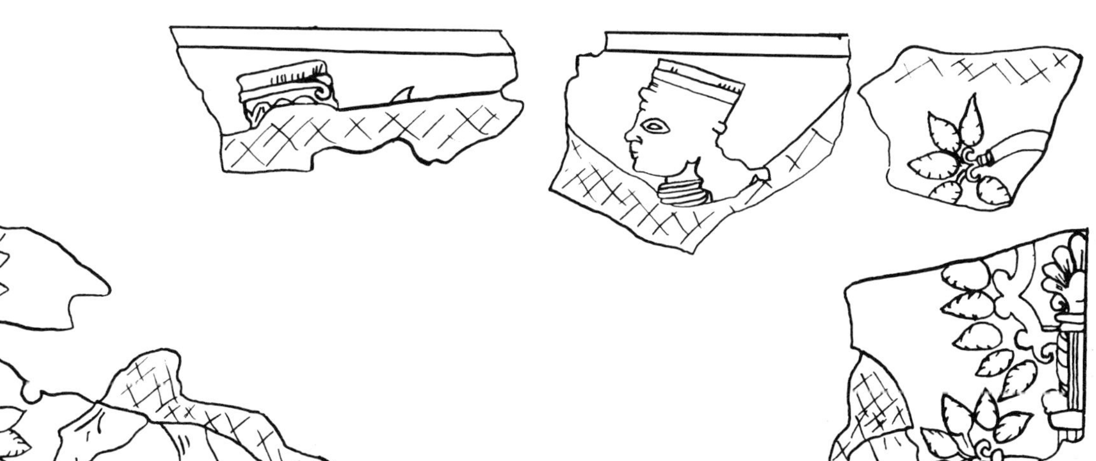

285A Bone; BB31 [1] (8); 64-724; MMA 65.163.33; ht. 5, w. 3.4, th. .5; Muscarella 1966, fig. 4.

B BB31 [1]; 64-725; T 25877; ht. 4.6, w. 2.3, th. .4.

C BB31 [1]; 64-723; MMA 65.163.35; ht. 2.2, w. 2.1, th. .25; Baer 1971, fig. 1, right.

D BB31 [1]; 64-725; T 25877.

Five fragments of concave-sided "cushion" plaques centered by a running ostrich with outstretched wings. Encircling the bird are chevron-decorated circles, with a pine cone at each quadrant. All are incised. There are at least three plaques represented. 285C is warped and burnt white. All may be bone.

286A BB31 [1] (8); 64-727; T; ht. 1.8, w. 5.1 (larger fragment); th. .3.
Two fragments of a narrow oblong band incised with running bustards (?), their wings outstretched, flanking trees. The trunks of the trees divide into roots that continue as a ground line under the birds on either side.

286B BB31 [1] (8); 64- ; UM 65-31-463; ht. 1.5, w. 2.3.
A fragment like the above two and probably from the same object.

287 AA31 [3] (5,N); 60-951; T.
Incised horned animal approaching or touching a tree, left. Horns are divided left and right, with one ear shown; the ear is incised from the same line that forms one horn. Rib marks are incised and an incised flame pattern is on the haunch. The right front leg is below a branch, the left is raised above the ground. Parts of three branches are preserved. The right section was left rough, probably for insertion into a slot. This piece and nos. 288 and 289 measure .2-.3 cm in thickness.

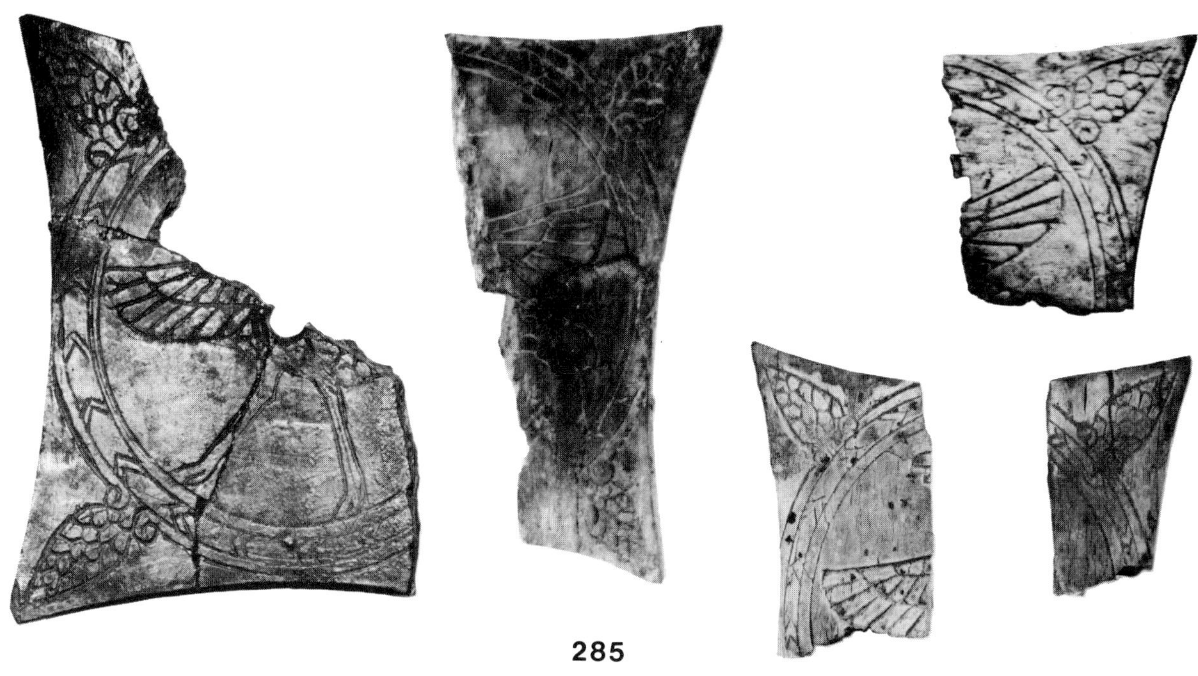

285

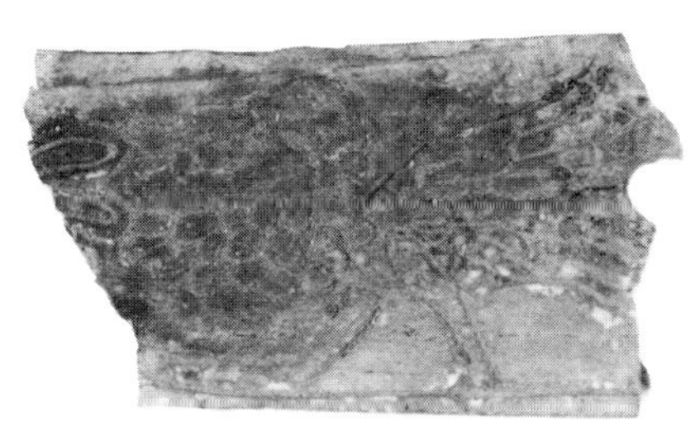

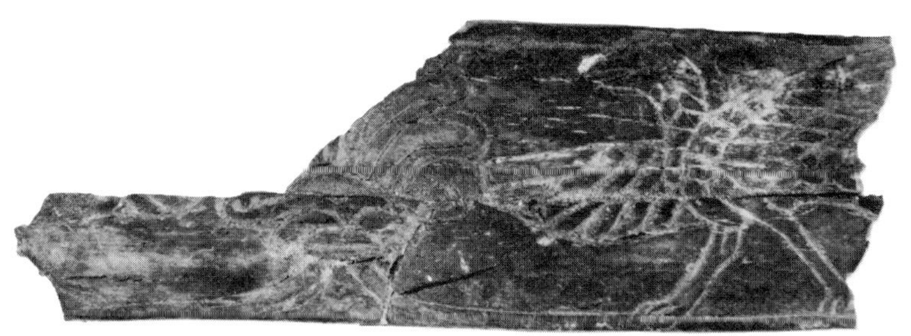

286A

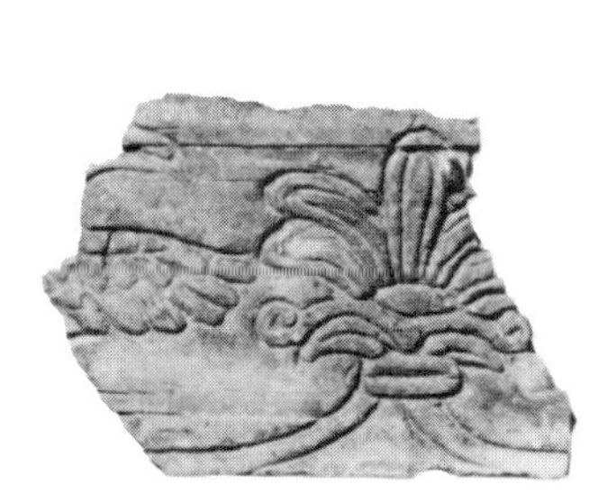

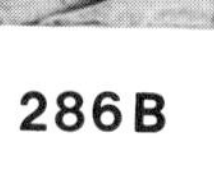

286B

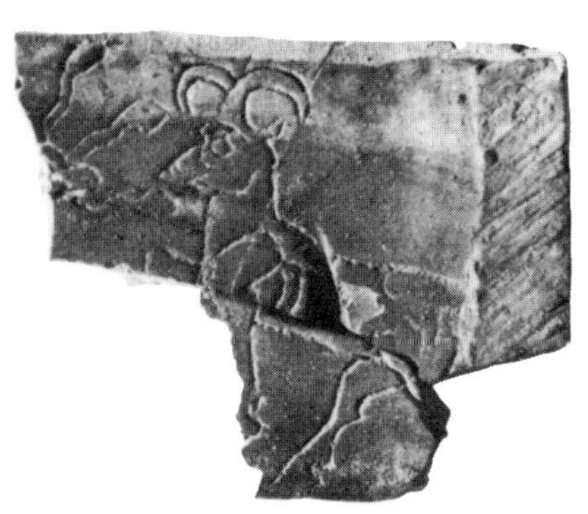

287

288 AA30 [3] (5,N); 60-951; T; drawing.
A small fragment depicting an animal exactly like no. 287 but moving right. It may be from the same scene: two heraldic horned animals facing a tree. The right edge is intact and the tree was incised on a separate fragment.

289 AA30 [3] (5,N); 60-951; T; drawing.
Lower part of an animal, right, walking on four legs and approaching a tree, of which only the tips of two branches are extant.

290 BB31 [1] (8); 64-772; UM 65-31-340; ht. 1.8, w. 5.9, th. .25.
Fragment of an incised oblong plaque like no. 286A, B, here with two kneeling goats flanking a tree of exactly the same type. Fine vertical scoring on the reverse.

291 W20 (area west of Tower 5, N of gate); 70-170; T; ht. 1.6, w. 2.6, th. .4.
A fragment preserving what appears to be the incised chest, wing and part of the leg of a winged creature, left. One wonders if this fragment was dropped by plunderers leaving the city.

292 BB32 [1] (8); 64-1048; UM 65-31-342; l. of largest fragment: 6, ht. 2.4, th. .5.
Five fragments of an incised oblong plaque depicting interlocking plants. The branches and roots are decorated with crosswise incisions.

293 BB32 [1] (10); 64-1048; MMA 65.163.34; l. 4.5, ht. 2.4, th. .5.
A fragment from the same plaque. It is burnt white. The reverse is smooth.

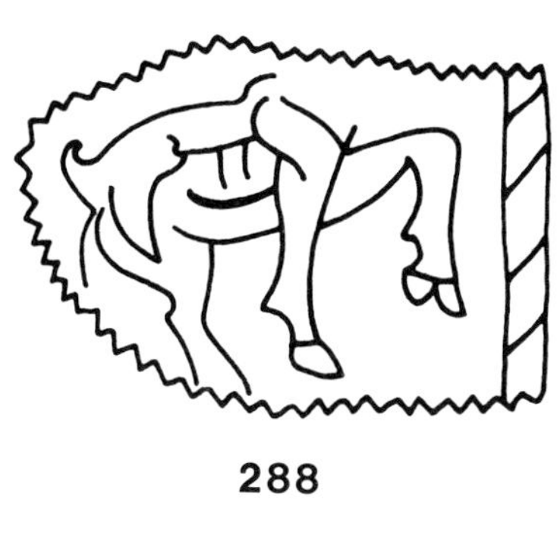

288

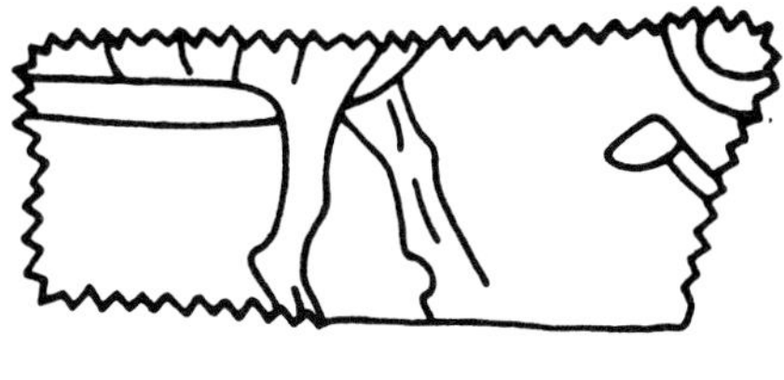

289

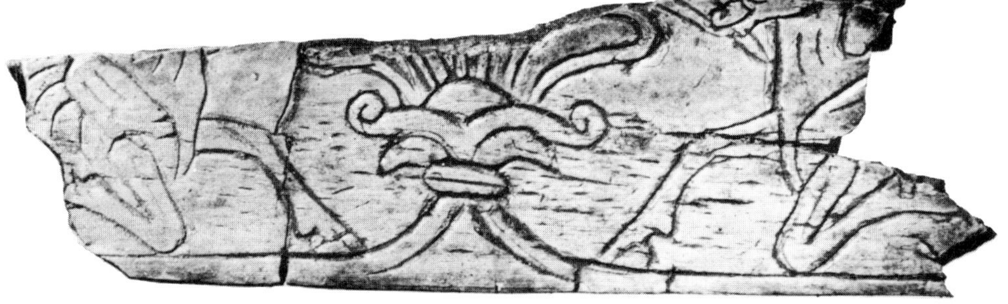

290

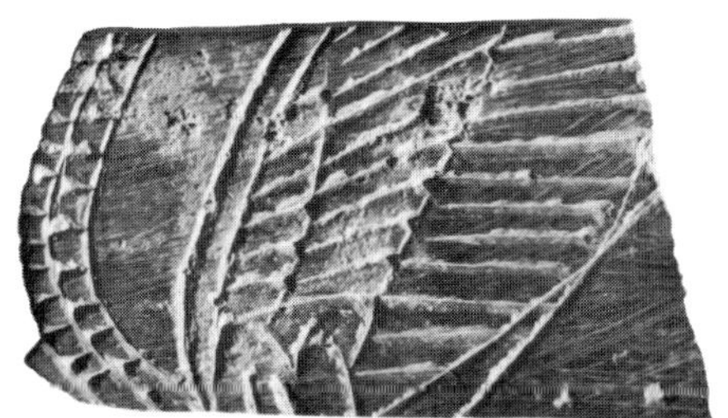

291

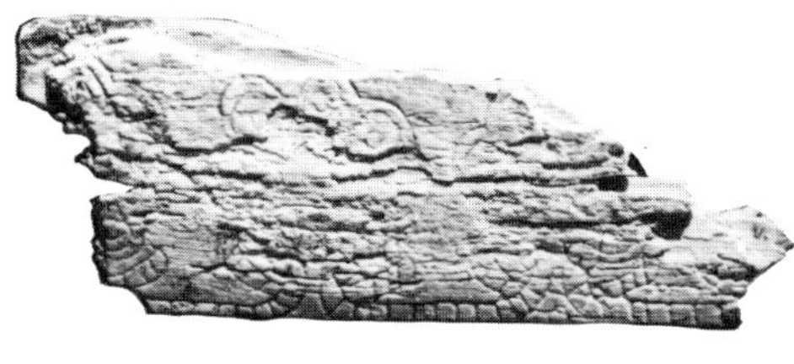

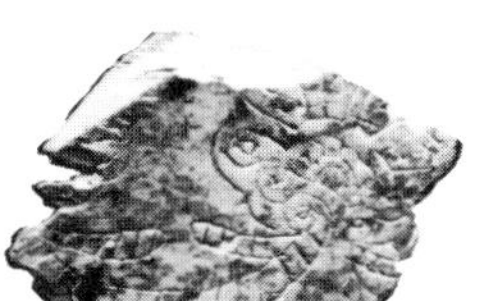

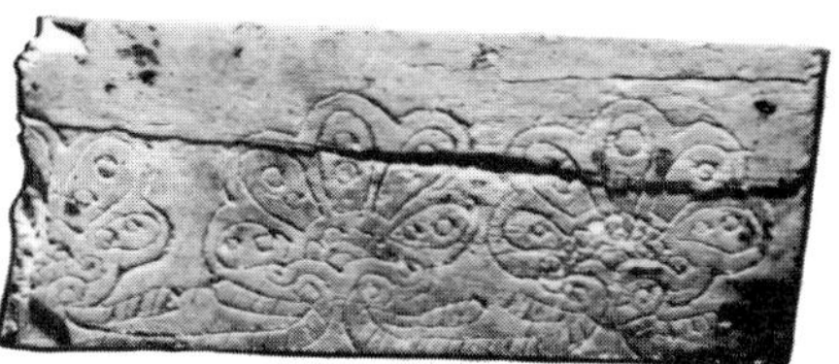

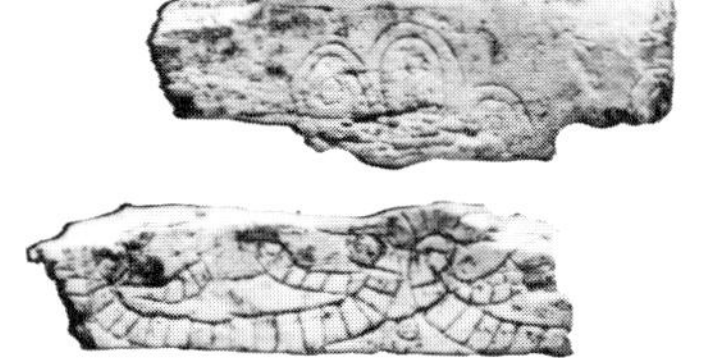

292

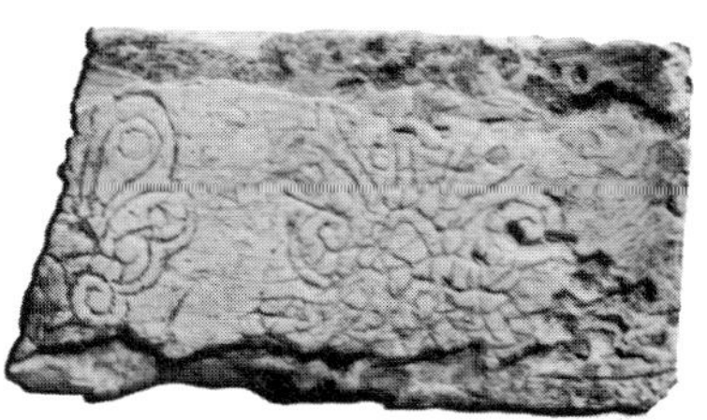

293

COMMENTARY

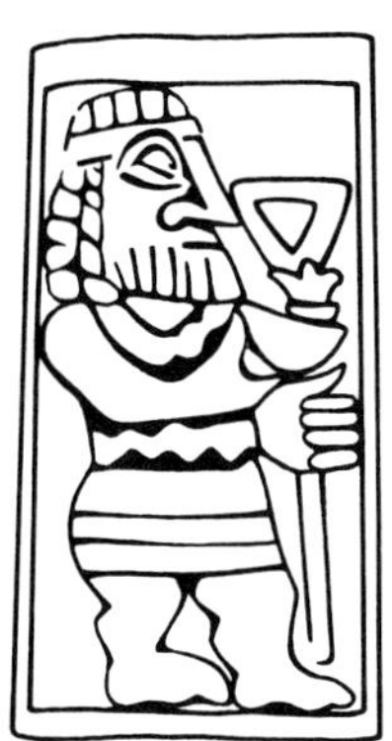

I

BATTLE SCENES: CHARIOTS, CAVALRY, WARRIORS

The majority of the battle scene fragments, those depicting chariots, cavalry, foot soldiers and archers, were recovered from the collapsed second storey fill in three rooms adjoining the great hall (Room 5) of BB II: Rooms 6, 7, 8; a few came from the area to the east of Room 7 and a scattered few were found in the eastern and northeastern area of the great hall (AA 30). Three isolated fragments were found in the fill of BB I. It may reasonably be concluded that ivories scattered so far apart, for example between Rooms 6 and 8, could hardly have belonged to the same object or to objects that were originally juxtaposed, even if we assume that in the collapse of BB II, objects from one area were scattered widely in different directions. Therefore, it seems more than probable that the ivories originally adorned several unidentified objects situated in more than one area or room in the second storey of BB II. We also know that two buildings contained objects decorated with battle scenes.

The scenes depicted represent battles with chariots, cavalry and foot soldiers—local and enemy,[1] taking part in mutual assaults; at least one scene has a representation of an enemy city under siege. Two of the siege fragments (nos. 69, 71) came from Room 8, the other (no. 70) came from an adjacent area in the great hall; it is not impossible that these fragments scattered from one area and that in fact we have only one siege scene.

The chariots, cavalry and foot soldiers move both to the left and right, although the majority move right. A series of chariots or cavalry and chariots followed each other (nos. 1, 3, 15, 18, 41, 47; nos. 21, 22, found together, seem to show four consecutive chariots, but this is not certain). Sometimes they overrun a nude enemy (nos. 1-4, 33, 40, 41); often foot soldiers precede or follow a chariot or the cavalry (nos. 19, 20, 34, 54, 58, 61, 67); at least one plaque depicted an overlapping of chariots or of chariots and cavalry (no. 14).

Except for one example of a four-spoked wheel (no. 16), all the chariots have six-spoked wheels; they all have an outer tire, and either a projection or a drilled hole representing the hub, with no indication of a linchpin. The axle is situated under the center of the chariot box; no. 4 seems to be an exception. The wheel with the four spokes (no. 16) is part of a chariot box that is not otherwise distinguished from the typical type and thus it is not certain that it belongs to an enemy—although, in fact, the possibility that it is an enemy chariot cannot be ruled out. In any event, four-spoked wheels are rare at this time (Moorey 1971, 104). Assyrian reliefs of the ninth century depict eight-spoked and six-spoked chariots together, the former definitely that of an enemy (Yadin 1963, 298, 386-7; Layard 1849, pls. 13, 14). Here the craftsman deliberately sculpted two sets of spokes, as is done also on the Hasanlu ivories. If no. 16 represents an enemy chariot we then have a battle scene in which both sides employed chariots as well as foot soldiers.[2]

The solid chariot box is tapered top to bottom and the top border is slightly convex; a curved unit

[1]By local I mean the victorious forces; by enemy I mean those the local forces defeat. The assumption underlying the discussion is that the local forces depicted may represent troops from Hasanlu itself.

[2]A fragmented seal from Room 7 of BB II (64-501) depicts a four-wheeled chariot under an unoccupied light box; the chariot is apparently drawn by a monster; a second monster and vulture follow. Because the seal is of ninth century date, contemporary with the ivories, it is of interest to note the use of the four-spoked wheel in both mythological and real-life scenes.

at the sides may be structural. The yoke pole at the chariot end is visible in several instances. No spears are attached to the rear of the box, nor are there any quivers at the sides. A pointed projection at the rear base of the box could be the buckle of a shield, although no shield is outlined. This projection slopes down and seems too pointed to be a step-up. One chariot (no. 15) seems to lack the projection, but this could be an accidental omission. The projection could also be the rear section of a partition within the box, separating the charioteer from the archer, or perhaps part of a unit closing the back for the protection of the occupants (cf. Littauer 1972, 147 f.; Karageorghis 1973, 73 f., 78 f., figs. 10, 11, VII).

Each chariot has two occupants, a charioteer who controls the reins and holds a whip, and an archer; apparently there were no spearmen in chariots (cf., however, no. 49). The charioteer is either in the background (no. 48) or foreground (nos. 7, 8). The archers of nos. 50 and 51 might be associated with chariots, although the latter could also be associated with a siege (cf. Layard 1849, pls. 13, 17). Except for no. 53, archers not associated with a chariot, quivers are not represented; they could, of course, be inside the box.

Two horses pull the chariot; a third horse, a spare, is never depicted and apparently was not used. In profile two heads and the body and feet of one horse are depicted. All horses, both chariot and cavalry, are stallions, ungelded, as testicles are always shown. The hair of the mane, stomachs and backs are rendered by either a twisted rope or a herringbone pattern; body hair is depicted by short incisions cut with a small triangular tool; and tails have vertical incisions (e.g., nos. 13-15) or a herringbone design (e.g., nos. 8, 9). Reins are linked directly to the horses' necks; in one case (no. 5) an additional set of reins is attached to a rein ring attached to the end of the yoke pole; no. 6 seems also to have a small rein ring, but this is not certain. Occasionally a round harness disc (nos. 2, 6), or tassel (no. 5) is shown either on the side or below the horse; and in two instances (nos. 5, 26; cf. 27), a feathered headpiece is worn by the horses. Some of the horses (nos. 6, 29, 30, 34; perhaps all), have an object pendent from their necks. The bases of these objects have rectangular incisions that could conceivably be small tassels or a depiction of incised decoration. The objects are bell-shaped and one is tempted to conclude that they are indeed bells. Yet, no clappers are depicted (cf. Hrouda 1953, pls. 26, 27) and the object might be no more than a decorative tassel, with its tuft suggested by the rectangular incisions. A few flaring bells and scores of rattle bells have been excavated at Hasanlu (Dyson 1968, 90), and they were probably placed on the necks of animals (horses too?). It seems to me that ultimately we must leave open the question whether or not the objects are actually bells, but at least we may accept the possibility and I have called them bells in the catalogue section. No bits (but cf. no. 19), blinkers, nose pieces, or elliptical objects connecting the chariot box to the end of the yoke pole are represented, nor are the horses protected by armor or breastplates. Characteristic of all the chariot horses is the fact that although they are represented in motion, their front and rear legs are depicted touching the ground, as if at rest.

The cavalry horses are illustrated singly, without an outrider or squire, perhaps because the cavalryman carried a spear rather than a bow and needed no help in steadying his horse. Cavalry horses are of the same style and type as the chariot horses: in body decoration, lack of bits, blinkers, armor, in the fact that they are stallions, and they too wear "bells" at the neck. No saddles or blankets are depicted and the cavalrymen must have ridden them bareback. Excavations at Hasanlu and nearby Dinkha Tepe have yielded many bronze and iron horse bits and (at Hasanlu only) several bronze breastplates—but no blinkers or nose pieces (Muscarella 1974c, 65 ff., 78, 80, fig. 36). As was the case with the chariot horses, the cavalry horses too override a nude enemy (no. 33). Although no depiction of a cavalry horse is complete, it seems from the horizontal position of the stomachs of nos. 33 and 38 that their front feet rested on the ground, as do the fragments of horses' feet, some of which may be from cavalry (nos. 42-45).

The cavalrymen seem to be dressed in the same manner as the foot soldiers but wear boots instead of sandals (*viz.* no. 33). The warriors with bows are represented as having different types of dress and hair styles. For example, the archer no. 48 has a belt and bandolier depicted in the same chunky units as his hair; no. 49, with spiral hair curls, wears a garment with a plain belt, fringed collar and sleeves; no. 51 wears a similar garment but one with a narrow decorated belt, and he has straight thick hair. Not enough is preserved of the heads to know whether or not they wore helmets (cf. the foot soldiers, *infra*); the left archer of no. 53 wears a fillet.

Regular foot soldiers wear a belted skirt with scalloped decoration on the borders and around the belt; the sleeves and bottom are fringed. The scallops might represent metal armor sections, many examples of which, in bronze and iron, have been found on the Hasanlu citadel. The soldiers also wear a flaring "feathered" helmet, often with an earflap made of leather (nos. 54, 55A, 57)—to judge from the triangular incisions, the same pattern found on the bodies of the horses; the back of the head and the face were not protected. These helmets do not appear to be metal, of which a few have been excavated at Hasanlu (e.g., Borchardt 1972, pl. 40: 2; Dyson 1961, fig. 14: a good Assyrian type). At least three of these helmets lack earflaps (nos. 59, 61, 62) and this suggests that earflaps were added separately. Such earflaps made of bronze or iron have been excavated at Hasanlu (and see Muscarella 1973a, 66 f.; figs. 27: 1, 28, for an example from Iron Age III Agrab Tepe); it is thus not surprising to find them depicted on the ivories. One warrior (? *infra*), no. 63, wears only a fillet. Of interest is the fact that none of the soldiers wears foot gear or armor (cf. the hunter on no. 178). Body armor, aside from the possible plates represented by the scallops, is not represented either. A pair of shoulder armor plates was found at Hasanlu (Dyson 1960, 10), but we do not know if they belonged to the local forces or to the attacking enemy, who we know penetrated into the citadel. Most of the soldiers (except for the trampled enemy and nos. 33, 49 left, and 55A) wear bracelets, which could be wrist guards except that other figures, not warriors, also wear them (*infra*).

The predominant weapon for the soldiers is the spear, no doubt socketed as may be judged from the representations themselves and from the many hundreds of iron and bronze examples excavated at Hasanlu. The spear is represented either naturally crossing over the body (nos. 19, 55A), or unnaturally, behind it (no. 54). No. 59 may wield a sword, and no. 61 a mace, but one cannot be certain. Nor is it clear what is in the hands of no. 63: the object seems to be a free-swinging mace, which, if so, gives us a rare illustration of the use of that weapon (Madhloom 1969, 61). No daggers are represented on any of the ivories. In addition to the spears mentioned above, many bronze and iron swords, and many bronze, iron, and stone maces have been excavated at Hasanlu, so they are not unexpected on the ivories. And that the bow was an important weapon of the local forces is attested by the excavation of many bronze and iron arrows and archers' rings (Muscarella 1974c, 80), and a few bronze quivers. Of interest is the fact that although many bronze axes were excavated not a single ivory depicts one in use. (Cf. Calmeyer 1973, 36 f., 189: C1; I have reservations about the authenticity of this piece: Muscarella 1977b, no. 70.) All the shields depicted are small and round with a raised outer edge; no central boss is evident. No such shields have been excavated at Hasanlu although one large bronze example was found (62-979).

Obviously, some of the warriors must represent the locals, others the enemy. It seems certain that the soldiers dressed in the scalloped garments and/or the "feathered" helmets are the locals, the victorious warriors, as is evidenced, for example, by the victorious representations of no. 33, and the vigorous position of nos. 54, 55A, 56. But nos. 59 and 61, dressed differently, also wear the "feathered" helmet, and they too are vigorously represented; perhaps they too are locals or their allies. The victorious soldiers seem to move from left to right, but the data are not sufficient for us to conclude that the soldiers of nos. 58, 62 and 63, who move right to left, must therefore be the enemy, especially because no. 62 wears the "feathered" helmet. Of the definite enemy we have those soldiers who are trampled by the chariot and cavalry horses. They are unfortunately nude and therefore without a uniform that can be identified. In addition, we have the spears of enemy troops, their bodies and faces broken away. But they too are barefoot (except, surprisingly, for those trampled, nos. 1, 33 [cf. no. 101]), and they also fought with spears and small round shields, as may be seen from nos. 21, 55, 62, 64.

There is only one example of a chariot horse that seems to be collapsing (no. 5: cf. no. 144), a definite sign according to the standards of ancient art that it is an enemy horse (cf. Mallowan and Davies 1970, no. 64; Layard 1849, pls. 13, 14). This horse has a double set of reins, one attached to a yoke ring, a tassel pendent below its stomach, and no body hair decoration, features not found on the other horses; it also has a headdress, found on only one other horse (no. 26; cf. no. 27); it is therefore possible that no. 26 might also belong to an enemy chariot. Assyrian artists sometimes distinguished their horses from those of the enemy by omitting a headdress on the latter (Layard 1849, pl. 13).

Finally, we meet the enemy in one other group of reliefs, on the siege scenes (nos. 69, 71): a female holding her hair in fear, and two figures embracing, also from fear.

Given the problem of the fragmentation of the ivories, it is not possible to place all examples into discrete units that conceivably could be the products of individual workshops. Yet it is clearly obvious that some of the ivories discussed are executed with the very same body proportions and outlines, and have the very same types of body incisions and specific details and structure for arms, legs, headdresses, hooves, wheels, and so forth, all of which allows them to be isolated within the corpus.

Isolating these fragments into discrete units may give us some indication concerning the number of local craftsmen, or better, local workshops operating at Hasanlu. By workshop I mean the production of one or more craftsmen who executed work of a basically uniform nature, with traits in common, distinguishable on the basis of these traits from the production of another workshop. We can never know if a single craftsman varied his execution and use of details from piece to piece, or from one scene to another, nor whether two or more closely allied craftsmen, say a craftsman and his apprentice, could, or chose to, create a number of reliefs indistinguishable from one another. Therefore, the word workshop, rather than single craftsman, is used to describe the artisans of those ivories that allow themselves to be placed into discrete units for the reasons given above. No attempt will be made to place every ivory fragment into a workshop both because of their fragmentation, and because I believe it is better to be conservative in this matter than to force the evidence, especially when my eye might not necessarily agree with what other eyes see.

Tentatively and subjectively, I would place the following fragments into discrete units: 1, 2, 3, 19-25, 28-30, 33, 171 (*infra*); 4; 5; 6; 13; 15; 16; for the warriors: 49; 50; 51; 53; 55A; 56; 59; 61; 62. Without attempting to justify each choice, I believe that one can observe, for example, that the horses' hooves and fetlocks, and the chariot wheel spokes of nos. 4, 14, 15, 16, are distinct from one another; that the body decoration and the manes of horses nos. 2, 5, and 6 are executed in a different manner; that the hair, noses, hands and thumbs, and arm structure of the warriors varies enough to justify separating them; and that the nude enemy soldiers vary in detail. Indeed, occasionally it seems that we may perhaps recognize the same hand at work, for example the horses' heads (and note the incised inverted V on the legs of nos. 1 and 22; cf. no. 14).

It does not, of course, follow that each unit represents a separate workshop, for reasons given above and because some fragments are those of horse's bodies, while others are parts of chariots, some of which surely belong together. Nevertheless, the inference to be drawn, speaking conservatively, is that there were several, perhaps a half-dozen local ivory workshops in operation. They shared a common corpus of ideas, motives and techniques, but, no doubt depending on individual skills and temperaments, came to slightly different resolutions.

Representations of cavalry and chariots in battle and siege scenes exist at Hasanlu not only on the local-style ivories and wood, but on local-style objects made of metal and on cylinder seals as well. Starting with the well-known gold bowl (Dyson 1960, 124; 1968, fig. 101),[3] we note that the chariots depicted there are lighter than those on the ivories. They are not solid and are drawn not by horses but by horned animals and bovines; also, they hold deities, not warriors. Obviously, these chariots are not battle vehicles involved in real-life situations; rather they served as vehicles for the gods and therefore would not be the same types as depicted on the ivories, although both types had six-spoked wheels. The double set of horns on the bovines suggests there were two animals represented; the other animals lack this feature but this may be an unintentional omission (cf. the doubled rams' heads under the nude goddess). The sole armed person, probably a god, holds a bow and wears a quiver. Clothing decoration, hair styles, and animal body decoration on the bowl are not totally different from those on the ivories (see *infra*). Moreover, all the gold bowl figures are barefoot, a feature common on the ivories.

---

[3]The Hasanlu gold bowl is actually not a bowl but a drinking vessel, a beaker or large cup. Because it has been called a bowl in all publications I continue that terminology here.

Of special interest in the context of the Hasanlu gold bowl is a remarkable copper beaker inlaid with silver figures recently acquired by the Louvre from the antiquities market (Amiet 1965, 235 ff.). In the upper of two friezes are two six-spoked light chariots each with a single deity; all the horses' feet are grounded. The lower frieze has a procession of unicorns. Both friezes are remarkable in that the upper reproduces the chariots and their deities represented in the upper part of the Hasanlu gold bowl, and the lower frieze reproduces the scene on the unicorn vessel from Marlik (Negahban 1964, figs. 109, 136, pl. XVI). If this vessel had been excavated rather than plundered in clandestine digging, it might have given us important information about cultural relations between Hasanlu and Marlik and perhaps even a third site. As Dyson (1968, 89) has pointed out, the technique of inlaying a precious metal into another metal, which occurs on the Louvre beaker, also occurs on the Hasanlu silver beaker (*infra*), and on a vessel from Marlik (Negahban 1964, fig. 108). On the basis of the unbridged spout of the Marlik vessel it would seem that it is the earliest in date of the three vessels, and that the Louvre and Hasanlu beakers are later, but not, to my mind, much later than the time the Hasanlu gold bowl was created.

In Muscarella 1972, 41, note 41, I briefly mentioned this vessel. Because of the existence of motifs found on both Hasanlu and Marlik vessels that occur on the unexcavated object, I was reluctant to discuss it until I had seen it. I saw it in 1973 in its case and am of the opinion that it is genuine. The Louvre vessel illustrates very neatly the problems involved for archaeologists and art historians when an important object appears without a provenience. For we shall never know where the vessel was found, whether or not it came from Marlik or Hasanlu, or near either.

It is not clear whether the gold bowl represents a different local style of workmanship within the vast Hasanlu repertory, or whether it is a slightly earlier production of the tenth/ninth century (Muscarella 1971a, 265; 1972, 42, notes 29, 30 for Porada's earlier dating; Porada 1967, 2978, note 16, and 1975, 390, now dates the bowl to 1250/1000 B.C.), or even the work of another neighboring atelier. But I suggest that the figures on the gold bowl are not foreign to those on the ivories. This is better appreciated when the ivories and the gold bowl are studied alongside other related, local-style material excavated at Hasanlu, and not studied in isolation without reference to the corpus of excavated objects.

A clay cylinder seal from Burned Building III (62-841), certainly not an heirloom, depicts in a lower frieze two five-spoked, light, open-boxed chariots, each controlled by one man. They are probably gods, for the chariots are drawn by leonine creatures with open mouths. Although the chariots and riders are not specifically related to the ivories in style and scene, they are related to the chariot scene on the gold bowl. Two small plaques from BB III (a total of twelve were found), one bronze (62-1059), the other iron (62-1055), with holes for attachment to a backing, depict in the former a chariot involved in a lion hunt, and in the latter, two chariots and a cavalryman galloping. The boxes on both chariots are light and staffed by one figure; spokes are not visible. The plaques are thus close to the gold bowl and clay seal, but the hunt (*infra*) and battle scenes relate them also to the ivories. In the bronze lion-hunting scene the chariot horse's front feet are raised off the ground, whereas on the iron plaque all the horses have their feet grounded—although there is no ground line. Only one head and two feet are depicted on these and the other metal plaques discussed here. On another bronze plaque from BB III (62-1061) a horseman hunts two goat-like creatures. The horse's legs are raised; this horse and the one on the plaque 62-1059 mentioned above are to my knowledge the only examples at Hasanlu where horses are depicted with their front feet raised.

On still another plaque, this one of silver (64-475) and broken, from Room 6 of BB II, there is depicted a man in a chariot. The man shoots with a bow. The horse is a stallion with all feet grounded; it has a round harness attachment on the body below its neck, and there is a triangular object pendent from its neck. Except for the fact that only one man staffs the chariot, the scene is like those on the ivories.

The electrum figures inlaid in two bands on the silver beaker from Hasanlu (Muscarella 1966, fig. 10; Dyson 1968, fig. 129; Porada 1967, 2972 ff.) are engaged in a battle or post-battle scene above, and a hunt scene below. The upper scene depicts a chariot, cavalry and archers, functioning together in one extended scene. The chariot is drawn by two horses of which both heads and the body of one horse are depicted; all the feet are grounded. The box is staffed by a charioteer and an archer and has six-spoked wheels. All these features relate the beaker scene to those on the ivories. Differentiating it from the ivories is the fact that there are crossed quivers on the box, a bird-headed yoke pole is shown, the archer shoots backward, the charioteer seems to wear a pointed helmet, and the body of an enemy is placed not under the horses but across the top of one wheel. These are features recognizable from Assyrian art and not otherwise represented at Hasanlu (Porada 1967, 2974 f.; Layard 1849, pl. 13; cf. pl. 11).

In the same battle scene is a horse attached by a tether to a dismounted cavalry archer who holds a man by his wrists. This man is not armed and may be a captured enemy; he wears the same clothing as the others, however, and has the same physiognomy and fillet, as does also the enemy on the wheel. They are followed by another archer who holds an arrow awkwardly by its end (Dyson 1964a, fig. 3), reminding us of the way the cavalryman of no. 33 holds his spear. Both archers on the beaker wear quivers, as they do on ivory no. 53, but details of body decoration and clothing of the beaker warriors are not paralleled on the ivories. Likewise, the body decoration of the animals is not the same as that of the ivory cavalry and chariot horses but is similar in general concept to that on other ivories, of apparent Iranian style, from Hasanlu (cf. nos. 214–221, *infra*), and on examples of Iranian metal work (Muscarella 1972, 25 ff.).

The lower scene shows the hunting of a bull, a lion and a third beast, by an archer who is dressed in the same clothing as the warriors in the upper scene.

The silver beaker, then, has some parallels and some differences when compared with the ivories, and it is executed in a slightly cruder fashion. Nevertheless, the scenes are not foreign in form and iconography to those on the ivories, and not, I suggest, chronologically distant (Porada 1967, 2972, 2977; 1972, 168; 1975, 393).

Another iron plaque (62-1057), part of the same BB III group discussed above, depicts six cavalrymen galloping right, three above and three below, without any ground lines. The metal is corroded but we can see that the men wear belts and boots but do not carry arms, and that all the horses' feet are grounded. Of further importance for our discussion is the fact that the men wear the distinctive "feathered" helmet worn also by the foot soldiers on the ivories. Three more bronze plaques from the same provenience and series as the others depict archers in battle. On 62-1058 three kneeling archers shoot right and are preceded by a small man walking right. On 62-1054 two archers wearing turbans (?) and quivers shoot from a kneeling position, back to back, just like the archers on no. 53; on either side and between them are other standing archers, without quivers. Finally, 62-1066 depicts two archers shooting left and two right, each group kneeling on a city-wall turret that projects above the walls. Thus this plaque must represent a siege scene, again duplicating a scene represented on the ivories.

There are still other metal plaques and some clay sealings with representations of horses all of which have their feet grounded even though they are in action. One sealing in local style, (64-658) has a horse with a triangular object pendent at its neck, perhaps a bell,[4] just like the silver plaque (64-475) mentioned above. Thus we see that this triangular object occurs on horses represented on the ivories, on metal plaques and also on seals, all of local style. If they are bells, they apparently are the earliest dated examples depicted on horses' necks in the Near East.

Summing up the evidence presented, it becomes clear that at Hasanlu battle scenes with representations of chariots, cavalry and foot soldiers, including archers, and siege scenes were commonly represented not only on the ivories but also on the locally made metal plaques, metal vessels, and cylinder seals. Moreover, specific details such as the grounded horses' feet, the triangular object at the horses' necks, the round harness disc, the "feathered" helmet, and so forth, were part of the artistic repertory at Hasanlu, and were not monopolized by one group of craftsmen. The local craftsmen working in different materials had the freedom to depict different types of chariots with one or more occupants, and different creatures drawing them, depending on the internal conditions of the scene represented. No mythological chariots occur on the ivories and on most of the other objects mentioned above, except the gold bowl and one or two sealings; rather most of the representations are concerned with real-life affairs. And although it is quite obvious that battle scenes occur out of doors, no background details—trees, rocks, rivers, hills—are ever depicted. This means that the actions of the figures themselves give the essence and reality to a scene with no subsidiary elements offered as clues to the locale of the action depicted.

Moving now from an examination of the internal local comparanda for the battle scenes depicted on the ivories to an examination of material from further afield in other areas of the Near East, it becomes readily evident that the Hasanlu scenes are by no means unique. In fact, they belong to a large repertory existing in the West, in particular in North Syrian and Assyrian art, and one may, I believe, talk of a *koine* of such scenes in the ninth century B.C.

Beginning with the Assyrian evidence first we note that battle scenes began to be represented in art by the late second millennium B.C., as known from the stone pyxis lid and apparently also the altar base of Tukulti-Ninurta I (1247–1207 B.C.) (Andrae 1938, pls. 49b, 51a; Güterbock 1957, 65, pl. 21:1) and continued with the "Broken Obelisk" and the glazed brick tiles of Tiglath-Pileser I (ca. 1100 B.C.) and those of Tukulti-Ninurta II in the early ninth century B.C. (Frankfort 1955, pl. 73a; Andrae 1923, pls. 6-9). The stone reliefs of Ashurnasirpal II (884–859 B.C.) and the bronze gates of his son Shalmaneser III (859–824 B.C.) are indeed the *Blütezeit* in Mesopotamia for such representations and, along with a few ivory plaques from this period (Mallowan and Davies 1970, pl. XVI), are the examples from Assyria that are most relevant to our discussion. The White Obelisk, if belonging to Ashurnasirpal II,[5] would be another ninth century Assyrian example of such scenes. What is of interest with respect to the Hasanlu ivories is that the Assyrians had a long tradition of representing battle scenes, that the partly contemporary (?) and partly earlier stone and bronze reliefs of Ashurnasirpal and Shalmaneser are vigorous and

[4]This sealing reminds us of a seal from Sialk B, where a horse also wears a bell at the neck (Ghirshman 1939, pls. 56, 96, S810). Note also a horse represented on a vessel (pl. 81) that has an object pendent from the neck: a bell?

[5]The date of this obelisk is disputed and there are good arguments presented by both those who claim it was made during the reign of Ashurnasirpal I and those who would date it to the time of Ashurnasirpal II. Recently Sollberger (1974) argued forcefully for the later date but Julian Reade (1975) argued equally strongly for the earlier period. Both Sollberger and Reade give an extensive bibliography; add to those who support a date in the time of Ashurnasirpal I, Porada (1967, 2974), Canby (1971, 37, note 37), J. Börker-Klähn ("Haartrachen," *Reallexikon* 1972: 28), Albenda (1972, 169); in the time of Ashurnasirpal II, Orthmann (1975, 315), Muscarella (*JNES* 35,3 [1976]: 210), J. M. Munn-Rankin (*Iraq* 36, 1/2 [1974]: 170, note 8).

extensive examples of these scenes, and that the Hasanlu ivory representations certainly must be examined against this background. Indeed, the existence of similar scenes both on the Hasanlu ivories and in the earlier and partly contemporary art of Assyria cannot be fortuitous and it seems logical to assume that the Hasanlu craftsmen were aware of their existence to the west. The similarities are seen at best in the general concept, which is closer to that of Assyria than to North Syria (*infra*), particularly in the representation in art of major battles, and cities under siege depicting together chariots, cavalry, archers and foot soldiers, all forming a continuous narrative (Güterbock 1957, 62 f.). To be sure, there are differences in motifs and details, differences that, as will be demonstrated below, document the fact that the ivory carvers were also stimulated by the art of North Syria.

The Assyrian chariot of the ninth century B.C. (*viz*. Hrouda 1963, 155, 158; 1965, 94 ff., pls. 26, 30, 61, 63; Yadin 1963, 298; Madhloom 1970, 12 ff., pls. 1, 2, 10; Littauer 1972, 154 f.) had a solid box resting on a six-spoked wheel, with the axle usually resting far back under the box, two crossed quivers on the side of the box, and a spear and shield placed at the rear. Usually two men, a charioteer and an archer, staffed the chariot; sometimes, presumably only in the king's chariot, a third man is shown. An elliptical object connected the chariot box to the end of the yoke pole, which terminated usually with some decoration such as a creature's head. At the time of Ashurnasirpal II there were usually three horses represented, the third apparently running free of the yoke (Littauer 1972, 153; Kantor 1962, fig. 3; Madhloom 1970, 16); on the White Obelisk, and on the Balawat Gates of Shalmaneser III only two horses are represented. All the horses' heads are shown, and a single foot for each; when sex is drawn, the horses are all stallions. In the great majority of cases, moreover, the front feet of the horses are raised off the ground to express motion and attack. This feature existed from the time when chariots were first depicted in Assyrian art (Madhloom 1970, pl. V). When walking, i.e., when not in battle, Assyrian horses usually have all feet on the ground, although sometimes here too one or both feet may be raised (Mallowan 1966, fig. 371c, g; Boehmer 1968, Biel 3:6). It is true that in a few instances Assyrian horses in battle or hunting have all feet grounded, but this is rare (Barnett n.d., pl. 164; Porada 1948, no. 661).

Assyrian chariot horses sometimes wear a frontlet (Kantor 1962, 96, fig. 3) and a feathered headdress (Budge 1914, pls. XVII, XVIII, XX, XXIII, XXV; Hrouda 1963, 97, pl. 29; Madhloom 1970, 14, pl. VIII), but apparently not bells, which became common later (Godard 1950, 102, fig. 87; Hrouda 1963, pls. 26, 27; Calmeyer 1969, 112, 115; Moorey 1971, 137 f.; cf. Wilkinson 1975, figs. 14, 14a). In battle scenes it was common to represent an enemy soldier, dead or wounded, under the horses' legs; sometimes he was clothed (Madhloom 1970, pl. II; Barnett n.d., pls. 144, 147, 150, etc.), other times nude (Barnett n.d., pls. 142, 150). In hunt scenes the animal is sometimes trampled by the chariot horses (Porada 1948, no. 660; Canby 1971, pl. XIII).

These Assyrian motifs clearly follow earlier Egyptian and Near Eastern art in many details, especially the vigorous chariot position where the king or another archer shoots at an enemy and where the horses' front feet are raised off the ground, sometimes trampling the victims (*viz*. Yadin 1963, 87 ff., 104 f., 186-88, etc.; Porada 1948, 971; Smith 1963, 34a, 38, 147c). The enemy trampled under the chariot goes back still further, to the third millennium B.C., as evidenced by the Ur Standard (Frankfort 1954, pl. 36; cf. pl. 34; Yadin 1963, 132-3). And it is interesting to note that the horses on the Standard are also stallions, a characteristic of chariot and cavalry horses all over the Near East. An Egyptian text of the fifteenth century B.C. confirms the preference for ungelded horses to draw chariots. Amen-em-heb tells us in his tomb biography that the Prince of Kadesh sent out a mare, presumably one in heat, to disrupt the Egyptian chariot horses. Only the courage of Amen-em-heb, who rushed out to dispatch the mare, prevented a catastrophe for the Egyptians (Pritchard 1955, 241). One wonders how common a tactic it was to send out mares in heat against enemy chariots.

Specific ninth century parallels with the Hasanlu ivories, aside from the general scheme, may be seen in the six-spoked wheels, the two horses in profile, a staff consisting of a charioteer and an archer, and a nude enemy trampled by the horses. A feathered headdress occurs on at least two horses represented on the ivories (nos. 5, 26 and 27?), but is lacking on the others; it was suggested that these horses with the headdress might be those of the enemy; no. 5 also has a decorated yoke-pole terminal that could be a version of an Assyrian type, or a form of a type represented at Malatya (Madhloom 1970, pls. I-III, VI, 5; an apparent example of a bronze terminal is in the Teheran Museum [Ghirshman 1964, fig. 168] said to come from Ziwiye). One may also note that the few apparent ninth century Assyrian ivory chariot scenes (Mallowan and Davies 1970, 15, 18, 26 f., 28 ff., nos. 55,

56, 62, 65, 66, 67) have no background scenery, although such scenery often occurs on the stone reliefs. Differences are more numerous: none of the Hasanlu chariots has crossed quivers on the box, nor a rear spear; none has the elliptical object connecting the box to the end of the yoke pole, and all the Hasanlu ivory horses have their front feet grounded, to my mind a significant feature.

Chariots represented on the few Assyrian ivories depicting battle scenes do not basically differ from those known from the stone reliefs and the bronze gates (Mallowan and Davies 1970, 26, no. 55; Barnett 1957, pls. XVIII, XXXIII, XXXIV).

Turning now to North Syrian art of the tenth and ninth centuries B.C. we note that in this region the chariots represented on reliefs also had a solid box resting on a six-spoked wheel that was placed either at the center or toward the rear of the box. Sometimes, but not universally, crossed quivers were attached to the box, and sometimes a spear and shield with a buckle were placed at the rear; and usually two men, a charioteer and an archer, staffed the chariot. An elliptical object occasionally joined the box to the yoke terminal, which sometimes was decorated; as mentioned above, no. 5 has terminals decorated like those at Malatya. The horses sometimes wore feathered headdresses and frontlets, although blinkers seem to be represented only on sculpture in the round (Bossert 1942, 905); no bells are represented (*viz.* Bossert 1942, 862, 863, 886; Orthmann 1971, pls. 24, 37a, b, 57a; Barnett 1957, pl. XVIII). A few of these details find parallels on the Hasanlu ivories but there are at least three specific motifs that distinctly relate the North Syrian chariot representations to those on the Hasanlu ivories: in most examples all the horses' legs are depicted grounded in action scenes (cf. however reliefs from Tell Halaf and Malatya: Orthmann 1971, pls. 11b-d, 42b; it is not clear if the front feet of the horse on pl. 42a are grounded or raised as they are on the same level as the lion's feet); a nude enemy is often under the horses' legs in a position definitely closer to the Hasanlu examples than are the Assyrian examples; and at Carchemish (later also at Sakçegözü) there is a guilloche border at the base of the orthostates. Moreover, the use of guilloche borders is very common on the ninth century North Syrian ivories from Nimrud (Barnett 1957, pls. XVIII-XX, etc.). To my mind, the existence on both the North Syrian reliefs and the Hasanlu ivories of the guilloche border, the same type and positioning of the trampled nude enemy, and, significantly, the grounded position of the horses' front feet, producing a static effect, in contrast to the dynamic Assyrian examples, is not fortuitous.[6]

To be sure, several of the details reported on the North Syrian reliefs and ivories—the elliptical object, the crossed quivers, the rear spear, details also found on the Assyrian reliefs—do not occur on the Hasanlu ivories; also, it was usual for the pairs of horses represented on the North Syrian reliefs to be shown as one horse, with one head, not the two that were surely there. More important, it was not characteristic of the North Syrian reliefs to represent major battle scenes with chariots, cavalry and foot soldiers juxtaposed (cf. Woolley and Barnett 1952, pls. 41-46, B 43a, for chariots and soldiers following one another). Reviewing the parallels between North Syrian art and the Hasanlu ivories against the details not shared—details that we have seen are shared with Assyrian art—still allows one to make a strong conclusion that North Syrian art strongly influenced the art of Hasanlu.[7]

The Assyrian cavalry appears in art for the first time during the reign of Ashurnasirpal II (Hrouda 1965, 100, 152), and continued to be represented often thereafter. The cavalryman carried a spear or a bow, or both (Madhloom 1970, pl. XXIV, 1; Reade 1972, 103). Usually two horses were depicted together, the second being either a spare mount (Barnett, n.d., 27), or the horse ridden by a squire (Budge 1914, fig. 122; Hrouda 1965, pl. 61:1). Often, a nude enemy is trampled by the horse (Hrouda 1965, pl. 62:1; Barnett n.d., pls. 147, 167).

The North Syrian cavalryman, less commonly represented than in Assyrian art, rode alone and carried a spear or a mace, or a bow (Vieyra 1955, fig. 95; Bossert 1942, 945); as with the chariot horses, all feet of the horse were grounded.

Little is preserved to us among the ivories (and the metal plaques discussed above) which depict the Hasanlu cavalry that allows for more than a general comparison with the Assyrian and North Syrian examples. As already pointed out, the Hasanlu cavalry are depicted as part of a large

[6]Moorey (1975, 27) sees Assyrian influence on ivory no. 1 here. It may be significant that both the Hasanlu and North Syrian guilloches have a central hole.

[7]Also probably derived from a North Syrian source are the chariot scenes depicted on ivories from Sparta in Greece, where in one case the horses' feet are flush with the ground and an animal is under the horses' legs (Dawkins 1929, pl. CXVI). The same source seems evident for chariots depicted on a bronze belt from Fortetsa on Crete (Brock 1957, 197 ff., pl. 168), where chariot horses have all feet grounded.

battle scene, more typical of Assyrian than North Syrian art. Only one foot of the cavalryman is shown on no. 33 (also on the metal plaques), a feature more common in Assyrian than in North Syrian art, although in both areas two feet may be shown (Farkas 1969, 60, 61, 63), and this is not necessarily significant. Of special interest, I suggest, are the grounded feet of the horses, a convention which makes us look to North Syria for references.

Very close parallels exist in Assyrian art for the representations of the siege of a city, nos. 69-71 (and also the bronze plaque, 62-1066). This is a common theme throughout Assyrian art of the ninth and following centuries, reflecting a continuity of an earlier stock theme (Yadin 1963, 96, 229). The woman holding her hair (no. 69) is neatly paralleled on a stone relief from Nimrud (Hrouda 1965, pl. 41:4; Muscarella 1966, fig. 17; for later examples, Barnett and Falkner 1962, pls. XXXVII-VIII, XLV, L, LI, XC). Warriors mounting a ladder placed against city walls (no. 70) are also numerous in Assyrian art from the ninth century onward on both stone and ivory reliefs (Barnett n.d., 142, 159, 160, 169; Barnett and Falkner 1962, pls. XXXVII-VIII, XL, LXI, LXXIX; Mallowan and Davies 1970, 35, no. 92).

A fragmented Assyrianizing ivory plaque, claimed to derive from Ziwiye, depicts a cavalryman and a fortress-city (Wilkinson 1975, figs. 13, 13a). Unfortunately, very little of the original ivory is preserved, so we do not know if inhabitants were depicted. I can find no other Assyrian or other example to parallel the couple holding each other (no. 71), but it is not foreign to the general theme of the Assyrian siege scene (cf. Mallowan and Herrmann 1974, no. 43, pls. L, LI; Layard 1849, pl. 62).

The "feathered" helmet, if that is what in fact it really was, has no prototype among the few helmets excavated at Hasanlu, nor can I find any exact parallels represented in art from other cultures. Many examples of helmets with attached crests are represented, as for example on North Syrians and Urartians (Barnett n.d., pls. 165, 169; Borchardt 1972, 103 f., pls. 26, 38:5, Beil E, F). These crested helmets are not dissimilar to bronze helmets and to several displaced crests excavated at Hasanlu (Borchardt 1972, pl. 40:2) but not represented in art there. Intriguing is an Assyrian-style ivory plaque from Nimrud depicting a battle scene (Mallowan and Davies 1970, no. 55). An enemy soldier wears a round helmet, perhaps made of leather, that has ear flaps and pointed objects projecting from the top. Mallowan and Davies call these objects crests but it seems that feathers are represented (also Barnett 1967, 2997; Borchardt 1972, 106, Beil E I A 4). This helmet is not like those depicted on our ivories, nor are they similar to those worn by Urartians on the Balawat Gates (*pace* Mallowan). Yet if feathers are represented on the Nimrud ivory they could be an Assyrian version of a helmet similar to, or the same type as, those on our ivories. Interestingly, but apparently without significance, the closest parallels for the Hasanlu ivory "feathered" helmet are those worn by Philistines (Borchardt 1972, 115 ff., pls. 16-18; cf. Barnett, 1967, 2998, who denies that the Philistine headdress is feathered).

Feathered hats or crowns, as opposed to helmets, occur on three ivory fragments, two perhaps from the same plaque (nos. 98, 102), in scenes that appear to be peaceful.[8] This type of headdress is well represented in ancient art from early times. For example, it is to be seen on a limestone plaque from Tello (Pritchard *ANEP,* 598); on a sphinx represented on the fresco from Mari (Strommenger 1962, pl. XXIX); on a Middle Assyrian ivory plaque from Assur (Moortgat 1969, 114, pl. 241); Babylonian kings of the Isin II period also wear them (Strommenger 1962, figs. 270-272; Seidl 1968, 45, 84; cf. Layard 1853, 508). In Iran the headdress goes back to the third millennium B.C. relief of Annubani and may also occur on a seal from Susa (Amiet 1966, 156a, c; Porada 1965, fig. 15). It appears on a bronze quiver of tenth/ninth century date, probably from Iran (Muscarella 1974d, no. 138), on a pin said to be from Luristan (Ghirshman 1964, fig. 96), and on a bronze tripod of unknown provenience (Moorey 1972, 143 f., pl. Ia).

A seated goddess on the White Obelisk of Ashurnasirpal I or II wears a feathered crown (Sollberger 1974, fig. 1); it is also depicted on Assyrian seals (Moortgat 1940, nos. 608, 610). In North Syria it is seen on reliefs from Tell Halaf and Malatya (Orthmann 1971, 121, 316, pls. 8b, 11f, 43b, d). Eighth century Assyrian Lamassu wear feathered headdresses, as do figures on seventh century reliefs, some of which depict Elamites (Madhloom 1970, 83, pls. XLIV, LIII; Barnett 1967, figs. 1063-65; Hrouda 1965, 46, pls. 7:8, 10).[8a] Falkner (1952, 131 f.)

---

[8]The feathered crown may also be represented on one of the figures depicted on the bronze tetrapod from Hasanlu, but if so, it seems to be of a different type from those on the ivories (Dyson 1964a, 6f., fig. 5).

[8a]I do not agree with Barnett (1967, 2998) that this type of headdress is represented at Sialk, period B; nor do I believe that there is any evidence to support his assumption that figures with feathered headdresses represented on the reliefs of Sennacherib and Assurbanipal are Medes and Persians, respectively (3002, 3005, figs. 1063-65). Further, and parenthetically, I suggest that

recognized such a headdress on the "Ziwiye" gorget. And later, of course, it is common at Persepolis where it is worn by Persians (Ghirshman 1964, figs. 226, 235, 236, 238). What its significance at Hasanlu was remains unclear, nor do we know if its occurrence there is a result of indigenous Iranian influence or of influence from the West—Assyria, Babylon and North Syria. Nevertheless, the feathered helmet was in use in Western Iran in the early first millennium B.C. as evidenced by both the Hasanlu bronzes and the ivories.

Ninth century Assyrian soldiers usually wore a short, knee-length tunic and either went barefoot or wore sandals (Madhloom 1970, 69, pls. XVI, XXXVII, XLV, XLIX, L). North Syrian soldiers also are shown either with or without sandals (Orthmann 1971, pls. 8d; 9d, 3; 25d; 28e, f; 29a; 31a-d; 57f; 61b). Barefoot soldiers are an old motif in Egyptian and Near Eastern art (*viz.* Strommenger 1962, figs. 72, 114, 117) and the warriors at Hasanlu fit into this background (cf. Wilkinson 1975, figs. 15, 17-19).

The closest parallels for the small round shield occur on the Balawat Gates where they are held by Urartians (Madhloom 1970, pl. XXVII). Relatively small shields are also carried by North Syrians (Bossert 1942, 945; 1951, 481), and by Assyrians or their auxiliaries (Madhloom 1970, pl. XXVII). Shields carried by hunters on the ivories said to come from Ziwiye are smaller and of a different type from those represented at Hasanlu (Godard 1950, figs. 80, 81, 83, 85, and pages 99 f.; Wilkinson 1975, 44, figs. 15, 15b, 17). Falkner (1952, 130) and Porada (1965, 127) see them as *Schlagring,* or brass knuckles. Furthermore, small shields have been excavated at sites in Luristan (Vanden Berghe 1971, 266; 1975, figs. 6-8, 15), demonstrating their actual use in combat.

Unfortunately, we do not have any textual information that would allow us to recognize the reasons for the existence of the warfare scenes on the locally made ivories. They could have been purely decorative, or even political in intent, copies of the type of scenes known to exist in Assyria and North Syria, and therefore a kind of art proper for royalty to possess. Inasmuch as Western reliefs reflected the power and glory of local royal families, it seems logical to assume that the same attitudes were appreciated by the ruler(s) of Hasanlu. Thus, we might conclude that not only were Western artistic values appropriated at Hasanlu; the political values were appropriated also. [See now Winter, 1977.] At the same time, the ivory reliefs could have been carved as representations of an actual historical event—or a conflation of a series of events—involving a successful campaign—or campaigns—of the local dynasty. The fact that it has been demonstrated that such scenes had their origin to the west, and were adopted by the local artists, does not, of course, preclude the conclusion, or suggestion, that the scenes depict an actual historical event of significance to the local people. One might speculate that it would be strange for the local ruler to have representations of a battle that involved a victorious foreign state. Therefore, I suggest that, although ultimately we do not know the reasons for the existence of such scenes, it is possible to interpret them as depictions of an historical event involving the ancient city of Hasanlu, celebrated locally and given continuous value by its representation in art. In short, we have the very same situation that existed with respect to Assyrian art and history. Moreover, evidence has been presented from the archaeological finds at Hasanlu that the local army employed horses, bows, spears, maces, body armor, and horse bells. No small shields have been excavated, nor a feathered helmet or headdress, but these may have been of perishable materials, especially the headdress, which seems to have been of leather (but cf. the metal crested helmets). Nor has any specific chariot equipment been recognized. Nevertheless, to a large extent, the artifacts depicted on the ivories are duplicated by the artifacts excavated in the same cultural context.

---

false historical and archaeological conclusions result from assigning ethnic identifications to figures represented in art without ancient attributions. Thus Barnett (2997 f., fig. 1055) identifies figures represented on a ninth century Assyrian relief as Iranians—which is pure guesswork, the same guesswork that led Sulimirski (*Artibus Asiae* XVII [1954]: 282 ff., fig. 1) to label these figures Scythians!

Calmeyer (1969, 156) states that an archer represented on an axe blade (his fig. 68) wears a "Federkranz," but my eyes do not see it; nor do I see this type of headdress worn by figures represented on a vase fragment from Bismaya, as Calmeyer maintains (157; see also Frankfort 1954, 19). He also refers (186) to a "Federkranz-Leute," which I do not believe can be supported by the evidence presented.

II

HUMAN HEADS AND BODIES: DRINKING AND PROCESSION SCENES

A large variety of bodies and heads depicted in local style and involved in drinking and/or apparent procession scenes exist on many fragments. Most were excavated in the fill of BB II Room 8 or the adjacent area of the great hall; a few others derive from Rooms 6 and 7 and the neighboring area to the east.

While the figures exhibit differences in details they nevertheless share other features in common. Nearly all the heads are executed in high relief with incised lines representing hair, eyes and sometimes the mouth. Eyes are usually oval, less frequently lozenge-shaped; sometimes a round dowel functioned conveniently as the eye. Noses are in relief and always prominent; sometimes they are sharp, other times fleshy; some noses are straight-bridged, others have an angle separating them from the brow. Ears when depicted are S-shaped and relatively large, in relief. Lips are usually rendered as a thick U on its side; a few are thin slits. Hair is rendered in several fashions: it is worn long and straight, short and straight, braided long or short; on some occasions it is worn short with chunky segments, and in spiral curls. The hair is usually held by a fillet. Beards are either scraggly, with thick incised lines, or they are thick and rendered in small chunky units. Faces without beards are always long and thin, with a prominent jaw. All the faces are in profile, never frontal.

A rough division of some of the heads into units based on general similarities in execution and details of physiognomy may be worked out although some units overlap each other and it is impossible to place every head in a specific unit. Heads in high relief, with thick straight hair that flares out at the neck, sharp pointed nose, thick beard, thick lips, and no ears: nos. 62, 76, 77, 78, 83; related are nos. 63, 81, 82, 120, 174 left. Some of these are certainly from the same workshop: nos. 77 and 78, 81, 82, 120. Others are clearly from different hands: cf. the fingers of no. 76 to 77 and 78; nos. 62 and 63 both have lozenge-shaped eyes but the latter is the better executed piece. Nos. 102 and 106 are fairly close to the others in hair and beard but are executed differently. No. 98 is also related, but the figures are rather crudely executed and have short fleshy noses and apparently undecorated hair. The warriors nos. 54, 55A, and 57 also have the flaring-out hair at the neck, the thick lips, straight-bridged noses, and scraggly hair.

Another unit has large fleshy noses, thin mouths, a long jaw, a large S-shaped ear, no beard, braided hair extending to the feet or to the small of the back, and a fillet: nos. 88-91, 92 left and right, and 93. Nos. 92 and 93, although probably from similar types of objects, are clearly from different workshops. These figures are all participants in a procession and may represent special functionaries. Nos. 96 and 111 and 112 are apparently also part of a procession. No. 96 has a scraggly beard and long straight hair, but is stylistically close to no. 89, and also to no. 92 center. Nos. 111 and 112 have the same heads and may be from the same plaque.[9]

Another unit that might be singled out consists of nos. 84, 85, and 87, perhaps also no. 86. They were executed in relatively low relief, have sharp noses, thin lips, S-shaped ears, flat heads with fillets or ribands. They too show some variation for nos. 84 and 86 have long thin braided hair, while no. 87 seems to have long straight hair.

The figures on no. 73, although definitely related to the other heads, form another unit. Their noses dominate their faces, only equalled by those of no.

[9]The objects carried by one of the men on no. 111 look very much like the arrow carried by the archer on the gold bowl.

71 and perhaps no. 69. There are no ears depicted, beards are scraggly, mouths only a slit, and their hair is rendered as short with a herringbone braid.

Other heads stand out as being almost unique within the corpus: nos. 75, 79, 80, 121, 122, and 97. The fact that there is such a large variety of heads with different details from one example to the next gives us a clear indication that the local craftsmen were not restricted by any artistic convention to producing one or two uniform types. Parenthetically one may add that this fact also makes it easier to accept the figures on the gold bowl and silver beaker as being part of the Hasanlu IV repertory of local forms, and not necessarily of a much earlier date or from a separate center.

Given the reservations expressed above when discussing the battle scenes that we have no controls concerning whether an individual craftsman might vary his execution and use of details from plaque to plaque, it would be rash to conclude that each head type or variety came from a separate workshop (cf. no. 174 where two different hair styles are depicted on the same plaque). Nevertheless, the evidence reinforces the conclusion suggested above that there were at least a half-dozen workshops, perhaps even more.

In addition to the full figures and isolated heads there are several headless bodies and parts of bodies that collectively give us important information about the activities depicted and probably practiced at Hasanlu. All the figures on nos. 73 and 74 drink from a beaker-like vessel held in the right hand and hold a staff in the left. Drinking from vessels held in the right hand is also depicted on nos. 75-78, 92 center, and 118. Nos. 98-101 carry staffs but do not drink, and they are apparently involved in a procession. Also seemingly involved in a procession are nos. 89-91, 96, 97, 111 and 112. Nos. 92 and 93, and perhaps 88, to judge from his gorget, may be involved in a presentation scene, or another procession. One may speculate that the seated figures of nos. 116-119 are also part of these scenes. Likewise involved in some type of procession are the "wheat bearers", nos. 112-114.

From the full figures and headless bodies it is possible to make some observations about the several different types of clothing represented: a knee-length garment with the bottom bordered and fringed, and a belt, is worn by the two standing figures on no. 73; the seated figure has no belt and has a decorated rear border. A knee-length garment with a thick-fringed hem and a fringe or decoration along the length is worn by nos. 102, 103, 107, 108, 116, 118, and apparently no. 109; the garment worn by no. 93 is similar, with a plain belt and a stitching or fringe along the length. A very short, groin-length kilt, pleated, perhaps with a belt, is worn by the figures of no. 92. A long ankle-length garment is also depicted: one with a wide belt, a fringed lower border, and with vertical and horizontal decoration is worn by no. 97; a plain garment with a wide decorated belt is worn by no. 89. A loose-sleeved garment is worn by no. 74, perhaps also no. 99; and a sleeveless garment is worn by no. 75.

Where visible the figures wear sandals except no. 97, and perhaps the standing figures on no. 73, who all seem to be barefoot, and no. 103 who wears boots (cf. no. 33). Most of the wrists have bracelets, except nos. 91b, 110, and 115, a feature also recognized on the warrior's wrists.[10] A few figures wear gorgets, nos. 88, 92, 93; only one figure, no. 80, a male, wears a necklace (cf. nos. 127 and 230); none wears a torque—a penanular necklace—a type excavated from Hasanlu IV and Dinkha II and III, the Iron I and II periods (Muscarella 1974c, 48, 80). Only one example of a brooch was depicted, that on a statuette, no. 127 (*infra*).

A few individuals have curved concentric lines on their joints, nos. 61, 65, 105, a feature found on other examples of Iranian art (Porada 1965, fig. 60; 1972, 166, figs. 1-4; Muscarella 1972, 25 ff., 41, note 21, figs. 1-11, 15, 16), and also on the Hasanlu gold bowl.[11]

Three non-ivory objects from Hasanlu, all published, have human representations that invite comparisons with the ivories. A bronze tetrapod stand (Dyson 1964a, 5 ff., figs. 4, 5) has eight human figures in relief, two on each of the four legs. The figures are no longer clear because of corrosion but one can see that they all wear calf-length garments with fringed borders; all but one or two (corrosion?) have belts, and at least three have some incised decoration at the rear below the belts. Their hats are high, either rectangular or rounded, turbans perhaps; one hat may have feathers. All the figures but one have a projection at the back of the neck that could be flaring hair. Facial characteristics are unclear but a few seem to have scraggly beards, a thin slit for a mouth and no ears. Although each figure holds a hand to his mouth no vessel is visible and the gesture

[10]Porada (1967, 2972, and 1972, 166) refers to parallel lines on the wrists of figures on the Hasanlu gold bowl and the silver fragments in the Sackler collection (*infra*) as wrist markings, which I suggest is incorrect. Many of the wrist markings on the Hasanlu ivories are in relief and can only be bracelets. Bracelets are very common in Iron II graves at Hasanlu and contemporary Dinkha Tepe (Muscarella 1974c, figs. 26, 36, 45, 48, and p. 80).

[11]Porada (1972, 164 ff.) accepts these curved lines as criteria for evidence of a late second millennium date. This is disproved by the Hasanlu ivories.

may be that of a supplicant. Their execution is not so neat as that of the ivories, no doubt reflecting the difference between casting and carving, but in deportment and in the type of clothing depicted they are related to the figures on the ivories and are probably contemporary.

The silver beaker with electrum figures, already discussed above, has warriors with shoulder-length straight hair held by a fillet. Their noses are sharp and long, eyes are round, and mouths and ears are not depicted. They wear either thigh-length belted kilts with tassels at the bottom (cf. kilts on the gold bowl), or knee-length belted garments, both types being richly decorated; they also all wear bracelets. The execution of the figures, including the animals, is more static and awkward than that of the ivories, and there are fewer facial details, but the face profiles and the hair styles relate them stylistically to the ivories.

Finally, there is the gold bowl. Here the figures seem related but are a step removed, so to speak. On the gold bowl the figures wear both thigh-length kilts and long ankle-length garments; the top figures have a stitch-like decoration on their clothing, reminding us of the same feature on no. 93. Fillets are worn by some of the figures and they divide the vertically striated crown hair from the straight hair below. (Note that the females' hair is distinguished from the males', being depicted by incised triangles.) All the figures wear bracelets and some arm and leg joints are outlined with concentric curved lines. There is also represented a figure seated on a throne that rests on a lion (cf. no. 118), and it is possible that the figure holding a cup in the top register is to be understood as drinking, rather than as pouring out a libation (cf. Mellink 1966, 71). Differences exist mainly in the types of scenes represented, none of which exactly matches a scene on any ivory; also the few ears depicted are not S-shaped, and the lips are always thin. Furthermore, the theme of the bowl's representations is distinctly religious or mythological, apparently each figure being a god or hero, whereas almost all of the ivory representations under discussion appear to involve humans.

Some silver fragments purchased on the antiquities market, and probably from a site in Iran, now in the Sackler Collection of Columbia University, depict a procession of warriors (Porada 1972, 163 ff.; 1975, 373, 392 f., Abb. 308). Their hair styles and large noses are similar to those on the Hasanlu gold bowl and to some on the ivories. The warriors' clothing is unlike that of any figure from Hasanlu, but the manner in which the procession is depicted finds a parallel with representations on glass vessels from Hasanlu (*infra*). Porada (1972, 170) dated the silver fragments to the twelfth or eleventh century B.C., but I suggest they could be a century or two later; their faces, hair, fillets, noses, concentric elbow lines, bracelets, and the procession itself, all occur in ninth century contexts at Hasanlu, on the gold bowl, the glass vessel, and on the ivories. (Later, Porada [1975, 392 f.] dated the fragments to the eleventh/tenth century B.C.)

The figures shown seated on a chair/throne are either kings or deities. Surely the figure on no. 118 is a deity, given the nature of the animal base. This motif is an old one, although less common than the representation of a deity standing directly on a bull or lion (*viz.* Kyrieleis 1969, 65 f.). The motif is very early in origin and occurs, for example, in the Early Dynastic period (Frankfort 1954, 23, fig. 12, two bulls; Orthmann 1975, Abb. 79b), on an Elamite seal of the second millennium (Amiet 1966, fig. 239B, a lion; cf. figs. 156A, 249), on Kassite and Mitannian seals (Smith 1963, fig. 153C, a bull; Porada 1948, nos. 575e, 1029, 1030 lions?),[12] and in early Assyrian art (Strommenger 1962, 95, fig. 179:3; Porada 1948, no. 854). It continues into the first millennium in Assyrian art (Porada 1948, no. 694), in North Syrian art (Vieyra 1955, fig. 51, a lion, and fig. 65, a bull), and in Urartian art (Barnett 1974, pl. XI, a bull). At Hasanlu itself we find it, aside from the ivory, on the gold bowl. A bronze quiver, not scientifically excavated but probably from Iran, depicts a male deity seated on a throne supported by a lion (Ghirshman 1964, fig. 423; Moorey 1975, fig. 7); he holds a cup for drinking, just like no. 118. This example may be contemporary or perhaps slightly later than the Hasanlu examples. Note that, aside from the sculptures (*infra*), no. 118 is the only recognized representation of a deity on the ivories, as no. 116 could be an important personage, perhaps a king.

Nos. 116 and 117 (also no. 119?) are apparently scenes where a king or other important person sits among his servants and guards. It is possible that these ivories could have represented a type of banquet scene, comparable to no. 73; if so, some of the fragments representing drinkers might have belonged to these plaques. Nos. 118 and 119 preserve parts of tripods, which would fit into a banquet scene. Indeed, the seated figure on no. 116 carries a staff, but in his left hand; if he held a vessel it

[12]Note that the seal no. 1030 (see also Strommenger 1962, 95, fig. 179) and an earlier Akkadian seal (Porada 1948, no. 239e) depict a woman holding a child on her lap, reminding us of a gold Hittite statuette of a goddess who holds her child on her lap (Muscarella 1974d, no. 125).

would have been in his right hand. A guard on no. 117 carries his spear head down, which surely suggests peaceful intent and a non-belligerent scene; beyond this we cannot speculate.

Some seals from the late second millennium at Tchoga Zanbil depict banquet scenes with the same features as on our ivories (Muscarella 1974a, 245, 249; Porada 1970, 57 ff., 65 f., nos. 61, 62). The scene is also depicted closer in time on the tenth/ninth century bronze beakers from western Iran (Calmeyer 1973, 18 ff., 34 f.; Muscarella 1974a, 239 ff., 245 f.), and at Sialk B, ninth/eighth century (Ghirshman 1939, pl. XCVI, S1975, 1521). It is also of interest to note here that the buttocks of the seated figure on no. 118 are decorated, outlined with a semicircular band, a common feature of seated figures on the bronze beakers.

In the West, banquet scenes are extensively represented in ninth century North Syrian art. Both one- and two-sided banquet scenes existed in North Syria, whereas in Iran they are usually of the former type. Both types existed earlier in Syrian and Hittite culture, for example at Ebla and at Alaca Hüyük and Yağri (Matthiae 1973, 483, fig. 156; Bossert 1942, 513, 516, 571), and this may account for the continuity of the two types in North Syria, although some features found on the North Syrian banquet scenes (Muscarella 1974a, 245, 246; 1970, 27, note 44) also occur on the Iranian scenes. No. 73 reinforces the conclusion that one-sided banquet scenes were preferred in Iran; and an ivory said to be from Ziwiye, in Assyrian style (Godard 1950, fig. 78), also depicts a one-sided scene.

In ninth century Assyrian art there are scenes where the king holds a vessel, sometimes to pour, other times apparently to drink, but these cannot be called banquet scenes (Porada 1948, 79 f., nos. 664-672; Mallowan 1966, fig. 21; Strommenger 1962, figs. 194, 195; cf. fig. 260, below, where the king pours rather than prepares to drink).

Representations of processions of a peaceful nature were not uncommon at Hasanlu, for aside from the ivories they are found there on three fragmentary glass vessels (von Saldern 1966, 10 ff., figs. 1-9; 1970, 209 f., 216 f., figs. 8-13; Porada 1972, 170 ff., fig. 8). None of the figures on the glass vessels carries a staff, nor is a seated figure preserved. And in head, dress, and body characteristics we find no relationship to the figures on the ivories. Von Saldern has argued for a ninth century date for the vessels "reflecting an older, Kassite style—and exported east" (von Saldern 1966, 23 f.; 1970, 210), while Porada (1972, 168 ff.) argues for a late second millennium date, seeing the vessels as heirlooms. Whatever the date of the vessels, which is an art historical problem, they were available to the ninth century craftsmen at Hasanlu. Thus, although no recognizable Kassite elements are evident on the ivories, it is not impossible that the procession scenes owe their inspiration to Kassite art. At the same time because of the common depiction of processions in ancient art one cannot automatically assume only one source of inspiration at Hasanlu, a situation obviously existing for other motifs noted there. In North Syria, for example, we find such scenes depicted on reliefs and ivories (Bossert 1942, 842-846, 911-914; Barnett 1957, pls. XVI, XVII, S3: eighth century?). The North Syrians themselves could have borrowed the procession scene from earlier Hittite examples (Akurgal 1962, pl. XIV, 75-80, 92, fig. 19) and not necessarily from the Kassites.

A rather close parallel between some of the Hasanlu procession scenes (nos. 98, 99, 100) and two joining ivory fragments said to have come from Ziwiye has been discussed by Dyson (1964a, 7, figs. 12, 13; see also Godard 1950, figs. 91, 92; Ghirshman 1964, fig. 135; Moorey 1967, 88 f.; Porada 1975, fig. 114). In addition to the general theme of the procession, one should note that the figures on the "Ziwiye" fragments hold staffs in both hands before the body, that they have vertically striated crown hair separated by a fillet from shoulder-length hair that flares out at the rear, and that they have sharp, straight-bridged noses, all features found on the Hasanlu ivories. In addition, the clothing on the "Ziwiye" ivory is very similar to that found on some of our ivories, in particular the zig-zag belt, the lower-border fringe, and the side decoration. Of further interest is the fact that no. 98 and the "Ziwiye" ivory are executed in the same crude manner (seen as Mannean by Barnett 1956b, 114; see also Falkner 1952, 130). Unfortunately, it must be understood that we do not know where in Iran the "Ziwiye" ivory under discussion (not to mention all the other objects said to come from that site) actually was found, and therefore, we are able to discuss it only in the context of an object without a provenience.[13] And

[13]Objects said to have been derived from Ziwiye exist in many private and museum collections. Not a single one of these objects has been excavated: they all came from dealers' shops. See my comments in *JNES* 35,3 (1976): 210, and Muscarella 1977a, *passim*. Porada (1975, 374) states that her Abb. 312a, b, an ivory plaque said to come from Ziwiye, is related to the Hasanlu local style, an opinion I cannot follow. However, the Ziwiye procession ivory discussed here in the text (her fig. 114) is dated by Porada to the eighth century and it is not cited as related to the Hasanlu local style.

Moorey (1967, 89, note 78) refers to a gold strip said

thus we may state that because of the parallels with the Hasanlu ivories there is no compelling reason why we may not assume a date in the ninth century or shortly thereafter for the "Ziwiye" ivory (cf. Ghirshman 1964, 102, for a seventh century date). Surely it reflects a cultural tradition similar to the one that lay behind the Hasanlu examples.

We do not know whether the figures of nos. 111, 113 and 114 were part of a procession or whether they stood alone, but the fact that two of the three fragments were found in Room 8 of BB II, along with many of the procession fragments, suggests they were part of a group. It is not clear whether they carry arrows or wheat. If the former, one is immediately reminded of the warrior on the gold bowl who carries a bow in his left, an arrow in his right hand; there, however, the arrow seems to be held merely as a weapon, rather than as a symbolic or charged object. If the figures do carry wheat, they fit into a pattern of early first millennium representations fairly common in North Syria, Tabal, Assyria, and later in Urartu. Stalks of wheat are held by worshippers or deities in scenes that seem to be concerned with vegetation rites (Bossert 1942, 796; Madhloom 1970, pl. XLIV, 3; Barnett n.d., pl. 1; 1974, pl. XI), or apparently at banquet scenes (Bossert 1942, 806, 808[?], 815), or in processions of indeterminate function (Bossert 1942, 846). Two figures on a North Syrian bronze plaque may also be carrying wheat (Barnett 1964, 1, pl. 2:2). Scenes of gods or humans holding wheat have an ancient history (*viz.* Seidl 1968, 136 ff.; Moortgat 1969, pl. 255; Porada 1948, 26 ff., nos. 207-214) and the Hasanlu examples may reflect the same sort of event depicted elsewhere, probably a religious or vegetation-fertility observance (cf. Muscarella 1974d, no. 74).

Representations of a mace held head down (no. 92) are not unique to Hasanlu. We see it on a probable ninth century banquet scene from Ördek Burnu in North Syria (Bossert 1942, 957), and on eighth century reliefs from Carchemish and Sakçegözü (Bossert 1942, 837, 888). In Assyria also it is depicted on eighth/seventh century stone and ivory reliefs (Barnett and Falkner 1962, pl. XXVII; Barnett 1957, pls. X-XIII, F1, F3).[14] Like other motifs so far discussed it has a long history (Porada 1948, 51 f.). The mace, like the scepter, represented rank and authority (Albenda 1969, 45 f., 52; Porada 1970, 8, note 8) and was carried head down probably to show deference or peaceful intentions. The mace carried by the Assyrian figure on no. 280 may also be held down as a sign of peaceful intent, and we may assume the same reason obtained for the spear held head down on no. 117. Spears are depicted with the head held down on second millennium B.C. seals (Porada 1948, 119, note 2, 913). And an Assyrian bowl of probable ninth century date now in the Bröckelschen Collection (Calmeyer 1964, no. 106, 45 ff., fig. 7) has an incised scene of tribute bearers bringing gifts to a dignitary who holds a spear with the head pointed down, an attitude assumed apparently to demonstrate peaceful intentions to the approaching figures. On a stone basin from Ebla (Matthiae 1975, fig. 156) the figures depicted behind a seated one are also, I believe, carrying their spears head down, peacefully, rather than holding them at the ready for battle; this interpretation best fits the peaceful nature of the banquet scene represented. It should also be noted that the two spears depicted on the Schimmel Hittite stag rhyton have their heads touching the ground (Muscarella 1974d, no. 123).

The scene represented on no. 92, probably also no. 93, two figures flanking a third, was very common in ancient art and it would be difficult to trace the Hasanlu example to one particular area (cf. Porada 1947, nos. 109, 187 ff.; 1948, 323 ff.; 1970, 8, 9, 15, pl. XIII, 4). Porada points out the problem involved in deciding whether the scenes depict a deity between two mortals, or a king between two subjects, or three lesser mortals, a problem that obtains equally for no. 92. There, however, the central figure does appear to be mortal, as are his two companions, and it is possible that we have a secular scene depicted, but one related in some manner to the deity standing on the lion above. Perhaps the

---

to come either from Ziwiye or Luristan (!) (Ghirshman 1964, figs. 92, 93) that has a scene "which might loosely be described as ritual presentation processions." He goes on to compare the figures depicted on the strip with those represented in the art of Hasanlu. I find the scene represented on the gold strip to be unparalleled in ancient Near Eastern art; in fact, it has so many events going on that the scene seems to be meaningless. And I find only the vaguest resemblance to the Hasanlu figures: the gold strip figures are very crudely drawn, have no ears, no mouths, strange hair and foot-gear, and the tree would be unique among trees depicted on excavated material. Thus, I believe that the gold strip should be treated cautiously and not be cited as definitely an example of ancient art (see Muscarella 1977a, 212 and 1977b, no. 55).

[14]The faces on the figures of F1 and F3 are beardless and are apparently not typically Assyrian—although at the same time I find it difficult to say they are not Assyrian. Barnett (1957, 183) says they carry swords, which I do not see; Brown (1958, 69) dated them to the eighth century, which seems convincing [Winter 1976a, 375, says the inverted mace is not an Assyrian motif; and on p. 482 she suggests that F1 and F3 were carved by North Syrians to suit Assyrian taste.]

central figure is given power and authority because of his position under the deity.

The *veneratio* representations on two bronze beakers from western Iran (Calmeyer 1973, 34 f., B1 and 2; Muscarella 1974a, 244, note 27) appear to be related in idea to the scene on no. 92 and certainly to nos. 73 and 74. On one beaker, B1, the attendant drinks from a vessel while he faces the king, who holds only a staff; on the other beaker, B2, three figures hold vessels, including the king, who alone holds a staff. While we cannot be certain that the central figure of no. 92, who alone holds a vessel, is the one carrying the mace, in the cases of nos. 73 and 74 the figures hold both a vessel and a staff.

The two subordinate figures on no. 92, one of the figures on no. 93, and the figure on no. 88 all wear gorgets on their chests. Among the finds from Hasanlu were several full-sized bronze gorgets, one small example in gold, and two small examples made from Egyptian Blue (all unpublished except for one of the latter, Dyson 1972, 46 f., fig. 6). Thus we have gorgets represented in art and as actual examples from the same site. Gorgets were apparently fairly extensively used in Iran. A superbly decorated large example in gold is said to have come from Ziwiye (Godard 1950, 19 ff., fig. 10); another, of bronze, is said to come from Luristan (Ghirshman 1964, 314, fig. 380b). Gorgets were also worn by ninth century Assyrians (Hrouda 1965, 57, pl. 52:2; Porada 1945, pls. I, X; cf. Ghirshman 1964, 308) and later they were adopted by Urartians, at whose sites we find them both excavated and represented in art (Bossert 1942, 1163, 1175; Akurgal 1968, 27, figs. 3, 12, 17, pl. XXXVa, b; Barnett 1963b, 196, fig. 44; Burney and Lang 1972, pl. 72). A gorget is apparently worn by an ivory winged youth from Nimrud (Mallowan 1966, 270, fig. 260). At least two human figures from North Syria wear them, a statue from Ain Arab and one from Ain et-Tell (Orthmann 1971, pl. 4b; Matthiae 1975, Abb. 411); the former also carries a staff. Thus, gorgets were usually, but not exclusively, worn by humans, probably as a badge of rank or office. They are still worn by officials in modern Iran and Africa as a sign that those wearing them are officials on duty.[15]

On most of the ivories, and on other objects where heads are depicted, short shoulder-length hair seems to be standard, although cut in different fashions (Dyson 1964, 5). Long braided hair seems to be represented in art at Hasanlu only on relatively few of the ivories. The braided hair may extend only to the small of the back (nos. 92, 93), or it may fall down to the ankles (nos. 88-91); nos. 69, 84 and 86 have hair of unknown length. Long straight hair, not braided, is also worn by a few figures (nos. 79 and 96).

Long braided hair reaching to the small of the back exists in Hurrian, Syrian, pre-Hittite, Hittite and Elamite art of the second millennium, and thus has no geographical limits (Bossert 1951, 588, 589; 1942, 383, 476, 581, 620; Amiet 1966, figs. 232B, 239, 305; Muscarella 1974d, no. 123, 125, 131). This type of hair occurs later also in North Syrian art (Bossert 1942, 928; 1951, 442, 443) and in Assyrian art (Mallowan 1966, fig. 371d). I know of no other representations of hair that extends down to the ankles. Unfortunately, it is not possible to recognize the figures with the ankle-length hair as males or females. Although no. 89 wears a long gown, no. 90 is bare-legged, and no. 97 makes it clear to us that males wore long garments. Note that no. 69 and possibly one or both figures of no. 71 are the only representations of females on the plaques.

Spiral curly hair, found on nos. 49, 61 and 174 right, is also known in the West, especially in North Syria and less commonly in Assyria in the ninth century (Madhloom 1970, XL, 2, 4, LXXX, 1, LXXXI, 4, 5a-b, XLII), and in the eighth and seventh centuries (Madhloom 1970, pl. XLVIII, 3, LIII, 4, LXVII, 6); it is also attested earlier in the Near East (Madhloom 1970, 86; Frankfort 1954, pl. 39C).

The lozenge-shaped eye depicted on a few of the ivories is of interest in that it deviates from the standard shape, which is oval. It would seem that the craftsmen had a choice and there is insufficient evidence to suggest that a different ethnic type was depicted. Nos. 62 and 63 could be the enemy but there is no independent proof to confirm such a suggestion. No. 121, apparently not human, has lozenge eyes, but no. 122, definitely not human, has oval eyes; see also the bull, no. 142. One is of course reminded of the lozenge eyes commonly represented at Sialk B to the southeast, which examples may be contemporary with, or slightly later than, the Hasanlu ivories. Here too round and oval eyes could be drawn by the same artisans (*viz.* Ghirshman 1939, pls. X, LXXXVI, XC, XCI). It would not be rash to see the lozenge eyes at both Hasanlu and Sialk B as reflecting a

[15]In 1973 at Ahwaz airport I saw it worn by airport police. See also *ILN*, Nov. 30, 1968: 15, photograph upper left. It was also worn by German military police during the Second World War, and continues in use at present. I do not share the view of Ghirshman (1964, 308) or Akurgal (1968, 27 ff.) that some cauldron-attachment sirens wear gorgets.

common artistic background, given the other parallels between the two sites (Muscarella 1973a, 70 f., notes 13, 14).

Lozenge eyes occur further west at Phrygian Gordion in late eighth century B.C. contexts on ivories of local style (Kohler 1964, pls. XIX, XX). These are later than the Hasanlu examples but, according to some opinions, may be roughly contemporary with, or slightly later than, finds from Sialk B, which floats chronologically between the late ninth and the late eighth—or even the early seventh century B.C. (Muscarella 1967, 70, notes 9-14; 1973a, 70 f., notes 13, 14).

No. 120, preserving only the head and one foot, is too fragmentary to allow us to strongly conclude that it is a representation of a bull man. The extant foot is indeed not human. We might expect horns on a true bull man (e.g. Loud 1939, pl. 10; Porada 1948, no. 980), but there are examples of bull men without horns (Porada 1948, no. 980; Harper 1969, fig. 7). Sometimes only bulls' ears are present without the animal horns (Porada 1975, 382, 386, pl. XXXIV, Abb. 295). And it is possible that a wall tile in the form of a human head with horns might be a bull man (Dyson 1960, 6; Porada 1975, 393, Abb. 309b: compare also Abb. 306, a bull man on a silver vessel; this vessel was not excavated but is probably genuine (cf. Muscarella 1977b, no. 194, which I now retract). Porada (1967, 70) has referred to the bull man as an Elamite feature (cf. Amiet 1966, fig. 299), even when it occurs in the art of Luristan (Moorey 1975, 21, fig. 1; Porada 1964, pl. 15; Pope 1938, pls. 28, 29; on these examples there are horns and human hands).

The tripods/tetrapods represented on nos. 118, 119 and 169 terminate in animals' feet: no. 119, a bull; 169, a lion; 118, unclear. On nos. 118 and 169 the tripod has no ground line and seems to float, but this feature is not uncommon in ancient art; it occurs, for example, on the Hasanlu gold bowl, and also in North Syrian art at Nimrud (Mallowan 1966, figs. 403, 404), and at Marash, Karaburçlu and Gaziantep (Bossert 1941, 808, 811, 813-815). The example from Gaziantep is of special interest because it allows us to speculate that a deity may be restored above the lion of no. 169. Animal-foot terminals are of course ubiquitous in the Near East (Kyrieleis 1969, 72 ff.) and the examples of stands excavated at Hasanlu, whether of bronze or terracotta, and the one represented on the gold bowl, terminate in animals' feet (Ghirshman 1939, pl. C, 16; Dyson 1959, 18; 1960, fig. 12; 1964a, fig. 4; Moorey 1972, 143 f.; cf. also a tripod from Kayalidere, Burney 1966, 96 f., fig. 20:1, restored by Kyrieleis 1969, 29 f. fig. 5, as a tetrapod). We do not know whether tripods depicted on the Hasanlu ivories had food placed on their surfaces, but if they were placed before a seated person, as is indicated by no. 118, food may confidently be restored. Judging from the complete example on no. 119, and also the incomplete no. 169, as well as the example depicted on the gold bowl, we may state that the Hasanlu tripods did not have a strut connecting the surface to the lower crosspiece, found in other areas (Bossert 1941, 813, 814; I do not count cross-legged tables where this feature is common, Muscarella 1974a, 241, 244).

The thrones/chairs on nos. 116-118 are all of the same type: undecorated; thick legs terminating in a rectangular foot; a crosspiece connecting the legs, which have square units at the joints; a slightly curving back; and no arm rests. These were without doubt made of wood, and fragments of wooden thrones/chairs were excavated from BB II. The square joints could have had metal frames but there is no indication of this on the representations; nor is there any indication that these thrones/chairs were covered with ivory plaques. Similar examples of such furniture are not at hand but thrones with curved backs were not uncommon. Throne Γ at Salamis on Cyprus of eighth cenutry date is of a different type from the Hasanlu examples but it has a curved back (Karageorghis 1973, 87, pls. LXI, LXII); so does a bronze model from Enkomi, also on Cyprus (Kyrieleis 1969, 80, pl. 12:3, 4). The eighth century throne/chair backs from SW.7 at Nimrud also have curved backs (Mallowan and Herrmann 1974, 3, 6 f., fig. 3). An eighth century throne represented on a relief from Zincirli shows the curve clearly, as does one on a ninth/eighth century pendant from the same site (Bossert 1942, 953; Vieyra 1955, fig. 122). Earlier, tenth/ninth century thrones represented on bronze beakers from western Iran sometimes illustrate a straight back, other times a curved one (Calmeyer 1973, 19, 23, A4, A10). That other thrones/chairs of the first millennium had square joints with metal reenforcements is demonstrated by furniture fittings of eighth century date from Urartian sites (Burney 1966, 98 ff., 108 ff., figs. 21:2, 23:3; Bossert 1942, 1180; Özgüç 1969, 68, pls. XIX, 1, XX, 1; Kyrieleis 1969, 24 ff., pl. 7:1). Three D-shaped bronze clamps from the seventh century site of Agrab Tepe, a few miles from Hasanlu, may also have been furniture fittings for a chair (Muscarella 1973a, 66 f., fig. 27:16).

A chair with joints is depicted also on the Hasanlu gold bowl, under the god with the hammer, and although not exactly like those depicted on the ivories it is clearly of the same construction.

III
HUMAN SCULPTURE IN THE ROUND

The five head fragments, nos. 123-126, 128, found widely separated in Rooms 6, 7, and 8, seem to be all of the same type and to share the same features; nos. 123 and 124 together yield information concerning what the heads looked like when complete. They are characterized by deep-cut oval eyes; thick brows, inlaid or in relief, that meet over the nose; thin lips; and prominent cheeks and jaws. The heads no doubt were locally made but to some extent reflect outside influences, especially in the mouth structure. The most obvious parallels seem to be some ivory heads from Nimrud, and other North Syrian figures in general. The "Ugly Sister" from Nimrud, now in the Metropolitan Museum (Mallowan 1966, 133, fig. 73) has the same pouting thin lips as our heads; so do a few other small female ivory heads from Nimrud (Barnett 1957, pls. LXX, LXXI, especially nos. S172-174, 198 and 199). Male and female stone heads from Carchemish, Zincirli and Tell Halaf are strikingly close to our ivories in the depiction of the mouth (*viz.* Bossert 1942, 824, 828, 902-904, 955; 1951, 448 ff.). The Nimrud ladies (cf. nos. 249, 250) do not have the prominent cheeks and jaws—a small chin was more characteristic of North Syrian heads—and the North Syrian males have beards, but their mouths are the same as on the Hasanlu heads. A similar mouth is noticeable on the second millennium statue of Idri-mi from Alalakh (Barnett 1957, 42; Strommenger 1962, figs. 174, 175). The same mouth may also be seen at Mari, both in painting and sculpture (Strommenger 1962, figs. 154, 164, pl. XXVIII). Thus the mouth type existed for some time in the West, and its occurrence in North Syria continued an old tradition.

The ivory heads, especially nos. 124 and 125 seem to have had a separately-made wig or headdress set on a narrow ledge at the forehead (cf. Harper 1969, 161, fig. 7); no. 124 has a hole at the back probably to help secure the added unit. It is also possible that the heads functioned as caryatids, as we know occurred at Nimrud (Barnett 1957, pls. LXXIII-LXXV). No. 125 is a complete unit and was never part of a statue; it may have functioned as a protome attached to a backing by three dowel holes arranged in a triangle at its back. An exact parallel for dowel holes arranged in triangular fashion on the flat backs of heads that also seem not to have been part of statues occurs at Megiddo (Loud 1939, p. 44: 190-194). The latter are dated to the late second millennium B.C. and attest to a continuity of a particular technique and function.

The prominent cheeks and jaws appear to be a local Iranian characteristic (Muscarella 1966, 130, fig. 23). This conclusion is strengthened by the wooden head no. 127. I know of no other parallel, even among the other locally made heads. Its preservation in such a fine state (and, of course, that of the other wood sculpture and plaques) is owed to the fact that it was burned and is now all charcoal. Burning also preserved the extraordinary wood sculptures from Ebla in North Syria, where fragments of a male, a female, and a lion attacking its prey, all from the late third millennium B.C., were excavated (Matthiae 1975, 487 f., Abb. 424, 425a, b; if ivory has been found at Ebla it has to date not been reported in the publications). At Samos, wood objects from the late seventh/early sixth century B.C. were found fairly intact because the area in which they were recovered had constant moisture (Kopcke 1967, 101). A statue of a female, presumed to be the goddess Hera, having a preserved height of 28.7 centimeters, wears a rather high polos, not dissimilar in form and outward flare to no. 127 (Kopcke 1967, 103 ff., pls. 45-47).

The remains of four wooden statuettes, all males, were excavated at Karmir Blur, of seventh/sixth century date; they are fairly well preserved even though they were not burned (Barnett 1952, 142, fig. 5; Piotrovsky 1970, figs. 29-34). These sculptures have no stylistic relationships to the Hasanlu heads, but they further attest to the existence of wood sculpture in the first millennium (cf. also Rudenko 1970, 85 f., 198 f.).

The face of no. 127 has a haunting quality that makes the piece one of the outstanding finds from Hasanlu. Of special interest is the brooch on the figure's left shoulder. Straight pins are worn by figures on the Hasanlu gold bowl, and many straight pins, but no brooches, have been found in the excavations at both Hasanlu and nearby Dinkha Tepe (Muscarella 1974c, 78, 80). None of the other figures represented on any material at Hasanlu wears pins or brooches, although the fact that the ivories are so fragmented might in part account for this. The closest parallel I can find for the brooch on no. 127 is the one represented on the near life-sized bronze statue of Queen Naparisu of the thirteenth century from Susa (Strommenger 1962, fig. 183).

The headdress of no. 127 is complete but for the top and we do not know whether it was flat or rounded, or very much higher than now preserved. In any event it is similar to, but not the same as, the tall hats worn by North Syrian priestesses and goddesses (cf. Orthmann 1971, pl. 45a, b; Bossert 1942, 810, 845, 846, 859, 866, 868), and also the hat on the wooden statuette from Samos mentioned above. It might also be a local variety of the relatively short polos worn by the Nimrud ladies, such as nos. 249 and 250, even though these are decorated.

What function did the heads under discussion have and were they humans or deities, males or females? Nos. 123, 124, 126 and 127 were probably all from free-standing statuettes. That some of the bodies were separately made is demonstrated by the tang on no. 124 (cf. Amiet 1966, fig. 217; Barnett 1957, pl. LXXI, U7), but the others were no doubt carved in one piece with the body. This seems certain from the evidence of nos. 127-129; nos. 128 and 129 are quite damaged so that no details are visible other than the fact that head and body were carved together. Recognizable parts of statuettes are not common (cf. nos. 251 and 252), although there must surely be parts of bodies among the many solid ivory fragments and splinters that were excavated.

There are also several fragments of feet preserved, either in place on their stands, nos. 92, 135, 95, or free standing, nos. 131-134. From this we know that some local-style statuettes were carved as parts of larger units while others were self-contained. The tang on the foot of no. 131 could have secured the statue either to a supporting stand or to a larger unit, like nos. 92 and 93, for example.

The question regarding the sex of the heads is not readily answered although the problem is not unresolvable. None is bearded and this certainly suggests that they are female. After the Sumerian period, when males were either bearded or unbearded, it was usual to depict males other than youths and eunuchs with beards, but not universal. In North Syrian and Urartian art, for example, some males could be represented without a beard (*viz.* Hogarth 1914, B4, 5, 7; Barnett 1957, pl. XVIII, XXII, XXIV, XXVI; Akurgal 1968, fig. 6; Piotrovsky 1959, figs. 68, 69); and an ivory unbearded head from Ugarit is assumed to be male (Matthiae 1975, 480, pl. XLVII). None of the Hasanlu heads has a specific female softness but this itself cannot claim them as male (cf. Orthmann 1971, pls. 13a, b, e; 43h), for it has been assumed that the harsh, farouche features recognized on some heads may indicate a ninth century date.[16] This is well illustrated by comparing the "Ugly Sister" and the "Mona Lisa," found together in the same well in Room NW of the North West Palace at Nimrud. The "Ugly Sister" has, as discussed above, a mouth and an austere face close to some of the Hasanlu heads (cf. nos. 123 and 124) and, as Mallowan and Frankfort pointed out, is close to faces on sculpture from Tell Halaf (Mallowan 1966, 134 f., fig. 73). Mallowan also suggested that the "Ugly Sister" was earlier than the softer, smiling "Mona Lisa," although he was reluctant to accept this conclusion as final. I think that on the basis of the evidence already presented by Mallowan and now on the evidence of the Hasanlu heads, it may indeed be concluded that the "Ugly Sister" was made some time before the "Mona Lisa."

The existence of the polos-like headdress, the brooch and a necklace on no. 127 points to the conclusion that this head is that of a female, and probably that of a goddess. The two Nimrud-type heads, nos. 249 and 250, are also females. And given the fact that most of the males depicted on the ivories and at least one in the round (no. 130) wear beards, it would be safe to conclude in the final analysis that all the heads in the round under discussion are those of females.

That at least one of the ivory heads wore elec-

[16]But it should be noted that severe faces may occasionally exist in the eighth century, as for example at Gordion (Young 1962, pl. 46).

trum earrings is neatly documented by a pair that was found in Room 7 of BB II; one had a fragment of ivory still preserved in its loop (Muscarella 1966, 135, fig. 36). Two more gold or electrum earrings, a pair, exactly the same type (70-405), were found just east of Room 7, and it is probable that they too belonged to an ivory head. Earrings on both males and females are of course commonly depicted in the ancient Near East, but on sculpture they are usually carved in one piece with the ears. A few statuettes of humans and animals, none, however, to my knowledge in ivory, do occasionally preserve a separately added earring (*viz.* Frankfort 1954, pls. 144, 152A; Negahban 1964, pls. I, X).

The statuette originally standing on the lion of no. 92 was a full figure in the round. There is no internal evidence concerning its sex but given both our knowledge of Near Eastern iconography (Moorey 1971, 203 f.) and the evidence presented above that the isolated heads were female, it may be suggested that the figure was a female. In fact, head no. 123 was found in the same room, 7, as the pedestal, and could have been the statuette's head. The figure, male or female—a female if no. 123 actually belongs to it—was obviously a deity, for it conforms to an ancient theme, that of a deity standing on an animal, found in many ancient cultures. I know of no parallel for the pedestal as a whole, but the combination of bare feet juxtaposed to a lion, both set over a cylindrical base, itself attached to another unit below, exists on an ivory from Nimrud (Barnett 1957, 210, pl. LXXVII, S251).[17] The feet on the Nimrud ivory do not rest on the lion but are next to it; yet, however different in arrangement these objects are from each other, one has the feeling that they are not unrelated in idea. The Nimrud ivory is not easily dated but it may be later than the more articulated and architecturally unified pedestal from Hasanlu.

The lowest unit of the Hasanlu pedestal obviously supported the upper ones but we have no clue about whether it was itself the base or was set on or into still another unit.

No. 93 seems to be the same type of object as no. 92, and is therefore to be tentatively restored with a deity above. It was found in an area close to no. 92 but on stylistic analysis seems to have been made in a separate workshop. Whether it was originally part of the same object as no. 92 or was, in fact, a separate object, with a similar function and use, unfortunately now eludes us.

From the evidence of the heads alone it is not possible to conclude whether they were human or divine. However, if my tentative suggestion that no. 123 was part of no. 92 is accepted, there is evidence, albeit tenuous, that the deity standing on the lion was female, and conversely that this head represented a goddess.

Head no. 124 came from Room 8, which also yielded foot fragments (no. 132) and hand fragments (no. 251). The latter appear to be imported objects and therefore are not part of no. 124, but one or two of the foot fragments could have belonged. Thus there is evidence for a separate statuette here, one that could have been that of a female deity. Nos. 128 and 129 are too fragmented to discuss meaningfully except that they give evidence for two more statuettes, be they human or divine.

The wooden fragment no. 95 and the wooden head no. 127 were found in adjacent rooms, 7 and 6, and it is tempting to see them as having been originally parts of the same statuette, separated when falling with the second-storey collapse. This suggestion is not subject to confirmation, but it is worth a tentative acceptance. There is in addition the wooden foot fragment no. 190, which, as stated in the Catalogue, is not clearly distinguishable as that of a human or an animal. Yet the apparent existence of a thong would suggest that the foot is that of a human, and thus one should tenatively consider it as another statuette.

It is obvious that we are in a weak position when we attempt to draw more than intelligent suggestions from the fragmented evidence at hand. Therefore it is not possible to securely know the absolute number of local deities represented at Hasanlu in ivory and wood. What is certain is that nos. 92, 93 and 95 give us a minimum number of three. Tentatively accepting no. 124 gives us a possible fourth. Stretching the evidence further, to what is admittedly a tenuous position, we may keep in mind nos. 128, 129, and 190 as possible candidates for representation of deities. And we still have nos. 123 and 127, which could have joined nos. 92 and 95. Therefore, it is possible to conclude cautiously that there were definitely three, and very probably seven —or even nine—representations of deities at Hasanlu in ivory and wood (see the discussion of the winged figures, *infra*).

No. 135 may be the remains of a nude female standing on a palm capital, perhaps a handle of some sort, examples of which exist at Nimrud (Barnett 1957, 108 ff., 209, pl. LXXVII, S236, S243). A similar fragment, but with two pairs of feet back to back, standing on a palm capital, was

[17]The Nimrud parallel for no. 92 was pointed out to me by Mrs. Vivian Mann of the Institute of Fine Arts, New York University.

found years ago on Crete, and is probably an import from North Syria, as pointed out by Kunze (1936, 221, pl. 84:11). I am not certain whether no. 135 was a local product or an import; the toes have a different structure from no. 92, but are similar to nos. 132 and 134, whose origins are also uncertain.

All that can be said about no. 130 is that a beard is evident and the figure is a male; there is nothing to indicate that he is a deity. Furthermore, it is not clear what the object is that is held close to his body; it looks like a shield or a tambourine. The herringbone hair and the foreshortened arm (cf. nos. 93 and 115) suggest that it was locally made, although this is not certain.

The activity of no. 94, and the type of head it had are lost to us. It is a plaque, not a sculpture, and represents a winged man or demon with a kilt that exposes his thigh. It is possible to conjecture, but without evidence, that the figure may have held a situla for libations (*viz.* Godard 1950, figs. 75, 76; Mallowan 1966, 595, fig. 575). It appears to have been locally made.

That there were more than several winged figures in the round is evident from the many wing fragments and from the fragmented figure no. 136. Some of these figures had their wings carved together with their bodies, *viz.* no. 136 and perhaps no. 140, while others, the majority, had their wings carved separately, attached by tangs or dowels to their respective bodies. One separately made wing, no. 138, is of wood and was part of a wooden statuette. Some of the wings are finely incised, nos. 140, 141; others have a high relief, nos. 137, 138, 140. On the evidence of no. 136, which seems to be of local manufacture, it is probable that all the wings were locally made.

I can find no other parallels for separately made wings in the first millennium B.C. (cf. Barnett 1957, 188, J3, pl. XV) but they do occur at Acemhüyük, in Anatolia, dated to the early second millennium (Özgüç 1965, 43, pl. XX, 2; Harper 1969, fig. 9) and at Mycenae in Bronze Age Greece (Poursat 1977, II, 14, pl. 1, no. 27). There are also the mosaic wing fragments from late second millennium B.C. Tchoga Zanbil (Amiet 1966, fig. 271), and, of approximately the same date, an ivory wing from Kamid el-Loz, Lebanon (Hachmann and Kuschke 1966, fig. 20:9). The Hasanlu wings could have come from genii or from deities; if the latter, then there were more representations of deities from Hasanlu than suggested above.

IV

ANIMALS, BIRDS, HUNTING SCENES

Various animals are represented in relief on the ivory and wood fragments from Rooms 6, 7 and 8 and adjacent areas: bulls and lions, some of which are winged, goats, stags and birds of prey. In some cases the fragmentation prevents an interpretation of the role some of the animals played; in others we are better able to recognize the context. Thus, we recognize animals grazing (no. 159); animals being hunted by men on foot or from chariots (nos. 145?, 170-176, 178, 180); a lion attacking a bull or stag (no. 181); lions in an heraldic position (nos. 162, 163, perhaps also nos. 164-166); a lion attacking a man or animal (no. 167); goats leaping, possibly flanking a tree (nos. 147, 148; a tree is by no means certain); a lion grappling with a sphinx or siren (no. 182); and heros fighting bulls and lions (nos. 183, 184-185; possibly also no. 142).

Grazing animals, including deer or stags, are a stock motif in first millennium art (*viz.* de Mertzenfeld 1954, pl. LXXXIX, 879, 880; XCVIII, 935; Barnett 1957, pl. II, 35, 37; Mallowan and Davies, 1970, pl. XXXV, 143; Mallowan 1966, figs. 435, 439, 561; Özgüç 1969, pl. XLIV). Sometimes deer are hunted, a motif with a long history (*viz.* Muscarella 1974d, no. 123; Bossert 1942, 521, 522, 764; Barnett 1957, pl. XVI, S9; Özgüç 1969, Pl. II, 1, 2). It is not clear if the stag on no. 156 is being hunted but he does not appear to be grazing. (Several sets of red deer antlers were excavated in the great hall of BB II, suggesting from the context that the animal was locally known and utilized in some manner other than just as a food source.)

No. 156 is clearly a local product, but the head and feet of no. 159 are unlike those of any other animal at Hasanlu and it was probably an imported ivory. In particular note the incised eyelashes. This feature is known to me only on some ivories in the Metropolitan Museum of Art (58.122.3, 5). They were said by the vendor to have come from Khorsabad but this information is totally without value. Body markings similar to those on ivories said to have come from Ziwiye, and which may be Iranian, suggest that the Metropolitan Museum ivories actually came from some site in Iran.[18] Two suckling calves from Arslan Tash have eyelashes incised on the eye corner alone (Thureau-Dangin 1931, pls. 38, 39: 67, 69), but the grazing stags from that site do not have incised eyelashes.

On contemporary North Syrian stone reliefs at Carchemish, Zincirli, Malatya and Tell Halaf, walking or hunted stags are fairly common (Orthmann 1971, pls. 33b, d, e; 42b; 56c, d; 57g; Moortgat 1955, pls. 69, 109), and this no doubt reflects earlier Hittite representations (Muscarella 1974d, no. 123; Bossert 1942, 521, 522). A stag is held by a ninth century Assyrian genius, presumably for a sacrifice (Barnett n.d., pl. 2), but stag hunting was not a typical Assyrian activity (cf. Porada 1948, nos. 601, 603, from the Middle Assyrian period). However, stags were represented, albeit not often, in ancient Near Eastern art as early as the third millennium B.C., and perhaps even earlier (Strommenger 1962, fig. 79; pl. IX seems to depict a stag). Eighth century examples of ivory stags occur at Arslan Tash (Thureau-Dangin 1931, pl. XXXVI, 61, 62), at Samaria (Crowfoot 1938, pl. X:8), and at Nimrud (Mallowan and Herrmann 1974, no. 103, pl. CIV).

[18]Some scholars have considered these ivories in the Metropolitan Museum to be forgeries, an opinion not shared by me. Recently, these ivories were tested in a laboratory where it was concluded that the organic composition was consistent with ancient ivory (Baer and Indictor 1975, 241 ff., figs. 1, 2).

Stags are also represented both in the round and in relief on Iranian vessels excavated in northwest Iran and dating to the late second or early first millennium B.C. (Negahban 1964, figs. 96, 103; Hakemi 1968, 63, pl. XXXIII; 66, 70, 72, pls. XXV, XXIX, for an example of a lion attacking a stag, said to have come from Gilan),[19] and at least one seal from Tchoga Zambil depicts a stag (Porada 1970a, no. 43). (Two grazing stags are represented on a bronze beaker but the date and authenticity of this vessel are not secure: Muscarella 1974a, 251; Calmeyer 1973, 105, fig. 98.)

To my knowledge, the only other example of stags represented in art at Hasanlu occurs on a remarkable terracotta vessel (Dyson 1961, fig. 8; 1967, fig. 1030). Unfortunately, the exact level in which this vessel was excavated is not secure, although Dyson now believes that it belonged in level III, seventh/sixth century B.C. (verbal communication; see also Muscarella 1971a, 265; *infra*).

The back of the stag no. 156 is outlined with a thick herringbone pattern, a pattern found on other ivory animals' backs (nos. 143, 145, 163, 168, 170, 172, 178). This herringbone pattern, incised or plastic, is also to be seen on some of the chariot and cavalry horses discussed above (nos. 2, 5, 6, 8, 9, 21, 33). These back manes extended from the head to the tail and are very characteristic not only at Hasanlu but elsewhere in Iran (Muscarella 1972, 41, note 18; Calmeyer 1973, H5, H7?; Hakemi 1968, 63, 81, pl. XXXIII; Canby 1971, 41 f.). The same thick herringbone pattern also occurs on the borders of North Syrian pyxides from Nimrud (Barnett 1957, pls. XVI, XXI-XXIII). Other animals on the ivories have the back outlined with a simple hatching or rope pattern (nos. 73, 142, 144, 146, 147). At Hasanlu we also find that the ubiquitous bronze lion pins have outlined backs (Dyson 1964b, fig. 9; Canby 1971, 42), reinforcing the conclusion that it was a local characteristic.

All the lions have their backs outlined in typical herringbone fashion except for no. 167, which has a thin ridge terminating in a small curl. This is a hair tuft, a motif that exists on other Iranian animals represented in art (Muscarella 1972, 41, note 19, figs. 9, 11, 15), and in a few cases, on Assyrian animals (Hrouda 1965, pl. 35:3, eighth century in date).

The winged lions are perhaps to be considered as lion-griffins, although no horns are depicted; other lions are natural creatures and are represented as being hunted. Thus lions are involved in scenes representing both the world of reality and that of mythology. Judging from no. 163 some of the winged lions were arranged in heraldic position; no. 167 has both feet raised and may be involved in a fight. The heraldic lions of no. 162 may also be fighting but the scene, two upright lions touching paws, is so common a theme in ancient art that another meaning is probably intended (cf. Herzfeld 1941, figs. 280-283; Muscarella 1966, figs. 18, 19). At Hasanlu was excavated an iron plaque (62-1060, now in the Metropolitan Museum of Art, 63.109.19) that depicts two upright lions touching paws; an animal is placed below them and here the lions might actually be fighting over the prey (cf. a sixth century plaque from Pazirli, Boardman 1970, 29 f., fig. 10, and the Achaemenid seals nos. 158, 162). An antler plaque from Karmir Blur, made locally or in the Caucasus further north, is strikingly similar to the Hasanlu ivory lions (Piotrovsky 1970, fig. 92; cf. also Rudenko 1970, fig. 45). The Hasanlu heraldic lions also remind us of scenes on Mitannian seals (Muscarella 1966, 129f., fig. 19; Porada 1947, nos. 174 ff.). And in the art of Luristan the motif occurs fairly often (*viz.* Moorey 1975, pl. IIIa; Pope 1938, pls. 44, 60).

Except for nos. 170 and 182, the lions' feet are depicted as distinctly clawlike. This feature, as well as the squared primaries of the wings, distinguishes this group of lions from those represented elsewhere. These feet are not always meant to be griffin's or eagle's feet, as is demonstrated by the existence of the same feet on the natural lion being hunted on no. 174 (cf. Porada 1948, nos. 268, 541, 596, etc.). A few of the lions (nos. 167, 168, 178; cf. 175) have a sickle-like hair tuft projecting from the legs, a feature common in Iranian art (Muscarella 1972, 41, note 20, figs. 9, 10, 11, 15; see no. 175).

Winged, snarling lions exist in both Assyrian and North Syrian art (Madhloom 1970, pl. CXIV, 1; Porada 1948, fig. 689e; Bossert 1951, 477). But it seems that the North Syrian form is closer as evidenced by the head type: the triangular hair tufts of the mane and its separation from the body by a narrow vertically decorated unit; also the lack of body "wings," and the bordered stomach and back (cf. Madhloom 1970, pls. LXXVI, LXXVII, LXXIX, LXXX; Kantor 1956, fig. 5; Barnett 1957, pls. XVIII, XXII, XXIV, XXV, etc.). The pose of the winged lions is also quite similar to that of griffins on stone reliefs from Carchemish (Orthmann 1971, pl. 33f.). It should also be remembered in this context that several North Syrian lion bowls were ex-

[19]This vessel was apparently not excavated and because of its strange motifs deserves more study. I find it difficult to come to a decision about whether or not it is authenic.

cavated at Hasanlu (*infra*), indicating a first-hand knowledge of North Syrian lions. And it should be noted that the triangles on the head of no. 92, a lion in the round, as well as the head structure and the occurrence of "warts," points also to a North Syrian background (cf. Akurgal 1949, figs. 35 ff., 45, 46; Madhloom 1970, pl. LXXX, 3). Triangles on the head occur also on an eighth century lion in the round from Altintepe in Urartu (Özgüç 1969, pls. 39-41; this may be a local Urartian product but it has a North Syrian background).

Winged lions are not foreign to Iranian art in areas other than Hasanlu. For instance, a double-headed example is depicted on a seal from Tchoga Zanbil (Porada 1970, fig. 40), a type similar to a winged lion on a gold vessel excavated at Kaluraz (Hakemi 1968, 65, pl. XXXIII), and to creatures depicted on objects from Luristan (Pope 1938, pls. 29A, 56E; Moorey 1975, fig. 1, pls. IIa, b, IVc). The Tchoga Zanbil example is dated to the thirteenth century B.C.; the Kalaruz vessel is either late second or early first millennium in date; and the Luristan examples are probably later than the Hasanlu ivories. The Hasanlu lions are not the same type as the other Iranian lions mentioned here, which are closer to Mitannian examples, as Moorey (1975, 23 f., fig. 6) has pointed out. The "Ziwiye" winged lions are later than the Hasanlu ivories (Godard 1950, figs. 16, 17).

Most of the lion plaques are clearly closely related to one another in all the details of carving and body decoration (nos. 163-167, 171-174; 176, 177, 179-181) and were made in one or more workshops by a few individuals; nos. 163 and 165 were probably made by the same hand. No. 171, because of the horse's mane, is connected with the workshop of other ivories, nos. 19-22, 28, 29, and possibly 23 and 24. No. 170 probably came from a workshop related to nos. 5 and 39, because they too have the same plastic herringbone outlines. The lion of no. 169 is more plastically rendered than the others; its ear is horizontal, not vertical, and it probably came from another workshop. No. 162 also obviously came from a different workshop, perhaps the same one that produced no. 185, to judge from the body structure and feet. The workmanship of nos. 168 and 178 suggests that they both came from the same workshop, and perhaps from the same hand.

No. 175, a scene in gold repoussé fitted over an ivory fragment, is no doubt of local manufacture. It is not so finely executed as the ivory work but the lion is the same creature as those represented on the ivories. A detail that slightly distinguishes the two lions on the gold band from the ivory lions is the fact that the former have a fully outlined shoulder, a characteristic more of metalwork than of ivories. Thus we see this type of shoulder represented on the silver beaker from Hasanlu (Muscarella 1966, fig. 10) and, in a more elaborate manner, on the Hasanlu gold bowl. This motif occurs on animals represented on other Iranian metalwork, and also in general in the art of North Syria and Phrygia (Muscarella 1972, 40 ff., note 65; Sams 1974, 180, 183 f.). A similar outlined shoulder also exists on the ivories nos. 142, a bull, and 156, a stag, and no. 170, a horse; but not on the ivory lions, which have a simpler outline (cf. a similar outline on no. 147). The gold band may not have been made by the same artisans who carved the ivories as it is cruder in technique and execution (*infra*). Nevertheless, it documents a close relationship of the various craftsmen working with different materials at Hasanlu.

Hunting scenes, individuals on foot fighting lions (nos. 172, 174, 175, 178, 180), or operating from a chariot or on horseback (nos. 170, 171), are standard Near Eastern motives occurring over a long time and over a wide geographical area. The closest contemporary examples, especially scenes involving a hunter in a chariot, are scenes common in both North Syria and Assyria on monumental and portable art (Bossert 1942, 764, 767; 1951, 474, 489; Strommenger 1962, figs. 202, 203; Albenda 1974, 1 ff.; Porada 1948, nos. 659 ff.). Although lions fight back on Assyrian reliefs I can find no example there of a lion in a twisted position as seen on no. 170 (cf. Canby 1971, fig. 4, pl. XIIa). This motif is not a common one before the later first millennium B.C. Amiet (1974, 247, notes 8, 9, 248, note 1) collects early examples from Iran, Byblos and Tell Agrab in Iraq. An example that may be contemporary or even earlier than the Hasanlu ivory is found at Tell Halaf, where a lion in a twisted position attacks a bull (Orthmann 1971, pl. 11e). Amiet (1974, 242 ff., pls. XV, XVI, 2) publishes a well-known Iranian bronze quiver which depicts two twisted animals. This quiver was not properly excavated and therefore has no objective provenience: Amiet asserts it is from Luristan, an attribution that is to my mind not necessarily secure. Two ivory fragments in the Metropolitan Museum, said to come from Ziwiye, which seem to be later than the Hasanlu ivories, have a similar twisted lion represented (Wilkinson 1955, 216, lower left; same as Wilkinson 1975, fig. 17b; Wilkinson 1963, fig. 16). Bodies of animals whose rear sections are twisted 180 degrees are very common in the Altai region, during the sixth and fifth centuries B.C. (Rudenko 1970, figs. 28, 51-54, 123-4, etc.). They also occur earlier, albeit rarely, in Bronze Age

Cretan and Mycenaean art (Davis 1974, 481, figs. 6, 7; Smith 1963, fig. 58).

The bulls (nos. 142, 150, 183), horses? (nos. 143-145), goats (nos. 147, 148, 152-155), birds (nos. 160, 161—probably made by the same hand) and the creature no. 146, are all of local manufacture. Some of these animals are part of hunting scenes (nos. 144, 145), others seem to be part of standard heraldic scenes (nos. 147, 149). Nos. 151, 157 and 158, while not apparently imports from the West, do not appear to be products of the same workshops that produced most of the other local ivories. Whether they were locally made in a separate workshop or came from another Iranian ivory-carving center remains unknown.

Mythological scenes where creatures fight a lion (no. 182), or a lion attacks a bull or other creature (no. 181) are all standard themes of ancient Near Eastern art (Barnett 1957, 72, 83 f.; Sams 1974, 176, 182; Calmeyer 1973, group M). Equally at home in Near Eastern art over a long period of time are the scenes represented on nos. 183, 184, 185, perhaps also 142. No. 183 depicts a hero grappling with a bull (cf. Porada 1948, nos. 140, 146, 169, 170, 172 etc.).[20] If one foot of the bull on no. 142 is raised to touch an opponent, then we may assume that here there was originally a scene similar to no. 183; one would assume also that the now missing horns were gripped by the hero's hand.

Hand-to-hand combat between a lion and a hero who wields a dagger to dispatch his opponent is also a widespread motif existing in Assyrian, North Syrian and Iranian art (*viz.* Porada 1965, pl. 15; Frankfort 1954, pl. 109; Orthmann 1971, pl. 9b; Barnett 1957, pls. XXII, XXIII, S2, 4, 30; Calmeyer 1973, D1; Moorey 1975, fig. 1), and thus continues an older tradition (*viz.* Porada 1948, no. 144; Barnett 1957, 66 f.; cf. Negahban 1964, fig. 104). The same motif, even with the foot of the lion touching his dispatcher, is found in neo-Elamite art and later in Achaemenid art, where it flourished (Ghirshman 1964, figs. 250-253; Amiet 1966, fig. 383; Boardman 1970, nos. 82, 115; cf. nos. 84, 85, 186, figs. 11, 13; Porada 1948, no. 826).

One of the three goats depicted on no. 73 has a human head and beard. This feature occurs on contemporary bronze Iranian beakers and has an older history in both Iran and Mesopotamia (Porada 1965, 32 f., 71, pls. 5, 15; Calmeyer 1973, 52 f., 68 f., 196, H1, 2, 12). The motif continues into Achaemenid times, with the body usually winged (Boardman 1970, 33, 34, nos. 101, 129-139, 198).

The head of the sphinx on no. 185 is unlike other human heads at Hasanlu, especially with the disproportionately large nose; but the lion's head and claws are similar to those on the lions of no. 162, and the sphinx's squared-off wing tip with its thick projecting upper border is the same as that found on other Hasanlu winged lions. Moreover, the incised concentric-circle design on the border is also found on no. 142. This design is not an unfinished guilloche but an independent decoration and is also found at Nimrud (Mallowan 1966, fig. 257; Barnett 1957, pls. LXIX, CXIX, CXXII, S169a, T22b, U4), and at Sparta (Dawkins 1929, pls. XCII:2, XCIV, XCV, CXII:2, CXXIV: c, d). And winged figures fighting other winged creatures such as griffins, lion-griffins or sphinxes are familiar to us from contemporary and earlier Near Eastern art (*viz.* Porada 1948, nos. 608, 610, 611, 650, 689; Barnett 1957, 76 f.).

No. 182 represents a battle between a lion and a sphinx or a siren, for which I can find no specific parallel. Sirens occur in eighth century North Syrian metalwork (Barnett 1964, 22—called a sphinx—fig. 6, pl. 2; Young 1967, 145 ff., fig. 1, pls. XIV ff.), and on ivory (Mallowan and Herrmann 1974, pls. XLVIII-LI); they are related to the bronze winged siren attachments found in various parts of the Near East and Europe in the eighth century (Muscarella 1962, 317 ff.; Herrmann 1966a, 30 ff.; for sirens in general see Dessene 1957, 88 f., nos. 213-218; Porada 1948, nos. 633, 634; for Achaemenid sirens see Boardman 1970, 28).

Nos. 182, 183, 184 and 185, in addition to the winged lions and the human-headed goat/ibex of no. 73, are the only local Hasanlu ivories that deal with mythological scenes; most or all of the other ivories are concerned with the world of reality. All the plaques with the mythological scenes were locally made.

---

[20]The Louvre has an unexcavated gold vessel with a scene similar to typical Akkadian representations of a hero fighting a bull (Amiet, *Syria* XLV, 3-4 [1968]: pl. XVII, 1-2). I find it difficult to come to a firm conclusion about the authenticity of this vessel. Compare also representations on bronze objects of men holding animals by the horns (Calmeyer 1973, C1, C6, III 3b′), all of which are unexcavated. I suggest they should not be quoted as ancient objects without further study (see my comments in *JAOS* 97, 1 [1977]. 79, and Muscarella 1977b, nos. 70, 195).

V

ANIMAL SCULPTURE

Nine examples of lion heads or bodies in the round are extant; counting the lion base of no. 92 and the fragment no. 95, there are eleven examples of these objects at Hasanlu. Without doubt no. 92 was locally sculpted, for aside from the evidence of the relief frieze below the lion, the latter exhibits certain features in common with the well-known Hasanlu bronze lion pins: in body position, in the placement of the tail between one thigh and the body, and in the geometric decoration of the outlined leg—on the pins with triangles (Dyson 1964b, fig. 9; 1968, figs. 123, 124; cf. the decoration on the ivory lion's neck), on the ivory lion with squares.

No. 187 may also be of local manufacture although I do not feel entirely secure on this matter. It is exquisitely carved, juxtaposing elaborate relief decoration with cutouts for inlay, and it is one of the finest pieces in the repertory. No similar object exists at Hasanlu, or elsewhere, to my knowledge, although the figure-eight design on the front leg is the same as that depicted on no. 170, a locally carved lion in relief. The flat base and dowel holes suggest that no. 187 was attached to a flat object, and it may have functioned as a decorative unit on the lid of a box, like the pyxis calves nos. 242-245. The compact pose reminds us of the Scythian-style animals depicted in relief on some objects said to have come from Ziwiye (Godard 1950, figs. 17, 23, 24, 33; Ghirshman 1964, fig. 142). Also, I think, it has a resemblance to the squat lions, albeit of different style, found on Luristan pins (Moorey 1971, nos. 318, 343, 345), and also on axes and swords (Pope 1938, pl. 50, E, 54, B). This squat, compact pose may be an Iranian concept. A lion on an ivory tube-pyxis from Nimrud, and apparently of ninth century date (Barnett 1957, pl. XXXVIII, S74) has a figure-eight motif on its shoulder, not dissimilar to those represented on nos. 170 and 187, which seem to be early examples.

No. 189 consists of a completely preserved lion protome and fragments of a second, forming a pair. One thinks of the ninth century Assyrian chairs and thrones with an animal-head protome at the ends of the seat (Frankfort 1954, pl. 89; Baker 1966, figs. 291, 292, 306; Kyrieleis 1969, fig. 7, pls. 1-4; cf. also the eighth century Barrekub's throne, Orthmann 1971, pl. 63c), but in these examples there must have been four heads, two in front, two at the back. It is possible that there were originally four heads at Hasanlu, two of which fragmented, or that our heads decorated an object other than a chair or throne. Seen from the front or side the protomes give the effect of a free-standing lion because they include shoulders and paws. As such they remind us of the portal lions common in North Syrian palaces. To my mind, the protomes, and also lion no. 92, reflect influences more from North Syria than from Assyria. The Assyrian ninth century lion had another type of mane pattern and a thick decorated ruff separating the head from the neck (Frankfort 1954, pl. 87; Madhloom 1970, pls. LXVI, 1, 2, LXXVII, 2; see also Freyer–Schauenburg 1966, 87 f.), which is not the case with nos. 92 and 189. The muzzle pattern, the nose wrinkles (separated by a T-shaped nostril on no. 92), the cheek swellings under the eyes, the forehead warts on a raised rectangular swelling, and the curve of the mouth as well as the high position of the ears, find their best parallels in North Syrian art (*viz.* Akurgal 1949, figs. 35, 38, 39, 41, 42, 47; cf., the mane pattern, Muscarella 1965, figs. 1, 2; 1974b, figs. 2, 3).

It is of further interest to note that when no. 92

is viewed in profile, it looks remarkably like the lion supporting the nude goddess on the Hasanlu gold bowl (Porada 1965, pl. 24). Moreover, the mane pattern of the lion beneath the mountain deity on the bowl is the same as that under discussion here.

Although there is no mane or body decoration on the head and face of no. 186, its head is not unlike those of nos. 92 and 189. Differences do exist: the plain raised ruff terminating at the ears, the "solid" mouth, and the ears, which consist of a crescent enclosing a "wart." This type of ear is not to be found on ninth century Assyrian lions, but rather in North Syria, where it is also usual for the ruff to terminate at the ears (*viz.* Akurgal 1949, 35, figs. 35, 41, 42, 45, 46, 48; also at eighth century Sakçegözü, pl. XXX); some of these, and still other North Syrian lions, also have "solid" mouths. Wartlike ears are found on an ivory lion from Samos that has been recognized as North Syrian by Freyer-Schauenburg (1966, 87 f., pl. 22; Akurgal 1949, 41, 75, pl. XXXVII, sees this ear type as Assyrian). Warts on the ear existed in Hittite art at Boğazköy and Alaca Hüyük (Akurgal 1949, figs. 27-29, 32, 33), the direct antecedent to the North Syrian usage.

Two distinctive details on no. 186 do however occur on ninth century Assyrian lions: the incised tulip design on the leg and the outlined shoulder with its smaller outlined fold of muscle (Layard 1849, pls. 6, 9, 10, 31, 32, etc.; Madhloom 1970, pls. LXXVI, 1, 2, LXXVII, 2). Neither seems to exist on contemporary North Syrian lions although a modified tulip design was known there (Akurgal 1966, figs. 88, 89; Orthmann 1971, pl. 12c; Barnett 1957, pl. XLIX, S78c).

The wart ear is also fairly common in later Urartian art, for example on a bronze lion protome from Karmir Blur and on bronze lion heads from Toprakkale (Piotrovsky 1970, figs. 64, 65; van Loon 1966, fig. 12, pls. XI, XIX). It occurs also on bronze lions in the round from Kayalidere and Patnos (Burney 1966, 75 ff., fig. 8; Akurgal 1968, pl. XXXVIIa, b). These two lions have in addition the small outlined fold of muscle on the shoulders as well as the tulip design on the legs, which relate them both to the Hasanlu lion no. 186 and to Assyrian lions. An extraordinary seated ivory lion in the round from Altintepe also has the wart ear.[21] Although it has a different pose and a solid mouth, no. 186 seems closest to the later Urartian bronze lions from Patnos and Kayalidere (even H.–V. Herrmann, 1966b, 109, seems to accept the Urartian bronze lions as locally made; also van Loon *apud* Burney 1966, 75).

Although discussed here with local-style ivories, no. 186 was probably an import, inasmuch as no other lion from Hasanlu has the wart ear and the tulip design. The specific center in the West whence the ivory might have come is not clear, given the mixed elements; I tentatively accept a North Syrian provenience, but leave the question of its origin open. One wonders if the Urartian bronze lions had their inspiration from Iran in lieu of, or as well as, from the West.

The gold bracelets in the Teheran Museum and in the A. B. Martin Collection have lions in the round that have "gabled" heads and ears with warts (Godard 1950, figs. 40, 41; Wilkinson 1963, figs. 11-13; Porada 1965, 134, pl. 39). Porada has called attention to the North Syrian background of the ear and has also mentioned the Karmir Blur lion protome. Van Loon (1966, 178), and Barnett (1956b, 112) have suggested that the bracelets are of Urartian manufacture: this may be so, but indeed they could

[21]Özgüç (1969, 87 ff., pls. A, 2, XXXIV, XXXV, figs. 39, 40), Akurgal (1968, 77, fig. 45) and Herrmann (1966b, 105 f., note 72) say this lion is not Urartian, rather provincial Assyrian (Akurgal) or North Syrian (Herrmann). Özgüç (1969, 85, note 71) believes that it and the other ivories from Urartu are examples of Urartian art, but made under the supervision of North Syrian craftsmen (see also van Loon 1966, 133 and Mallowan 1966, 377, note 16). The Altintepe lion is unique and it is not easy to reach a consensus. Herrmann, *loc. cit.*, rightly rejects calling the other Altintepe and the Toprakkale ivories Urartian; they are imports—which opinion I accept—except for the Altintepe lion, about which I am not sure. The couchant ivory lions from Altintepe (Özgüç 1969, 83 ff., pls. A, 1, XXXVI, XXXVII, figs. 43, 44) are also a problem with respect to ultimate origin. Yet given the opinion that all—or most—of the other ivories so far found in Urartu are probably imports, can one accept the seated and couchant lions, pieces of very sophisticated manufacture, as made by Urartians? Some bone objects from Karmir Blur might be locally made and so might the wooden statues, none of which are so fine as the ivories discussed above (Piotrovsky 1970, figs. 29-34; 88-92, maybe 93, 94).

The Urartian ivories mentioned here apparently do not pre-date the eighth century B.C. That ivory objects existed in Nairi in the ninth century is attested by a text of Ashurnasirpal II (Luckenbill 1926, I, para. 501) where an ivory couch overlaid with gold is mentioned as booty given to the Assyrians. Unfortunately, we do not know if in this instance Nairi equals Urartu. Further we do not know if the couch was made of plain ivory plaques and legs, nor if the couch was a locally made product or an import from the West. Later, in the eighth century, Sargon II took as booty from Musasir ivory staves, daggers, cups, tables, a couch and other ivory objects (Luckenbill 1926, II: para. 172-174). Again, the original source of these products is not known.

easily have been made within Iran, inspired by North Syrian, Urartian, and even Iranian prototypes. The bracelets are said to have come from Ziwiye, but there is in fact no proof of this, and they could have come from there or from another site within Iran (cf. also Godard 1950, fig. 48; Muscarella 1977a, 199 f., note 6, 201). In any event, there is no strong reason—based on present information concerning Urartian goldwork—to consider these objects as products of an Urartian atelier, where to date nothing like them has yet been excavated (see also Wilkinson 1963, 282). I can find no parallel for the mane decoration of no. 188 and am not sure whether it is an import or a locally made piece.

VI

TREES, PLANTS, MISCELLANEOUS

The rectangular plaques with trees in relief, nos. 191-197, were probably used to decorate boxes or even the surfaces of furniture. All appear to have been locally made and represent a local variety of an Assyrian or North Syrian prototype. A fragmentary silver plaque from Hasanlu (64-862, BB II) has in relief two trees of the same type as represented on the ivories, except that the trunk, decorated with vertical incisions like the ivory examples, has no branches.

An incised tree from Nimrud (Barnett 1957, pl. CXX, T21) has the same top as ours but does not have the side branches—reminding us of the Hasanlu silver plaque. The volute motif at the base of our trees reminds us of similar features on a tree represented on a bronze vase probably from Iran (Muscarella 1972, fig. 9, top).[22] The volute at the base and also the raised bands on the trunk and a splayed top flower, are typical of branchless trees from Tell Halaf (Moortgat 1955, pls. 78, 79a); and related, but often more elaborate trees, are known in Assyrian art from the Middle Assyrian period onward (Strommenger 1962, pls. 186, bottom, 187, middle, 193).

Most of the miscellaneous items may be dealt with briefly. No. 200 probably represents joints from a small piece of furniture; nos. 201 and 202 appear to be box lids with bronze knob handles, and no. 203 seems to be a box fragment. No. 204 must be an inset from a flanged dagger or sword handle, other examples of which exist in stone at Hasanlu and elsewhere (Calmeyer 1969, 122, note 396, figs. 60-63; Moorey 1971, fig. 13).

The function of nos. 207-213 was probably as inlays and borders for boxes or plaques. Similar rosette discs and guilloche bands are fairly common in the ivory repertory of other sites (*viz.* Barnett 1957, pl. CXXII, T18; Crowfoot 1938, pl. XXI, 7; Loud and Altman 1938, pl. 56:71; Loud 1939, pl. 15: 74-79; de Mertzenfeld 1954, pls. XVII, 203, LIX, 502, 503, XCVII, 924-927, CVIII, 987; Özgüç 1966, 43, pl. XX, 4; Poursat 1977, II pl. IX, 119, 121). I can find no parallels for the pronged objects, such as no. 211; the fact that the one fully preserved example is decorated on both sides suggests that it was not an inlay. Its shape suggests that it was meant to be a turret.[23] The bands, no. 198, may have framed boxes or decorated plaques; two have finished upper borders but two were obviously larger than now preserved. All that can be said of no. 199 is that a flower, apparently from a tree, is depicted; no other examples of such flowers are preserved. I am not certain that nos. 198 and 199 are local products.

The eye insets, nos. 205 and 206, belonged to a statuette of a human, I suggest, rather than to an animal (cf. Harper 1969, fig. 3); each once held an iris inlay. It appears that they came from a fairly large statuette, larger it would seem than those preserved to us. Solid eye insets are known from Arslan Tash (Thureau–Dangin 1931, pl. XLIII, 86) and examples very much like ours were excavated on Crete and at Delphi (Kunze 1936, 224, pl. 86:28, 33, 34; Amandry 1939, 91 ff., fig. 7, pls. XIX-XXII). At Delphi some of the eyes were found detached, others *in situ* in ivory heads.

The function of the fragments no. 213 bis eludes me. The design reminds one of the hair on some of the North Syrian female heads although our fragments do not appear to be heads. Furthermore, it is not certain that these pieces are local products.

[22] J. Vorys Canby has called to my attention that the plant in the upper left of Muscarella 1972, fig. 10 is very similar to Canby 1971, pl. XIII, c.

[23] One is reminded of the strange pronged architectural units excavated by the Tilias at Persepolis (A. Britt Tilia, *Studies and Reconstructions at Persepolis and other Sites of Fars* [Rome, 1972], 61, text fig. 2, figs. 128, 129, pl. F).

VII

IRANIAN IVORIES

The winged bulls in relief, nos. 214-221 stand out from the other ivories at Hasanlu both because they are among the best-executed pieces in the repertory and because on the basis of style they appear not to be products typical of the local workshops. They may be separated into two distinct groups. The first consists of nos. 214-217 and 221; the second of nos. 218-220. The bulls of the first group apparently walk one behind the other (see no. 215); there is no evidence that they were placed in heraldic positions. Although their surfaces are quite worn and the pieces very fragmented, certain features are clear: thin elegant legs with curled hair tufts on the front; a straight vertical chest; a ruff separating the head from the neck; thick double-outlined eyebrow over a round eye; horns thick at the vertical base, that then curve out horizontally; a generous supply of spiral curls at the ruff, throat, stomach and chest; a single curl at the forehead and at the base of the tail; the tail projecting upward, then falling straight down; wings neatly divided into zones that terminate in round units decorated with a neat herringbone pattern. It is not clear whether the bodies were decorated in any manner but one sees at least that on no. 215 there is a row of incised circles on the thigh. An elaborate tree or plant characterized by rosettes with a drilled center separates one bull from the other.

The second group of bulls, much better preserved in details than the first, is characterized as follows: relatively short angular legs elaborately decorated with incisions; a wavy chest outlined by a thick border; a plain ruff separating the head and neck; thick multiple-outlined eyebrows over an oval-shaped eye drawn vertically; a muzzle that touches the chest; an absence of curls on any part of the body; the whole body divided into units—stomach, back, haunch—by neat incised lines; flesh folds on the neck and chest represented by incised lines; wings that are bordered by bands terminating in triangular units, and which have no internal divisions or feather pattern.

I suggest that both groups of bulls are to be accepted as examples of Iranian ivory carving, each group coming from a different workshop, perhaps even a different site. Iranian elements in the first group consist of the occurrence of curls on various parts of the body, and the leg hair tufts (Muscarella 1972, 41, figs. 9, 10, 15; Calmeyer 1973, F5, H3, L1, 2, 4, M1; cf. Wilkinson 1975, 45, fig. 17); the incised circles on the haunch (Calmeyer 1973, H2, 6, 12, L1, 4, M3); the curve of the horns (Muscarella 1972, 36, 41, figs. 10, 11); and the general deportment of the walking bulls (Negahban 1964, pl. XII, figs. 111, 140; compare also the tails, horns and wings). The Iranian elements of the second group are more obvious, especially in the division of the body into units (Muscarella 1972, 40 ff., figs. 9-11, 15, 16; 1974a, 242 f., 247), the wavy chest, the bordered wings, and the outlined projecting shoulder (Calmeyer 1972, groups H, L and M; Muscarella 1972, 31 ff., 40 f., figs. 9-11; 1974a, 239, 242, pl. 46, fig. 1). A few more minor details reinforce the Iranian background: there is an incised inverted V on the front corner of the eye, a feature that also exists on the bulls drawing a chariot on the Hasanlu gold bowl (Dyson 1959, 18), and on winged bulls represented on a gold vessel from Marlik (Negahban 1964, pl. XII, figs. 111, 140); incised chevron markings exist on the legs of no. 165, markings also found on bulls represented on bronze beakers (Calmeyer 1973, L3, 4; Muscarella 1974a, pl. 50, fig. 19); and it should be noted that the wings of the second group are plain, like those on the beakers.

The trees of the first group are fairly easy to reconstruct: they have a thick vertically incised lower unit with side volutes from which sprouts a straight, narrow chevron-decorated trunk that terminates in a large flower. From the trunk and top spring rosette flowers attached to stems; the latter may be plain (no. 215) or decorated (no. 217). In basic structure and form the trees are quite like contemporary Assyrian examples and are probably derived from them (Barnett n.d., pls. 3, 7; Porada 1945, pl. VII). However, I can find no parallels for the rosette (cf. Amiet 1966, fig. 271, from Tchoga Zanbil). All that remains of the tree placed with other fragments in no. 221 is part of the trunk and two volutes. This fragment was found close to no. 218 and may have belonged to that fragment; its high relief—cf. no. 215—supports this suggestion. Note that all the fragments of the first group were found in BB II Room 10; all but no. 220 of the second group were found in the neighboring Room 8; moreover, in the first group the figures are about twice the height of those in the second. This all suggests that the two groups may have decorated separate objects.

Although it has been concluded that the bull fragments were manufactured in Iranian workshops, it is obvious that they were not products of the workshops that produced the other ivories from Hasanlu. Moreover, they reflect far more than any of the other Hasanlu ivories an intimate knowledge of the metalworkers' skill and techniques in the precision of the drawings and the use of decorative details. Indeed, as demonstrated, decorated metal vessels present the best parallels. This does not necessarily mean that the same artisans who made the decorated metal vessels also made the ivories, although this is not an impossible concept. The one example at Hasanlu of metalwork closely associated with ivory carving, no. 175, is cruder in execution than any of the ivories and suggests either that an ivory carver not skilled in metalwork created this piece, or that a local metalworker, not involved in ivory carving, made it. In any event, no. 175 was not the inspiration for the craftsmen who carved the bulls. These craftsmen most certainly had fine metal vessels at hand and were skilled enough to translate the same features and details from metal to ivory.

Where were these ivories carved? Two suggestions present themselves: they were made at Hasanlu by the best and most skilled craftsmen and thus represent a "court style"; or they were imported from another area within Iran, which, judging from the style, was probably in northwestern Iran, anywhere from the western and southern shores of the Caspian to the Zagros. Because these ivories with their distinct style represent a small percentage of those from Hasanlu, it would seem that the second suggestion is the more probable. Thus, these ivories give us a clue that one or more ivory carving centers existed in northwestern Iran in addition to Hasanlu. (For another possible Iranian piece, see no. 221 bis.)

VIII

NORTH SYRIAN IVORIES

VIII. A: LION BOWLS

The lion bowl no. 222 from BB II has already been published and needs no further comment here (Muscarella 1974b). In the 1974 season at Hasanlu fragments of apparently three separate ivory lion bowls were excavated from BB V (223-225). The wings of no. 223 have no cross-hatching design; this is lacking also on the tip of the tail of no. 224, so it is possible that this small fragment is part of 223, although we cannot be sure. However, the claws of nos. 224 and 225 are both from left feet, and are therefore from separate bowls. Thus there are possibly three, certainly two, ivory lion bowls from BB V. Whereas no. 222 has wings that are cut out to receive inlays, similar to the pyxides wings (*infra*), the wings of no. 223, probably those of a bird, are solid, in relief (cf. Muscarella 1974b, figs. 1, 3b). The winged creatures of no. 224 and apparently no. 225 (only their tails are extant), also seem to be birds, not sphinxes, which apparently exist on no. 222. Birds with solid wings are found on ivory lion bowls from Nimrud (Barnett 1957, pls. XLIX, S87a, b, here with a hand at the base), on a bowl from Samos (Freyer–Schauenburg 1966, pl. 28; Muscarella 1974b, figs. 4a, b), and on a bowl from Tell Halaf (*infra*; cf. also a stone bowl in the Louvre, *Syria,* XLI, 1964, pl. XIV, 3-4, known to me only from the publication). The fragmentary lion claws of nos. 224 and 225 are the same type as no. 222, a type known on some ivory lion bowls from Nimrud (Barnett 1957, pl. XLIX, S78a, b), as well as on other ivories there (Mallowan 1966, fig. 453). The spread-out paw with the sharp nails is to be seen in ninth century Assyrian art, on the Black Obelisk of Shalmanezer III and on the incised garment decoration of kings (Madhloom 1970, pl. LXXVII, 2; Canby 1971, pls. X, c, XI, c, XIII, b; fig. 2). It also occurs on ivories said to have been found at Ziwiye (Godard 1950, figs. 82, 83).[24]

Hasanlu has now yielded a total of five or six lion bowls: one of Egyptian Blue with two sphinxes below the rim and covered with gold foil, one of stone (fragmentary) with two lion cubs at the rim (Muscarella 1965, figs. 1-3, 10), and three, possibly four, of ivory, one apparently with two sphinxes, the others apparently with birds below the rim. Two of the bowls, the Egyptian Blue example and no. 222, were recovered from BB II, the stone bowl was a surface find, and the others came from BB V. Thus at least two of the major buildings contained these objects, whose function is still not fully understood to everyone's satisfaction.

To the list of excavated bowls presented in Muscarella 1974b, 25, one should now add nos. 223-225. In addition, one should also add a steatite fragment from Tel Zeror that preserves only a lion's claw (Ogawa 1971, 25 ff.), and an ivory fragment from Tell Halaf that was published years ago but not previously recognized (Hrouda 1962, 9, pl. 10, 59a-c). This latter piece preserves one of the two winged birds originally placed at the rim of the bowl, but nothing of the lion. It is similar in type to the Hasanlu bowls nos. 223-225, and to the example from Samos.[25] In addition I believe

[24] The lion (and all the other decoration) in repoussé and incised on a bronze bucket in the Metropolitan Museum of Art (Wilkinson 1963, figs. 14, 15) is a modern addition, as was established by laboratory analysis (Muscarella 1977a, 211; *idem* 1977b, no. 162).

[25] I do not think it is of value to list the many non-excavated bowls that continually turn up in dealers' shops and in collections. They are all without provenience and add nothing to our knowledge about the bowls and their function; some seem to me to be of modern manu-

that an ivory bowl from Crete (known to me only from photographs) is a lion bowl and not a female body joined to a lion's head (Kunze 1936, 222, pl. 84, 14), nor a swimming lady (Barnett 1957, 44, note 9; Galling 1969, 100 ff.; cf. Muscarella 1970, 119 f.; cf. also Freyer–Schauenburg 1966, 120 f., note 676).

In my discussion of the Hasanlu stone lion bowl (Muscarella 1965, 41 ff., 45 f.) two stone parallels were brought forth, one from the Kofler Collection, the other purchased at Sandilieh by C. L. Woolley and now in the Ashmolean Museum. In fact, a third, ivory, example exists, one I belatedly recognized; it is a fragment excavated by Loftus at Nimrud (Barnett 1957, 197, pl. L, S82) and consists now only of a lion cub overlooking the rim of the bowl. The fragment should be restored with a second cub overlooking the rim, as well as the central lion at the tube end, and it is therefore the same type as the Hasanlu, Kofler and Sandilieh bowls. Thus, there are at least four lion bowls of this type (cf. Barnett 1957, pl. L, S83), two of which derive from excavated contexts.

VIII. B: PYXIDES

Turning to the pyxides we note that there are fragments representing approximately eight to ten separate objects; except for nos. 228, 237 and 238, from BB V, all were recovered from BB II, from the neighboring rooms 6 and 7. That there are as many objects as stated may be suggested from the following comments. Nos. 226 and 229 both have insets at the base, but they are of a different thickness, and they have different double-banded base lines. No. 227 could belong to no. 226, but it has no inset and faces the same direction; nos. 231 and 232 also seem to be from separate pyxides, but we do not know for certain that there were not four sphinxes depicted on each pyxis.[26] No. 230 alone has a necklace and is from a different area than the other pyxides from BB II. No. 231 is also thicker than nos. 226 and 227, and no. 229 has no inset. Nos. 234 and 235A have different types of carving of the shoulders, ears and hair, although no. 235B could belong to no. 235A. No. 236 has a zig-zag base, unlike nos. 226, 227 and 229, but similar to no. 234. No. 237 is from BB V, but is not part of no. 238, although it could belong with no. 228. No. 238 is from a different area than all the other BB II fragments.

The decorated pyxides allow themselves to be divided into four groups: 226-233, 236; 234-235A, B; 237; 238. The first group represents a homogeneous unit and was probably made in the same workshop. Collectively they may be briefly described: two couchant sphinxes are in heraldic position with a plant or palm frond separating them. One wing is extended forward to touch the palm, the other, extended backward, rests along the body; both are carved in the champlevé technique—with drill holes extant—to receive inlays. The front feet are extended, the rear tucked under the body, in a natural position for animals at rest. Bodies and legs have incised decoration that includes the distinctive flame pattern, neatly hatched triangular tufts at the lower rear part of the body, and a lozenge design on the coverts of the wings, which are solid. Tails curve up gracefully and frame a (now missing) element, probably a tree. The faces are fleshy and without beards; the nose is fairly thick, almost straight-bridged; lips are thin; the chin small; large eyes are oval with inlaid pupils, and fill the area between the nose and ears; heart-shaped ears partly overlap a soft pointed cap; the hair is straight, curling up at the ends into a spiral curl, overlapping the wing; a zig-zag band in relief forms the upper border, narrow bands the lower, and no. 236 alone has a lower zig-zag border (cf. no. 234); only one sphinx, no. 230, wears a necklace. The decorative zone, perhaps even the whole pyxis, was originally covered with gold foil. The decorative zone is confined to the lower half of the vessel; a plain convex section above the upper zig-zag becomes vertical and ends in a ledge, the lip, which projects and is flat. In section the lower decorated zone projects slightly more than the plain vertical area just below the lip.

Pyxides of the second group are similar in style, format and composition to those of the first, and were also covered with gold foil. Here the sphinxes have the same couchant position, the same wing type, body decoration, faces and ears. However, their hair is rendered in chunks, like an Egyptian wig, and they wear no hat, only a fillet; a small difference is also noticed in that the covert of the wing has a square rather than a lozenge decoration. There are at least two pyxides of this group at Hasanlu, both of which were made in the same workshop, perhaps by the same individual.

The question naturally arises whether the hat and

facture. Only excavated bowls or those not excavated that have a distinct or rare motif, and that are without doubt genuine, should be published (see Muscarella 1977b, 190 f., nos. 234-237).

[26]Cf. Barnett 1957, 192, S13, pl. XIX, where three sphinxes are depicted; and S18, pl. XXI, where four sphinxes are depicted.

hair differences between the two groups suggest that they came from two different centers, or workshops, or whether the differences merely reflect different sexes. Male sexual organs are not commonly depicted on representations of sphinxes and except for beards it is not usually apparent if a sphinx is male or female (Dessene 1957, 87; Calmeyer 1973, 64, H5; cf. Harper 1969, 160 f., figs. 4, 5, 8, called female). A sphinx on a blinker from Nimrud (Orchard 1967, no. 41) has both a beard and male sex and also chunky-style hair. And on a cylinder or pyxis of the tall type, also from Nimrud (Barnett 1957, 195, pls. XXXIII-IV, S50), there are unbearded sphinxes with the spiral curl who have distinct male sex depicted (Barnett calls them female). Thus male sphinxes could be bearded or not, and have hair that is short and chunky or straight with a curl.

Other sphinxes have breasts making it clear that they are females (Dessene 1957, 112, 115, 147; cf. 123, 129 f., 149 f.). Although the Nimrud (and Hasanlu) pyxis-sphinxes depict no sexual organs Barnett assumed that they were females (Barnett 1957, 8 f., 142, 191 f.). It is certain that females with straight hair and lower curl are represented at Nimrud (*viz.* Barnett 1957, pls. XCIII, S336, XXIII, S26, XXVI, S20). A pyxis from Nimrud of probable ninth—but possible eighth—century date depicting musicians (Mallowan 1966, fig. 168) shows in the same scene males with chunky hair next to females with straight hair and a curl, and here there is no doubt that the hair style is a sexual distinction. Yet on another pyxis from Nimrud, this one perhaps of eighth century date, and also depicting musicians (Barnett 1957, pl. XVI, S3), all the figures have the same chunky-style hair. Some seem to be clearly males, but are some females, as Barnett suggests? Their dress might indicate that they are all males, although the question may be left open.

Further complicating the issue with respect to hair depiction and sex is a silver plaque from Zincirli (von Luschan 1943, pl. 47e) where there is a beardless male who has the same hair and hat as on our first group of pyxides. He faces a female who has the very same hair style but a fillet rather than a hat.

The evidence therefore suggests that both males and females could be depicted with straight hair ending in a curl, and that males often were depicted with chunky hair. And the ninth/eighth century Nimrud pyxis depicting musicians shows us that the artist would at times differentiate males and females in the same scene by giving each a particular hair style. This pyxis also demonstrates to us that there need be no chronological difference nor separate workshops involved merely because the sphinxes at Hasanlu have distinct hair styles—a situation that may also be inferred from no. 174 of the Hasanlu corpus. Why a distinction in hair and hat styles exists at Hasanlu on the pyxides must for the present remain an open question. One may tentatively see the sphinxes with the hair curl and hats as female (nos. 226, 227, 230), the others as male (234, 235A, B), but the lack of uniformity in these matters prevents one from arriving at more secure conclusions. [Winter 1976, 340 f. suggests that our second group depicts males.]

The third group, represented by only one example, no. 237, apparently originally depicted two standing or walking heraldic sphinxes placed above a guilloche border. The fourth, no. 238, probably depicts one or more walking bulls. Parenthetically, it should be mentioned here that the small fragments, nos. 240 and 241, might have been from plain undecorated pyxides or another type of box. The holes at their bases seem to indicate that they had added bottoms (cf. Barnett 1957, fig. 17). If these examples are pyxides then we have a fifth, plain, group.

The Hasanlu pyxides are of course the very same types that were excavated at Nimrud, and are typical "Nimrud ivories." For the first group we may cite as stylistically exact or close parallels Barnett 1957, pls. XIX, S13, XX, S16, XXV, S23c (cf. S23c to no. 261); other pyxides have the very same facial types (Barnett 1957, pls. XXVIII, XXIX, S12). For the second group there are no specific pyxis-sphinx parallels but the face and hair type are close to those represented on other pyxides (Barnett 1957, pls. XVII, S3, XXIII, S28; Mallowan 1966, fig. 168). Also, the wings of the Hasanlu and Nimrud sphinxes have the same drill holes. Minor differences between these Nimrud and Hasanlu pyxides exist: on the Nimrud examples some of the hats have a band tied in a knot at the rear; a different type of tree separates the sphinxes; the upper line of the wings is higher relative to the heads; and the sphinxes occupy the full, straight wall, rather than only the lower section of the pyxis. Also of some interest is the fact that only two of the Hasanlu examples, nos. 237 and 238, have guilloche borders, common at Nimrud, while the others have zig-zags, not occurring on the Nimrud examples. The zig-zag design does exist on a pyxis lid from Nimrud (Mallowan 1966, 173), attesting to its use there. Also, the heights of the Nimrud examples vary from one that is the same height as no. 231 (S2, 5.8 cm.), to others that are larger, 8 and 8.5 cm. (S20, S1), presumably because of the size of the tusk chosen at the time of manufacture. Nevertheless, the overall similarities between the Hasanlu and Nimrud pyxides are so outstanding that even if there may be a question that they came from the same workshop, they surely came from the same center, probably from neighboring workshops. That they are of North Syrian origin is certain: the eyes, nose, mouth, chin, hats, and body decoration are well attested in North Syrian art (*viz.* von Luschan 1943, pl. 47d, e; Kantor 1956, fig. 5; Orthmann 1971, pls. 8d, 28b, 61b, c). [For a good discussion of these pyxides as typically North Syrian now see Winter 1976b.]

An exact parallel for no. 237 of the third group also exists at Nimrud (Barnett 1957, pl. XX, S17; cf. S14 and pl. XII, S6, S18; the latter wears a necklace exactly like no. 198). I suggest that there can be no doubt that the same hand made both S17 and no. 237, as line for line they match precisely. For no. 238 one may refer to Mallowan 1966, figs. 438 and 551 for the closest parallels.

A few "frit" or faience pyxides of local manufacture from Susa continued the tradition of decorated pyxides within Iran. One pyxis has winged sphinxes (Amiet 1966, fig. 375) that are framed at the top by a guilloche border. Although distinctly Elamite in style, this pyxis is obviously related in its decoration to both the Nimrud and Hasanlu pyxides, and may safely be considered as derivative from them. Porada (1965, 70) dates the Susa examples as roughly contemporary with the Nimrud and Hasanlu examples, but they may actually not pre-date the eighth century B.C. What is not known to us is whether the Susan artists knew of the pyxides from their possibly earlier occurrence within Iran (Hasanlu) or because of direct Elamite contacts with Assyria.

An incised bronze pyxis from War Kabud (vanden Berghe 1968, 133 ff., 169, fig. 30:4, pl. 35) has four scorpion sphinxes and four fortresses depicted. The hair and eyes, and the foot and wing positions of the scorpion-sphinx clearly derive from the North Syrian sphinxes depicted on the ivory pyxides. However, none of the ivory pyxides has a similar creature depicted nor a representation of a fortress, the latter, at least, more commonly found on Assyrian works of art. It is therefore probable that the War Kabud pyxis, although ultimately derived from a North Syrian prototype, may actually have had a more immediate Assyrian background (van Loon 1972, 68); the type of incising may further reinforce this conclusion. Thus, if my conclusion is viable, the War Kabud pyxis may not be brought forth as a definite example of a North Syrian import or an example of North Syrian influence in Luristan (*infra*).

The zig-zag border pattern on the Hasanlu pyxides occurs on other ivories from Hasanlu (nos. 73, 116). It is found earlier on ivories from Megiddo (de Mertzenfeld 1954, pls. LVII, 483, LX, 521) and from Kamid el-Loz (Hachmann and Kuschke 1966, figs. 18-20), and on a few combs at Nimrud (Barnett 1957, pl. LXIX, S169); also on some ivories said to have come from Ziwiye (Godard 1950, figs. 91, 92). These latter ivories are probably Iranian works and the zig-zag might be derived from the Hasanlu examples. Later Achaemenid ivories from Susa also have the zig-zag pattern (Amiet 1972, figs. 22, 23). In addition, it should be noted that the pattern is to be found on several Greek ivories from Sparta (Dawkins 1929, pls. CXXVI ff.).

I am not absolutely sure that the fragment no. 238 is from a pyxis. It has the same lozenge wing-covert as the pyxis-sphinxes and is also covered with gold foil, but this does not preclude its coming from a plaque (cf. Barnett 1957, fig. 11). Likewise, as already stated, it is not clear whether the fragments of nos. 240 and 241 are from a plain pyxis. (For other possible pyxides see nos. 259, 261).

It has been mentioned that several of the pyxis fragments at Hasanlu have small holes at their bases to secure the separately made bottoms in place. Holes for small dowels also exist on the Nimrud pyxides, but there they were placed slightly above the base within the design area itself (Barnett 1957, pls. XIX, XXII; the former also had a dowel on the body of the sphinx, probably for a repair). A Middle Assyrian ivory pyxis from Assur and two pyxides from second millennium Alalakh have similar holes at their bases (Orthmann 1975, Abb. 256; Woolley 1955, 290, pl. LXXVII); one of the Alalakh pyxides also has a guilloche border, a forerunner of the later Nimrud examples. Ivory pyxides from Mycenaean Greece also have separately made bottoms attached to their bases by dowels; in some cases the bottom was inset into the pyxis, in others it was joined to it outside (Davis 1974, 482, figs. 15, 18; Shear 1940, 283, 287, figs. 27, 31. Poursat 1977, II, pls. XXV, XXIX, XXXVII, XLII). The fact that a pyxis, wherever made, was usually carved from the hollow part of a tusk, made necessary a separate base (but cf. Poursat 1977, II, pl. I, no. 41).

The recent excavations by Mallowan at Nimrud have allowed us to interpret the small couchant calves (nos. 242-245) as handles on the pyxis lids (Barnett 1957, 64 f., fig. 19; Mallowan 1966, 219, fig. 173; also figs. 174-175). The Hasanlu examples are easily matched in style, form and body decoration, as well as in the form of the slots for attachment at the base, to those from Nimrud and they were probably made in the same workshops. A few minor differences exist, for none of the published Nimrud examples apparently has the elaborate curls found on the back of nos. 242 and 243, nor do they have the very neatly incised triangular hair pattern found on the bellies of the Hasanlu calves. This distinctive hair pattern occurs, however, on numerous examples of North Syrian art, on ivory plaques, on ivory and stone lion bowls, on ivory pyxides, and on stone, metal and terracotta objects (Hrouda 1962, pl. 9, 49; Barnett 1957, 47, fig. 11, pls. XVIII-XXI, XXXVIII, XCVIII; von Luschan 1943, pls. 9i, 10h, 14h; Barnett 1956a, 236, pl. XXIIIc; Moortgat 1955, pls. 38, 44, 46-48, 109, 118; Kantor 1962, figs. 5, 6). It is of some interest to point out here that couchant calves and other animals executed in Greek style have been excavated at Perachora and Sparta (Dunbabin 1962, pl. 174; Dawkins 1929, pls. CXLVIII-CXLIX); these are surely derived from the North Syrian couchant calves, those under discussion here (see also Muscarella 1970, 119).

There are fragments of more than half a dozen "lids" (nos. 246-248) from BB II and BB V, where pyxides were excavated. Which of these belongs to a particular pyxis is not possible to establish. Moreover, it is not easy to sort out which of these objects were lids and which may actually have been bottoms. No. 248 seems to be a lid, because of the position of the holes on its decorated surface. Most of the fragments are decorated on both sides, which may suggest that they are lids.[27] No. 246A has no cuttings for surface handles and might be a bottom. Both fragments of no. 247 have dowel holes on their edges suggesting that they are bottoms, but one fragment has gold foil on its edge, which seems strange for a bottom that would be hidden in the inset of the base. Perhaps the bottoms were also covered with gold foil that was tucked up over the edge; cf. also no. 246B. In any event, it is certain that lids and bottoms must have existed, whether or not we are able to recognize and distinguish one from the other.

Parallels for the Hasanlu "lids" are easily found at Nimrud (Barnett 1957, pls. XIX, XXI, XXX, XXXI). A rosette on no. 248 was blocked out but left unfinished and drilled, probably for the attachment of a calf handle; this would explain why the area was not completed. The presence of gold foil makes it clear that we are not dealing with an unfinished object.

[27]The base of the Egyptian Blue goblet, unpublished except in part (Porada 1965, pl. 33), has a rosette design similar to that of the lids/bottoms discussed in the text.

A stone pyxis lid from Carchemish (Woolley 1921, pl. 28c) has a guilloche border like some ivory examples, and its edge is decorated with rosettes similar to those on the border of no. 248 (cf. Barnett 1957, fig. 19 and no. 269 below). Similar rosettes are also to be found on some of the ivories said to come from Ziwiye (Wilkinson 1975, 12). Moreover, it is a favorite filler ornament in early first millennium metal work from Iran (Muscarella 1972, figs. 1-10, 13-15; Moorey 1975, pls. I, II, fig. 7). Still earlier examples exist (de Mertzenfeld 1954, pls. VII, LIII, LIV, LXXV: second millennium).

The function of the shell object no. 221 bis is not certain although examples of exactly the same object are known, one from Tabarak, near Ispahan, according to Herzfeld (1941, 139 f., fig. 254 left), another excavated at Nimrud (Barnett 1957, 85, pl. XVII, b; Rimmer 1969, pl. XXII, c). Herzfeld suggested that the shell, along with others he published, was a shield buckle. Barnett, challenging this interpretation, suggested that the shells were clappers or castanets; he was followed in this interpretation by Rimmer (Barnett 1963a, 84; Rimmer 1969, 40). Mallowan (1966, 125, note 3, 452) disagreed with Barnett and noted that there were no abrasions on the rim of the shells. Whatever function no. 221 bis had, it was certainly carved in the same workshop as the examples from Tabarak and Nimrud; it is also probable, as suggested by Barnett (1963a, 84), that the workshop was in Iran; the style of the carving, however, suggests that the workshop was not at Hasanlu. I have tentatively placed it in the catalogue in the Iranian ivory section.

VIII. C: HEADS, STATUETTES, ANIMALS

Nos. 249 and 250 need little discussion. They are imports from the West, perhaps even from Nimrud itself. Many examples were excavated at Nimrud and one was excavated at Tell Halaf (Hrouda 1962, 3, pl. 9, no. 46); each is slightly different from the others, although there can be little doubt that they were made in closely related workshops. To my knowledge none of the published heads with poloi from outside Hasanlu have the zig-zag hair on the forehead, but other ivory ladies have this feature (Barnett 1957, pl. LXXI, S182). These heads were sometimes found detached from the statuettes' bodies; other times they were found intact, and seem to have been used as caryatids (Barnett 1957,

103 ff., 206). The faces of both the Hasanlu examples are austere and farouche (Brown 1958, 69; Mallowan 1966, 135), typical of the Tell Halaf and Nimrud heads, and characteristic of female heads that are of ninth century date; the eighth century examples are usually softer and more sensuous. Among ancestors of these heads, as has been recognized by others, is an ivory head from the second millennium at Megiddo; the Nimrud and Hasanlu heads are further indications of continuity into the first millennium (de Mertzenfeld 1954, pl. XXV, 342; also pl. XXIV, 342b; for the polos cf. Bossert 1942, 540).

No. 250 was found in the vicinity of no. 252, which includes what seems to be the legs and an arm of a statuette, and a small fragment that seems to be the ankles, complete with anklets, and shins of a nude female. Statuettes with free-standing legs and arms are known from Nimrud (Barnett 1957, pls. VI, LXXVII, S236, S241, S239, fig. 65, C39), as are also females with legs joined together and wearing anklets (Barnett 1957, pls. LXXV, S217, LXXXIX, S294; Mallowan 1966, fig. 549). Whether one or more of the fragments belongs to head no. 250 is not known but, I think, may be accepted as probable. In any event, BB V had at least one imported statuette.

The two fragments of no. 251 are from imported female statuettes, whose hands are held against the body, as, again, we know at Nimrud (Barnett 1957, pls. LXXIII-LXXVI: cf. also Schauenburg 1966, pl. 32.

The fragment of a kilted male, no. 254, was carved in the round and represents a figure striding to his left. This fragment is definitely an import; the kilt type, with the fabric coming to a point at the center is typical of many kilts depicted in art at Nimrud and elsewhere in the West (Barnett 1957, pls. XVIII, XXII, fig. 20, S1-4; Mallowan 1966, 531 f., figs. 443, 446; Bossert 1942, 769, 770, 775, 776, 796, 856). The lozenge pattern, with small lozenges set within a larger one, is exactly paralleled on several North Syrian ivories from Nimrud (*viz.* Barnett 1957, pls. XXIII, S28, and p. 67, fig. 20—mis-labeled—, XXVIII, K1; cf. pls. XXVI-XXVIII, S20, 12ee; Mallowan 1966, 218, fig. 168, 541, fig. 463). In some examples the lozenge border is beaded, in others, plain like no. 254. At least two examples of this lozenge-decorated kilt exist on works of art from the Aegean. One occurs on an ivory fragment from Delphi (Amandry 1939, 105, pl. XXXV, bottom row); this piece appears to be of Greek workmanship judging only from the photograph. The other example occurs on a hero depicted on an orientalizing locally made bronze quiver from Fortetsa on Crete (Brock 1957, 193 ff., pl. 169). Both objects are excellent examples of North Syrian motifs borrowed by the Greeks.

Whether no. 254 was winged or not we cannot say, but the fragmented sculpture in the round, no. 253—also depicting a kilted male, but with a different decoration—preserves part of his wings. The activities of these figures are lost to us. Neither do we know what kind of head they had.

The four lions, nos. 255, 256, 257, 258, two heads and two bodies, are all imports from the West, again probably from North Syria. The function of nos. 255 and 256 is not certain, except that the former was probably a protome and the latter may also have been one. As such they probably served as end pieces on a chair or table, as Mallowan and Thureau-Dangin suggested for similar lion heads from Nimrud and Arslan Tash. Both Hasanlu heads have excellent parallels abroad: no. 255 is neatly matched by a lion's head from Nimrud (Barnett 1957, 219, pl. XCVIII, S358) in the cut-out sections on the forehead, eyes with gold leaf inlays, incised triangular tufts of hair, incised horizontal muzzle lines, and separately made ears. This head and ours could easily have come from the same workshop, even from the same craftsman's hands. Another head from Nimrud (Mallowan 1966, fig. 74) is a different type from the two just discussed, but it has inlays on the head, and may have separately made ears.[28] This head is probably later than the other Nimrud head and the Hasanlu example. No. 256 shares with no. 255 the separately made ears and the triangular tufts, but does not have the cut-outs. No. 256 has an exquisitely carved mane, finer than any other example at Hasanlu, including no. 258. It was cut by a master craftsman. The base of this ivory has a bottle-shaped slot; and both the slot and the head itself have excellent parallels at Nimrud (Barnett 1957, 174, fig. 14; pl. XCVIII, S359).

It is not possible to know whether no. 255—and its Nimrud counterpart—had small dots on the upper muzzle, which exist on nos. 256 and 258. This feature appears on three lion heads from Arslan Tash, which are of a different style from ours (Thureau-Dangin 1931, pl. XLIII, nos. 89-91; Thimme 1973, no. 29 for another probably from Arslan Tash).[29] These Arslan Tash heads are later than ours (*infra*),

[28] Mallowan (1966, 135) says "The ears are thrown back," but the caption to his fig. 74 says "The ears were separately added."

[29] Head no. 89 in Thureau-Dangin's photograph seems to have a separately made ear, but I can find nothing in the text about this.

and they have "warts" that are stained, reminding us of staining on the "Mona Lisa" ivory from Nimrud (Mallowan 1966, 130, n. 14), surely of eighth century date. A bronze lion-griffin protome, probably from Iran, now in the Norbert Schimmel Collection, has dots on the muzzle and lips, showing that this feature was not limited to ivories (Muscarella 1974d, no. 139; cf. no. 145 bis).

No. 257, a fragment of a lion's body, also has good parallels at Nimrud: the neat triangular tufts of the mane and stomach, and the incised vertical markings enclosed within a rectangle on the side of the body (*viz.* Barnett 1957, pls. XVIII-XX, XXII, LXVII, XCVIII, XCIX: cf. from Hasanlu nos. 229, 243, 244). Of some importance is the existence of the stitch-like markings on the lion's back, a motif found on the backs of the couchant calves from the pyxis lids (Barnett 1957, pls. CI-CVI), on sculpture from Tell Halaf (Orthmann 1971, pls. 8f, 11e-g, 12a, c) and on ivories from Tell Halaf and Hama (Hrouda 1962, pl. 9, no. 49; Barnett 1957, 47, figs. 11, 12). Note also that lions in relief on pyxides from Nimrud (Barnett 1957, pls. XVIII, S1, XXVI, S20) have the very same body-hair details, which help us date these pyxides to the ninth century. The austere, farouche and thin lipped face of the female holding the two lions upside down on S20 also supports an early date. Other pyxis-lions from Nimrud share the body markings, again helping us date them to the ninth century (Barnett 1957, pls. XXII, S2, 4, XXIII, S8, XXIV, S10).

No. 258 was probably a handle or a finial; at least it joined another object at the end where there is a smooth rim instead of a tail and a dowel hole at the side. The closest parallels are two rampant lions in the round from Nimrud (Barnett 1957, 218, pl. XCVIII, S353, 354), one of which has a tube opening at its tail end. Compare also an ivory finial said to have come from Ziwiye (Wilkinson 1975, fig. 35). No. 273 might also have been used as a handle or finial, perhaps the end of a fly whisk.

The lions depicted on nos. 260 and 261, of which only parts of bodies are extant, are clearly of a different style than the other lions from Hasanlu, and are obviously not of local manufacture. The closest ivory parallels for the body details, flame pattern, hair tufts, eyes and ears, are again from Nimrud (Barnett 1957, pls. XX, S14, 17, XVIII, S1, XXV, S23c, XXVI, S20, XXVIII, bb, XCVIII, S353, 354). The standing, passant position of our lions also is similar to other North Syrian lions represented in stone (*viz.* Bossert 1942, 852; Akurgal 1949, 50, fig. 46).

No. 261, preserving only part of the rear of the lion/sphinx, has the same body patterns as found on the pyxis-sphinxes; it may be part of a pyxis, but it is too fragmentary and thin for us to be certain. At the same time, however, it should be pointed out that it is exactly paralleled by the rear of the sphinxes on pyxides from Nimrud (Barnett 1957, S17, S14, Pl. XX). No. 259, also from BB V, preserves only part of a bull's foot next to a vertical raised border. Although definitely an import from North Syria, the fragment is too small to enable us to decide whether it is from a plaque or from a pyxis (cf. Barnett 1957, S51, S143, pls. XXXV, LXII).

VIII. D: BOXES, HANDLES, MISCELLANEOUS

Several of the bones and ivories are box-like in appearance but may in fact have been handles or fittings of some sort. Numbers 262 and 263, both bone, found in adjacent areas, are the same type of object although the latter lacks the duck's head. A fragment of exactly the same type of object, much worn from use on the lower guilloche border, was excavated at Nimrud (Barnett 1957, 222, pl. CXXII, S388). Number 264, also bone, has plain walls and a bulge, and probably served the same function as the previous objects. None of these fragmentary objects preserves holes for attachment so that if they were handles the object to be secured was sleeved into them; the lack of holes, which would be necessary to secure a bottom, also suggests that they were not boxes.

Problems of identification and function exist for nos. 265 and 266, but here the narrowness of the opening suggests that they were handles. Nos. 267 and 269 are too fragmentary to allow for more than a general designation of boxes/handles. Numbers 258 and 273 should also be kept in mind as possible handles of an elaborate type.

Barnett (1957, 210 f.) has suggested that the "palm capitals," i.e., no. 272, were "undoubtedly used on tops of staves or on the heads of the women figures . . . [and] to have probably supported the lotus capitals . . . ," i.e., nos. 270-271. No. 272 has a wooden plug still *in situ* in its bottom, so that only the upper opening could have held a tenon from another object. Many examples of palm capitals have been recovered from Hama and Nimrud (de Mertzenfeld 1954, pl. CXVI, 749; Barnett 1957, 46, fig. 9, pls. LXXVII, LXXVIII, LXXIX, especially S236, S243, and S259b, an almost exact parallel to ours); it is not mentioned if any have wooden plugs. Another palm capital was found at Toprakkale associated with a statuette of a nude female, to which it may have belonged (van Loon 1966, 132, pl. XXXIV); these ivories, I believe, were imported into Urartu. Another palm capital was excavated at Gordion (unpublished) from the eighth century Phrygian level; its publication may make it possible to decide whether or not it was locally made or an import from North Syria. Still another example was excavated on Crete, probably imported from North Syria (Kunze 1936, 221, pl. 86:19).

Fragments of similar palm capitals, but with a double row of "petals," are in the Abegg Collection in Switzerland, and are said to come from Ziwiye (Wilkinson 1975, 51 ff., figs. 24-27). Note also that the same palm-capital motif was used in later Urartian furniture mouldings of various types (Akurgal 1968, figs. 3, 55, pl. XXXIII, b).

Palm capitals from Nimrud were placed on the top of female statuettes' heads and also served as supports for statuettes (Mallowan 1966, 210, fig. 146; Barnett 1957, 207, 210 f., pls. LXXIII-LXXV, LXXVII); further evidence that such capitals served as bases for statuettes is given by ivory reliefs from Nimrud and Gordion (Mallowan 1966, 538 f., fig. 458; Young 1962, pl. 46), and also from the existence of no. 135.

The wooden plug in the base of no. 272 seems to preclude its having been on top of a statuette (unless, of course, the plug is in fact a broken tenon), although it could have served as a support under one or under a lotus capital. The top outer diameter of no. 272 is essentially the same as the outer diameter of the base of the lotus capital no. 270. This object has a plug in the top of the cavity; it is not known what it may have supported. In short, the evidence from Hasanlu does not allow us to make finer distinctions than those presented by Barnett.

Lotus capitals were fairly common at Nimrud (Barnett 1957, 211, pls. LXXIX-LXXXI), from where our examples probably came; one or more were also recovered from the Phrygian debris at Gordion (unpublished); and one was found on Crete (Kunze 1936, 221, 227, pl. 86, no. 19).

A few ivory examples of champlevé patterns were recovered from Hasanlu. They include nos. 276-278, and a small fragment with a triangular floral pattern (no. 267). Another fragment, also with a floral pattern, was acquired from a dealer's shop in Nagadeh, the closest town to Hasanlu, and most certainly comes from Hasanlu IV (no. 268). Champlevé ivories were excavated at Zincirli (von Luschan 1943, pl. 72, P), Samaria (de Mertzenfeld 1954, pl. XIX) and Nimrud (Mallowan 1966, figs. 474, 475, 500-502), all probably eighth century in date. A fragment is also said to have come from Ziwiye (Godard 1950, fig. 89). Two small Egyptian Blue gorgets, mentioned above in a different context, and perhaps imports from Assyria, also are decorated in champlevé patterns (Dyson 1972, fig. 6).

Problems with respect to function obtain for nos. 274, 275-279. No. 275 has no central hole for inserting a stud and it may have been a small cosmetic dish such as the larger example (diameter 12.5 centimeters) from Megiddo (Loud 1939, pl. 26:14b). Objects nos. 276-279 might be buckles, not necessarily for shields, or handles from boxes, or even chariot box attachments, as originally proposed for similar objects by Mallowan (1966, 125). Although Nimrud has shells with designs like that of no. 279 I can find no parallels for nos. 276 and 277 but tenatively place them with the North Syrian group. None of the Hasanlu shells has writing on its surfaces (cf. Barnett 1963a, 82-84). No. 274 may simply be buttons or other clothing decorations.

IX

ASSYRIAN IVORIES

Nos. 280-293 present a homogeneous unit as they are all readily recognized as Assyrian objects made by Assyrian artisans and they are imported pieces at Hasanlu. Their classic Assyrian characteristics executed either in low relief or in incised technique and their superb workmanship indicate that they came from one of the royal or canonical workshops (cf. Canby 1971, 41 ff., 47).

Far too few fragments of no. 280 exist to allow us to determine whether it was originally a rectangle or whether its lower section was curved like no. 281. The height of the figure would have been about 17 or 18 centimeters, using the lower line of the arm as a mid-point; adding 2.5 centimeters from the figure's head to the top edge gives a height for the plaque of at least 20 or 21 centimeters; and if the base were decorated, this would have added several more centimeters. The size of our plaque, and the figure depicted, is smaller than an ivory rectangular plaque in relief of Assyrian style from Nimrud, but larger than another example, incised, from the same site; both Nimrud plaques may represent a king (Mallowan and Davies 1970, nos. 1, 7, pls. I, II).

No other ivory plaque known to me has a border decorated with tassels, although similar tassels were common on lower borders of Assyrian garments (*viz.* Strommenger 1962, figs. 191, 192; 1970, figs. 2-5, pls. 1, 2, 4, 6).

There is no indication that the figure on no. 280 was winged: one would expect to see parts of the wings in the space behind the left arm or in the upper left corner (cf. no. 281). Thus it would seem that the figure is a human. He wears a fillet but it is not possible from this to conclude that he is a king rather than some other important person, since both in the ninth century wore fillets (Hrouda 1965, 44; Madhloom 1970, 67 f., 76, pls. XVI, XXXIV, 2, XLI, 3). This fillet is now very worn and smoothed but one is able to see that the upper edge is rippled, implying that the fillet was braided (cf. Madhloom 1970, pl. LXV, 3). A swelling at the front suggests that there was originally a rosette here, now much eroded.

The nature of the scene, a distinguished figure carrying both a staff and an animal for sacrifice, and the elaborate fillet, suggests that we may indeed have before us a representation of an Assyrian king. Unfortunately, not enough detail is preserved to allow us to identify which king he is, Ashurnasirpal II, his son Shalmaneser III, or still another. A study of the beard structure does not lead to definite conclusions, although this is one area where we might expect a clue. Our figure has three rows or layers of curls below the face-beard, terminating at a point high on the chest, just below the shoulder line. These features seem to me to be more common in Ashurnasirpal's reign than during that of his son. Although in both reigns two layers of curls are common, at least one example from the earlier reign has three layers (Mallowan 1966, 97, fig. 43; also Madhloom 1970, 85, note 1). And in Shalmaneser's reign the beard length seems to be longer, extending lower on the chest than it did earlier (cf. Strommenger 1970, fig. 2 with figs. 5, 6). At the same time we note that on the throne dais of Shalmaneser, found at Nimrud, the beards of the Assyrian and Babylonian kings are not long (Mallowan 1966, fig. 371). Furthermore, on a relief of Adad-Nirari III (809-782 B.C.), the beard is fairly short (Oates 1968, pl. XXXVII). The Hasanlu plaque exhibits signs of wear suggesting that it was in use for some time, but whether it took 60 or 30 years to become worn eludes us, and thus the identification of the king remains an open question. That he is either Ashurnasirpal II or Shalmaneser III—if he is a king indeed—seems most probable. The well-known ivory plaque from Nimrud considered by Mallowan and Davies (1970, 2, 16, pl. 1) to be Ashurnasirpal II, does not help us in our conclusions, as the beard and the iconography are not the same as ours.

Nos. 281 and 282 share the same shape, with a squared top and rounded bottom, and the same general scheme of decoration: a large upper zone with a figure, separated by a decorative band from a smaller lower zone depicting a kneeling goat. The figures in the main upper zone of both plaques stand on a mountain pattern that itself rests on a guilloche band.

The figure of no. 281, like no. 280, carries an animal in the left hand but, instead of a staff, he carries in his right hand a flowering branch, also top down. This figure is winged and he is dressed differently from no. 280, judging from the few elements of clothing preserved. If no. 281 wore a fillet it is no longer extant, but we know from his wings that he is not human but a genius. The figure of no. 282 is less preserved and we do not know if he too had wings. He faces right and holds a mace close to its head while his right hand is held out palm open. This scene is paralleled on Assyrian ivories at Nimrud (Mallowan and Davies 1970, pl. XI, 306).

No. 283, although quite small and badly burned, preserves part of an incised kneeling goat; it is clearly the remains of a plaque like nos. 280 and 281. It too was found in BB IV East indicating that there were at least three Assyrian plaques in that building.

Plaques similar in both shape and decorative scheme exist at Nimrud (Mallowan and Davies 1970, nos. 201, 202). There, however, the main zone has a winged griffin, the lower zone winged bulls; both the upper and lower borders are decorated and the horizontal band separating the zones has a different pattern than the Hasanlu examples. A further difference is that the guilloche design of the Nimrud plaques moves left to right, that of the Hasanlu ones right to left. The Hasanlu examples are also smaller than the Nimrud examples, 10 centimeters compared with 17 centimeters.

Scenes depicting a striding figure holding an animal in one arm and an object in the other are a fairly common motif in Assyrian art (Mallowan and Davies 1970, pl. XXVI, 90, 91). Usually a winged deity or genius holds a goat or stag (Barnett n.d., pls. 1, 2) and either wheat or flowers in the other hand, often in an upright position. In the Sargonid period there is a representation of the king holding a goat and flowers (Hrouda 1965, pl. 36:3). Examples of a king or winged deity holding flowers in a lowered position also exist but these figures carry no animal (Madhloom 1970, pl. LXVII, 5; Budge 1914, pls. XVIII, 2, XXXVIII, 1, XXXIX). The usual position for holding the animal is that depicted on no. 281, where the arm crosses over the animal's body and is placed under the front legs; the position of no. 280, where the arm passes under the rear legs is unique.

Plaques of this type are considered to have been used to decorate furniture, chairs or thrones, or perhaps even couches (Mallowan 1966, 251 ff.; Mallowan and Davies 1970, 3, 4; Hrouda 1965, pls. 14:1, 16:3), and it is very probable that our plaques were employed in the same manner.

I can find no parallels for a figure walking directly on a mountain pattern as exists on our plaques, although an ivory fragment of Assyrian manufacture from Nimrud preserves human feet placed above a narrow band that rests on a mountain pattern (Barnett 1957, pl. CXVIII, V7; cf. Ghirshman 1964, fig. 404).

The sphinxes of no. 284 are probably female, judging from the type of necklace and the hat. They surely were framed by trees but we do not know if they flanked a tree or an animal. Heraldic sphinxes were of course a common motif in ancient art (e.g. Porada 1948, nos. 972, 980, 985, 995; Dessene 1957, pls. VII ff.; Mallowan and Davies 1970, pl. XXXVII) but no ivory plaque similar to ours has hitherto been recorded. However, ivories said to have come from Ziwiye, of different style and of a later date than ours, depict heraldic female sphinxes wearing necklaces, with heads facing backward, and flanking a central rosette (Wilkinson 1975, figs. 1, 1B); and an unpublished ivory fragment in the Teheran Museum, also said to have come from Ziwiye, has two facing heraldic sphinxes flanking a tree. In this context one should also compare the gold plaque attributed to Ziwiye that also has heraldic sphinxes flanking a tree (Wilkinson 1963, figs. 2, 3). Contemporary or slightly earlier depictions of heraldic sphinxes occur on decorated bronze beakers of Iranian manufacture (Calmeyer 1973, 64 ff.); and late second millennium B.C. examples are on seals from Tchoga Zanbil (Porada 1970a, nos. 13, 88-90).

While I can find no exact parallel for the elaborately decorated concave-sided or cushion plaques, no. 285, both the shape and the running ostrich with outstretched wings are at home in Assyrian art. At Nimrud the shape is attested in ivory (Mallowan and Davies 1970, pl. XXXIII, 125), and ivory plaques of different shape have the ostrich (Mallowan and Davies 1970, 45, pl.

XXXVI). The cushion-shaped panel also exists as a decorative element in Assyrian wall painting (Mallowan 1966, 11, 443, fig. 308); slightly later examples occur in North Syria (von Luschan 1943, pl. 53 a, f; Thureau-Dangin 1931, XLVIII, 1). Equally at home in Assyria are the representations of running bustards, no. 286A, B, also incised on ivory (Mallowan and Davies 1970, pls. XXXVI, 157-159; Barnett 1957, pl. CXVIII, VI). The Hasanlu bustards rest on a ground line formed from the plant roots; this detail, as well as the scene itself, is paralleled in all features by clothing designs incised on Assyrian royal reliefs (Porada 1945, pl. IX; Budge 1914, pl. L, 1, LIII, 2).

Ostriches depicted as being hunted or captured are found on tenth/ninth century B.C. bronzes that probably came from Iran (Calmeyer 1969, figs. 86, 87; 1973, C4, 160 ff.). These bronzes with ostrich depictions are apparently of Iranian manufacture, unlike the Hasanlu ivory examples, which are imported.

Kneeling or rampant goats flanking a small tree or plant (nos. 287-290) are also commonplace in Assyrian art, represented on ivory, metal, pottery and stone. At Nimrud this motif occurs in wall painting, on a silver bowl and on ivory strips like ours (Mallowan 1966, figs. 357, 373; Mallowan and Davies 1970, pl. XXXVIII, 161, 162; cf. pls. XXXIV, XXXIX, 133-141, 161-168); allegedly from Ziwiye are ivories with the same motif (Godard 1950, figs. 66, 70). On none of these ivories do the roots of the tree form the ground line, but this feature does occur in clothing decoration (*viz.* Budge 1914, pl. LI, 2; Godard 1950, fig. 67; *supra*), and on a glazed vessel from Assur (Andrae 1923, pl. 2).

These Assyrian ivories may have been the models for some of the local products (nos. 147, 148; cf. Moorey 1971, 244 f.). It will be recalled that a superbly made Egyptian Blue goblet with representations in relief of griffins and goats flanking a tree was found together with the ivories in the debris of BB II (Dyson 1962, 6, fig. 5; 1968, fig. 109; Porada 1965, pl. 33). This goblet does not appear to have been a local product and was imported from the West, probably also from Assyria.[30]

The incised sphinx no. 291 is too fragmentary to reveal its function in a particular scene, but the object was an import, again probably from Assyria (cf. Mallowan and Davies 1970, pl. XXXVII, 160).

For rows of plants similar to those represented on nos. 292 and 293, see the incised examples from Nimrud (Mallowan 1966, figs. 216, 217; and Mallowan and Davies 1970, nos. 161, 162, 180).

[30]Lumps of Egyptian Blue were found at Nimrud (Mallowan 1966, 408). It is possible that all the Egyptian Blue objects from Hasanlu are imports from Assyria, for example, Muscarella 1966, figs. 30, 31, 33 (*infra*).

MATERIALS, WORKSHOPS, USES

That the same artisans who carved the ivories also worked with wood and bone is attested at Hasanlu. Bone was naturally better suited for narrow tube-like objects and handles, sword pommels, or eye inlays (nos. 73—incorrectly called ivory by Porada 1965, 238, n. 13—204-206, 262-264, 270); wood was more extensively used for carving both flat reliefs and sculptures, i.e. the same types of objects carved in ivory (nos. 7, 38, 39, 44-46, 50, 95, 127, 138, 143, 190). Only the burning of the wood to charcoal at the time of the final catastrophe secured its preservation, and surely other examples of wood carving perished in the fire or disintegrated within the citadel debris. This situation, wood and ivory carving executed by the same artisans, fits into a general pattern known from other Near Eastern sites. A relevant text from the UR III period at Ur refers to a sculptor's shop that produced both ivory and wood objects (Legrain 1947, 259; see also Barnett 1957, 158; Philippe 1965, 164). Because of local environmental conditions Nimrud yielded only rare examples of wood (Mallowan 1966, 255 f.), while at Phrygian Gordion the protective nature of the clay covering the tumuli and the City Mound allowed for better preservation of wood alongside ivory (Kohler 1964, 58 f.). Peculiar local conditions at Samos (Kopcke 1969, 100 ff.) and in the Altai region (Rudenko 1970, 239 ff.) also made possible the preservation of locally made wood objects. The rare, burned, and therefore preserved, late third millennium B.C. wood sculptures from Ebla (Matthiae 1975, 487 f., Abb. 424, 425a, b; see also *Archaeology* 34 [1977]: 246 ff.; *Biblical Archaeologist* [Sept. 1976] 103 f., 111, fig. 14) are patently sculpted in the same manner as ivory (as of the time of this writing no ivories have yet been reported from Ebla). A few wooden objects have also been preserved at Karmir Blur (Piotrovsky 1970, figs. 29-34), some of which may have been locally made. Several bone objects, a sphinx, a human face (cf. the Altintepe ivory examples, Özgüç 1969, 86, pl. XLV, 1-2), a turret, a comb, tubes, kitchen utensils, were also recovered from Karmir Blur (Piotrovsky 1962, figs. 54, 55, 57, 59, 60 [called ivory in Piotrovsky 1970]; van Loon 1966, 137), but very few ivory objects (cf. Altintepe). It would seem that the seventh century Urartians used bone more extensively than the earlier workers in North Syria, Assyria, and Iran.[31]

A wooden statuette now in the Teheran Museum was said to have been found at Ziwiye (Ghirshman 1964, 124, fig. 173), for which provenience of course there is no proof ("an object that came as a complete surprise"!, *ibid.* Muscarella 1977a, 202). Because parts of the statuette are missing, in particular the face, it is difficult to date the object; all we know is that we have a wooden statuette that may have been made in ancient Iran.

Shell carving was apparently a minimal activity at Hasanlu but not uncommon at Nimrud (Mallowan 1966, 396 ff., 407), where the existence of a shell-working atelier was suggested.

Many stone bowls, sword pommels, buttons, door bolts (?), maces, and the like, were excavated at Hasanlu, but, aside from an imported second millennium Kassite stone vessel, obviously an heirloom (64-656; Dyson 1972, 46), there are no examples of decorated or relief stone work of any kind. It has often been stated that ivory, wood and stone carving are related activities, both in ancient and modern times (Barnett 1957, 45, 64, 167;

[31]Bone was also used more extensively than ivory in Sparta (Dawkins 1929, 203 ff., pls. XLI ff.); perhaps there was a shortage of ivory in Greece and Urartu at this time.

Porada 1970b, 98; 1975, 365, 366; Mallowan 1966, 484; Kunz 1916, 93). In the discussions of certain body markings found on North Syrian ivories it was noted that specific parallels are often found on large-scale stone reliefs from North Syrian sites; it was also noted that Assyrian ivories share the same scenes and motifs found on the large palace reliefs from Assyria. It does not follow from this that the same craftsmen who carved the ivories carved the larger stone reliefs, even though it may be argued that the same artisans sometimes worked with both materials (e.g. Mallowan 1966, 484). If, however, we restrict ourselves to observations concerning *Kleinkunst*, we are better able to see the relationship between stone and ivory work and to recognize a few cases in which the same artisans seem to have worked in both stone and ivory.

The same specialized artisan who made the plain stone pyxis from Tell Tainat (Oriental Institute, unpublished) might easily have made the plain ivory pyxis from Tell Halaf (Barnett 1957, fig. 17); and the now fragmentary decorated stone pyxis and lid from Carchemish (Woolley 1921, pl. 28) could conceivably have been carved by an ivory worker.[32] The North Syrian stone and ivory lion bowls were made in the same or neighboring ateliers and it is conceivable that they might have been made by artisans who made one time an ivory bowl, another time a stone bowl. The evidence of the existence of related stone and ivory bowls and pyxides at least demonstrates a close working relationship between the workers in the two materials. Nevertheless, from the evidence at Hasanlu itself there is no indication that the local ivory carvers also worked on stone objects, portable or otherwise.

Kantor (1956, 173 f.) has presented the position that, inasmuch as the style of animal body details on North Syrian orthostate carvings is basically the same as that found on the local ninth century B.C. metalwork and ivories, which continued a tradition that began centuries earlier, the latter must have been the inspiration for the stone workers. Both Porada (1967, 2977; 1970b, 98) and Usshishkin (1971, 24 ff.) have supported this conclusion. On the other hand, Moorey (1967, 88) and Mallowan and Herrmann (1974, 46 f.) have taken the opposite position, namely that the ninth century B.C. ivory carvers copied from the slightly earlier reliefs, i.e. that *Kleinkunst* was copied from or depended on monumental works of art for its stimulus and inspiration. It is difficult, if not impossible, to actually document which artisans or works of art influenced which others in the tenth/ninth centuries B.C. in North Syria, for it would be arrogant to assume that we know all the artistic sources available to a given artisan working on a stone or ivory relief. Nevertheless it is certainly reasonable to accept the suggestion of Kantor that artistic traditions and motifs were carried down from the late second millennium into the first on ivories, providing that some were available, not buried in mounds.

Another issue, however, is pertinent to this discussion. One would have to know whether in the ninth century it was the ivories or the stone reliefs that were in fact carved first in order to resolve the issue. Unfortunately, our knowledge on these matters is not so firm as we would wish, for we know only that the Hasanlu, North Syrian and Assyrian ivories, the best dated corpus available at present, were made sometime prior to about 800 B.C., but how many years prior eludes us. And we are still debating the exact dates for the reliefs at Tell Halaf and some at Carchemish, which may have been carved in the first half of the ninth century. [Winter 1976a, 158 ff. also argues for an early ninth century date for these reliefs; see also pp. 351 ff. for a discussion of the priority problem.]

Eventually, by about 800 B.C. it would seem that the various groups of artisans used a commonly held repertory of motifs and themes without a conscious copying by one group from another. The evidence from Hasanlu itself certainly suggests, at least for that site, that the local ivory workers were stimulated by their knowledge both of other ivories and of the monumental North Syrian and Assyrian stone reliefs.

The evidence at Hasanlu also suggests that at that site the metalworkers and ivory carvers were not the same artisans. While some of the motifs and scenes are shared by the local-style ivory and metal objects, as has been pointed out several times, they do not always share the same lines and fineness of details. In fact, the workmanship on no. 175, on the bronze and iron plaques, and on the silver beaker, are inferior to the work on the ivories. For good parallels with respect to shared quality and details on ivory and metalwork there are the superbly carved bulls of nos. 214-221 and the metal vessels brought forth as comparable works. As suggested above, I believe that these ivories were probably

[32]Note that the stone pyxis purchased by Herzfeld at Mahmudiye, near Baghdad, and definitely of North Syrian origin, copies motifs found on North Syrian reliefs (Muscarella 1970, fig. 11; cf. Orthmann 1971, pl. 70 c; 21 c, 27 b, 33 e, 43 i, 45 a, 56 c, d, 57 c, 61 c, 66 d). The execution of the pyxis is cruder than that on ivories and therefore one does not know if it was carved by an ivory worker. [In her dissertation Irene Winter also deals with the relationship between the stone and ivory pyxides, Winter 1976a, 355 ff.]

not locally made, and that it is more probable they were consciously copied from fine metal examples at hand, than carved by the same artisans who also made metal repoussé.

In this context one should also mention again the close relationship between the metal plaque from Zincirli and the ivory pyxides from Nimrud and Hasanlu (Muscarella 1966, figs. 5, 6). But inasmuch as the same facial and head type also exists on the stone reliefs of Carchemish (Orthmann 1973, pl. 28b), it may be possible to conclude that separate artisans worked the different materials using a common artistic repertory.

No ivory workshop area has been recognized at Hasanlu—not necessarily surprising as the factories and workshops were probably located in the city proper, and not on the citadel.[33] Not a single one of the Hasanlu ivories appears to be unfinished. As stated above, the pyxis lid no. 248 certainly has one or more rosettes that were blanked out but not completed. But a dowel hole was drilled in this area and it would seem that some object, perhaps a couchant-calf handle was set in place here, thus precluding the need to finish the rosettes. Moreover, the edge of the lid has gold foil *in situ*, which would hardly have been added to an unfinished object. Two plaques with animal reliefs, nos. 148 and 287, have unworked borders at the right. No. 287 is an import (apparently from Assyria) and surely not unfinished; thus it would seem that the unworked border on this object, and on no. 148, was meant to be inserted into a slot where it would not be visible.

Barnett (1957, 52, 223) published some examples of alleged unfinished ivories from Nimrud. A few are definitely unfinished, S399, S402 and S403; but S400 seems to be a fragment of a couchant calf, originally complete but fractured in the destruction of Nimrud; and four fragments of a pyxis, said to be unfinished, are discussed but not illustrated. And Mallowan suggested that because tusks were found in a room at Nimrud along with what he considered to be unfinished ivories, the room might have been an ivory workshop (Mallowan 1966, 112; but cf. 483). These particular ivories are to my mind, judging from the photographs, not unfinished but rather crudely incised plaques (see Mallowan and Davies 1970, 40, nos. 118, 119; Barnett 1957, 26, 133, note 1: cf. these to unprovenienced ivories —said to be from Ziwiye—in Wilkinson 1975, 63, figs. 34, 34a, 34b). Nevertheless, tusks' having been found in this and in other rooms at Nimrud (Mallowan 1966, 112, 483; Layard 1853, 195), joined with the evidence of the unfinished ivories presented by Barnett, plus the existence of the Assyrian-style ivories excavated there, surely makes it likely that ivory carvers did work at Nimrud. Textual and sculptural evidence documenting the importation of ivory tusks to Assyrian cities, including Nimrud, in the reigns of Ashurnasirpal II and Shalmaneser III, further supports this conclusion (Barnett 1957, 114 f.; n.d., pls. 152c, 165; Budge 1914, pl. XX; Mallowan 1966, 445 ff., 472, 477, 479; Luckenbill 1926, I, para. 476, 625).

Barnett (1963a, 84; cf. Strøm 1971, 115) cited Riis (*Gnomon* 35, 1963, 206) that there were "ivory chips" found at Hama, which to Barnett were "evidently from a workshop," and thereby added documentation to Barnett's thesis that Hama was the major North Syrian ivory-carving center. Riis referred to these fragments as "Werkstattabfülle," and also thought they supported Barnett's thesis. While it is very possible that Hama was in fact *one* of the North Syrian cities that manufactured ivories, these still unpublished chips do not prove unequivocally that there was a local atelier. For, in view of the hundreds of ivory splinters of all sizes and shapes found at Hasanlu, it is quite possible that the Hama chips could also have come from fragmented, completely finished ivories; publication may help resolve the issue. Moreover, if level E at Hama, from which level the chips derive, was in fact destroyed by Sargon II in 720 B.C., the chips can tell us nothing about workshops at Hama in the ninth century. Barnett also referred to ivory tusks "marked for sawing up" from al Mina (Barnett 1957, 167, note 1); this, if it can be confirmed, would imply that ivory was being worked at that site (date?).

As mentioned above, Barnett (1957, 46 f.; 1963a, 81 ff.) has taken the position that the ivories of North Syrian style found at Nimrud derived from one center, from Hama. This conclusion was originally based on stylistic similarities between ivories found at Hama and Nimrud, but was later supported by inscriptions published by Millard (1962, 42 ff.). Unfortunately, none of these inscriptions, which state either "Hamath" (hmt), or "Lu'ash" (l's), a neighboring city, exist on documented ninth century ivories. Moreover, a Hittite hieroglyphic inscription of Urhilana, King of Hamath in the ninth century, found on a *shell*, has no relevance to *ivory* carving at Hama. Barnett's leap from an inscribed shell to proof of an ivory atelier

[33]At the same time it should be noted that axe and tool molds have been found on the citadel. The only possible evidence for an artisan's shop, that of a metalworker, was excavated on the eastern slope of the citadel mound.

at Hama clouds the issue. That Hama had an atelier in the eighth century may indeed be accepted on the basis of the ivory inscriptions, although it is also possible that the name represents a shipper's label, rather than a "made in Hama" seal (Freyer-Schauenburg 1966, 57, 69; cf. Mallowan 1966, 452). The ninth century ivories excavated at Hama (*infra*) do not constitute proof that there was an atelier there at that time, although there is equally no proof that there was no atelier.

Actually, one can say very little about the existence of ivory worshops in particular North Syrian cities. If an openwork ivory chariot is found at Zincirli (de Mertzenfeld 1954, pl. CXXXII, 1142) and a similar one is found at Nimrud (Mallowan 1966, fig. 462), can we know—aside from art historical analysis—whether one was made in Zincirli and shipped to Nimrud, or the other brought to Zincirli from Nimrud, or both made in a third site? We cannot. Nor can we state that because gold and silver metalwork from Zincirli, cited above, has physical features very close to those on the Hasanlu and Nimrud sphinxes, the latter were therefore made in Zincirli. In the discussion of these pyxides, a stone relief of sphinxes from Carchemish that has the same features was cited. Carchemish, like other North Syrian states, gave ivory and tusks to the Assyrians as tribute in the ninth century (Luckenbill 1926, I, para. 476). No ivories to speak of were excavated at Carchemish, and none of certain ninth century date (Woolley and Barnett 1952, pl. 71 f.), but obviously ivory existed there if it was sent to Assyria (although by itself this fact does not prove ivory was carved there). And what of Hattina, a state which also sent ivory to Assyria (Luckenbill 1926, I, para. 477, 585, 593; Mallowan 1966, 446, 449)?[34] In short, we know from the texts and from representations in art that more than one North Syrian state sent carved ivory and tusks to Assyria but we do not know if each of these states had its own ateliers. A discussion concerning the specific centers of manufacture of the North Syrian ivories found at Nimrud and Hasanlu is not the aim of this study, but I firmly believe that the evidence does not support the suggestion that there was only one center of production [an opinion also argued by Winter 1976a, 262, 366 ff., 378]. To be sure, Zincirli and Carchemish are strong contenders for recognition as ivory-working centers, as is also the site of Nimrud itself, but beyond these suggestions I choose not to speculate. [Winter 1976a, 513, 361 f. sees Carchemish as an ivory-carving center.] Compounding the problem is the fact that most of the North Syrian ivories known to date from the ninth century were excavated at Nimrud and Hasanlu; Tell Halaf and Hama preserve only a few examples (*infra*). This could mean either that most of the North Syrian ivories were exported, or that more lie under the ground, still unexcavated.

The techniques of carving, attaching, and decorating the ivories with gold at Hasanlu do not differ from those recognized on ivories from other centers. The local artisans felt perfectly free to carve one scene across several pre-cut plaques, allowing parts of a single figure to be carved on separate plaques. This same freedom existed, for example, on ivories from Arslan Tash (Thureau–Dangin 1931, 97, 102 f., 108, 112, 121 f., nos. 15-17, 22, 26, 39, 44, 75-77), Nimrud (Mallowan 1966, figs. 209-211, 215, 581), Salamis (Karageorghis 1973, pls. LXVIII, LXIX, CCXLII), and on ivories said to have come from Ziwiye (Godard 1950, figs. 84, 85 and p. 100; Wilkinson 1975, figs. 1, 2, 9, 14-18). Moreover, this same technique was practiced by the sculptors of the Assyrian stone reliefs (Smith 1963, 119 f.; Barnett n.d., fig. 25), and by the sculptors of some stone reliefs from North Syria, at Zincirli, Carchemish, Karatepe and Sakçegözü (Vieyra 1955, 78, fig. 77; Bossert 1942, 915, 940, 943, 944, 946, 949; 886, 888; Woolley and Barnett 1952, pl. 55a). It is assumed that the stones were set in place before carving and therefore it would not be unusual for the sculptors to treat the separate slabs as one wall surface. If the ivory plaques, however, because of their fragility and small size, were carved before being set into their final position, there must have been a cartoon or preliminary layout. This manner of working, if used, would demonstrate a high degree of skill and sureness on the part of the artisans.

None of the Hasanlu ivory plaques has been preserved in its complete shape. From the limited evidence of the fragments it would seem that there was no standard size; rather the plaques seem to have been cut to fit horizontal and vertical positions as needed. Some of the horizontal plaques are 4, 4.5, and 6 centimeters in height (*viz.* nos. 21, 178, 5), and no. 1 was originally more than 9.5 centimeters in length.

The tools used at Hasanlu can be inferred only from the internal evidence of the ivories themselves and these seem to be the same used by ivory carvers at other centers (Barnett 1957, 157 f.; Mallowan 1966, 483 f.; Philippe 1965, 164; Kunz 1916, 257 ff., 266 ff., 289): saws, drills of various diameters,

[34] Irene Winter has informed me that the Oriental Institute in Chicago has ivory fragments from Çatal Hüyük and Tell Tainat. [Winter 1976a gives an inventory of North Syrian ivories and their proveniences. Now see also Winter 1976b.]

punches, files, chisels, hammers and compasses. Occasionally, tool marks of unusually small gauge are faintly visible, i.e. nos. 74 (below the wrist), 80 (at the tip of the nose), 90 (in front of the leg), 123 (on the face), etc. Drills of different diameter are the most visible of the tool marks, in wings, eyes, or dowel holes. Some of the ivories are highly polished; in a few cases fine scratches or grinding striations are still discernible with a magnifying glass, i.e. nos. 69, 79, 90, 123, etc. The textured surface on some animal bodies, nos. 2, 6, 9, 11, 19, 21, 28, 29, 33, and on the leather earflaps, no. 55A, was incised by a small triangular punch, the same type of tool used on Assyrian-style ivories said to have come from Ziwiye (Wilkinson 1975, figs. 15b, 17). This triangular marking goes back a long time as it was used to represent skin in the third millennium B.C. at Tepe Yahya and Shadad in Iran (Porada 1975, Abb. 279a, fig. 108; both stone; cf. also a stag on a Hittite relief, Muscarella 1974d, no. 132).

The finished plaques were attached to a backing by means of glue and ivory or, less commonly preserved, wooden dowels. Dowels were placed usually in an undecorated part of the plaque but sometimes they are found within a decorated section, cutting through the design, i.e. nos. 55A, 120, 195, 216, 281; sometimes they were conveniently placed within the area of the eye, i.e. nos. 79, 86, 88, 96, 214. Apparently the best position to securely fasten the plaques was picked, disregarding, where deemed necessary, the decoration. Bottle-shaped slots were employed at times to join sculpture to another unit, i.e. nos. 245, 256; the same type of slot exists also at Nimrud (Barnett 1957, figs. 64, 87). Glue may be inferred from the presence of rocker or irregular scoring on the backs of most of the ivories, which was executed apparently to form a grip for the glue; some ivories have a relatively smooth back with no obvious scoring. A black substance found in the eye sockets of nos. 124 and 249 was no doubt used to secure the inlaid eyes; this could be bitumen and reminds us of the black substance that was used to hold the Altintepe lion together (Özgüç 1969, 83, 87).

Rocker scoring may occur on more ancient ivories than is known at present, as the backs of ivories are rarely published or discussed. An ivory writing tablet from Nimrud (Mallowan 1966, fig. 257) preserves a neat example of rocker scoring that facilitated the adhesion of the wax coating. The occurrence of this distinctive pattern at Nimrud and on the local-style ivories at Hasanlu gives us a further indication about the sharing of knowledge among craftsmen of different areas. To be sure, more often crude, irregular cross-hatching seems to have been employed at Hasanlu and elsewhere (*viz.* Crowfoot 1938, 47; Amiet 1972, 189; Thimme 1973, XIV, XX:R; for Mycenaean ivories see Poursat 1977, I, 254).

A number of Hasanlu ivories still preserve traces of a gold foil overlay, but whether all the ivories were gold covered remains unknown. Gold foil overlay on ivories was very common from all over the Near East and from different periods (Thureau–Dangin 1931, 113; Loud and Altman 1938, 69; Barnett 1957, 20, 23, 63, 155; Thimme 1973, XIV; Karageorghis 1973, 93, 96; Özgüç 1969, 80, 82 f.; Harper 1969, 156, 160 ff.); none of the ivories said to come from Ziwiye has gold overlay (Wilkinson 1975, 10) but since not a single example was excavated by archaeologists it is possible that the clandestine diggers—at whatever site or sites the ivories were in fact found—removed it. Textual evidence regarding gold overlay reinforces the archaeological information (I Kings, X: 18; Güterbock, 1971, 3, 4; Mallowan 1966, 649, note 3; Barnett 1957, 114; Thureau–Dangin 1931, 139; see note 21).

Staining (or painting) apparently did not exist on any of the Hasanlu ivories although it was a technique known at Nimrud (Mallowan 1966, 130, note 14; 408 f., fig. 335; Barnett 1957, 64; see Kunz 1916, 264 f.), and apparently also at Arslan Tash (Thureau–Dangin 1931, pl. XLVI). Staining seems to have occurred in earlier periods as well, and is attested in Hittite texts (Güterbock 1971, 2, 5, 7; Rost 1961, 209 f.; cf. also *Iliad* IV:141), where white and red ivory are mentioned. A red color for ivory could presumably result only from staining as it is not one of the colors that would develop from burning. The color range of the Hasanlu ivories is predominantly grey or black, with brown and white less common, and clearly resulted from the fire that destroyed the citadel. Laboratory tests have shown that when ivory is subjected to higher and higher temperatures it will change from its natural cream or white color to yellow, then brown, brown-black, black, dark grey-blue, and finally back to a white color (Baer and Indicator 1971, 1 ff.; cf. Loud and Altman 1938, 96 f.). Examples at Nimrud also turned black from the destruction fire (Barnett 1957, 159; Mallowan 1966, 130, 146, 434); and ivories probably from a burned room at Acemhüyük consist of grey, white, pink and orange colors (Harper 1969, 158); the pink and orange were apparently produced deliberately by iron oxide. The Khorsabad ivories were burned brown, blue, black and white (Loud and Altman 1938, 96 f.), all the expected colors. See also Poursat 1977, I, 256, for Mycenaean burnt ivories.

None of the Hasanlu ivories preserves alphabetical signs or marks of any kind. Alphabetical signs are found on ivories from Nimrud, Samaria and Arslan Tash, and are assumed to be fitters' or carvers' marks (Millard 1962, 49 f.; Orchard 1967, pl. XLIII; Barnett 1957, 161; Mallowan 1966, 594 ff.; Crowfoot 1938, 6 ff.; Thureau–Dangin 1931, 91 ff.).

The question concerning the specific function of the Hasanlu ivory plaques arises, but it is easier asked than answered. The ivories were scattered in the fill mixed with other objects in the debris of the destruction, which made it impossible to relate them to any object or material to which they may have been attached. Charred wood in fragments and splinters was ubiquitous but it was never possible to connect it with any ivory. Remains of a wooden chair or throne were found on the floor of the great hall of BB II at the south end, just below the raised platform before Room 6, but no ivories were found juxtaposed. Therefore, any conclusions with regard to the function of the plaques can only be suggestions based on comparative material and textual references from elsewhere.

Taking the textual evidence first, we find that ivory furniture is mentioned fairly commonly in ancient literature and historical documents. The best known, of course, are the Biblical references to Solomon's throne and to beds and houses of ivory (I Kings, X:18; XXII:39; Amos VI:304; XXII:15). Homer mentions Odysseus' bed of inlaid ivory and Penelope's silver and ivory throne (*Odyssey* XXIII:200; XIX:56-57). Assyrian tribute lists from the ninth through the seventh centuries B.C. refer to ivory beds, chairs, couches, tables, staves and vessels (summarized in Barnett 1957, 114 f.; Mallowan 1966, 477 ff.). Still earlier literature presents evidence for the existence of ivory objects. Ur III texts that discuss ivory workshops (Legrain 1947, 228 f., 259) mention ivory statuettes, animals, birds, sheathes, ear plugs, and an ivory bed and some chair feet. Texts from the Larsa period mention ivory combs, pectorals, spoons, boxes, and inlaid furniture, imported from Telmun (Oppenheim 1954, 7 f., 11). Ivory-inlaid chairs are mentioned in an early second millennium B.C. text discussed by Leemans (1968, 216). And a text from Ras Shamra refers to beds belonging to a queen that were decorated with ivory plaques (Schaeffer 1954, 38; Barnett 1957, 117). Moreover, Mycenaean Linear B tablets from Pylos mention furniture of ivory or inlaid with ivory, as well as ivory feet on tables (Vermeule 1964, 174 f.; Baker 1966, 248 f.), perhaps reflecting influence from the East. Hittite texts also refer to ivory combs, hair pins, figurines of eagles and lions, containers (pyxides?), drums, and chairs, tables, and beds; ivory was also used as inlays (Güterbock 1971, 2 ff.).

Excavated material has neatly supported the textual evidence. An ivory bed of the second millennium from Ras Shamra has decorated panels (Schaeffer 1957, 51 ff., pls. VII-X); at Nimrud plain ivory plaques have been identified as the edging of a couch (Mallowan 1966, 396 f., fig. 321); Karageorghis excavated an ivory bed in the dromos of Tomb 79 at Salamis on Cyprus (Karageorghis 1973, 11, 89, 92 ff.), where the frame consisted of plain plaques and the head of decorated plaques. It is also very probable that the bed of Ashurbanipal in the famous garden scene is decorated with ivory plaques (Strommenger 1962, fig. 241; Barnett 1957, 118, fig. 46). Finally, there are the two bed frames from Arslan Tash which were decorated with plain ivory plaques.

Tomb 79 at Salamis has also yielded both plain and decorated units from a fine ivory chair, as well as wooden chairs and stools (Karageorghis 1973, 11, 88 ff., 91 ff.). The ivory panels from Room SW.7 at Nimrud have been identified as belonging to chair backs (Mallowan and Herrmann 1974, 3 ff., 38 f., 64). Also from Nimrud are ivory chair legs; and a group of ivories, some with curved bottoms like nos. 281 and 282, and assumed to be from furniture, were excavated close to the royal dais in the Ezida; moreover, a text on a plain ivory strip specifically mentions that it was part of a throne of Shamshi-Adad V (Mallowan 1966, 249 ff., 408 f., 594, figs. 335, 596; Barnett 1957, fig. 77).

Ghirshman (1964, 101 f.) asserts that the ivory fragments allegedly from Ziwiye must have been from a throne or bed. This identification is based not on archaeological evidence, which is non-existant, but rather on Ghirshman's opinion that the "Ziwiye Treasure" derived from the tomb of a Scythian prince who must have been buried with his furniture. If we knew, in fact, whence the ivories derived, and in what situation and juxtaposition, we might be in a position to arrive at intelligent suggestions (cf. Godard 1950, 80 who refused to speculate about "les ensembles décoratifs auxquels elles appartenaient;" cf. also Wilkinson 1975, 10; Muscarella 1977a, 200, 201, 202, 215).

Detached ivory furniture legs or other units from various sites in Egypt, from the earliest times (Baker 1966, 20 ff.), and from the second and first millenniums B.C. in the Near East have also been excavated (de Mertzenfeld 1954, pls. XLIV, CX, CXXVII, CXXVI; von Luschan 1943, pls. 62c, 63; Harper 1969, 160; Schaeffer 1954, 54, fig. 5; Barnett 1957, 119 f.; Hrouda 1962, 53, pl. 43; 1965, pls. 13, 15; Karageorghis 1973, 119). Ivory inlays from a footstool are known from a Mycenaean grave (Vermeule 1964, 173, 219); and other ivory fragments from Mycenae may have belonged to furniture (Baker 1966, 250 f.). At Gordion wooden beds, screens, tables and stools, all without ivory decoration, but some with intricate wooden inlays, were excavated within Tumulus P and MM (Young 1974, 3 ff.; Baker 1966, 226 ff.); but in Megaron 3 on the city mound several decorated ivory plaques were recovered juxtaposed to charred wood of unknown use (Young 1960, 240, pl. 60, fig. 25 a-c; Kohler 1964, 59 ff., pls. XIX-XX). Thus, at Gordion, wooden furniture may have been predominantly unadorned with ivory, which, because of the woodworking skills practiced there, may have been considered superfluous. But that some wood furniture, or other object, was covered with ivory is attested by the Megaron 3 evidence.

More difficult to document from excavations are examples of doors or walls decorated with ivory. An inscription of Tiglath-Pileser III from Nimrud refers to ivory-decorated doors (Barnett 1957, 113), and Kunz (1916, 36) reminds us of the ivory door panelling at Haghia Sophia, attesting to the continuity of the practice. Crowfoot (1938, 1) and Barnett (1957, 60, but cf. 113) have suggested that the ivories from Samaria decorated the walls, because of the admonitions of Amos (III:15) against Ahab's "house of ivory." Unfortunately, we do not know what that term really means, whether it meant that there was ivory wall panelling or a house filled with ivory furniture. At Nimrud Mallowan believed that some walls had been decorated with ivory plaques; he found some decorated ivories apparently embedded in mud bricks, which might imply that some ivories were in fact used as wall decoration (Mallowan 1966, 416, 480, 519 f., fig. 424; Orchard 1967, iii; Barnett 1957, 113 f.). In another passage Mallowan (1966, 293) said that a wall in Hall AB6 had been decorated with plain ivory panelling set over a wooden frame. The evidence for ivory wall panelling at Nimrud is indeed tenuous but certainly not ruled out.

Given the lack of any juxtaposition of the Hasanlu ivories to a recognizable piece of furniture, or to walls and doors (no longer in evidence because of their collapse), it is virtually impossible to draw meaningful conclusions about their specific uses, aside, of course, from pyxides, handles, lion bowls and statuettes. All of the ivories from Buildings I, II, IV and V came from the fallen upper storey, presumably the living quarters of the local dignitaries. Without getting into a discussion about the function of the buildings, especially BB II, where most of the ivories were recovered (and of course BB I where both the gold bowl and silver beaker were found), we may legitimately assume from the ivories and the total corpus of objects recovered that we are talking about royalty and their personal possessions. Royalty liked small portable luxury items as well as decorated thrones and furniture, and, presumably, also decorated walls. And considering the textual and archaeological evidence from other sites, it seems a fair conclusion to assume that the Hasanlu ivories probably were used in the same way: to decorate beds, chairs, stools, boxes, and perhaps even walls.[35] The distribution of the ivories in the fill of the various buildings, and over a large part of BB II, suggests that many objects were involved. It should also be noted that the ivories from BB II derived from the collapse of the rooms at the east and south and that none was found in the fill of the rooms at the west and north; the few examples from the great hall area were no doubt scattered there when the superstructure collapsed. This provenience pattern signifies that the ivories were in use in limited areas of the building and perhaps we may conclude that the living and recreation areas of the occupants were confined to the east and south.

Of further interest is the fact that no plain ivory plaques were recovered at Hasanlu, which might indicate that no bed frame of ivory existed, although a head board of decorated ivory is not precluded. Also, unlike the ivory hoards from other sites, Samaria, Nimrud, Megiddo, perhaps also Arslan Tash, the Hasanlu ivories had not been thrown away or placed in a storeroom; rather, they were in use up until the very moment the citadel at Hasanlu was destroyed.

[35]Some of the small bronze and iron plaques mentioned in the section on chariots and warriors might also have been used in the same manner as the ivories. For ivories used on horse reins or trappings see *Iliad* V:583.

FOREIGN TRADE AND RELATIONS

From the previous discussions and comments concerned with foreign parallels it will be quite clear that the Hasanlu ivory artisans had an intimate knowledge of, and were consciously influenced by, the art and culture of both North Syria and Assyria. In fact, we may easily conclude that the knowledge of ivory carving itself at Hasanlu—and the motives depicted—resulted from its prior existence in the West and the subsequent spread of that knowledge eastward. That is, local ivory carving workshops at Hasanlu were established only after contact with points west had occurred; there is no reason to suppose that ivory carving developed at Hasanlu independent of outside stimuli. Ivories in the round have been excavated at Susa and Tchoga Zanbil in Elam, where they are dated to the second millennium B.C. (Amiet 1966, 285, 479, figs. 217, 271, 325, 337). Whether they were locally made or imports from Mesopotamia is not obvious but in any event it does not seem possible on stylistic and chronological grounds to connect this early group with the later production at Hasanlu. Nor does it seem possible to connect the Hasanlu ivories with the majority of the later ivories said to come from Ziwiye, as they were created under Assyrian influences. However, at least one of these ivories (Godard 1950, fig. 91) can legitimately be claimed as an indigenous Iranian product; it is closely related in style and detail to some of the Hasanlu ivories (*infra*), although its place of manufacture is not known to us (see note 13).

With regard to Assyrian art it has been demonstrated that the local artisans were aware of specific representations on the stone reliefs at Nimrud, created there to glorify royal power—the massive battle scenes with chariots, cavalry, soldiers, and besieged cities. It has also been mentioned that the same scenes were represented on Assyrian ivories found at Nimrud. But it is significant that not one of the Assyrian ivories recovered from Hasanlu depicts a battle scene, siege scene, or chariots of any kind, nor do any of the locally made ivories depict ostriches, figures carrying an animal, or heraldic sphinxes, scenes depicted on the imported Assyrian ivories. These facts reinforce the suggestion that the larger, non-portable stone reliefs in Assyria, rather than the minor art of Assyrian ivory (at the very least not the examples present at Hasanlu), played the crucial role as the source of inspiration available to and accepted by the local workers.

The Assyrian presence at Hasanlu is further documented—aside from the influences and the imported ivories—by other objects excavated there: painted wall tiles of distinctively Assyrian shape and decoration (either imported or carefully copied local pieces), helmets, a fork held by addorsed lion heads and many Assyrian cylinder seals (Dyson 1959, 14; 1961, fig. 14; 1965b, 199; Moorey 1967, 88; Porada 1965, 120). It is possible that the Egyptian Blue lion bowl, albeit a characteristically North Syrian type (Muscarella 1974b, 28, fig. 1), may actually have been made in Assyria. This may be inferred both from the style of the sphinxes on the sides of the bowl, and from the fact that the material was not ordinarily used to manufacture such bowls; Egyptian Blue, moreover, has been found in a raw state at Nimrud (Mallowan 1966, 408, 482). And it is also possible that the other Egyptian Blue objects, a goblet, a decorated beaker, a cosmetic stand, furniture legs, a blinker-like object, gorget fragments (Muscarella 1966, figs. 30-33; Dyson 1967, fig. 5; 1968, fig. 109; 1972, 45 f., fig. 6; see note 30) as well as still unpublished bracelets and a lion-headed vessel, were all imported from Assyria. However, these objects deserve more study before we can be firmer in our conclusions about Assyrian origin (Dyson 1972, 46).

The same situation with respect to actual imports and artistic influences obtains for North Syria. For not only do we have in hand at Hasanlu the many North Syrian ivories, we have a stone lion bowl, and other stone bowls of apparent North Syrian types. (A unique painted vessel, mentioned above, not from a secure stratigraphical context [Dyson 1961, fig. 8; 1967, fig. 1030, pl. 1485E; Muscarella 1971a, 265; 1972, 39, note 9] has very good parallels at Carchemish and Hama.) Many of the locally made ivories and metal reliefs reflect a knowledge of North Syrian art—chariot horses and nude enemy, lion types, body decoration, the *Knielauf* and "Humbaba" motifs (Dyson 1967, fig. 1034; Muscarella 1966, 127 ff.; 1971a, 264 f.; see also note 36 below). Here also, the primary evidence for influences seems to derive from the non-portable stone reliefs, although the portable ivories and metalwork from North Syria clearly played a role.

Although it has been demonstrated that many of the elements and motifs on the Hasanlu ivories have good parallels in the West, and that imports from that area exist in some quantity, relations with other centers within Iran might be adduced. This conclusion is primarily documented by the few groups of winged bulls, nos. 214-221, which I have suggested were not locally made nor imported from the West, but which seem to have been carved elsewhere in Iran. There is also the possibility that the stylized shell, no. 221 bis, may have been made at an Iranian site, not Hasanlu. There is also the possibility that nos. 151, 157, 158 and 159 may also not have been made at Hasanlu, although of this I am not sure. Where within Iran these sites are to be located remains unknown at present. A few specific details have also been mentioned as best fitting into an Iranian background, for example the hair tufts on animals' legs, and concentric lines marking body joints. What is not so clear, however, is whether one can be anything but general in comments relating certain of the ivories to specific areas within Iran. Thus, no. 127 (wood) wears a brooch that tentatively could be brought forth as an Elamite feature, and the compact lion no. 187 was related to similar lion types from Luristan. My present opinion is that these elements should be kept in mind as possible indications of contacts with or influences on areas to the south but that they are in themselves not sufficient evidence to allow us to draw stronger conclusions.

Most of the parallels that were presented, other than those specifically Assyrian or North Syrian, for the various motifs and scenes depicted on the ivories are Near Eastern in general, not specifically Iranian; that is, they are elements recognized as existing in more than one culture. For example, the feathered headdress and helmet occurs in Iran and was worn by Elamites and Persians, but it also occurs earlier in Mesopotamia and Iran. Therefore, I do not think we may automatically assume that this headdress may be traced directly from Hasanlu to Elam (or vice versa) and to the Persians. Perhaps when the final publication of all the Hasanlu material is available we may be in a better position to discuss cultural relations between Hasanlu and other areas within Iran.

How, we must ask (if not answer to everyone's satisfaction), did the North Syrian and Assyrian material and motifs get to Hasanlu? Several hypotheses, each of which, in part at least, answers the question, present themselves to one's mind, and it would be of some value to briefly review them here. The starting point is the facts at hand, namely that Hasanlu had actual objects and artistic influences from two distinct cultural areas to the west. Because textual evidence is lacking we have no objective information about the mechanism of the distribution and stimulation from west to east, hence the hypotheses: a) North Syrians and Assyrians independently came to Hasanlu, the merchants brought goods, the artisans ideas and motifs; b) Merchants and artisans from Hasanlu traveled west and brought back both goods and motifs; c) Most of the objects, many of which are definitely luxuries, especially the ivories, were gifts sent independently by North Syrian and Assyrian kings and rulers to gain the good will and friendship of the authorities at Hasanlu, perhaps to establish a trading post or to cement relations with a military ally; d) The Assyrians alone, merchants and envoys, came to Hasanlu and brought all types of goods, some of which were North Syrian objects obtained by tribute and as booty.

Indeed, one could accept variations of the hypotheses a, b, and c: the goods came directly via the movement both ways of merchants and envoys, the knowledge of the reliefs via local craftsmen traveling west, or, further, even that the North Syrian and Assyrian ivories at Hasanlu were made there by fugitive or traveling craftsmen from their respective countries; but there is no objective information, no textual evidence. We know from literary sources that craftsmen traveled as envoys sent by their rulers, or as captives transported to foreign areas, or even as fugitives from their native lands (Dyson 1965, 199; Moorey 1967, 88, 136; Sasson 1966, 46 ff., 51 f.;

1968, 46 ff.), and therefore I consider it necessary and relevant to ask the question whether North Syrian and Assyrian craftsmen were actually present at Hasanlu, or whether artisans from Hasanlu traveled west to North Syria and to Assyria. However, although the question must be asked, I do not think that it may be answered, i.e. the question is indeed pertinent but the answer eludes us. This is because we are dealing with foreign objects and apparent foreign influences, which—although obvious with regard to their background—do not reveal the dynamics of their transit to Hasanlu. And lacking texts, we cannot form categorical historical conclusions.[36]

There are strong arguments, both historical and archaeological, that can be brought forth to support hypothesis d, namely that no North Syrian, merchant or artisan, ever came to Hasanlu, and that all West-East contacts and trade was in the hands of the Assyrians, working perhaps with the local merchants. All the Assyrian objects obviously came from Assyria, or at least from Assyrian craftsmen. The Assyrian plaques nos. 280-284 are presumed to have decorated one or more elaborate chairs or thrones and as such might be eliminated as a normal item of trade; rather they might be considered as a gift from a king, as "status" items (Wright 1974, 4). That thrones and chairs, some of ivory, were given as gifts by Near Eastern kings is well established in ancient literature (Muscarella 1967, 59; Smith 1963, 32; Luckenbill 1926, 1, para. 410, 475). It should be re-

---

[36]Parenthetically it should be noted that if my suggestion (Muscarella 1966, 123) that certain architectural features at Hasanlu—the *bit hilani* portico—derive from North Syria is acceptable, it could be argued that merchant activity alone cannot explain them. Apparently the Assyrians did not copy the *bit hilani* until the eighth century (Luckenbill 1926, II: para. 73). In addition, it is tempting to suggest, for example, that the differences between the manufacture of pyxides at Nimrud and at Hasanlu, discussed in the text (Chapter VIII), can be brought forth as evidence that the latter pieces were made by North Syrians actually working at Hasanlu. Moreover, it is also tempting to suggest that North Syrians at Hasanlu were responsible for transmitting knowledge both of their homeland's architectural features and of the stone reliefs. But it might easily be argued that differences between the pyxides may merely reflect different workshops, or craftsmen within a workshop, in North Syria or Nimrud, and by itself is not an indication that the workshop was at Hasanlu. And if there is not clear-cut evidence at Hasanlu for a local North Syrian workshop staffed by immigrant craftsmen we cannot assume that a knowledge of the reliefs or of architecture came through their presence. In short, if there actually were North Syrians at Hasanlu, we do not know it and cannot draw that conclusion to the exclusion of others from the evidence at hand. Thus, in the text I raise the issue as an hypothesis, not as an historical reality.

Moorey (1967, 88 and note 70; also 1971, 269) refers to Assyrian and North Syrian influences and craftsmen in Iran in the ninth and eighth centuries B.C. Unfortunately, two of the objects he cites as alleged examples of Assyrian material found in Iran were in fact purchased from dealers: furthermore, they are forgeries. One is the decoration on a bronze bucket mentioned in note 24 above; the other is a scene on a bronze bowl in the Oriental Institute of the University of Chicago (Muscarella 1977b, no. 216 bis). Frankfort's assumption that the aberrations in both the iconography and execution of the "Assyrian" figures indicated that the scene was a provincial product made in "one of Assyria's eastern provinces," was accepted by Moorey. Even if not forgeries, unprovenienced, purchased objects can never be used to yield information regarding cultural relations between two areas.

In his review of vanden Berghe 1968, Maurits van Loon (1972, 68) strongly concluded that certain objects excavated at War Kabud in Luristan were derived from North Syria and could "hardly be the result of trade alone," and represented "massive North Syrian influence." These objects came to Iran, according to van Loon, in some manner connected with deportations of North Syrian "craftsmen to Assyria and points beyond." However, of the objects considered to be North Syrian—pointed-base jars, glazed vessels, crenelated bronze mace heads, bronze/iron mace heads, omphaloi, rosette bowls, and fibulae—*all* have parallels in Assyria and are not specifically North Syrian products (although some of these types of objects may have been made there also), as vanden Berghe (1968, 122 ff., 141 f., 165 ff., 171 f.) demonstrated, giving relevant bibliography. Crenelated bronze mace heads (some clearly cosmetic vessels with feet), bronze/iron mace heads, as well as omphaloi and glazed vessels, are also known from Hasanlu IV. Moreover, it is not certain from the texts cited (van Loon 1972, 68, n. 17) that North Syrians were deported to Luristan. Sargon II did deport people from Commagene to the borders of Elam but it is not established which border is meant. A reference from the time of Sennacherib regarding an unnamed people sent to Ellipi, according to Levine (1974, 104 ff.) to be located in northern Luristan (but still not definitely located), cannot be presented as evidence that North Syrians were sent to Luristan. And an earlier reference from the time of Tiglath-Pileser III, stating that 30,000 people from Hamath were deported to Assyria—not Iran—continues an older practice of conquering Assyrian kings who brought back prisoners to their homeland. Therefore, I believe that the archaeological and historical evidence presented to document North Syrian elements and presence at War Kabud actually does not exist.

Further, Calmeyer (1969, 87 ff.) correctly points out that the winged sun disc on certain bronze helmets that were purchased from antiquity dealers have North Syrian features. His conclusions, however, based solely on information supplied by the dealers (I believe that actually only one dealer is involved), that the helmets were found in Iran (see also Borchardt 1972, 107 f.) and that they testify to some form of contact between Iran and North Syria or Urartu, must be rejected: no one knows where the helmets were found nor how many hands they passed through before their sale (see my comments in *JAOS* 97, 1, [1977]: 80).

called that many elaborate North Syrian chair backs (from thrones?) were found in Room SW.7 at Nimrud, and these were probably there as booty or gifts sent to the Assyrian king (Mallowan and Herrmann 1974, 39). Therefore, one could suggest, as an explanation for the presence of the Assyrian plaques at Hasanlu, that Assyrians themselves brought the furniture as a gift from their king. Moreover, it is significant, to my mind, that most of the North Syrian ivories at Hasanlu have their parallels at Nimrud in Assyria, where, it is generally assumed, the ivories excavated were either locally made by North Syrians or were imported from North Syria. In this context it would not overreach the archaeological evidence to accept the probability that the North Syrian objects recovered at Hasanlu arrived directly from an Assyrian city, perhaps even from Nimrud.[37] The Assyrians would thus be the source both for all their own products that reached Hasanlu (direct contact trade) and for all, or most of, the North Syrian products (exchange trade) (Lamberg-Karlovsky 1972, 222 f.; Larsen 1967, 172). North Syria traded extensively with Mesopotamia for centuries before the ninth century as we know from various economic texts (Sasson 1966, 168 ff.). This trade definitely continued into the first millennium B.C., albeit at this time the royal annals place emphasis on booty and gifts. That Assyria could keep North Syrians and other Westerners out of her eastern provinces and satellites, including regions in western Iran, during the ninth century B.C., is clear from our knowledge of the history of this period. On the other hand, at least by the late eighth century B.C. North Syria traded with Phrygia, Urartu and Greece, areas that Assyria could not control, or could not continuously control. And it is of interest to note in this context that North Syrian ivories reached these areas, and, significantly, that each of these areas subsequently developed local ateliers and styles of ivory carving, a situation we have noted occurred earlier at Hasanlu.

To date there is no evidence from ninth century North Syrian sites that any Iranian objects were imported, objects that might represent North Syria's share or reciprocity of alleged trade with Iran. The islands of Samos and Crete have yielded some Iranian objects most of which seem to fit into a broad ninth-to-seventh century context (Jantzen 1972, 74 ff.; Muscarella 1973b, 236 f.). A bronze spouted vessel, a typical bronze Luristan standard, and an Iran-style ibex or goat from Samos, and an openwork pendant from Crete are surely imports from Iran. Other bronze objects from Samos that are probably Iranian include an openwork rattle-bell, a pendant, and seven goats. The spouted vessel could be ninth century in date although later examples exist. I believe that these objects reached the West by the same route used in the ninth century, across the Zagros passes directly to the coast. Inasmuch as there is no evidence for Urartian materials traveling across Anatolia in the eighth and seventh centuries (Muscarella 1962, 1970), there is no reason to assume that Iranian objects traveled north to Urartian territory and then west across Anatolia via the Black Sea. And it should be noted that the trans-Zagros routes have been used from Islamic times up to the present by both merchants and nomads, each group carrying goods to and from Iran. In any event, the Iranian imports on Crete and Samos do not necessarily yield information about similar materials reaching the West in the ninth century (Muscarella 1977, 31-57).

Ninth century Iranian objects that reached Assyria are better documented. I have discussed elsewhere (Muscarella 1971, 264 f.) the fact that ninth century Hasanlu contained rhyta, omphalos bowls (which existed in Iran earlier in the second millennium, Muscarella 1968, fig. 16; 1974c, 43 f., fig. 7) and attachment handles for vessels, types of objects that were also used by Assyrians. I argue that it is possible these objects may represent original Iranian products that were imported and adapted by Assyrians after their trips to, or contacts with, Iran. Thus, while we have no recognizable evidence for Iranian material imported to North Syria in the ninth century we may have evidence for such material being imported to Assyria at this time. This evidence, albeit negative with respect to North Syria, reinforces the suggestion that Assyria had a trade monopoly with Iran.

Another matter deserves to be discussed with respect both to Assyrian relations with Iran and to the problem of Assyrian control of trade with Iran: Did Assyrian armies get to the Solduz valley in the ninth century B.C.? In their annals Assurnasirpal II and his son Shalmaneser III mention campaigns to Gilzani, Zamua and Hubushkia; the latter king also refers to his penetration of Mannaea and the Nairi Lands, including the "Sea of Nairi Land," and "the Upper and Lower Seas of Nairi." Where were Gilzani, Zamua and Hubushkia? Kinnier Wilson (1962, 110 f.) places Gilzani and Hubushkia west and southwest of Lake Urmia; Levine (1972, 120) leaves

[37]Dyson (1972, 44) stated that the pyxides and a female head, all of North Syrian origin, were examples of Assyrian influence at Hasanlu. This position can be maintained only if we accept the Assyrians as the vehicle for bringing such objects to Hasanlu. [Winter, 1976a, 414 f., independently arrived at the conclusion that Assyria was responsible for the redistribution of North Syrian objects to Hasanlu.]

the question open but places Zamua in eastern Iraq (1973, 16 ff.; cf. for example Moorey 1967, 89, who places it near Ziwiye). And if Gilzani is near Zamua, then it might be farther south of Lake Urmia than Kinnier Wilson allows. Furthermore, if, as Levine (1974, 113 ff.) suggests. Mannaea probably extended from Lake Urmia in the north[38] to Lake Zeribor in the south, how far north, how close to Hasanlu, did Shalmaneser's armies penetrate (or at least his influence extend)?

Further complicating the problem of ninth century geography is the meaning of the expressions "Land of Nairi," and "Upper and Lower Seas of Nairi," and, indeed, their relationship to the site of Hasanlu itself. "Nairi" is a term used both as a geographical designation (*viz.* Kinnier Wilson 1962, 111, note 135) and/or as a political unit. Therefore the "Lower Sea of Nairi" need not, for most of the ninth century, equal the "Lower Sea of Urartu." Nevertheless, by the last few years of the ninth century, by 810-805 B.C., there seems to be no doubt that the state of Urartu extended as far south as the Solduz and Ushnu valleys (Muscarella 1971b, 47; 1974c, 82; Levine 1973, 20 f.), and that at this time, at least, the "Lower Sea of Nairi" surely represented Lake Urmia. But what of the preceding period? Several times Shalmaneser refers to the "Sea of the Land of Nairi" (Luckenbill 1926, I, para. 598, 606, etc.; Hulin 1963, 51, 59); was this Lake Van? In 843/2 B.C. Shalmaneser refers to both Seas of Nairi conquered by his armies (Kinnier Wilson 1962, 95, 102). In this formula was the Lower Sea in fact Lake Urmia and the surrounding valleys, and was it conquered by the Assyrians in 843/2? Hulin (1963, 59) accepts this but also believes that as early as 859 B.C. the "Sea of the Land of Nairi" was Lake Urmia. The question for us here is: did Shalmaneser actually "conquer" Hasanlu in 859 and/or in 843/2 B.C.? Needless to state, the answer is not readily available, but it would seem that if Shalmaneser's term "Lower Sea of Nairi" is Lake Urmia, then Hasanlu was within the area claimed to have been conquered by the Assyrians at some time before the major, final destruction.

A relevant problem is that concerned with the understanding of the word "conquered" as used by the Assyrians. One could interpret the word to signify "controlled" which would mean that Assyrian armies need never have physically entered the Urmia area. Whatever meaning is to be inferred, at least we may interpret the word conquer to mean that the Assyrians considered the Urmia area to be within their sphere of influence for some decades before the destruction of Hasanlu, apparently by the invading armies of an expanding Urartu. Levine (1973, 21, note 90) has pointed out that Assyrian influence at Hasanlu does not necessarily indicate Assyrian conquest.[39]

Another point must be made. Although the evidence suggests that these conclusions concerning Assyrian control of East-West contacts are probable, I believe that not all the information is yet available. The questions concerning the mechanics of cultural contacts or "long distance" trade (Wright 1974, 4) between North Syria and Hasanlu should not be considered as fully answered. The primary reason is what I have stated before, the apparent evidence that Hasanlu craftsmen knew at first hand the North Syrian reliefs. If this evidence were not as obvious as I think it is, I would have no objection to accepting without reservation Assyria's total intermediary role between North Syria and Iran. Thus, although I favor hypothesis d as the major force in the exchange between the West and Hasanlu, I do not think we should rule out the possibilities expressed in the other hypotheses.

The raw ivory used by the local craftsmen at Hasanlu could also be explained as coming from Assyria, which in turn got its supplies from Syria and Phoenicia as booty or gifts. The Hasanlu ivories have not been analyzed to determine whether they are of Indian or African origin (if in fact this can be established beyond doubt). Barnett (1948, 11,

[38]It is not clear, however, if this situation existed in the ninth century B.C. as well as the eighth. In the eighth century the Solduz area might have been part of Uishdish (Levine 1974, 105); was it so in the ninth century? The earliest reference to Mannaean on the Urartian side is on the Tashtepe inscription set up by Menua (ca. 805-790 B.C.).

[39]Still-unpublished information from Hasanlu might have some bearing on this question; all the five buildings excavated to date (originally built in Period IV C) were burnt and destroyed (end of Period IV C) and subsequently rebuilt (Period IV B) at a time before the final major destruction (end of Period IV B), presumably by the Urartians. The earlier destruction could have been caused by an Assyrian attack. See now Dyson and Pigott 1975 for a report of the 1974 excavations. (After this monograph was completed I received Elizabeth Childs Johnson, Urartian Influence Upon Iranian Architecture in the Early First Millennium B.C., *Marsyas* XVII [1976]: 21-38. The credits state that I "offered many helpful suggestions in composing the final draft of the present paper." What is not stated is that the numerous criticisms, suggestions and comments I offered concerning the chronology of the Urartian and Iranian sites discussed, the nature, sequence and chronology of the architecture and fortification walls of Hasanlu IV [e.g. that the latter were now published as belonging to Period III!], and still other items, were *totally* ignored in the final draft as published. I am in disagreement with many of the paper's claims and conclusions.)

note 4) states that some of the Nimrud ivories are from Indian tusks and (1957, 168) that some of the Samarian examples are from African tusks; on the other hand Mallowan (1966, 484) states that Syrian elephants were the source for the Nimrud ivories. Given the evidence for trade with the West, it is probable that Hasanlu got its ivory from that direction rather than from India, with which area there is no evidence for any contact.

Recently Collon (1977) has suggested that for centuries antedating the first millennium B.C. Indian elephants were imported to the West to replace the extinct Syrian elephant and that it was from these elephants that western craftsmen derived their ivory. She admits that it is not possible to know when the alleged trade began—although she believes that it may have coincided with the chlorite trade in the third millennium—and so it seems that we can draw no conclusions for the Hasanlu ivories. Yet, even if she is correct the conclusions suggested above that ivory came to Hasanlu from the West would not be obviated.

Trade and/or strong cultural contacts and relationships between the southern Lake Urmia basin and areas to the west extend back in time to the second millennium B.C., ca. 1800–1600 B.C. as evidenced by the existence and extent of the Khabur Ware Culture (Dyson, 1965, 193 ff.; Muscarella 1968, 188 f., 194 ff.; 1974c, 35, 52 f.; [Kramer] Hamlin 1974, 125 ff.). This culture extended from Syria across the Near East to its easternmost extension around the southern shores of Lake Urmia. Its existence at Dinkha and Hasanlu seems to be a cultural expansion rather than simply a matter of trade relations. For our purposes the geographical extent of this culture indicates quite certainly that Northwest Iran, Mesopotamia and North Syria were trading and in contact with each other long before the ninth century. Thus the occurrence of contacts in the ninth century was not a new phenomenon but essentially a continuation of an older situation.[40]

What raw goods or mineral products, if any, the ninth century city of Hasanlu may have exchanged with the West in return for its luxury imports is not at present known to us. An Islamic source refers to lapis lazuli in Azerbaijan but there are no modern traces allowing for verification of this statement (Herrmann 1968, 27), and therefore we are in no position to discuss this material as an item of Northwestern Iranian trade. Furthermore, no lapis has been found at Hasanlu or Dinkha from any period, which would be strange if it were an item of export. The evidence available at present suggests that by the third millennium B.C. lapis was traded from Afghanistan southwest to Elam and from there to the West (Herrmann 1968, 28, 53). Lapis jewellery is reported from Kalaruz (Hakimi 1968, 65) but not from Marlik. The presence of worked lapis jewellery does not in itself document that Kalaruz was active in the lapis trade but its absence from the very rich site of Marlik suggests that the area of the South Caspian was not on a lapis trade route.

The southern Urmia basin has also been brought into a discussion concerning the tin trade routes between Iran and Mesopotamia during the Early and Middle Assyrian periods. There is much literature on this subject but in fact no one has yet been able to document to everyone's satisfaction that there was a tin route passing from some still undetermined place in Iran to the southern Urmia area and then across the Zagros to Mesopotamia. What has been proven beyond doubt, because of textual evidence, is that in the early second millennium B.C. Elam received tin from some area still to be determined and that from there it was shipped to southern Mesopotamia which in turn moved it north and west (Dossin 1970, 97 ff.; Muhly 1973, 407 f.). Thus we know that there was a southern route for tin moving from Iran to Mesopotamia: but is there evidence for a northern route, Urmia to Mesopotamia? Leemans (1968, 205, 207, 210) argued strongly that such a route existed, disagreeing with Garelli who had earlier suggested a southern route. Muhly (1973a, 409), while recognizing the existence of the southern route, agreed that a northern one was possible and he specifically mentioned Hasanlu as one of the sites on the route. He was thinking of course of early second millennium Hasanlu, about which, unfortunately, we know very little, and his suggestion cannot be supported. Larsen (1967, 4, 172) also referred to the presence of tin in northwestern Iran and believed there was a northern route into Mesopotamia because of a letter of the eighteenth century B.C. excavated at Shemshara in northern Mesopotamia. This letter was written from someone requesting tin from the local ruler, and because Shemshara is near northwestern Iran, Larsen believes the tin came from there. Muhly and Leemans, and more recently Hamlin (1974, 132), also refer to the Shemshara letter as evidence that tin came from northwestern Iran.

There is still confusion however, about whether or

[40]This is of special interest when it is realized that the Habur Ware culture in Northwestern Iran ceased to exist ca. 1600 B.C. It was replaced after about 100 years by a Grey Ware culture called Iron I. Some traces of continuity exist but the Iron I remains clearly reflect a new culture possibly representing a new people coming into the area (Muscarella 1974c, 52 f.). Who these people were remains a major problem for Iranian archaeologists.

not tin does in fact exist in northern Iran, or existed there in the past, or indeed, passed through that area at any time in antiquity. And, according to the latest information, we do not know the source of the tin handled by the Elamites (Muhly 1973a, 409). However, that tin may exist in eastern Iran has recently been documented by geological surveys.[41] In the eastern Lut mountain range, in the area extending roughly from Birjand to Zahedan, geologists have found deposits of cassiterite tin ore and also stannite, an ore containing both copper and tin; copper, lead and zinc were also reported from the same areas. In addition, old mine workings extending for a distance of 2000 meters were discovered; the dating is still uncertain. This area, which now assumes major importance in Iranian archaeology, is close to, or north of, several major Bronze Age sites, Shahr-i-Sokhta, Shad-Dad, Tal-i-Iblis, Tepe Yahya and Bampur. That this eastern region was the source of the Susa tin is yet to be established, but at least one can now talk of specific tin and stannite sources within Iran.

A Middle Assyrian text of the thirteenth century B.C. (Iron I in Iranian archaeological terminology) from Tell al Rimah specifically cited Nairi to the north of Mesopotamia as a source of tin (Wiseman 1966, 175, 183; Leemans 1968, 209). That Nairi continued to be a source of tin in the ninth century B.C. is confirmed by a text of Ashurnasirpal II (Landsberger 1965, 288; Leemans 1968, 209; Luckenbill 1926, I, para. 501). Recent work at Metsamor in the Caucasus suggests that tin was plentiful there in the late second millennium (Burney and Lang 1972, 73, 90; Mkrtiachan 1967, 76); and some of the eighth century Urartian bronzes, bowls for example (Piotrovsky 1970, fig. 63), are known to have a high tin content, which explains their color and high polish. There is a five hundred year time span between the Shemshara and the al Rimah letters and therefore we cannot automatically conclude that Shemshara in the early second millennium B.C. received its tin from Nairi. And given the known contemporary south-to-north tin itinerary, from Assyria to Anatolia, it is not improbable that Shemshara in fact got its tin supplies from the south.[42]

It must also be noted that although tin bronze is attested in Northwestern Iran by the early second millennium (Moorey 1969, 135), no evidence exists for the presence of tin ore at the extensively excavated sites known from that area, in particular Hasanlu, Dinkha Tepe, Geoy Tepe, Haftavan, or Yanik Tepe near Tabriz. It would seem, therefore, that there is no evidence at hand that Hasanlu at any period was involved in a putative tin trade between Iran and Mesopotamia and we cannot hypothesize that tin played any role in the exchange of goods in the ninth century.

In the first millennium tin was available to Assyria from areas to the north, east and west. Aside from that from Nairi, tin was given as booty to Assurnasirpal II and to Shalmaneser III by Gilzani (Luckenbill 1926, I, para. 441, 589) and from Zamua (Luckenbill 1926, I, para. 457). During the same period tin was very plentiful in North Syria, in the Khabur area and on the Phoenician coast, a great amount of which came to Assyria as booty (Luckenbill 1926, I, para. 443, 469, 470, 473, 474, 475, 477, 479, 518, 525, 593, 596, 603, 610).[43] Whether Hasanlu played a role in getting the tin to Gilzani and Zamua we do not know nor do we know where these

---

[41]J. Stocklin, J. Eftekharnezhad and A. Hushmanzadeh, *Central Lut Reconnaissance, East Iran* (Teheran, 1972). This reference along with relevant information was supplied to me by Professor James Muhly. (Unfortunately, for no explainable reason, I did not read Muhly's extraordinarily important book *Copper and Tin* until the present work was in proof. On pages 292 ff., 302 ff., 317, 325, 337, 451, n. 588, he vigorously argues for the existence of a tin route from northwestern Iran, south of Lake Urmia, across the Zagros to Assyria, and he mentions Hasanlu and Dinkha Tepe as sites "associated in the overland trade route which brought the tin of northwest Iran into northern Mesopotamia" [303; incidentally, he disassociates the lapis trade from this northern route, 303 f.]. Nevertheless, given the lack of firm evidence that tin actually exists in northwest Iran, and the total absence from *any* excavated site in the area of tin ore or ingots or any other relevant evidence for the presence of tin in trade, plus the evidence given in my text, I find that I cannot alter my opinion. It should also be noted that Muhly himself [305] states that "it must be admitted that the evidence for this overland tin trade is very incomplete and fragmentary." And further [306], concerning tin in northern Iran, that "the present lack of any geological evidence must be recognized." In any event, Muhly is discussing the second millennium B.C., whereas we are concerned here specifically with ninth century B.C. Hasanlu and its source of wealth, which, on the basis of all the available evidence, cannot be associated with a putative tin trade. For reference to tin in eastern Iran see Muhly 1976, 98, where it seems to be belittled.)

[42]Hittite texts refer to tin (*viz.* Pritchard 1955, 348 f., 358), the source of which by this time might have been Nairi. However, one cannot eliminate the old established southern route, especially because Hittite texts also refer to lapis lazuli, which probably came from the South. That trade with Elam existed is documented by a text that refers to jasper coming from Elam (Pritchard 1955, 356). Also note that "Nairi" might also include parts of the Caucasus, where tin exists.

[43]Luckenbill translates the word *anakku* as lead. It is now recognized that this word means tin (Landsberger 1965). Tin may not have come from Elam in the first millennium.

areas got their supplies; speculation does not help us resolve the problems. What is significant, however, is that tin was available to the ninth century Assyrians from all quarters of the Near East, not from areas to the east alone.

Suggestions regarding the nature of goods and materials that Hasanlu may have exported to the West are at present only guesses. The few artifacts mentioned above that may have come to Assyria from Iran do not by themselves appear to be the only items sought by the Assyrians. From the Assyrian texts of the ninth century we know what Assyria wanted from states that must have been geographically close to Hasanlu and that were perhaps similar in economy—Zamua, Gilzani, Mannáea, Hubishka. These states collectively traded or gave as booty cattle, horses, camels, grain, copper, tin, silver, gold, garments and so forth. It seems that the Hasanlu area was as fertile in antiquity as it is today and therefore grain, cattle, and horses might have been, in part at least, the commodities traded, for the Assyrians could never get enough of these products (Moorey 1971, 115 f.). Renfrew (1969, 154) states that "trade is a two-way process," but he also points out that "reciprocity cannot always be demonstrated." Thus if Assyria were mainly importing animals and food the archaeological record could not possibly furnish evidence of such transactions.

One more comment is both necessary and relevant. Hasanlu is a site that is not only accessible, without geographical barriers, to the western and eastern shores of Lake Urmia and points north, but it is also accessible to areas east and south. Furthermore, and significantly, it is also close to several passes, especially the Kil i-Shin, that links Iran to Iraq. In this respect it commands a natural setting for an entrepôt or caravan stop. This advantage, under a powerful and astute ruler would make Hasanlu a city that could control or monitor movements of goods both within Iran and between northwestern Iran and Assyria. It is therefore conceivable that, aside from any specific local items traded with Assyria, Hasanlu's importance and wealth might have resulted primarily, or in part, from her geographic position. Certainly in this context Assyria through conquest or treaty would want to have political influence at Hasanlu, influence that is reflected in the archaeological record. What the archaeological record cannot tell us, I submit, is whether trade by itself led directly to the importance of Hasanlu, or whether the geographical importance of Hasanlu led to the growth of trade.

In the final analysis we do not have all the answers to the question concerning Hasanlu's wealth, having only one side of the equation—the objects and architecture excavated—but both the fertility of the Solduz valley and the geographical setting of the site must surely have played some role, and should be accepted as furnishing some, if not all, of the answers. As a final comment we may surely note that the evidence for trade and strong cultural "contacts" and relationships between Hasanlu and points west attests to a cultural collision that must have deeply affected both the cultural and political life of the local inhabitants. [Now see Winter 1977 for a penetrating discussion of this problem.]

HASANLU AND OTHER IVORY GROUPS

At some time in the ninth century B.C. after a hiatus of about two hundred and fifty years ivory carving again began to flourish in the Near East (Kantor 1965, 171). That this renaissance resulted at least in part from a knowledge of earlier carving seems a reasonable assumption, and Kantor has presented evidence for this conclusion. Both from Biblical sources and Assyrian texts we have information about the prevalence of ivory carving in the ninth century. Solomon had his ivory throne, Ahab his ivory house;[44] and Tukulti-Ninurta II (ca. 890-884) received an ivory chair and other ivories from an Aramaean city; Ashurnasirpal II and Shalmaneser III received many ivory objects and tusks from North Syrian, Phoenician, and even Urartian cities. There was, therefore, even before the discovery of the Hasanlu ivories, no doubt among scholars that in the ninth century B.C. finished ivory products were present in various areas of the Near East and that some of these found their way to Assyria.

Many archaeologists have attempted to recognize which of the many ivories excavated at various sites might be the examples, or the companions, of those discussed in the texts. Here, of course, is the problem, for since the initial publications of the ivories from Nimrud, Hama, Samaria, Zincirli and Arslan Tash, scholars have disagreed about whether some or all of these ivories were in fact made in the ninth century. The issue is not merely one of stratigraphy, which would preclude discussion (*viz.* Hasanlu), but one of stylistic and historical interpretations: Nimrud was destroyed in the late seventh century, Hama presumably in 720, Samaria presumably in 722; the building which contained the ivories at Zincirli was in use until the seventh century; and the building in which the ivories were recovered at Arslan Tash was apparently built by Tiglath-Pileser III (745-727) (Barnett 1957, 125 ff., 133; Mallowan and Davies 1970, 39 ff.; Freyer-Schauenburg 1966, 68; Frankfort 1954, 190 ff., 260, note 134). The date of the final deposition of the ivories was not necessarily considered to be the date of their manufacture.

The fact that the ninth century textual evidence exists and also the occurrence of the name Hazael on plain ivory plaques at Arslan Tash and Nimrud have led some scholars to accept a ninth century date for some of the decorated ivory groups, while other scholars have argued on stylistic and stratigraphic grounds that most of the decorated ivories are in fact eighth century in date. Thureau–Dangin (1931, 135 ff.) accepted the Hazael inscription at Arslan Tash as that of the Biblical king and therefore proof that the ivories found there were made in the ninth century; he has been supported in this view by de Mertzenfeld (1954, 33, 126), Barnett (1957, 126 f.), Millard (1962, 41), Thimme (1973, viii, xv, xvi), Matthiae (1975, 490 f.), and in part by Mallowan (1966, 329, 452, 598), and Mallowan and Herrmann (1970, 50 ff.). On the other hand, Frankfort (1954, 190 ff., 260, note 134) refused to see these ivories as earlier than those from eighth century Khorsabad. And Brown (1958, 69) held that it was not clear which of the decorated ivories belonged to the bed, and that on the basis of style the Arslan Tash ivories could be eighth century. Frankfort and Brown were followed in their stylistic arguments by Freyer-Schauenburg (1966, 68; also Strøm 1971, 239, note 168). Of interest is the fact that the inscription of

[44]Even if it is assumed that the relevant Biblical references were written later than the ninth century it does not necessarily follow that the information about the use of ivory in Palestine is lessened. The Assyrian texts allow no doubts about the production of carved ivory after 900 B.C. One wonders, of course, who worked the ivory mentioned in the Old Testament, and one also wonders if this ivory was plain or decorated, *infra.*

Hazael is not on a decorated plaque, and, perhaps significantly, the same situation exists for the Hazael plaque at Nimrud. It will be recalled that there were remains of two beds at Arslan Tash, both of wood with plain ivory veneer (Thureau–Dangin 1931, 89 f.). Therefore, it is quite possible that the Hazael inscription belonged only to the plain ivory beds; this resolution would satisfy those who believe the inscription is indeed ninth century, as well as those who see the decorated ivories from Arslan Tash as eighth century in date. There is no compelling reason to connect the decorated ivory plaques with the inscribed plain example.

While the Samaria ivories have no juxtaposed inscription, Crowfoot (1938, 1 ff.) assumed that they derived from the ninth century palace of Ahab, some short distance away from the find spot. Again de Mertzenfeld (1954, 33, 63) and Barnett (1957, 125) accepted this date, followed by Mallowan (1966, 474 ff., 556, 656, note 120), who believed, however, that some of the larger and cruder pieces could be eighth century (see also Mallowan and Herrmann 1974, 39 f., and Matthiae 1975, 490; Strøm 1971, 238, note 168). The same scholars who challenged the early dating of the Arslan Tash ivories also challenged a ninth century date for the Samaria examples, again because of style and because of their stratigraphic context. Although it is not inconceivable that a few of the Samaria ivories are ninth century heirlooms (*viz.* Crowfoot 1938, pls. VIII: 1-5, XI: 1 [?]), the evidence is not so certain as one would wish.

The Zincirli ivories have generated less discussion. They were found in a building in use for a long time and conclusions about their dating cover the general range of ninth/eighth century B.C., without firm opinions being expressed (Barnett 1957, 125 f.; Mallowan and Herrmann 1974, 41 ff.; Strøm 1971, 115 does suggest an eighth century date). A fragment showing part of a chariot that may have six spokes could be the earliest ivory in the group (de Mertzenfeld 1954, pl. CXXXII, 1142). It is close in detail to a fragment from Nimrud, which Mallowan (1966, 541 f., fig. 462) dates to the mid-eighth century or earlier. Six-spoked wheels usually are a ninth century B.C. attribute, but do occur on Nimrud ivories that must be eighth century in date (Mallowan and Herrmann 1974, 46 ff., 68 f., pl. III). Thus the Nimrud and Zincirli chariot plaques could easily be of eighth century date.

The few ivories from Hama have not aroused the controversy associated with the other groups even though they were found in Level F, apparently destroyed in 720 B.C. There is agreement among scholars that these ivories were heirlooms from the ninth century (cf. de Mertzenfeld 1954, 33, 109, eighth century), because the body markings of the animals—flame pattern and belly motif—relate them closely to stone reliefs of the ninth century (Frankfort 1954, 192; Kantor 1956, 173; Porada 1970b, 98; Strøm 1971, 115). Here again style rather than stratigraphy plays a strong role in determining date.

One of the very few ivory groups, aside from Hama, that claims a consensus accepting a ninth century date is the assemblage from Tell Halaf, at least those ivories definitely known to have come from the cremation graves under the statue of the seated female (Strøm 1971, 115; Hrouda 1962, 9 f., 117, pl. 9; Moortgat 1955, 12 f.). Thus, in addition to Hrouda and Moortgat, Frankfort (1954, 191), Brown (1958, 69), Barnett (1957, 44, 49), Freyer-Schauenburg (1966, 120), and Porada (1970b, 98) agree on the basis of both style and stratigraphy that the Tell Halaf ivories are ninth century in date (cf. de Mertzenfeld 1954, 140, eighth century). It should be noted in passing that the Hasanlu stylistic evidence reinforces the conclusions that the Hama and Tell Halaf ivories are of ninth century manufacture.

What emerges, then, from the preceding discussion is that the only western site in the Near East that produced ivories securely dated to the ninth century on the basis of stratigraphy is Tell Halaf. And the only other group of ivories from the same area that are accepted with no controversy as ninth century products, albeit without stratigraphic support, is that from Hama. Ivories from the other sites mentioned, on the other hand, have been subject to much discussion and controversy, with no consensus regarding their date. Therefore, aside from the few Tell Halaf ivories, those from Hasanlu form the major corpus of ivories yet known that are stratigraphically secured to the ninth century B.C. Their value and importance in this respect, speaking here only of chronology and not of art history, is major. For, being a large and varied corpus of dated material, they present objective criteria for helping scholars decide which ivories hitherto floating in a time range of a hundred years, are in fact ninth century products. The Hasanlu ivories form a chronological and stylistic corpus against which other ivories may be judged and compared. Thus, for example, in the discussions of the various parallels brought forth from Nimrud for many of the Hasanlu ivories it becomes clear that a ninth century attribution for the former is considerably strengthened.

The particular types of ivories from Nimrud chronologically affected by the Hasanlu corpus may be reviewed briefly. Some of these were previously recognized as ninth century products but the Hasanlu evidence should preclude further controversy (except, of course, in cases of continuity): "farouche" female heads with a polos; kilted male sculpture; lion plaques and sculpture with triangular-tufted manes and stomachs, flame patterns and back "stitching"; lion bowls; pyxides decorated with sphinxes, with their lids and calf handles; lotus handles and palm capitals; certain lion heads with inlays and dotted muzzles; and certain examples of grazing animals. Some of these ivory types are known not only from Nimrud but also from Hama and Tell Halaf. Although most Assyrian ivories are not difficult to date on the basis of style, it is of value to have a group such as the Hasanlu assemblage to provide stratigraphic confirmation.

Those types of ivories known elsewhere which do not appear at Hasanlu may also be significant in a discussion of ivory chronology. Not a single example of a "Phoenician" ivory exists at Hasanlu;[45] and there are no examples of winged griffins, winged sun discs, nude frontal females, women at a window, or palm plaques—all motifs common at other sites. Nor are there any recognizable horse frontlets or blinkers. While one cannot base categorical conclusions about chronology on the lack of these types and motifs at Hasanlu, it is possible in some instances, I believe, to use the negative information as a guide. For, given the fact that so many imported ivories from the West, from North Syria and Assyria, found their way to Hasanlu, it is surprising that there are no Phoenician ivories, especially since they were present at Nimrud. This absence may indeed be fortuitous, or it may be, as I believe, that in fact none existed in the ninth century, before the destruction of Hasanlu.

Fragments of Phoenician ivories have been excavated in the Etruscan Bernardini Tomb, dated sometime about 700 B.C. or later (Barnett 1957, 129; Freyer-Schauenburg 1966, 55; Strøm 1971, 133 ff., 154, 218, note 8). And recently, examples of Phoenician ivories were excavated at Salamis on Cyprus from a tomb fairly well dated close to 700 B.C. (Karageorghis 1973). Here we have two of the best-dated groups of such ivories ever excavated. Thus, the combined evidence of the absence of these ivories at ninth century B.C. Hasanlu and their presence in late eighth and seventh century contexts in Italy and at Salamis, suggests that the date of the "Phoenician" ivories is to be set in the second half of the eighth century, not earlier. The argument from the Hasanlu site is *ex silentio* to be sure, but joined with the firm Salamis and Italian evidence is of value.

A problem still to be resolved is the existence of the Biblical and Assyrian evidence that Phoenicia had ivory objects, evidence that cannot be ignored. A tentative resolution may be that the Phoenicians in the tenth/ninth centuries carved ivory only for furniture and that they did not carve decorated plaques and sculpture until the eighth century, copying a technique used by North Syrian artisans earlier. Again I repeat that the Hazael inscriptions are on plain ivory panels, which may be significant in a discussion of the dating of decorated Phoenician ivory carving.

Carrying this line of reasoning further, I believe it is possible to suggest that the absence at Hasanlu of the North Syrian, non-Phoenician ivory types found at Arslan Tash, Zincirli, and Samaria, not to mention Khorsabad, as well as of certain types found at Nimrud, supports the conclusion that these particular ivories are in fact eighth century products. Gordion, where again good dating is at hand, presents further archaeological support for an eighth century date for the North Syrian harness attachments with a frontal nude female under a sun disc, and for sphinxes with bodies in relief and head *en face* (Young 1962, pls. 46, 47; cf. Mallowan 1966, figs. 458, 549; Orchard 1967, pls. XX, XXI, XXVIII-XXXII).

[45]*Pace* W. Culican, *Syria* 27 (1970): 65, 75, 76; see Muscarella 1977b, 177 f. [For a discussion of differences in style between North Syrian and Phoenician ivories now see Winter 1976b.]

CONCLUSION

Perhaps the most important contribution of the Hasanlu ivories to Near Eastern art history and archaeology is their very existence. The ivories were scientifically excavated from several major public buildings within a specific site and therefore they have an objective, not a putative, provenience.[46] Given the present sorry state of Iranian archaeology, where so many objects—both genuine and forged—in collections and publications are said by dealers to have come "from Iran," or even from a specific site or mound in Iran, the known provenience of the Hasanlu ivories is significant and refreshing. To recognize the full thrust of this statement one has merely to contrast the value of the Hasanlu material with, for example, that of the hundreds of objects of different materials—gold, silver, bronze, ivory, terracotta—some of them ancient, others of apparent recent manufacture, said by dealers to have come from Ziwiye. Not a single one of these objects has ever come out of the ground in the presence of an archaeologist and yet many scholars accept them as archaeologically derived from Ziwiye (Muscarella 1977a). One may place in the same category of putative provenience many objects said to have come from Amlash, Ardebil, Marlik (aside from those excavated by Negahban), Luristan, Urartu and so forth.

[46]Had the Hasanlu ivories been found by clandestine diggers and circulated via the antiquities market to sundry collections and museums, no scholar would ever have been able to know that the local style and the North Syrian and Assyrian ivories were in fact originally juxtaposed in one particular Iranian city. And, it need hardly be mentioned, no one would ever have known the historical and archaeological information associated with their discovery. Some authorities would undoubtedly have assumed that the North Syrian ivories "obviously" derived from Nimrud, that the Assyrian examples derived from some site in Iraq, and that the "local-style" ivories came from the site suggested by the vendor, or at best, from an unknown site, somewhere in the Near East. Compare the "Khorsabad" ivories in the Metropolitan Museum, mentioned in the text, and the "Ziwiye" ivories, also mentioned.

Aside from the objective provenience, the Hasanlu ivories also have a fairly well-established chronological position: They were manufactured some time before the destruction of Hasanlu, which most probably took place a few years prior to 800 B.C. Consequently, they form a corpus of material that is invaluable for dating other ivory groups, as well as works of art in other materials. Moreover, the ivories both in quantity and quality are at present the second most important group known from the ancient Near East, second only to the Nimrud corpus.

The collection also provides us with a large group of objects that one may legitimately assume were made by the people who inhabited Hasanlu. We see them portrayed on the local-style ivories in scenes of warfare and siege, wherein chariots, cavalry and foot soldiers participate, employing swords, bows, spears, and probably maces; in hunting scenes, lions pursued by chariots or hunters on foot, or animal hunting animal; in ritual scenes depicting seated personages, perhaps in banquet scenes, and people drinking; in a procession and perhaps in introduction scenes. Moreover we have mythological scenes where a hero fights a bull, a lion attacks a sphinx, a genius fights a sphinx; and depictions of winged lions. The local style also includes statuettes of deities, in some cases standing on a lion; sculptures and reliefs of animals such as lions, stags, birds, goats, horses and bulls. These representations present historical, religious and genre scenes that must have had meaning and significance to the local people.

Humans represented on the local-style ivories usually have thick, outlined lips (sometimes thin mouths), large oval eyes, prominent noses and large ears. They wear their hair in various styles and lengths, often with a fillet or feathered headdress. They have thick sandals, sometimes boots, or no footwear at all. Only one figure, a statuette, no. 127, wears a brooch and a necklace. Jewellery, aside from bracelets, a few gorgets and one example of a necklace, is not worn by the relief figures; some of the statuettes had separate earrings.

The figures are always shown in profile. There is never any background detail or filler ornaments; all scenes are represented against a bare background. Figures are placed close to, but free of, one another, with rare instances of overlapping. The execution of all the plaques is predominantly in high relief with a generous use of incision to depict body and clothing details. Animals in relief are distinguished by thick outlines along the back and incised body details with a moderate tendency towards stylization.

The activities and details on the local-style ivories occur also on other apparently locally made objects excavated at Hasanlu: seals and seal impressions, metal plaques, a gold relief (no. 175), the silver and electrum vessel, and also the gold bowl. The locally made objects were created under the influences of Western, specifically North Syrian and Assyrian, art; ivory carving itself was learned from the West. Various hands are recognizable on the local-style ivories and it may be estimated that there were at least a half-dozen, probably more, workshops functioning at Hasanlu.

The majority of the ivories recovered are of the local style, followed in quantity first by ivories imported from North Syria, and then by ivories imported from Assyria. None of the Assyrian ivories seem to have been copied locally at Hasanlu, but a few of the North Syrian examples may have influenced the local workshops. These include animal sculptures and reliefs, particularly of lions, and human sculptures in the round. Both Assyrian and North Syrian motifs, however, were freely used by the local artisans, who appear to have had an intimate knowledge of the art of these cultures. The Assyrian ivories at Hasanlu seem to have been limited to furniture plaques while the North Syrian ivories are more varied and include pyxides, lion bowls, animal and human sculpture, some reliefs, and lotus and capital handles. Further, two groups of relief plaques depicting winged bulls were neither locally made nor imported from the West. Rather, it seems that they were made in other workshops within Iran, in areas still to be identfiied.

Although a few motifs on the local-style ivories appear to be characteristic of Iranian art, there seems to be no indication that the local artisans functioned under strong Iranian influence. Several of the motifs that occur in Iranian art are also found in Mesopotamia and North Syria, *viz.* feathered headdresses, procession and introduction scenes, banquet scenes, deities on animals, long hair; others, however, are indicative of a more specifically Iranian background, *viz.* hair tufts and concentric circles at body joints.

The strong Western influences, it is postulated, came partly from first-hand knowledge of the stone reliefs in North Syrian and Assyrian buildings and partly, perhaps mainly, from a close relationship with Assyria, which probably controlled all East-West contact and trade. Lacking archaeological and textual information we are not able to identify the products that were exchanged for the ivories and other objects that reached Hasanlu. Tin and lapis lazuli can be eliminated as exports because of a lack of solid evidence; horses and agricultural products were probably major items in the exchange, and possibly Hasanlu's geographic position athwart the trade routes enhanced its role.

The established chronological position of the Hasanlu ivories within the ninth century B.C., together with the presence of certain North Syrian types and the absence of any examples of the "Phoenician" ivories, helps date other groups. Thus some ivories from Nimrud, Tell Halaf and Hama now take their place as ninth century in date; others from Nimrud and elsewhere can be placed later. And "Phoenician" ivories are seen as eighth century products, manufactured after the destruction of Hasanlu.

REFERENCES

Akurgal, Ekrem
1949
Spaethethitische Bildkunst. Ankara.

1962
The Art of the Hittites. New York.

1966
The Art of Greece: Its Origins in the Mediterranean and Near East. New York.

1968
Urartäische und Altiranische Kunstzentern. Ankara.

Albenda, Pauline
1969
Expressions of Kingship in Assyrian Art. *JANES* 2 (1): 41-52.

1972
Ashurnasirpal II Lion Hunt Relief, BM 124534. *JNES* 31:3, 167-178.

1974
Lions on Assyrian Wall Reliefs. *JANES* 6: 1-27.

Amandry, Pierre
1939
Rapport Préliminaire sur les Statues Chryséléphantine de Delphes. *BCH* LXIII (1): 86-119.

Amiet, Pierre
1965
Un Vase Rituel Iranien. *Syria* 42: 235-251.

1966
Elan. Auvers-sur-Oise.

1972
Les Ivoires Achéménides de Suse. *Syria* 49: 167-191, 319-337.

1974
Un Carquois du Luristan. *Syria* 51: 243-251.

Andrae, Walter
1923
Farbige Keramik aus Assur. Berlin.

1938
Das wiedererstandene Assur. Leipzig.

Baer, N. S., and N. Indictor
1971
The Effect of High Temperature on Ivory. *Studies in Conservation* 1: 1-8.

1975
Chemical Investigations of Ancient Near Eastern Archaeological Ivory Artifacts. *Advances in Chemistry Series* 138: 236-245.

Baker, Hollis S.
1966
Furniture in the Ancient World. New York.

Barnett, R. D.
n.d.
Assyrian Palace Reliefs. London.

1948
Early Greek and Oriental Ivories. *JHS* 68: 1-25.

1956a
Ancient Oriental Influences on Archaic Greece. In *The Aegean and the Near East,* edited by Saul S. Weinberg: 212-238. Garden City, New York.

1956b
The Treasure of Ziwiye. *Iraq* 18: 111-116.

1957
A Catalogue of the Nimrud Ivories in the British Museum. London.

1963a
Hamath and Nimrud. *Iraq* 25: 81-85.

1963b
The Urartian Cemetery at Igdyr. *Anat. Studies* 13: 153-198.

1964
North Syrian and Related Harness Decoration. In *Vorderasiatische Archäologie*, edited by K. Bittel, 21-26. Berlin.

1967
Assyria and Iran. In *A Survey of Persian Art*, edited by A. U. Pope, XIV: 2997-3007. London.

1974
The Hieroglyphic Writing of Urartu. In *Anatolian Studies Presented to Hans G. Güterbock*: 43-55. Istanbul.

Barnett, R. D., and M. Falkner
1962
The Sculptures of Assurnasirpal II, Tiglath-Pileser III, and Esarhaddon from the Central and Southwest Palaces at Nimrud. London.

Boardman, John
1970
Pyramid Stamp Seals in the Persian Empire. *Iran* 8: 19-45.

Boehmer, R. M.
1968
Zum weissen Obelisken Ashurnasirpal I. *BJV* 8: 207-209

Borchardt, Jürgens
1972
Homerische Helme. Mainz.

Bossert, H. T.
1942
Altanatolien. Berlin.

1951
Altsyrien. Tübingen.

Brock, J.
1957
Fortetsa. Cambridge, England.

Brown, Llewellyn
1958
Review of *A Catalogue of the Nimrud Ivories in the British Museum* by R. D. Barnett. *PEQ:* 65-70.

Burney, Charles
1966
A First Season of Excavation at the Urartian Citadel of Kayalidere. *Anat. Studies* 16: 55-111.

Burney, Charles, and D. M. Lang
1972
The Peoples of the Hills. New York.

Calmeyer, Peter
1964
Altiranische Bronzen der Sammlung Bröckelschen. Berlin.

1969
Datierbare Bronzen aus Luristan und Kirmanshah. Berlin.

1973
Reliefbronzen in babylonischem Stil. Munich.

Canby, J. V.
1971
Decorated Garments in Ashurnasirpal's Sculpture. *Iraq* 33: 31-53.

Collon, Dominique
1977
Ivory. *Iraq* 39: 219-222.

Crowfoot, J. and G.
1938
Samaria-Sebaste, 2: *The Early Ivories.* London.

Davis, Ellen
1974
The Vapheio Cups: One Minoan and One Mycenaean? *Art Bulletin,* December: 472-487.

Dawkins, R. M.
1929
The Sanctuary of Artemis Orthia. London.

Delougaz, P. P., and H. Kantor
1972
New Evidence for the Protohistoric and Protoliterate Culture Development of Khuzestan. In *Memorial Volume Vth International Congress of Iranian Art* and Archaeology: 14-23. Teheran.

Dessene, A.
1957
Le sphinx étude iconographique. Paris.

Dossin, G.
1970
La route de l'etain en Mesopotamie au temps de Zimri-Lim. *Revue d'Assyriologie et d'Archeologie* 44 (2): 97-106.

Dunbabin, T. J.
1962
Perachora, II. Oxford.

Dyson, Robert H., Jr.
1959
Digging in Iran: Hasanlu, 1958. *Expedition* 1 (3): 4-17.

1960
The Death of a City. *Expedition* 2 (3): 2-11.

1961
Excavating the Mannaean Citadel of Hasanlu. *ILN,* Sept. 30: 534-537.

1962
The Hasanlu Project. *Science,* Feb. 23: 1-11.

1964a
Ninth Century Man in Western Iran. *Archaeology* 17 (1): 3-11.

1964b
In the City of the Golden Bowl. . . . *ILN,* Sept. 12: 372-374.

1965a
Hasanlu Excavations, 1964. *Archaeology* 18 (2): 157-159.

1965b
Problems of Protohistoric Iran as Seen from Hasanlu. *JNES* 24 (3): 193-217.

1967
Early Cultures of Solduz, Azerbaijan. In *A Survey of Persian Art,* edited by A. U. Pope, XIV: 2951-2970. London.

1968
Hasanlu and the Solduz and Ushnu Valleys: Twelve Years of Exploration. *Archaeologia Viva* I (1): 82-101.

1972
The Hasanlu Project, 1961-1967. In *Memorial Volume Vth International Congress of Iranian Art and Archaeology,* 39-58. Teheran.

Dyson, Robert H., Jr., and Vincent C. Piggott
1975
Hasanlu. *Iran* XIII: 182-185.

Falkner, Margarete
1952
Der Schatz von Ziwiye. *AfO* XVI: 129-132.

Farkas, Ann
1969
The Horse and Rider in Achaemenid Art. *Persica* 4: 57-76.

Frankfort, Henri
1954
The Art and Architecture of the Ancient Orient. London.

Freyer-Schauenburg, B.
1966
Elfenbeine aus dem samischen Heraion. Hamburg.

Galling, Kurt
1969
Ein phönikisches Kultgerät aus Kreta. *Die Welt des Orients* 5: 100-107.

Ghirshman, Roman
1939
Fouille de Sialk. Paris.

1964
The Art of Ancient Iran. New York.

Godard, Andre
1950
Le Trésor de Ziwiyè. Haarlem.

Güterbock, Hans
1957
Narrative in Ancient Art: Anatolia, Syria, Assyria. *AJA* 61 (1): 62-71.

1971
Ivory in Hittite Texts. *Anadolu* XV: 1-7.

Hachmann, R., and A. Kuschke
1966
Bericht über die Ergebnisse der Ausgrabungen in Kamid el-Loz (Libanon) in den Jahren 1963 und 1964. Bonn.

Hakemi, Ali
1968
Kaluraz. *Archaeologia Viva* I (1): 63-65.

Hamlin, Carol Kramer
1974
The Early Second Millennium Ceramic Assemblage of Dinkha Tepe. *Iran* 12: 125-153.

Harper, Prudence
1969
Dating a Group of Ivories from Anatolia. *The Connoisseur,* November: 156-162.

Hermann, Hans-Volkmar
1966a
Die Kessel der orientalisierenden Zeit. Berlin.

1966b
Urartu und Griechenland. *JdI* 81: 79-141.

Herzfeld, Ernst E.
1941
Iran in the Ancient East. Oxford.

Hogarth, D. G.
1914
Carchemish, I. London.

Hrouda, Barthel
1962
Tell Halaf, IV. Berlin.

1963
Die assyrische Streitwagen. *Iraq* 21 (2): 155-158.

1965
Die Kulturgeschichte des assyrischen Flachbildes. Bonn.

Hulin, Peter
1963
The Inscription on the Carved Throne Base of Shalmaneser III. *Iraq* 25 (1): 48-69.

Jantzen, Ulf
1972
Samos, VIII: *Ägyptische und orientalische Bronzen aus dem Heraion von Samos.* Bonn.

Kantor, Helene
1956
Syro-Palestinian Ivories, *JNES* 15 (3): 153-174.

1962
A Bronze Plaque with Relief Decoration from Tell Tainat, *JNES* 21 (2): 93-117.

Karageorghis, Vassos
1973
Excavations in the Necropolis of Salamis, III. Nicosia.

Kohler, Ellen
1964
Phrygian Animal Style and Nomadic Style. In *Dark Ages and Nomads ca. 1000 B.C.,* edited by Machteld Mellink: 58-62. Istanbul.

Kopcke, Günter
1967
Neue Holzfunde aus dem Heraion von Samos. *Ath. Mitt.* 82: 100-148.

Kunz, G. F.
1916
Ivory and the Elephant. New York.

Kunze, Emil
1936
Orientalische Schnitzereien aus Kreta. *Ath. Mitt.* 61: 218-233.

Kyrieleis, Helmut
1969
Throne und Klinen. Berlin.

Lamberg-Karlovsky, C. C.
1972
Trade Mechanism in Indus-Mesopotamian Interrelations. *JAOS* 92 (2): 222-229.

Landsberger, Benno
1965
Tin and Lead: the Adventures of Two Vocables. *JNES* 24 (3): 285-296.

Larsen, Mogens T.
1967
Old Assyrian Caravan Procedures. Istanbul.

Layard, Austen H.
1849
The Monuments of Nineveh. London.

1853
Discoveries in the Ruins of Nineveh and Babylon. London.

Leemans, W. F.
1968
Old Babylonian Letters and Economic History. *JESHO* 11: 171-226.

Legrain, Leon
1947
Ur Excavations Texts, III. London, Philadelphia.

Levine, Louis D.
1973
Geographic Studies in the Neo-Assyrian Zagros, I. *Iran* 11: 1-27.

1974
Geographic Studies in the Neo-Assyrian Zagros, II. *Iran* 12: 99-124.

Littauer, Mary
1971
The Figured Evidence for a Small Pony in the Ancient Near East. *Iraq* 32 (1): 24-30.

1972
The Military Use of the Chariot in the Aegean in the Late Bronze Age. *AJA* 76 (2): 145-157.

Loud, Gordon
1939
The Megiddo Ivories. Chicago.

Loud, Gordon, and C. B. Altman
1938
Khorsabad, II. Chicago.

Luckenbill, D. D.
1926
Ancient Records of Assyria and Babylonia, I, II. Chicago.

Madhloom, T. A.
1970
The Chronology of Neo-Assyrian Art. London.

Mallowan, Max
1966
Nimrud and its Remains, I, II. London.

Mallowan, Max, and L. G. Davies
1970
Ivories in Assyrian Style. Ivories from Nimrud, II. London.

Mallowan, Max, and Georgina Herrmann
1974
Furniture from SW7, Fort Shalmaneser. Ivories from Nimrud, III. London.

Matthiae, Paolo
1975
Syrische Kunst. In Orthmann 1975: 466-493. Berlin.

McEwan, C. W.
1956
Soundings at Tell Fakhariyah. Chicago.

Mellink, Machteld
1966
The Hasanlu Bowl in Anatolian Perspective. *Iranica Antiqua* 6: 72-87.

de Mertzenfeld, C. Decamps
1954
Inventaire commenté des Ivoires phéniciens. Paris.

Millard, A. R.
1962
Alphabetic Inscriptions on Ivories from Nimrud. *Iraq* 24 (1): 41-55.

Mkrtiachan, Boris
1967
The Mystery of Metsamor. *New Orient* 3: 76-78.

Moorey, P. R. S.
1967
Some Ancient Metal Belts: their Antecedents and Relations. *Iran* 5: 83-98.

1969
Prehistoric Copper and Bronze Metallurgy in Western Iran. *Iran* 7: 131-153.

1970
Pictorial Evidence for the History of Horse-Riding in Iraq before the Kassite Period. *Iraq* 32 (1): 36-50.

1971
Catalogue of the Ancient Persian Bronzes in the Ashmolean Museum. Oxford.

1972
A small Tripod-Stand from Western Iran. *Iran* 10: 143-146.

1975
Some Elaborately Decorated Bronze Quiver Plaques made in Luristan, c. 750-650 B.C. *Iran* 13: 19-29.

Moortgat, Anton
1940
Vorderasiatische Rollsiegel. Berlin.

1955
Tell Halaf III Die Bildwerken. Berlin.

1969
The Art of Ancient Mesopotamia. New York.

Muhly, James
1973a
Tin Routes of the Bronze Age. *American Scientist*, July-August: 404-413.

1973b
Copper and Tin. Hamden, Conn.

1976
Supplement to Copper and Tin. Hamden, Conn.

Muscarella, Oscar White
1962
The Oriental Origin of Siren Cauldron Attachments. *Hesperia* 31 (4): 317-329.

1965
Lion Bowls from Hasanlu. *Archaeology* 18 (1): 41-46.

1966
Hasanlu 1964. *MMAB* XXV (3): 121-135.

1967
Phrygian Fibulae from Gordion. London.

1968
Excavations at Dinkha Tepe, 1966. *MMAB* XXVII (3): 187-196.

1970
Near Eastern Bronzes in the West: the Question of Origin. In *Art and Technology,* edited by S. Doehringer, D. G. Mitten, A. Steinberg: 109-128. Cambridge, Mass.

1971a
Hasanlu in the Ninth Century B.C. . . . *AJA* 75 (3): 263-266.

1971b
Qalatgah: an Urartian Site in Northwestern Iran. *Expedition* 13 (3/4): 44-49.

1972
A Bronze Vase from Iran and its Greek Connections. *MMAJour* 5: 25-50.

1973a
Excavations at Agrab Tepe, Iran. *MMAJour* 8: 47-76.

1973b
Review of *Samos,* VIII, by U. Jantzen. *AJA* 77 (2): 236-237.

1974a
Decorated Bronze Beakers from Iran. *AJA* 78 (3): 239-252.

1974b
The Third Lion Bowl from Hasanlu. *Expedition* 16 (2): 25-29.

1974c
The Iron Age at Dinkha Tepe, Iran. *MMAJour* 9: 35-90.

1974d
(Editor) *Ancient Art—The Norbert Schimmel Collection.* Mainz.

1977a
'Ziwiye' and Ziwiye: The Forgery of a Provenience. *JFA* IV (2): 197-219.

1977b
Unexcavated Objects and Ancient Near Eastern Art. In *Mountains and Lowlands,* edited by Louis D. Levine and T. Cuyler Young, Jr. 153-207. Malibu.

1977c
The Archaeological Evidence for Relations between Greece and Iran in the First Millennium B.C. *JANES* 9: 31-57.

Negahban, Ezat
1964
A Preliminary Report on Marlik Excavation. Teheran.

Oates, David
1968
The Excavations at Tell al Rimah, 1967. *Iraq* 30 (2): 115-138.

Ogawa, H.
1971
A Steatite Bowl from Tell Zeror. *Orient* 7: 25-48.

Oppenheim, A. Leo
1954
The Seafaring Merchants of Ur. *JAOS* 74: 6-17.

Orchard, J. J.
1967
Equestrian Bridle-Harness Attachments. Ivories from Nimrud I, 2. Aberdeen.

Orthmann, Winfried
1971
Untersuchungen zur späthethitischen Kunst. Bonn.

1975
(Editor) *Die alte Orient,* Propyläen Kunstgeschichte II. Berlin.

Özgüç, Nimet
1966
Excavations at Acemhöyük. *Anadolu* 10: 29-52.

Özgüç, Tahsin
1969
Altintepe, II. Ankara.

Philippe, J.
1965
Matière et travail des ivoires. In *Miscellana Pro Arte,* H. Schnitzler Festschrift: 163-167. Düsseldorf.

Piotrovsky, B. B.
1954
Vanskoe Urartu. Moscow.

1970
Karmir Blur. Leningrad.

Pope, Arthur Upham (Editor)
1938
A Survey of Persian Art, IV. New York.

Porada, Edith
1945
The Great King, King of Assyria. New York.

1947
Seal Impressions from Nuzi. New Haven.

1948
Corpus of Ancient Near Eastern Seals in North American Collections, I: *The Collection of the Pierpont Morgan Library.* Washington.

1959
The Hasanlu Bowl. *Expedition* 1 (3): 19-22.

1965
The Art of Ancient Iran. New York.

1967
Notes on the Gold Bowl and Silver Beaker from Hasanlu. In *A Survey of Persian Art,* edited by A. U. Pope, XIV: 2971-2978. London.

1970a
Tchoga Zanbil, IV: *La Glyptique.* Paris.

1970b
Review of *Tell Halaf,* IV, by Barthel Hrouda. *Artibus Asiae* 32 (1): 97-99.

1972
Problems of Iranian Iconography. In *Memorial Volume Vth International Congress of Iranian Art and Archaeology,* 163-182. Teheran.

1975
Iranische Kunst. In Orthmann 1975: 363-398. Berlin.

Poursat, Jean Claude
1977
Catalogue des Ivoires mycéniens du Musée d'Athènes, I, II. Paris.

Pritchard, James B. (Editor)
1955
Ancient Near Eastern Texts Relating to the Old Testament. Princeton.

Reade, Julian
1972
The Neo-Assyrian Court and Army: Evidence from the Sculpture. *Iraq* 34 (2): 87-112.

1975
Ashurnasirpal I and the White Obelisk. *Iraq* 37 (2): 129-150.

Renfrew, Colin
1969
Trade and Culture Process in European Pre-history *Current Anthropology* 10 (2/3): 151-169.

Rimmer, J.
1969
Ancient Musical Instruments of Western Asia. London.

Rost, Liane
1961
Zu den hethitischen Bildbeschreibungen. *Mitt. des Instituts für Orientforschung* 8 (2): 161-217.

Rudenko, Sergei
1970
Frozen Tombs of Siberia. Berkeley.

Sams, Kenneth
1974
Phrygian Painted Animals: Anatolian Orientalizing Art. *Anat. Studies* 24: 169-196

Sasson, J. M.
1966
A Sketch of North Syrian Economic Relations in the Middle Bronze Age. *JESHO* 9: 161-181.

1968
Instances of Mobility among Mari Artisans, *BASOR* 190: 46-54.

Schaeffer, C. F. A.
1954
Les fouilles de Ras-Shamra/Ugarit, 15[e], 16[e], 17[e] campagnes. *Syria* 31: 14-67.

Seidl, Ursula
1968
Die babylonischen Kudurru-Reliefs. *Baghd. Mitt.* 4: 8-220.

Shear, T. Leslie
1940
The Campaign of 1939. *Hesperia* 9 (3): 261-307.

Smith, Sidney
1938
Assyrian Sculptures in the British Museum. London.

Smith, W. S.
1963
Interconnections in the Ancient Near East. New Haven.

Sollberger, E.
1974
The White Obelisk. *Iraq* 36 (1/2): 231-238.

Strom, Ingrid
1971
Problems Concerning the Origin and Early Development of the Etruscan Orientalizing Style. Odense.

Strommenger, Eva
1962
Fünf Jahrtausende Mesopotamien. Munich.

1970
Die neuassyrische Rundskulptur. Berlin.

Thimme, Jürgen
1973
Badisches Landesmuseum Karlsruhe: Phönizische Elfenbeine. Karlsruhe.

Thureau-Dangin, F.
1931
Arslan Tash. Paris.

van Loon, Maurits
1966
Urartian Art. Istanbul.

1972
Review of vanden Berghe 1968. *Bibliotheca Orientalis* 29: 66-69.

vanden Berghe, Louis
1968
Het Archeologisch Onderzoek naar de Bronscultuur van Luristan. Opgravingen in Pusht-i Kuh I: Kalwali en War Kabud (1965 en 1966). Brussels.

1971
Excavations in Pusht-i Kuh (Iran). *Archaeology* 24 (3): 263-271.

1975
Le Necropole de Čamahzi-Mumah. In *Proceedings of the 4th Annual Symposium of Archaeological Research in Iran*: 337-367. Teheran.

Vieyrà, Maurice
1955
Hittite Art. London.

Vermeule, Emily
1964
Greece in the Bronze Age. Chicago.

von Luschan, Felix, and W. Andrae
1943
Ausgrabungen in Sendschirli, V: *Die Kleinfunde.* Berlin.

von Saldern, Axel
1966
Mosaic Glass from Hasanlu, Marlik, and Tell al Rimah. *JGS* 8: 9-25.

1970
Other Mesopotamian Glass Vessels. In *Glass and Glassmaking in Ancient Mesopotamia,* edited by A. Leo Oppenheim: 203-228. New York.

Wallis Budge, E. A.
1914
Assyrian Sculpture in the British Museum. London.

Wilson, J. V. Kinnier
1962
The Kuraba'il Statue of Shalmaneser III, *Iraq* 24 (2): 90-115.

Wilkinson, Charles K.
1955
Assyrian and Persian Art, *MMAB* XIII (8): 213-226.

1963
Treasure from the Mannean Land, *MMAB* XXI (5): 274-284.

1975
Ivories from Ziwiye. Bern.

Winter, Irene (see Addendum)

Wiseman, D. J.
1968
The Tell al Rimah Tablets, 1966, *Iraq* 30 (2): 175-205.

Woolley, C. Leonard
1921
Carchemish, II. London.

1955
Alalakh. Oxford.

Woolley, C. L., and R. D. Barnett
1952
Carchemish, III. London.

Wright, G.
1974
Archaeology and Trade, Addison-Wesley Module in Anthropology 49.

Yadin, Y.
1963
The Art of Warfare in Biblical Lands. New York.

Young, Rodney S.
1960
The Gordion Campaign of 1959: Preliminary Report. *AJA* 64 (3): 227-243.

1962
The 1961 Campaign at Gordion. *AJA* 66 (2): 153-168.

1967
A Bronze Bowl in Philadelphia. *JNES* 26 (3): 145-154.

1974
Phrygian Furniture from Gordion. *Expedition* 16 (3): 2-13.

ADDENDUM

Winter, Irene
1976a
North Syria in the Early First Millennium B.C., with Special Reference to Ivory. Ph.D. dissertation, Columbia University 1973; Ann Arbor, Mich.: University Microfilms.

1976b
Phoenician and North Syrian Ivory Carving in Historical Context: Questions of Style and Distribution. *Iraq* 38 (1): 1-22.

1977
Perspective on the 'Local Style' of Hasanlu IVB: A Study in Receptivity. In *Mountains and Lowlands,* edited by Louis D. Levine and T. Cuyler Young, Jr.: 371-386. Malibu.

UNIVERSITY MUSEUM MONOGRAPHS

Francis R. Steele
1 THE CODE OF LIPIT-ISHTAR
1949. 28 pp. 7 pls.

Samuel Noah Kramer
2 SCHOOLDAYS: A SUMERIAN COMPOSITION RELATING TO THE EDUCATION OF A SCRIBE
1949. 19 pp. 4 pls.

J. Alden Mason
3 THE LANGUAGE OF THE PAPAGO OF ARIZONA
1950. 84 pp.

Arthur J. Tobler
4 EXCAVATIONS AT TEPE GAWRA, VOLUME 11
1950. ii + 260 pp. 182 pls.

Carleton S. Coon
5 CAVE EXPLORATIONS IN IRAN 1949
1951. ii + 125 pp. 33 illus. in text. 15 pls.

John H. Moss, in collaboration with Kirk Bryan, G. William Holmes, Linton Satterthwaite, Henry P. Hansen, C. Bertrand Schultz, W. D. Frankforter
6 EARLY MAN IN THE EDEN VALLEY
1951. vi + 124 pp. 32 figs. in text. 9 pls.

Samuel Noah Kramer
7 ENMERKAR AND THE LORD OF ARATTA: A SUMERIAN EPIC TALE OF IRAQ AND IRAN
1952. iv + 55 pp. 28 pls.

J. L. Giddings, Jr.
8 THE ARCTIC WOODLAND CULTURE OF THE KOBUK RIVER
1952. x + 144 pp. 43 figs. in text. 46 pls.

Dorothy Hannah Cox
9 A THIRD CENTURY HOARD OF TETRADRACHMS FROM GORDION
1953. v + 20 pp. 1 map in text. 8 pls.

Ward H. Goodenough
10 NATIVE ASTRONOMY IN THE CENTRAL CAROLINES
1953. 46 pp. 4 figs. in text. 1 map.

John Howard Young and Suzanna Halstead Young
11 TERRACOTTA FIGURINES FROM KOURION IN CYPRUS
1955. x + 260 pp. 3 plans. 17 figs. in text. 75 pls.

Daris Ray Swindler
12 A STUDY OF THE CRANIAL AND SKELETAL MATERIAL FROM NIPPUR
1956. v+40 pp. 8 pls.

Machteld J. Mellink
13 A HITTITE CEMETERY AT GORDION
1956. xii+60 pp. 30 pls.

Linton Satterthwaite
14 STONE ARTIFACTS AT AND NEAR THE FINLEY SITE, NEAR EDEN, WYOMING
1957. iv+22 pp. 5 figs.

Edwin M. Shook, William R. Coe and Vivian L. Broman, Linton Satterthwaite
15 TIKAL REPORTS, NUMBERS 1 - 4
1958. vi+150 pp. 26 figs.

Rudolf Anthes, with contributions by Hasan S. K. Bakry, John Dimick, Henry G. Fischer, Labib Habachi, Jean Jacquet
16 MIT RAHINEH 1955
1958. vi+93 pp. 18 figs. in text. 45 pls. Map.

James B. Pritchard
17 HEBREW INSCRIPTIONS AND STAMPS FROM GIBEON
1959. vi+32 pp. 12 figs.

William R. Coe
18 PIEDRAS NEGRAS ARCHAEOLOGY: ARTIFACTS, CACHES AND BURIALS
1959. x+245 pp. 69 figs.

Edmund I. Gordon, with a chapter by Thorkild Jacobsen
19 SUMERIAN PROVERBS: GLIMPSES OF EVERYDAY LIFE IN ANCIENT MESOPOTAMIA
1959. xxvi+556 pp. 79 pls.

Richard E. W. Adams, Vivian L. Broman, William R. Coe, William A. Haviland, Ruben E. Reina, Linton Satterthwaite, Edwin M. Shook, Aubrey S. Trik
20 TIKAL REPORTS, NUMBERS 5-10
1961. iv+225 pp. 73 pls.

Robert F. Carr and James E. Hazard
21 TIKAL REPORTS, NUMBER 11
1961. Portfolio of 10 maps and iv+24 pp.

James B. Pritchard
22 THE WATER SYSTEM OF GIBEON
1961. viii+34 pp. 48 figs.

Porphyrios Dikaois, with contributions by J. Lawrence Angel, M. Stekelis, F. E. Zeuner and A. Grosvenor Ellis, S. P. Dance
23 SOTIRA
1961. xiii + 252 pp. 122 pls.

Daris R. Swindler
24 A RACIAL STUDY OF THE WEST NAKANAI
1962. viii + 59 pp. 9 pls. 3 figs.

James B. Pritchard
25 THE BRONZE AGE CEMETERY AT GIBEON
1963. x + 123 pp. 100 figs.

James B. Pritchard, with contributions by William L. Reed, Douglas M. Spence, Jane Sammis
26 WINERY, DEFENSES, AND SOUNDINGS AT GIBEON
1964. viii + 85 pp. 100 figs.

Rudolf Anthes, with contributions by Ibrahim Abdel Aziz, Hasan S. K. Bakry, Henry G. Fischer, Labib Habachi, Jean Jacquet, William K. Simpson, Jean Yoyotte
27 MIT RAHINEH 1956
1965. x + 170 pp. 21 figs. in text. 69 pls.

Frances James
28 THE IRON AGE AT BETH SHAN: A STUDY OF LEVELS VI - IV
1966. xviii + 369 pp. 128 figs.

Froelich G. Rainey and Carlo M. Lerici, with the collaboration of Orville H. Bullitt, *et al.*
29 THE SEARCH FOR SYBARIS 1960-1965
1967. xix + 313 pp. 26 pls. Map supplement: 8 maps.

Ina VanStan
30 TEXTILES FROM BENEATH THE TEMPLE OF PACHACAMAC, PERU
1967. vii + 91 pp. 5 tables. 78 figs.

Carleton S. Coon, in collaboration with Harvey M. Bricker, Frederick Johnson, C. C. Lamberg-Karlovsky
31 YENGEMA CAVE REPORT
1968. 77 pp. 35 pls.

J. L. Benson, with contributions by Edith Porada and J. Lawrence Angel
32 BAMBOULA AT KOURION: THE NECROPOLIS AND THE FINDS. EXCAVATED BY J. F. DANIEL
(published by the University of Pennsylvania Press)
1972. xvi + 252 pp. 74 pls.

Eliezer D. Oren
33 THE NORTHERN CEMETERY OF BETH SHAN
(published by E. J. Brill, Leiden)
1972. xx + 307 pp. 84 figs.

J. L. Benson, with contributions by Edith Porada and E. A. and H. W. Catling

34 THE NECROPOLIS OF KALORIZIKI: EXCAVATED BY J. F. DANIEL AND G. H. McFADDEN FOR THE UNIVERSITY MUSEUM, UNIVERSITY OF PENNSYLVANIA, PHILADELPHIA
(published at Göteborg as volume XXVI of Studies in Mediterranean Archaeology)
1973. 202 pp. 63 pls.

James B. Pritchard, with contributions by William P. Anderson, Ellen Herscher, Javier Teixidor

35 SAREPTA: A PRELIMINARY REPORT ON THE IRON AGE
1975. ix + 114 pp. 63 figs.

Robert J. Sharer (General Editor)

36 THE PREHISTORY OF CHALCHUAPA, EL SALVADOR
(published by the University of Pennsylvania Press)
1978. 3 volumes.
VOLUME I xv + 194 pp. 26 tables, 87 figs. (8 maps in pocket).
VOLUME II: xx + 211 pp. 12 tables, 38 figs.
VOLUME III: xvii + 226 pp. 9 tables, 39 figs.

Robert J. Sharer (General Editor) and Wendy Ashmore (Volume Editor)

37 QUIRIGUA REPORTS, VOLUME I: PAPERS 1-5
1979. ix + 73 pp. 4 tables. 24 figs. Site map.

John Bockstoce

38 THE ARCHAEOLOGY OF CAPE NOME, ALASKA
1979. xiii + 133 pp. 3 maps. 3 tables. Frontispiece. 28 figs. 9 pls.

Irene J. Winter

39 A DECORATED BREASTPLATE FROM HASANLU, IRAN: TYPE, STYLE, AND CONTEXT OF AN EQUESTRIAN ORNAMENT
Hasanlu Special Studies, volume I
1980. xiv + 105 pp. 1 map. Frontispiece (color). 79 figs. Folding plate.

Oscar White Muscarella

40 THE CATALOGUE OF IVORIES FROM HASANLU, IRAN
Hasanlu Special Studies, volume II
1980. xi + 231 pp. 2 plans. Frontispiece. 293 figs.

James B. Pritchard

41 THE CEMETERY AT TELL ES-SA'IDIYEH, JORDAN
1980. xii + 103 pp. 2 tables. Frontispiece.
46 pls. 29 figs. in text.

Saul S. Weinberg

42 BAMBOULA AT KOURION: THE ARCHITECTURE
(In preparation)

Rodney S. Young, with contributions by K. DeVries, E. L. Kohler (Editor), J. F. McClellan, M. J. Mellink, G. K. Sams
43 GORDION EXCAVATION REPORTS, VOLUME I: THREE GREAT EARLY TUMULI
(In preparation)

Christopher Jones and Linton Satterthwaite
44 TIKAL REPORTS, NUMBER 33A: THE MONUMENTS AND INSCRIPTIONS
(In preparation)

UNIVERSITY MUSEUM PAPERS

Keith DeVries (Editor), with contributions by Margaret Thompson, Homer A. Thompson, Eugene Vanderpool, Keith DeVries, Hans G. Güterbock, Ellen L. Kohler, Machteld J. Mellink, George M. A. Hanfmann, Crawford H. Greenewalt and Lawrence J. Majewski, Robert H. Dyson, Jr., and G. Roger Edwards
1 FROM ATHENS TO GORDION: THE PAPERS OF A MEMORIAL SYMPOSIUM FOR RODNEY S. YOUNG
xix + 168 pp. Frontispiece. 144 figs.

UNIVERSITY MUSEUM CATALOGUES

Philip P. Betancourt
1 THE CRETAN COLLECTION, VOLUME I: VARIOUS SITES
(In preparation) 3 volumes.